The Making of an Ecologist

The Making
of an Ecologist

My Career in Alaska Wildlife
Management and Conservation

David R. Klein
Edited by Karen Brewster

University of Alaska Press
Fairbanks, Alaska

Text © 2019 University of Alaska Press

Published by
  University of Alaska Press
  P.O. Box 756240
  Fairbanks, AK 99775-6240

Cover and interior design by Paula Elmes.

Cover photos (L–R):
  Dave Klein with a large bull reindeer he harvested to weigh and take samples from to determine
  the animals' health and body condition as part of his research on the reindeer population of St.
  Matthew Island, 1957. Courtesy of Dave Klein.

  Dave Klein collecting lichen samples within a vegetation plot on St. Matthew Island, 2012.
  Photo by Rich Kleinleder.

  Dave Klein overlooking Blåsø Lake in northeast Greenland,1987. Courtesy of Dave Klein.

  Most of the 2012 St. Matthew Expedition team. L–R: Mirianne Alpin, Aaron Poe, Heather
  Renner, Marc Romano, Tony Degange, Monte Garroute, Rich Kleinleder, Steve Delehanty,
  Dennis Griffin, and Dave Klein. Photo by Rich Kleinleder.

  Dave Klein and Ulf Marquard-Petersen loading a tranquilizer dart for muskoxen at Cape
  Copenhagen, North Greenland, 1987. Courtesy of Dave Klein.

Back cover photos:
  Dave Klein outside on his deck at his home in Fairbanks, April 2014. University of Alaska
  Fairbanks, Todd Paris.

  Painting of Dave Klein by his friend and colleague, João Bugalho, former Director of Wildlife
  Management for Portugal. Painting done in 2006. Photo of the painting by Karen Brewster.

The reindeer herd graphic used in chapter introductions was adapted by Paula Elmes from a photo
Dave Klein took of a group of bull reindeer on St. Matthew Island in 1963. The muskox image used
on section dividers is a stock image supplied by Adobe Stock.

Library of Congress Cataloging in Publication Data

  Names: Klein, David R., author. | Brewster, Karen, editor.
  Title: The making of an ecologist : my career in Alaska wildlife management and conservation /
    by David R. Klein and edited by Karen Brewster.
  Description: Fairbanks, AK : University of Alaska Press, 2019. | Includes bibliographical
    references and index. |
  Identifiers: LCCN 2018060360 (print) | LCCN 2019008750 (ebook) | ISBN 9781602233928
    (ebook) | ISBN 9781602233911 (pbk. : alk. paper)
  Subjects: LCSH: Klein, David R. | Wildlife management–Alaska. | Ecologists–Alaska–
    Biography. | Wildlife conservation–Alaska. | Natural History–Alaska. | Alaska–
    Environmental conditions.
  Classification: LCC QH31.K59 (ebook) | LCC QH31.K59 A3 2019 (print) | DDC
    333.95/416092 [B] dc23
  LC record available at https://lccn.loc.gov/2018060360.

Contents

Acknowledgments

This project would not have been possible without contributions from other people. We wish to express our thanks to: Mark Madison, Historian, US Fish and Wildlife Service, National Conservation Training Center Archives/Museum in Shepherdstown, West Virginia, for his support of this project and for providing a transcriptionist; Wendy Contreal from the US Fish and Wildlife Service National Conservation Training Center for transcribing sixty hours of audio into 838 pages of transcripts; the Alaska Chapter of The Wildlife Society for supporting some of the oral history interviewing; David's former graduate student and retired biologist with the Alaska Department of Fish and Game, Pat Valkenberg, for assisting with some of the oral history interviewing; Dan Roby, Ned Rozell, Marc Romano, and Rich Kleinleder for giving us permission to use some of their photographs; Heather Renner and Marc Romano of the Alaska Maritime National Wildlife Refuge for assisting with photograph identification; and William Schneider for his never-ending enthusiasm, guidance, and reviews.

And most importantly, we would like to thank our families and friends for their encouragement and support, and for their patience while we isolated ourselves and worked diligently for a number of years to complete this book.

David Klein sitting in his office at
the Arctic Health Research Building
on the UAF campus surrounded
by decades of collected books,
papers, reports, photographs,
memorabilia, and master's and
doctoral theses, 2014. UNIVERSITY OF
ALASKA FAIRBANKS, TODD PARIS.

Foreword

by David Klein

Although I never met Aldo Leopold, who died in 1948, he had a posthumous influence on me as a mentor. When I was an undergraduate studying wildlife, my professor was trained under Leopold, so he brought that perspective to the classroom and we used Leopold's book *Game Management* (Leopold 1933) as a textbook. Aldo Leopold was clearly the father of wildlife management, having published the first book on it. He also developed an understanding of wildlife ecology and the relationship of land-use practices, began to see the role of predators in the ecology of the southwestern states, and became an activist trying to educate the public, including ranchers, hunters, and the US Forest Service (Warren 2016). All of this laid the groundwork for a then-emerging national program of conservation and management of our wildlife resources and protection of their natural habitats. I connected with this approach and applied what I had been learning to my own work.

Leopold's legacy formed the basis for the growth of the wildlife profession in the latter half of the twentieth century, and influenced my life and professional development in many ways. He influenced me mostly in terms of learning about wildlife management, but also in philosophy. The example of his life and the ideas he developed and eloquently wrote about captured my admiration. The evolution of his thinking from a narrow, agency-biased perspective to a broader, more ecologically based view of the world coincided with my own shifts from being an academically trained biologist focused on a career in wildlife management to that of being an ecologist.

The term *ecology* was first coined by Ernst Haeckel, a German biologist, evolutionist, and artist at the end of the nineteenth century (Haeckel 1900; Stauffer 1957), and since has become a branch of biology that focuses on the relationships of organisms to one another and to their physical surroundings. Ecologists study whole ecosystems and the interconnections among elements within that system that come together to form our integrated natural world. My father, who was not a trained scientist but was curious about the natural world, was strongly influenced by Haeckel through the English translation of his book *The Riddle of the Universe at the Close of the Nineteenth Century*, which provided strong support for Darwinian evolution and associated natural selection (Haeckel 1900). I was influenced by listening to my father discuss these ideas at the family dinner table.

As I advanced in my education, the study of integrated natural systems and the connections between animals, plants, habitat, and climate perfectly fit my interests in herbivores and their relationships to plants. I also wanted to know how the plants responded to grazing and may have evolved to stay resistant to overgrazing or heavy browsing, and also how the animals adapted to changes that were going on in the environment. Ecosystems are inherently complex, and being an ecologist meant looking at all the related variables.

To be an effective ecologist, you need to be a good observer. Leopold certainly was a keen and objective observer of the land and the life it supported. He saw examples of how humans used and abused the land, and realized that these could be models from which we could learn. I feel like I have been a successful ecologist because the minute I step into the natural environment, I am seeing things and trying to figure it all out. It's just how I see the world; I have this psychological need to explain things. If I see something, I ask, "Well, why is it that way?" I'm always curious, and I think it's important to continue to be curious no matter what age we are.

A lot of nature study is like detective work. It's just about being a keen observer and having the ability to interpret what you see and figure out what it all means. I do not think I know more than other people that are out observing the environment. For example, Native people are generally ecologists, because they have been learning the hard way about the importance of observation. Or in the old days, naturalists would get familiar with the natural world and then try to explain things. Some naturalists eventually became scientists, like Adolph and Olaus Murie, and were so much better scientists because of previously having been on the ground observing things. They may have been handicapped in many ways, compared to the world today and our advanced technology and research methodology, but what they did is still relevant. However, there is more to being an ecologist than just being a good observer. It is also about knowing enough about how ecological systems work that you can answer seemingly complex environmental questions.

Wildlife biologists are confronted with ecological complexity—often unique to our own regions—that makes our work both interesting and challenging. Through travel, we can step back from the myopic view of our own research or management activities and open our minds to understanding how other systems function, be they ecosystems or human societies, and be able to compare familiar systems with those newly encountered. The opportunity to travel widely, both in North America and abroad, advanced my own education beyond that gained formally in the classroom and from the written word. For me, this experience inevitably led to a greater depth of understanding of my own local environment, from the ecological relationships of wildlife species that have been the focus of my work to the human involvement in their management. Travel also led to the establishment of professional contacts and collaborations with individuals whose educational and cultural backgrounds differed from my own, and exposed me to their ideas and solutions to problems. By increasing our understanding of others, we increase understanding of ourselves.

I appreciate that my interest in ecology and being curious about the natural world came from my parents. They both enjoyed the natural world and so this was emphasized during my childhood. And my grandfather, who had been a farmer, taught me a lot about the outdoors, nature, plants, and animals. The idea of becoming a scientist or ecologist was influenced by the fact that both of my parents were keen observers. For example, sometimes when I was a boy and the stars were out, we would go outside and learn some of the constellations from my dad, so I got fascinated with that.

I remember my dad saying, "Just imagine how small you are relative to the universe. We're only seeing a portion of it." This made me think about how we are so insignificant, and that it was important to remember that humans and planet Earth are not the center of the universe. I appreciated these kinds of experiences.

I feel like my choice to be an ecologist has been the right path for me, although there were times when I was fascinated with other fields of endeavor, such as architecture, horticulture, and agriculture. But then I think that being a biologist has important advantages, because in biology you learn about yourself as well as about the rest of the environment that you live in. To me, if you know more about yourself, you get along better in the world than if you don't. And ecology, of course, helps you to understand your place in the world even more.

After such a long career, I feel like I have the ability to share what I've learned as an ecologist and I enjoy doing that. For example, in recent years, I appreciate having gone on nature walks with my neighbors' kids and their moms with a desire to teach the kids how to observe the natural world and to think for themselves about the meaning of what they're seeing. When they point something out and ask me about it, I get a thrill out of saying, "Well, what do you think? Why are those berries together in a little pile? Did someone put them there?" They look up at me and then one of them will say, "Some animal did that." Another one will ask, "What kind of an animal?" I reply, "Well, let's look closely and see if we can figure it out together." I see that there's a vole dropping there, so I show it to them, and they say, "Yeah, it was a vole." Then they feel so good about having figured it out themselves. It builds their self-confidence. I like to see kids get excited like this and to see them learn.

And then, of course, there is the great satisfaction I gained from teaching at the university, and guiding graduate students in the development of their research projects and helping them obtain new understandings of complex biological and ecological questions. I have appreciated being the one to stimulate their interest and inspire them to become future scientists and ecologists. Also, exposure to these young people and the opportunity for enthusiastic exchanges of ideas allowed me to become a better ecologist. I am proud that so many of my former students went on to have successful careers in wildlife management and conservation, especially in Alaska, and have become well-informed and involved citizens.

David Klein and Karen Brewster
on the beach in Homer, Alaska,
May 2015. PHOTO COURTESY OF KAREN
BREWSTER.

Introduction

by Karen Brewster

Kick, glide. *Scrinch, swoosh.* Kick, glide. *Scrinch, swoosh.* These are the blessed sounds I hear on a sparkling and sunny late-winter day as I push my cross-country skis along the deeply grooved tracks of the Estle Connector Trail in the northern part of the University of Alaska Fairbanks (UAF) campus. It is midafternoon on a Friday, a time when I often do not see other skiers as most people are at work. With my Monday through Thursday work schedule, I have the luxury of a private playground.

As I glide up the trail, I notice a lone figure in the distance. Given my measured pace, I am surprised when I catch up to this tall, lanky man. After following him for a while, I become frustrated with his slow pace and step out of the track. As I start to pass, I turn to say something and realize I recognize him. It is David Klein, a longtime Alaska wildlife biologist known for his work with caribou, reindeer, and muskoxen. Although I can't pinpoint if we've ever actually met before, I certainly recognize him and am aware of his background. Despite Fairbanks having a population of 100,000, within certain liberal circles it remains a small town and many of us end up crossing paths again and again in a variety of contexts.

Although David is eighty years old, in the winter he still commutes by skis the couple of miles from his home to his office on campus. In the summer, he bicycles. When I realize it is David, my frustration at his slow pace transforms into admiration as I am impressed that he is out skiing at all at his age. With his long legs, his motion is smooth and graceful. As I ski up alongside, I begin a conversation about the glorious day, the beauty of the snow-shrouded trees, and the quality of the skiing. I do not introduce myself but speak in a familiar tone as if we know each other. I doubt he recognizes me bundled against the cold. Little of my face is visible with my hat pulled down to my eyebrows and my fleece neck gaiter covering my mouth and nose like a bank robber. He responds in a friendly tone, as he would to any conversation from a fellow skier, never letting on that he might not know who I am. I slow my pace to remain skiing alongside him and continue chatting, but soon I get cold and sadly have to ski faster in order to warm up. We say our farewells and off I go, stepping into the tracks ahead of him.

This is one of my first and favorite memories of David Klein. I doubt he remembers that encounter. I first really got to know David a few years later at weekly "Marching and Chowder Society" lunches: a group of six to ten people who met for lunch once a week at a rotation of dining venues in Fairbanks. At age forty-eight, I was the youngest member. Everyone else was retired, many of them professors emeriti. Conversation amidst this highly educated and liberal crowd ranged from local events to state or national politics, to the latest happenings at the university, to deaths of friends or colleagues. It was always lively, entertaining, and informative. David fully participated by reflecting on local environmental or political issues, discussing historical events in relation to something current, or sharing details of a recent trip. I also would stop to talk with David when I ran into him at the grocery store, public lectures, or environmental events. The more we spoke, the better we got to know each other, and I realized that I walked away from every conversation having learned something new.

After sitting next to David at the lunch table for a few years, one day he casually broached the subject of helping him put together a book about his life. "My children have been bugging me to do this for a while now, but I'm too busy still trying to write scientific papers," he said. David had read the life history book I had just completed of Ginny Wood (Brewster 2012), so he was familiar with my style, and thought I could help him. After a few meetings to discuss possible approaches to the book, we decided to just jump in feet first and start recording.

I was a bit nervous to interview David. I was intimidated by his somewhat formal speaking style and the fact that he was a scientist. I am not a scientist and knew little about wildlife studies or management, and was worried that I would not be able to follow his explanations or stay engaged with his detailed stories. David also had specific ideas about what he envisioned in a book about his life. This was a lot of pressure for me; different from my previous two life history books (Brewster 2004, 2012), where after the interviewing was completed the narrators were not involved in the book production due to medical issues or death. In addition, I was close friends with these people before we began recording, and they trusted me to represent their lives in a way in which they were comfortable. In comparison, David and I only had a superficial understanding of each other before starting this project, and our approach was more businesslike. Despite all this, I decided to help David. I knew he had made contributions to scientific understanding of Alaska ecosystems, had administered the Alaska Cooperative Wildlife Research Unit at the University of Alaska for thirty-five years, and that he had observed many changes in his over sixty years in Alaska. I thought his life and the role he played in Alaska history was something that others could learn from.

Scientific Accomplishments

The purpose of this life history book is to highlight the life and accomplishments of a pioneering Alaska scientist. The focus is not on his scientific findings per se, but to tell the stories of how this science was done, to show the inspiration behind the research, and to expose the thinking underlying particular scientific theories.

As an ecologist, David Klein sees the connections between people, plants, animals, and the land, and applies this to all aspects of his life and the world. He has contributed to the field of wildlife studies by emphasizing the importance of animal-habitat relationships. More specifically, it involved thinking about how the plant influences the animal as well as how the animal influences the plant. His research was focused on ungulate species in the Arctic (caribou, muskoxen, and reindeer) and their behavior and adaptations to this extreme environment. This meant looking at things like the food they eat, where they go to get quality forage, how they behave, if they migrate seasonally, and how they respond to predation.

David worked on so many research projects over the years that it is impossible to cover it all in this book. For those who want a more comprehensive scientific explanation of specific research results, we would refer them to the many papers David published in scientific journals and conference proceedings. Finally, it is important to David that people recognize that he has not been the only one to do research on these animals, nor by any means is a sole expert. He collaborated with many colleagues and graduate students both in Alaska and around the Arctic with whom credit should be shared.

David's earliest research in Alaska focused on deer ecology in Southeast Alaska. His findings verified that old growth forests in the southern and northern extremities of Southeast Alaska provide critical deer habitat. This resulted in development of the then novel, but now widely accepted, concepts that deer selectively feed on the highest-quality forage available during the summer growth period, preferring to forage on alpine tundra rather than shaded forest floor vegetation. He was also able to show that limited capability for animals to feed under high-density conditions had direct results on body size, and that there was a relationship between forage biomass and animal numbers.

The major component of David's research has emphasized the interrelationship of caribou (and secondarily reindeer) with their food sources, stressing nutritional relationships, variations in forage quality, and plant responses to grazing. He also was involved in explaining differences in migration patterns between large and small caribou herds and identifying energetic costs of insect avoidance by caribou. Much of his research has been interdisciplinary, involving biologists, social scientists, and local residents. For instance, he was involved in evaluating the effectiveness of caribou management systems in Alaska and Canada from the viewpoints of indigenous subsistence hunters and government agency managers.

In addition, David conducted research on muskox ecology in the Alaska Arctic, where he compared grazing strategies of muskoxen and caribou, investigated muskox habitat and forage selection, and looked at the influence of snow on winter habitat use and possible competition with caribou. Research results were used to develop recommendations to minimize impact on muskoxen and assure protection of their habitat from oil and gas exploration in Alaska and Greenland.

Another aspect of David's scientific work relates to consequences of northern development on wildlife. Results demonstrated both the adaptability and limitations of wildlife populations when confronted with large-scale development projects. For example, research findings indicated how oil field infrastructure may influence access by caribou to insect-relief habitat and clarified how caribou respond to obstructions and disturbances.

David Klein has been recognized by a number of awards, including meritorious service from the US Department of the Interior, special recognition from The Wildlife Society, performance awards from the US Fish and Wildlife Service, and the 1999 Aldo Leopold Award from The Wildlife Society (The Wildlife Society 1999 and 2005). He also has been a role model for many younger leaders of today's conservation movement by mentoring university students into becoming recognized and productive scientists and responsible citizen activists in their own right.

Interviewing

On the evening of November 4, 2013, I drive up to David Klein's small, secluded house immersed in a tight-knit forest of stunted, skinny black spruce trees. His backyard abuts the undeveloped northern section of the university campus and its network of trails. David built this house in 2000, after having built two previous homes in other parts of Fairbanks with now former wives. He selected this location because it was close to campus where he could enjoy a rural location, privacy, and the opportunity to ski right from his door.

Stepping into the living room from the enclosed arctic entry, the birch wood interior emits a golden glow that engulfs you like a sunset. One wall is a huge built-in bookshelf housing rows and rows of David's eclectic collection of books, and David's "desk"—a large rectangular table—sits under a large picture window and is covered with piles of papers, stacks of mail, and magazines. A large mounted muskox skull hangs above as if overseeing the happenings below.

Although long since retired, David remains engaged with science and political issues. He stays attuned to the latest in scientific inquiry by reading journal articles and is still working on writing a few articles of his own. He avidly reads the daily newspaper and writes letters to the editor or to politicians on key issues. And he stays in close contact with former students and colleagues by email. When not outdoors skiing, biking, hiking, gardening, or splitting wood, or going to campus to meet colleagues or attend lectures, David works on his computer at his desk where he gains inspiration

David at his desk in his house, 2014.
UNIVERSITY OF ALASKA FAIRBANKS, TODD PARIS.

from watching forest creatures and birds at the feeder hanging off his porch. Staying connected to nature is essential for his well-being.

In order to get to know each other better, David and I visit over dinner before turning on the recorder for our formal interview. I set up the recorder on a small table that stands between me sitting on the old futon couch and David who sits in his hard wooden desk chair facing me. I connect one microphone to his collar and the other to my shirt, and we're off and running. Three hours later I have to cut it off. It is now ten o'clock. And we haven't even gotten past his childhood!

This pattern continued over the course of a year and resulted in twenty-five interviews. I started each interview with a question about a general subject or theme that we had previously agreed would be the evening's topic. David talked for two to three hours. As a professor, he was accustomed to lecturing on a topic, and his conversational style sometimes followed this pattern. This can be challenging if you expect a conversation where you have the opportunity to respond and engage in a back-and-forth discussion, but I accepted it, since within the oral history context the person talking about his or her life is the main subject of the interaction. However, there are times when it is important to ask follow-up questions, so there were moments when I was challenged to find ways to interrupt to get clarification. As I became more comfortable and relaxed around David, I gained the confidence to just jump in to ask about something I didn't understand or to bring him back when I felt he got too far off topic. David took this in stride and just kept on talking.

As a scientist, David is focused on detailed observation, and as an ecologist, he sees the world as a complex system of interconnected variables. This may be one explanation behind his storytelling style, where he provides a fine resolution of description and shares many side stories related to an event or backgrounds of the people involved. His presentation is particularly jam-packed when the topic is science or ecology. All of the scientific facts can be hard to absorb. The associations between things come to him so fast that he often jumps into a related concept before fully explaining the first. For example, when talking about population dynamics of deer on islands in Southeastern Alaska, David quickly shifts to talking about their predators: wolves, brown and black bears. Always seeing linkages, talking about bears gets him thinking about the salmon that bears eat and changes topics once again to explain how nutrients leaching out of rotting salmon nurture the old-growth forest system.

This diverging tendency created challenges in the oral history interviews. I would often feel that David was taking us off the main trail into the weeds; that he was off the map we had been following. I worked hard to stay engaged along the side trails, and amazingly, if I was patient enough, he often came back around on his own. In these moments of diversion, I would sometimes lose focus and realize that I wasn't listening carefully. This was embarrassing. I didn't want it to look like I wasn't interested. I respected David's knowledge and appreciated this opportunity to become better informed on subjects new to me. But, I also was continually thinking about the audience for a future life history book. The story of his life's work had to be told in a way that would hold the attention of readers who were not necessarily scientists. I did not think that they would be as interested in all the details that

David found so fascinating and critical to the telling of his life. With this in mind, I was already mentally editing his narrative into a shorter form that would maintain a sense of how this man thinks and connects information.

The retelling of memories is a personalized art form. As fiction writer Isabel Allende says: "Memory is fiction. We select the brightest and the darkest, ignoring what we are ashamed of, and so embroider the broad tapestry of our lives. Each of us chooses the tone for telling his or her own story" (Allende 2001:303–4). For some people, weaving a good yarn takes precedence over accuracy. For David Klein, he relays the past in the form of facts rather than a flowing literary narrative. Nevertheless, it is important to remember that our stories are based upon a continual relayering of meaning as we are influenced by audience, setting, current events, or interests (Schneider 2002, 2005, 2008). A life history is a created negotiation between narrator and oral historian (Grele 1975; Finnegan 1992; Schneider and Morrow 1995; Yow 1997; Portelli 1998; Schneider 2002, 2005, 2008). The constructed narrative is influenced by the experiences, ideas, and biases the researcher brings to the questioning and his or her responses to the narrator. Mandelbaum (1973) and Schneider (2008) note that life histories often are framed in terms of turning points that resonate through the rest of a person's life.

With David Klein, construction of this life history also included his own predetermined ideas of what he wanted to talk about. Before we even started the interviewing, David already had a plan in mind. And for both of us, we knew this was a life history focused on his public life and scientific career, that we would not be talking so much about his private and family life. There is brief mention of his first wife, Arlayne, and his children, Martin, PeggyEllen, and Laura, in the early years as they relate to David's activities. As with many academics or scientists, this book highlights David's professional experiences and accomplishments.

David William Cohen (1994) reminds us that memory is as much about forgetting as it is about remembering, and making these decisions about which facts to leave out and which to put in means there is a difference between "history as lived" and "history as recorded" (Tonkin 1992). This is certainly true for David Klein. This life history can only offer a glimpse of a very complicated man with a long and rich life. It has only been possible to tap the surface of his mind and memory.

Building Connections

By the end of 2014, after a year of conducting interviews, I felt that David and I had enough material and decided it was time to stop recording. As I spent time working with transcripts and David drafted his own chapters, we periodically met for dinner. These visits and sharing experiences with David outside of the formalized interview setting allowed us to stay connected and expand our friendship.

Some oral historians warn against becoming too involved in the lives of their narrators (Yow 1995; K'Meyer and Crothers 2007). I disagree. I believe friendship is critical to something as personal as a life history. The life history relationship is based on mutual trust. With friendship, comes trust and deeper understanding. As a friend, I feel a sense of responsibility in how I retell the stories. It was important to me to build these connections with David.

I made two trips with David, during which spending time with him and his family provided new insight into who he was. In May 2015, we drove thirteen hours to Homer to visit his daughter PeggyEllen and celebrate his eighty-eighth birthday. It became a narrated journey through Alaska's landscape as viewed through the lens of David's past. Near Kenai Lake, he pointed to the top of a craggy cliff where he had studied mountain sheep in the 1950s. And we located the old enclosure hidden in the woods just off the Seward Highway where research had been done in the 1960s and 1970s to document the rate of vegetative growth when herbivores were excluded. And in June 2016, there was a sudden whirlwind camping trip to Nancy Lake Campground, located halfway between Homer and Fairbanks, to meet PeggyEllen to exchange cars after David had to leave his broken-down Volvo in Homer for repair. The three of us engaged in interesting conversation and had fun together, which allowed me to catch a glimpse of what it would have been like to be on one of his field research trips.

In August 2016, at age eighty-nine, David moved out of his home into the Raven Landing retirement community. No more cutting firewood,

In May 2015, David revisits an enclosure built in 1960 by the US Forest Service on the Kenai Peninsula to compare browsed and unbrowsed winter moose range. PHOTO BY KAREN BREWSTER.

planting a garden, clearing brush in the yard, or cleaning out gutters. No more clearing snow from the driveway or worrying about slipping on the ice. While David misses the exercise these chores provided, he knows that as his balance and stability decline, it is safer to make the change sooner rather than later. More time for thinking, reading, and writing. At Raven Landing, David has reveled in the intellectual engagement of dinner conversations with other educated and like-minded senior citizens. And he has been invigorated by the physical activity and camaraderie of a group who regularly plays Ping-Pong together. He even competed on a mixed-doubles team at the Alaska International Senior Games in August 2017 held in Fairbanks.

Putting It All Together

Hearing about events firsthand in the words of someone you know brings the past to life in a more personal way than just words on a page. In this vein, David Klein's stories were well suited for oral history. They represented the "behind-the-scenes" details of how science is carried out and how scientific understandings are formed. This is something rarely discussed among scientists (Estes 2016) and not well understood by nonscientists. David's life provided an opportunity to record a perspective on what it means to be an Alaska scientist.

Transcribing the sixty hours of audio recorded during our twenty-five sessions (Klein 2013b–d, 2014a–v) and editing it to create a smooth and engaging narrative has been a long and arduous process. Eight hundred and thirty-eight pages of transcripts were created by Wendy Contreal from the US Fish and Wildlife Service National Conservation Training Center Archives/Museum in Shepherdstown, West Virginia.[1] I then reviewed and corrected each transcript while listening to the associated interview. To help build the overall narrative, I also utilized previous oral history interviews with David in the UAF Oral History Archive (Klein 1985 and 2002). While somewhat repetitious, these older interviews did contain different stories or

---

1. The original recordings and final transcripts are archived at the Oral History Program, Alaska and Polar Regions Collections & Archives, Elmer E. Rasmuson Library, University of Alaska Fairbanks. The final transcripts are also archived at the US Fish and Wildlife Service National Conservation Training Center Archives/Museum.

alternative explanations than were in my interviews. Given this wealth of material, it was particularly tough to determine what was most relevant to the main storyline versus what could be cut. To David, it was all key to the retelling of his life.

Producing a life history involves selection, since "only a very small part of all that the person has experienced can possibly be recorded" (Mandelbaum 1973:177). Moving from interview to published account involves countless decisions, many of which affect the tone and often the meaning of the final account (Horne and McBeth 1998). I have sought to maintain a sense of the conversation and David's personal style, but it is worth remembering that we speak and tell stories differently than we write and "that for all of our efforts, this is not the original telling. It is our representation of the telling" (Schneider 2002:147). The term *oral biography* attempts to bridge this gap by preserving voice and story while providing context for future genera-tions (ibid.:114). The goal is to "make sure that the way the story is retold and represented to new audiences remains true to the original intent of the telling" (ibid.:137).

While we have created a document based on David's retelling of events that shaped his life and career, his detailed review and editing of the oral-based chapters has additionally influenced the account and produced an expanded collaborative project. As the editor, my job has been to help make the narrative engaging, which at times meant making tough decisions about removing distracting or confusing sections or rewriting pieces for clarity and brevity. David then reviewed the stories, deleting pieces he found unneces-sary and inserting details missing from the interviews, including citations to related articles. Given that David's editing already created a narrative with a more written tone than I was used to in my previous oral history work, I gave myself permission to make additional editorial changes in sentence structure and flow that I would never have done in the past. This level of ed-iting begs the question as to whether this is still an oral biography. I suggest that it is, because despite the reader being a bit further removed from the original telling, I am confident that we have retained the underlying mean-ing of David's words and stories.

The current expectation within the field of oral history is that a life his-tory will be a co-created document that sets the narrator's stories within the context of broader historical themes (K'Meyer and Crothers 2007). David Dunaway calls this an "oral memoir," in which a narrator tells his or her own story and a writer adds explanation and footnotes (Dunaway 1991). However, in this book, I have abided by David Klein's wishes and diverged from this methodology by adding only minimal contextual footnotes, instead incorporating such material into the main text. Also divergent from a standard life history, references are given to related published literature. Detailed discussion of the science is left to these more appropriate sources and interested readers are directed to specific articles for full scientific analysis.

By combining the spoken word with the written, this book brings new meaning to what it means to be a collaborative life history project. David has been a prolific and talented writer who wanted a book about his life also to include his writings on topics related to the application of scientific knowledge to public policy and philosophy. These essays appear in the third part of this book, *The Human Perspective: Essays by David Klein*. Although there is a change in tone from the oral-based chapters to these written pieces, they remain relevant to the larger themes of David's life. They provide a window into his mind and demonstrate the shaping of his views and values at a deeper level than what the oral history interviews alone were able to capture.

Finally, given the wealth of information included in David's stories, the original manuscript was much longer than what appears here. In order to appeal to a more general audience, we realized that it had to be shortened for publication. However, we did not want to lose the valuable historical record that David's life represents, so have chosen to archive the original manuscript under the same title at Elmer E. Rasmuson Library at the University of Alaska Fairbanks so that readers wishing more detail can access it.

Legacies

David Klein's stories are a touchstone for thinking about how Alaska's landscape and cultures have changed over the last sixty-eight years. His outlook, philosophy, and approach toward sustainability, wildlife management regimes, and conserving our natural world serves as an inspiration to us all as we move forward in an ever-changing global society.

David's experiences also provide insight into how science can play a role in environmental advocacy, which is especially timely given the current debate about causes and impacts of climate change. As a scientist, he felt he could be most effective by applying his training to the presentation of unbiased scientific data. Even in 2018, at age ninety-one, David continues to advocate. For example, he has been pushing for creation of a new state park in the Quartz Lake–Shaw Creek Flats area, about eighty road miles southeast of Fairbanks, where he owned a recreational cabin for over forty years and is concerned about declining water levels contributing to deterioration of fish habitat and growing motorized threats to the area's rich fish and wildlife habitat (Sherwonit 2012; Klein 2013a).

David Klein has the ability to synthesize various disciplines and perspectives, and sees a connection between nature and humanity. He has passed this thinking on to his students, and emphasizes the importance of education if we are to create a more sustainable world. As an optimist, David continues to look toward a brighter future, and hopes that his stories and his legacy in science will inspire the next generation to keep moving forward toward ensuring the survival of our fragile planet.

EARLY INFLUENCES

The chapters in this section are based on oral history interviews and offer insight into David's earliest influences that built toward his becoming an ecologist and wildlife biologist in Alaska. The stories show how childhood experiences shaped his appreciation of nature and development of outdoor skills, how his educational training formed the underpinnings of his ecological perspectives, and how he fell in love with Alaska and chose to make it the focus of his research.

David (left) as a child with his
older brother Dick, and older
sister Elizabeth (Betty), circa 1930.

1
Learning to Love the Outdoors

I was born in Fitchburg, Massachusetts, on May 18, 1927. My parents were living in a suburb called Lunenburg. My father was working in Fitchburg as a machinist for Iver Johnson Arms and Cycle Works, a company that made firearms, motorcycles, and bicycles. I have a sister, Betty (Prior), six years older than me, who lives in Florida, and my brother, Dick, who was two years older than me, passed away in September 2017.

My father was Ferdinand Klein. He was born in Brooklyn, New York, in 1891 and grew up there. To make it simpler, sometimes he went by Fred, but my mother called him Bud. His parents had immigrated to New York City from Neuchâtel canton, the French-speaking part of Switzerland. My grandfather's birth certificate shows that although he was born in Switzerland he was of German heritage. The woman he married, my grandmother, was French and living in Switzerland at the time. My grandfather apparently was trained as a gold worker and watchmaker in Switzerland and did similar work after arriving in the United States in Brooklyn and Attleboro, Massachusetts.

I was never able to get enough information about my grandparents or their coming to this country. My father never talked much about his parents or his family background. He had a sister, but as adults they did not get along very well together, and he did not keep track of her. The perplexing questions in my mind have been why my grandfather's family left Germany and moved to Switzerland at the time that they did and why my grandmother left France and went to Switzerland. Similarly, why did they choose to leave Switzerland and come to the United States? During my life

David's parents, Ferdinand and Norma A. (Peverley) Klein, in the backyard of their house in Buckland, Connecticut, circa 1944. COURTESY OF DAVID KLEIN.

some have assumed that I was Jewish because of the surname Klein, but it is a common surname on both sides of the border between France and Germany. My father, however, never gave any indication that there was any Jewish background in our family or that it might have been why his parents left Switzerland.

My mother, Norma Alberta Peverley, was born in 1893 in Syracuse, New York. Both sides of her families had immigrated to Canada from England generations before, and then from Canada to upstate New York. My mother's father, Reginald Richard Peverley, preferring to be called Richard or Dick, had left school precipitously, left home, and "rode the rails" west to Chicago, where he got a job in the stockyards. He learned the butchering trade there, then returned home and ultimately owned his own butcher shop in Cambridge, Massachusetts. He lost his wife, Elizabeth Cottrell Peverley, and oldest daughter, Rita, during a contagious disease outbreak, and raised his remaining daughter, Norma, as a single father.

I do not recall ever hearing how my parents met specifically, but it was in Cambridge. My mother had post–high school secretarial training and some training in art, and held jobs in the Boston area in accounting and painting decorative floral designs on fine china. My grandfather had the foresight in that regard to support her training to increase her likelihood of finding employment as a woman. My father was working as an intern in the Boston area to become a small tool machinist. In those days, if you wanted to become a professional in any field, especially mechanics or carpentry, you worked as an intern. Having this type of experience greatly increased your chances of getting a job and earning a higher salary. What I do know is that when my father was courting my mother he often invited her on weekends to go for a boat ride in Boston Harbor. He rented a rowboat and enjoyed fishing, while my mother read a book, which she said helped her avoid seasickness.

My father was very knowledgeable and had very broad interests. He had a good high school education and was extremely well read. By the time he was in his thirties, he had such broad capabilities that he was known as a Renaissance man by family and friends. My father was a pacifist, but was supportive of the war effort during World War II because of Nazism and what was happening to people in Europe. He was a good citizen in terms of being well informed, and believed in supporting our government. He was a fiscally conservative Republican of the old school, but as an outdoorsman he was very much supportive of protection of the environment, which is something that influenced my developing an appreciation for nature.

My mother was kind and loving. Understanding would be a good term to describe her. They were very close and had a very good relationship. He was such a hard worker and much of it was tied to providing for the family, encouraging growth of the children and their education, and supporting his wife and her Christian values. My mother was moderately religious, and the church that she attended and wanted us to go to was Congregationalist. I assume that my father had leanings toward Christianity, but I think he was more of a deist. He was tolerant of religious beliefs, but he didn't believe in organized churches, partly because they were always in conflict with one another, so he was not an active church member; he went on special occasions for cultural and family reasons. One thing I know for sure is that my father definitely believed in evolution, although it wasn't a particularly popular view at that time among Christian Protestants. Although more liberal, the Congregationalists had not yet really bought into evolution, and Methodist and Lutheran churches were considered too conservative to accept evolution. My dad would kid my mom about the existence of evolution. I remember him talking at the dinner table about something he'd read about evolution in the Sunday *Boston Globe* newspaper, or when we'd talk about something related to nature, he would explain it in an evolutionary context. Or then there was a time when we were planning to visit the Brooklyn Zoo in New York City, and he turned to my mom and said, "You can see your relatives there, the monkeys." She smiled. She knew he was teasing her. She never directly said that she did not believe in evolution because that wasn't as important to her as living a life that was good for the family and avoiding conflict with her husband. They were both tolerant of the other's understandings and got along fine.

During the Depression, my father was laid off from Iver Johnson Arms and Cycle Works. It had looked like he had a good future there, but then they cut back nearly everything except the firearms and bicycles and the company virtually folded. They recovered a little bit during World War II, but they did not survive. So my family moved to Hartland, Vermont, which was a small community on the Connecticut River. It had one store, one gas station, a post office, and a tiny town hall. We were able to rent an old farmhouse with land and have a large garden, chickens, and occasionally raised a calf for veal. My father had trained himself to be a jack-of-all-trades, and was a good electrician, plumber, carpenter, and machinist, so was able to find small part-time jobs. He found enough work to help us get by financially, but we were living as much off the land as possible.

My parents chose Hartland because my grandfather, my mother's father, was living on a small subsistence dairy farm near there. His farm was about four miles from our farmstead. Shortly before he retired and sold his butcher business in Cambridge, Grampa got remarried to a widow named Ida. She was warm, loving, and a wonderful cook, and even though she actually was our step-grandmother, I thought of her as a grandmother since I had never known my real grandmother. Grampa had six milking cows and a team of horses, cut and stored his own hay, and raised and cured silage for the cows.

He and Ida did the milking by hand and put the milk cans in a spring that ran through the cellar to cool down the milk before they took it to the dairy in the village to be pasteurized.

My grandfather also had a large vegetable garden, an apple orchard, and made maple syrup. It was really fun for us kids to go visit during sugaring time. He collected the sap from the maple trees into buckets that he then poured into a larger wooden container that he hauled around on a low sled pulled by a horse. Ida would be boiling the sap down in a special shed where the steam would be finding its way out under the eaves. As the sap was boiling down, Ida let some thicken beyond the syrup stage, and then would throw a ladleful of it on the snow to turn into maple candy for us kids to eat. It was wonderful. Whenever we went to visit Grampa, we always came back with great quantities of apples and maybe some meat. My parents didn't want to be dependent upon him, so they did their best to get by during the hard times of the Depression, but it was nice to have him and his farm there as an emergency fallback if they needed it.

Grampa loved having a small farm. He did most of the work himself, enjoying the diversity of activities and independence associated with farming. As a young boy, Grampa was a wonderful role model for me. When asked what I wanted to be when I grew up, my unhesitating response was "a farmer."

My childhood was like nirvana. It was rural New England. Hilly, pine forest, small farms, and small villages. I did not know what city life was like, except as described by my parents and they preferred rural living. I went to the four-room schoolhouse in Hartland for first and second grade, which was within walking distance from our home. For fun as kids we did the usual things, like playing games with other kids like Kick the Can, throwing a baseball, or chasing games. I do remember an unfortunate experience I had with a close friend whom I often spent time with after school. One day, we were hanging around the town hall, which was a small red brick building in the center of town with low windows to let light into the first level. It was a nice place for little boys that liked to wander around on the only concrete sidewalks in town. While absorbed in physically active talk, I accidently bumped a window and broke the glass. The first reaction was that we should run like hell. We knew that to replace a big window like that would cost a lot of money. But then we thought, "No, this was an accident. I did not try to do it!" So I went home and told my mom what I had done and she understood that it was not a willful act, and she said, "Well, you have to tell them that you did it." She took me by the hand and we walked back down to the town hall. We went up to the front desk inside and my mom said, "My son has something to tell you." I was probably close to tears and I said, "I broke the window. I did not mean to." My mom said, "You know, we'll pay for it." I do not know how much it cost, but it was probably substantial for our budget at the time. My mother certainly got across her message that if you do something like that, then you have to take responsibility. You can't just walk away. Of course, she also was teaching me the concept of respect and that it was wrong to destroy someone else's property.

In 1936, we moved to Connecticut because my father had found a full-time job in Hartford with a company making parts for Sikorsky helicopters. During these pre-war years, it was realized that helicopters would be increasingly useful for the military and would probably have an important role to play in future wars. My father was a machinist and worked his way up into management. He must have been good at his job, because fairly early on they put him in charge of supervising a big section of the workers. During the Second World War, my father was able to stay home and work and not go into the military because he was in what they called "an essential job." Helicopters were very important for the military and the parts were in high demand, so the company was very busy. He soon was working twelve-hour shifts and paid overtime for over forty hours of work per week. I didn't see much of my dad when he was working those long shifts, but it was financially beneficial to our family because he received extra pay for working overtime. When he worked night shifts, the only time we saw him was at dinnertime. He slept during the day when we were at school, and then he got up and had dinner with us and then went to work. My parents both felt that it was important that we had at least one meal a day where we sat down and discussed things together as an entire family. To me, those mealtime get-togethers were the key to our strong family relationships.

In Hartford, we moved into a big complex with six apartments in one building. Moving from the country in Vermont right into this apartment complex was one of the toughest parts of my childhood. I was only in the third grade and had a hard time with the intense human presence of the city. Not long after we had moved into the neighborhood when I didn't yet know the city, I got lost after becoming separated from my brother when we were running away from a gang of "mean" kids. Once I realized that I didn't know where I was, I thought, "Well, I'll go and get help from a policeman." But then it occurred to me, "I don't know my address or phone number. All I know is my name." And we had just moved into the neighborhood so my name didn't have any meaning. It was starting to get a little dark, and I was wondering how anybody would find me. I was starting to get frightened and felt like crying. I had never been lost before. When we lived in the country, I would have known my way home, because I knew the terrain and could read the different signals. But I had not yet learned how to interpret landmarks in the city, so it seemed more like a wilderness to me than the woods. Then I saw my dad coming down the street. That was such a wonderful feeling!

We stayed in that apartment in Hartford for a few years and then found a house to rent that had a big yard, an orchard, and the landlord had beehives. I learned a lot about bees, stimulating my interest in learning more about their social complexity and their importance as pollinators. It was not a bad place for my brother and me. There was a river at the back of the property that offered challenges and risks for us, even though our parents had declared it off-limits because it was heavily polluted.

By 1939, my parents were financially able to buy an old run-down house and some land in Buckland, Connecticut, which was a twelve-mile commute each way for my dad to Sikorsky Helicopters in Hartford. Buckland was a quiet town of about two or three hundred people. It had a post office, one store, a gas station with a repair shop, and was surrounded by agricultural fields mostly growing high-quality tobacco for cigar production. Once again we were able to have a large garden and chickens. My dad loved to plant, so much of the food we ate was harvested from that garden. It was not until the end of the Second World War that freezing vegetables was a preservation option, and there were no supermarkets where fresh vegetables and greens were available in the winter, so we didn't eat fresh vegetables until spring and summer. But we did have a large root cellar, where carrots, beets, turnips, and potatoes were stored, and my mother canned a lot of fruit and vegetables like peas, corn, and green or wax beans.

The Klein's house in Buckland, Connecticut, with the garden, chicken coop, and at left a garage and workshop that David's father built. COURTESY OF DAVID KLEIN.

I remember in the Depression years, as well as during the war, subsistence living made sense. My father had read a lot about home gardens and self-sufficiency, and strived to do things in an energy-efficient way. It wasn't a question of fossil fuels and greenhouse gases back then, it was a question of the cost of commercial fertilizers. If you had a natural fertilizer available, such as chicken or cow manure, why not use it? He worked the soil by hand in small vegetable plots in our yard, and fertilized them by stirring in compost and the manure from our chickens.

My brother and I had the not-very-enjoyable job of cleaning out the accumulation of manure in the chicken shed. We didn't like the work, but we did it because we knew that our effort was critical to the garden's productivity. It smelled awful. After a while you got used to it, but if you didn't change your clothes before you went to school, they knew you'd been out in the chicken shed. Dick hated it worse than I did, so I frequently negotiated with him over who did other chores related to the chickens. I enjoyed the feeding, egg gathering, and adding dry wood chips to the nest boxes and floor, leaving the job of keeping water for the chickens for Dick. He liked the latter task even though it was harder work carrying the water to the henhouse, but it was less time consuming than the chicken chores I chose. I said, "Well, I'll do all the other chores for most of the time, but you have to take over major responsibility for the cleaning." I did end up giving him a hand, because to do it by yourself was psychologically depressing, because it was so much to do, and so messy. Overall, my brother was a good guy, but as a big brother, a lot of times, he took advantage of me. But on the other hand, I got away with quite a bit, too.

After my step-grandmother, Ida, died, my grandfather sold his farm in Vermont and he moved in with us in Buckland. Since my father was working a lot and commuting, my grandfather took over the gardening responsibilities and handled other chores around the place. Grampa was about seventy, was still in pretty good health, wanted to stay active, and loved outside work. For instance, we had a wood-fired furnace in the basement that heated the house, so my grandfather salvaged wood for it from trees that had blown down in the 1936 hurricane that came up through New England. Then he used a sledgehammer and wedges to split the wood into chunks that would fit through the furnace door. Sometimes my brother and I would go out after school to help him, and he showed us how to use the big crosscut saw to saw through huge trunks of oak by hand. I was very attached to my grandfather. I used to hang out with him and help him because I always was interested in learning this kind of outdoors work.

Childhood is important in shaping one's subsequent life, but for some of us it is more important than for others. In my case, my mother, my father, and my grandfather had a tremendous influence on me through their genes and through the environment they created for me. Both my parents loved nature. My father was an ardent hunter and fisherman, but he also loved just to be outdoors. My father was such a handyman that both my brother and I wanted to be like him. But as a machinist, he was largely constrained to indoor factory jobs, so he used to advise my brother and me to "find some other job." My grandfather and my parents all enjoyed getting their hands in the soil and gardening. In addition to the vegetable garden, my mother always had lots of houseplants and a big flower garden. She also enjoyed and knew

L–R: David's grandfather Reginald "Dick" Peverley, David's sister Betty, and David's father Ferdinand in Buckland after Grampa Dick came to live with the Klein family, circa 1943. COURTESY OF DAVID KLEIN.

a lot about wildflowers. In the springtime, when the wildflowers were starting to come out, she'd say, "Who wants to go for a walk with me and maybe see some wildflowers?" I usually always said, "Yes." So my mother played an important role in nurturing my fascination with wildflowers and later interest in botany. Both my parents encouraged my interest in understanding the flowers, learning the names, and looking at why the plants were related to one another. I remember one Christmas after my parents were back on their feet financially when I was given a beautiful book on wildflowers of the northeastern states and Audubon's book, *Birds of North America*. Receiving these books was the best present ever, and they were my pride and joy.

My mother also loved to go for Sunday afternoon drives so she could appreciate the New England landscape. She especially enjoyed this in the fall when foliage colors were at their peak. My mother never learned to drive herself, so my father would take her. As a young kid, I always wanted to go along, whereas it was boring for my brother because they drove so slowly on small back roads, and he wanted to be doing other things. We also did a little bit of camping together as a family in a camping trailer that my father had built, which helped encourage my enjoyment of being outdoors and my sense of adventure. However, one time when we were camping at the beach on the coast of Long Island Sound, my brother and I got into a little trouble. Dick and I would normally spend much of the day out in the shallow, wadeable water in the bay where there weren't any waves coming in, so it was safe for children. But we found a short chunk of a large log that we nailed a driftwood outrigger to and we paddled out into the deeper water of the bay. When my parents saw that we were out much too far, my brother got chewed out worse than me, because he was older and so was supposed to know that because I couldn't swim I shouldn't have been out that far.

My mother certainly supported my interests in aesthetics, landscaping, and art. She had training in art before she was married which helped with her job painting floral designs on china. She played her talent down by saying, "Well, I was just copying." But she wasn't. She did have pictures and flower displays to work from, but she had a nice eye for perspective and was good at drawing. I was adept at copying complex pictures of buildings and landscapes, but slow in the process. When we moved to Hartford, my mother suggested that I might benefit from some art lessons. Our family was still recovering financially from the Depression, but she convinced my father that a few art lessons would be just what I needed. I think I was eight or nine years old. I was shy and I did not have appreciation for the capabilities or talents that I might have had. I knew that I liked to draw and my family appreciated it, but I was very slow and meticulous.

Well, that was a disaster for me. There were six of us in the art class, and the teacher, who was a young woman, gave us an assignment where you'd have three minutes to draw big freehand things with different colored crayons. She'd say, "Okay, you have the paper. Now, I want you to take a colored crayon, and make a slash like this on the paper. After a couple of those things, see how nice a curve you can make to it." Then she would go around looking at what we had all done. She'd say to me, "Oh, no, that doesn't look very good." This was not what I expected from the class. This had nothing to do with my interests and capabilities. This was just not my way of doing things.

My mom came and picked me up and she said, "Well, how did it go?" I really felt bad, because I felt there must be something wrong with me because I didn't feel like I connected at all with the class. I told her what happened. That I had thought the teacher would let us do our own thing and then correct us. But this woman didn't understand me at all and I didn't understand what she was trying to do. I said, "She was a nice young woman, but I thought it was a waste of money because she was just telling me I was doing everything wrong." I basically felt that she was the wrong person to teach me; that if it had been a different teacher it might have worked. But I certainly appreciated that my mom and dad made this effort to pay for special lessons.

Among my siblings, I was the most oriented toward the land, although my brother did enjoy hunting. As the oldest son, Dick received Dad's advice and training that enabled him to become a competent hunter and fisherman, whereas when I became old enough to get such training and encouragement Dad no longer had the time to focus on my presumed hunting and fishing aspirations. On the weekends we might have time together, but it was more by chance. He was always busy with all these things to do on the house, and he just didn't have time to go hunting and fishing. You might conclude that this unanticipated loss of Dad's focus of attention was a sore spot from my perspective. But I did not see it that way. It was a negative for me in some respects, because I didn't get Dad's influence and attention as much, but I did learn a few things about how to shoot and hunt from my brother. He had a single shot .22 and a pump shotgun, and had become competent enough as a hunter so that he could go out hunting with my sister's Scottie dog that was a pretty good bird dog. Dick would hunt for rabbits in the fields by our house and occasionally pheasants. One minor problem occurred when he was using the single-shot 12-gauge shotgun and wounded a pheasant so it couldn't fly. The dog ran after it but was not trained to kill a wounded bird, so Dick ran to it and tried to hit the pheasant with the stock of the gun. He hit the ground instead and broke the stock.

The other person who had a big influence on me during my childhood was a man named Arthur Percival Curtis, known by friends as AP. He was a great-uncle through my mother, and we saw him and his wife quite a bit. He was financially well off, at least partly because he owned the patent for a unique finger rest that Iver Johnson adopted in 1933 for all of their revolvers. AP was a well-educated man with a wonderful library that contained books focused on conservation and good management of wildlife. He had been an ardent hunter, but he was also very supportive of better game laws, prevention of overshooting, the need for a migratory bird treaty, and the beginning of wildlife conservation. He helped foster my interest in these subjects because he gave me books on environmental conservation and related management of habitat for specific wildlife species, especially small game and nongame migratory birds.

AP also inspired my interest in world cultures and diversity. On one of his visits, when I think I was in third grade, AP was impressed by my level of understanding of world geography, and learned that it came from my stamp collecting. He said that such worldliness was a valuable asset for business. He had saved lots of stamps from foreign countries with the intent of giving them to a serious stamp collector. He said I qualified and sent them to me, along with future ones he received. I excitedly waited for those foreign stamps to arrive.

As kids, we did a lot to create our own entertainment, and a lot of it was doing fun things outside, even in the winter. For example, in Vermont, there was a steep slope where the driveway made a turn that was perfect for sledding. Since we couldn't afford toboggans, we would find pieces of cardboard that you could sit on and slide down with. That was fun. We built snowmen and snow forts, and had snowball fights. I have been an ardent cross-country skier as an adult, but cross-country skiing did not exist as such when I was a boy. Even if it had existed when we lived in Vermont, our family would not have been able to afford to buy skis. We tried to improvise once using barrel staves as skis, but their surfaces were too rough to slide. In Connecticut, we would venture out onto the new forming ice of local ponds. The type of ice skates that had built-in boots were far too expensive for us, so if we had skates at all they were the kind that clamped onto the sole of your shoe and had a key that you used to tighten the screws. But we sometimes ran around on the ice and slid and played something like hockey with or without ice skates on, especially on new ice forming in the fall, which was fun because it would sag under your weight. Once you got familiar with it, you could just run across these places and the ice would go down and you'd hear it crack a little bit but it wouldn't break like older ice would. There was an official ice skating pond not far away from where we lived in Buckland, where we would sometimes go to skating parties or play a little bit of hockey with homemade hockey sticks. That was fun.

In elementary school, I didn't focus enough on some of the basics like language, reading, and spelling, and I was slow in starting to read. Even by the time I was in seventh and eighth grade, I did not read very much, partly because if I had free time I preferred to be outdoors rather than being indoors reading a book. The same was true with things like math. I'd get by, but just barely, because I wouldn't do an adequate job. I didn't do my homework well. And I was sometimes disruptive in class. If the teacher turned her back, I teased the student next to me or whispered something to someone. I was not paying attention.

The worst thing I did in grammar school was on one spring day when it was sunny and warm outside. Our teacher was called out of the room and she left with the idea that she'd be back in a couple of minutes, so she said, "I'll be right back." Well, we sat there, but then it dragged on for more than, I guess, six or eight minutes. Some of us more adventurous ones were up at the big open windows looking out and watching the traffic go by. I suggested that I could jump from the window down the eight or nine feet to the grass below without hurting myself. The other boys said, "Nah, nah, you can't do it." I figured, well, since the teacher was gone I could jump out and run around and come back before she got back in the room. So I got up on the windowsill and I leapt out and landed on the lawn. The teacher walked in just as I was going out the window. She rushed to the window, but it was too late. I was already out.

This teacher was never too severe, but after this incident she sent a note home to my mom. Apparently, she explained how embarrassing it was because a friend of hers had been driving by and saw a student leaping out the window of her classroom. She acknowledged that she shouldn't have been out of the room for that long, but emphasized that in any case I shouldn't

David (left of and in front of the teacher) with his eighth grade class, graduating from Buckland School, circa 1940. Mrs. Pierce is the teacher standing in the back. COURTESY OF DAVID KLEIN.

have jumped out the window. She felt so bad because it was so embarrassing to her and that it wouldn't have happened if she had her classroom under control. But it wasn't under control; she was out of the room. My mom explained the whole thing to me as well, and said that I should have thought about the teacher. I was pretty good about thinking about the concerns of other people so I got the message. I really felt bad about it. I don't remember whether I actually apologized to the teacher, but she was aware that I realized that I shouldn't have acted as I did. But earlier on, she had sent notes home that said, "Dave is not keeping up with studying and practicing spelling. He is doing very poorly on his spelling." She'd say, "I know he can do better. It's very disappointing to me that he's not living up to his capabilities."

The Jesters, David's high school buddies at the flag pole in front of the old main building of Manchester High School, 1945. L–R: Randy Toop, John Hansen, Sidney Cushman, David Klein. COURTESY OF DAVID KLEIN.

I then went to Manchester High School, from which I graduated in 1945. It was a good school, but it was about four and a half miles from where we lived. There was no school bus, but there were public buses that came through Buckland to North Manchester with a connection to South Manchester where the high school was. The bus stop was on the main road just two blocks from where we lived. That's how I got to school unless during good weather in spring and fall when I could ride my bike.

I had many good experiences in high school. These were largely through the friendships I made. Friendships have always been important in my life. There were five of us who were really close friends and hung out together a lot. We even had our own intramural basketball team. We called it the "Jesters," because we all had a good sense of humor and just had fun playing; it did not matter so much to us whether we lost or won. We lost most of the time because we didn't practice much, but we had a good time. Although the personalities involved were diverse, bonds of friendships made in high school seemed to last. We have maintained our friendship over the years, getting together once every five or so years back in Connecticut where the majority still live. For me, high school offered the opportunity to break away from family bonds that emphasized conformity to explore relationships with others of diverse backgrounds. High school, therefore, was a new, unique, and exciting experience.

Our close comradeship was facilitated somewhat by the fact that only one of the five of us had an automobile. He was a dairy farmer's son with extra gas rations so he could get to school and back quickly enough to still be involved in the milking. It was an old, but functional, sedan that he drove around to pick us all up, and we all chipped in to buy gas. The first thing he'd do when we got in the car was say, "Okay, twenty-five cents."

In high school, I was a C student, but I started to get interested in polar exploration and then geography, and biology was one of the few courses I got a good grade in. The teacher encouraged us to make drawings of leaves and other plant parts to compare differences between major plant groups. I loved doing that. I learned a lot about biology but also was able to use my art capabilities. I always had a keen eye about landscape and architectural design and had a real appreciation for art. But I would've been bored being an artist and not being able to move around in the environment and learn more about it.

Mechanical drawing was another course in high school that I enjoyed and did well in. One of my close buddies, John, was also in the class, and we were the only two that got As. The teacher appreciated our high-quality drawings and liked that we were good learners, but he didn't encourage the other students to come to us if they had a problem. So when the teacher would go out of the room to take a smoke break during our two-hour lab, John and I, who had finished our assigned drawings early, would offer to help other students. They would gather around our drawing tables seeking help with drawing tools and making mathematical conversions to enlarge or reduce the drawings from actual size to fit on the appropriate size paper. John's desk was close to the door and they could hear the teacher's footsteps as he came down the hallway, so they could quickly return to their own desks. But as he came into the room and saw several students gathered around my desk, he would say, "Klein, how can the students get their work done if you are talking to them?" I felt I would only add to the confusion if I responded that we were assisting the other students because he was not there to answer their questions. I was honored, however, to get an A, even if a disruptive one. The teacher later acknowledged that our class was one of the best he had had because we worked together. It was maybe the only A I got that year.

When I was in high school, it was understood that the allowance we got was very minimal, because most of my father's income was badly needed just to feed us and pay for the house and the heating and all of that. So I tried to find small jobs to earn some of my own money. When you had your own money, then you could decide how you wanted to spend it, whereas your parents were still paying for your clothes and everything else. Plus, you learned a work ethic. One of the ways I earned money was to shovel neighbors' driveways after school in winter. And I had a bicycle paper route, but houses that subscribed to the paper were few and far apart, so I got plenty of exercise but the financial return was low. One summer, I worked for a surveyor who was laying out a new housing development. I learned how to set up the transit and use it to lay out batter boards to mark the locations of house foundations and roadways. It was heavy on math, which I was not strong in, but I learned in spite of that. The surveyor was kind of stern, but he really was a nice guy and he liked helping students that were working for him. That was good training for me. It was gratifying to recognize that what I had learned in the mechanical drawing class had direct application in building at the community level.

Other summers, I worked in the tobacco fields. High-quality shade grown and broad leaf tobacco was grown in the Connecticut River Valley near where I lived. Working in the tobacco fields at harvest time was one of the best ways for us high school students to earn some spending money because we were paid by the hour and, if you put in the hours, you made quite a bit. It was hard work and you would come home with the smell of nicotine all over your fingers that was difficult to wash off. The stain would be there for two to three weeks. But it was outdoor work and you worked hard as a team, so you weren't by yourself.

I earned enough money through all these little jobs that eventually I was able to buy a car with my high school buddy who lived next door. It cost us twenty-five bucks. It was a 1924 Dodge touring car that originally had a canvas top that was long since gone, so it was wide open to the weather. This was at the beginning of the Second World War and we couldn't buy gas without ration coupons, so my friend got us a job through his uncle, who was a manager for one of the tobacco companies, where we spray-painted some of their tall tobacco curing barns. The company provided us all the equipment and paint, as well as enough gas to run our car, a compressor, and to clean out the painting equipment at the end of each day. We tried to be super conservative with the gas so that we might have a little leftover that we could use later for our car. It was a shame to waste a couple of gallons of gas to clean paint equipment, so we had the great idea to strain the gas through cheesecloth and pour it into the car. That worked fine for a while, until all the fuel lines and carburetor clogged up, and we had to use so much fresh gas to flush it all out that in the long run we didn't end up saving anything by trying to recycle. We did not try that again.

Since gas was hard to get, we also used kerosene for fuel. It's close to diesel. The car would run on kerosene, but it wouldn't have much power so hills could be a problem. I remember one weekend, four or five of us guys were going out to a friend's cabin at Coventry Lake and all chipped in what money we could to buy gas, but we didn't have enough to fill up the tank, so we mixed in some kerosene. To get there, we had to go over a long, gradual hill. We had a good start on the hill, but it was questionable whether we were going to make it. By the time we were almost to the top, the Dodge didn't have much power left and was going pretty slowly, so my buddy said, "You guys have to get out and push or we're not going to make it." There was a car behind us, and at first they were pissed off that we were holding up traffic, but then it appeared funny to see all of us out there pushing. We made it over the top and were home free; it was all downhill from there. Despite this difficulty, we did have a great time.

We occasionally would drive the Dodge to school if the weather was good in the spring. It was such an antique car that others saw it as a unique junker that fit our jocular sense of humor. But there were a lot of prankish kids. One day, unbeknownst to us, some of our friends had rigged the car with a loud firecracker wired to the sparkplug that would explode when we started the car in the school parking lot. My friend Ray put the key in and

David in Boy Scout uniform
around age fourteen.
COURTESY OF DAVID KLEIN.

there was a loud *kaboom* and smoke poured out from under the hood. We immediately leapt over the side and ran like hell. We thought the whole thing was going to explode and catch on fire. Then we heard all this laughing. They sure got us on that one.

Also, when I was in high school I became active in Boy Scouts. When we lived in Vermont, I had been too young for Boy Scouts. The minimum age was twelve. My father volunteered as an assistant leader with a regional troop because he thought that Boy Scouts provided good training for living close to and appreciating nature. I did not do Cub Scouts either, because it was too hard to organize getting there after school or on weekends.

When we moved to Connecticut, I joined a Boy Scout troop that met in the basement of the Congregational church my mother attended and where we went to Sunday School. I was really excited about Boy Scouts mainly because of the camping, hiking, and opportunities for learning about nature and outdoor skills. Boy Scouts was a good experience for me, but the part I did not care for was the military aspect. The Boy Scouts was started by Lord Baden-Powell, who lived in Rhodesia at the time when it was under British rule, and he believed that Boy Scout training made good soldiers and military leaders.

The other aspect of the Boy Scouts that was hard for me to accept was that it was racially and culturally discriminatory. This was before the civil rights movement, but in New England we never thought about the racial issue. We had a black boy in our troop and nobody was concerned about that. We thought of him as one of us and a nice guy that everybody liked. As kids, we had limited understanding of or interest in racial discrimination. Of course, also in those days there were the Boy Scouts and the Girl Scouts and there was no opportunity of an advanced level of scouting that was co-ed. Also I wasn't so keen on the religious aspect of the Boy Scouts. The Boy Scout motto was, "In God we trust," and the expectation was that you believed in God. It wasn't a big issue when I was younger, but by the time I was older, it was becoming an issue for me. What do you do when there is a prayer at the start of the meetings when you don't believe in it? Do you involve yourself in the prayer or just close your eyes? I just couldn't bring myself to do that.

After I had been in the scouts for a while and moved ahead in the different grades from tenderfoot to first class, and then star, I volunteered to be a Cub Scout leader. We met in someone's home where you were in charge of the meetings, but the house's mother had oversight over the activities and the cubs' behavior. We did hikes with these young Cub Scouts and taught them the basics that they would need once they eventually went into scouting. I loved all that. I liked kids, in general, and liked scouting.

I was sort of a super achiever in the Scouts because my ultimate goal was to be an Eagle Scout. I liked the merit badge concept where you developed a skill and refined it enough to meet the specific requirements to earn the badge. You had to have a minimum of twenty-one merit badges in order to be an Eagle Scout, and athletics was one of the core requirements. Being on a school team was the only route to the athletics merit badge, and the swim and track coaches at Manchester High School were the only persons authorized by the regional Boy Scout Council as advisors and examiners for this. This turned out to be problematic for me since I would have to stay after school for practice and the bus would be my only way home. Our family only had one car, which my dad used to go to work, and since it was during the war we did not have enough gas to spare for an extra trip to come get me. Taking the bus would get me back home from practice close to 9:00 p.m., which would violate the family plan of having dinner together every night, as well as reduce the time I had for doing homework. I told the coaches, "I can't be on a team because I can't stay after school." The attitude of both coaches was, "Well, that's the only way you can earn the athletics badge. We don't have time to do something special for you." So that was that. I was not able to become an Eagle Scout. I was frustrated and disappointed because this was something I had really wanted.

During the war, Boy Scouts were asked to join the Civil Patrol to help protect our communities. Our main task was to walk through neighborhoods at night with an adult civilian—usually an older male who for health or other reasons was not in the military—to make sure people had their shades down and were abiding by the blackout and curfew rules. At that stage of the war, we'd been told there were German submarines off the coast of New England and we never knew whether German planes might fly over, so there were blackouts. If someone did not have their shades down and their lights were lit, we would knock on the door and remind them about the blackout. I felt good about doing this as a contribution to the war effort, but the experience taught me that I was not comfortable with the military or the militaristic style of the Boy Scouts.

Later in my life, my early discomfort with the Boy Scout's racial and religious discrimination and its military emphasis grew. Following military service in the Second World War and Korean War, I had become a pacifist and disapproved of the Boy Scout national organization's mission of glorifying the military in peacetime. I also strongly disapproved of its record of segregation of black Boy Scouts in separate troops in the south even during the civil rights movement. And I was uncomfortable with the continuing emphasis on fundamental Christian beliefs as an essential part of being a

Boy Scout, and reluctance to accept gender equality. Although I benefited from involvement in Boy Scouts when I was a boy and felt it would also be similarly beneficial for my son, I did not want to color my son's view of the Boy Scouts by my own complex association with it. In the 1970s, I tended to choose the hypocritical route of remaining mute in any family discussions that might threaten my son's pride in achieving Eagle Scout status.

In terms of my own religious development, as I said, my mother was moderately religious so when we were children we went to Sunday school at the Congregationalist Church, because that's what my mother wanted, and my dad agreed to it. When we were about ten or eleven years old, my father felt that we should be free to make our own decision as to whether we wanted to continue with Sunday school. I respected him very much for that, and my mother felt it was reasonable. I made the decision to no longer attend Sunday school, but my mother was still active in the church, so I continued attending church occasionally. At the same time, I was connected to the church to some extent because my Boy Scout troop met in the basement. And then during the Second World War, when I was in high school, the church had a youth group for teenagers that I enjoyed, probably mostly because it facilitated socializing with girls. We'd do things like put on plays, which I enjoyed acting in, or there were evening group activities like playing Ping-Pong. Sometimes we would do outings on weekends to play softball or have picnics. Since this was during the Second World War when there were few young men around, there was a surplus of young women, many of whom enjoyed socializing. This made the church youth group an even more enjoyable situation for me. I got a lot of attention from women that I may not have consciously appreciated at the time.

The church deacons wanted us in the youth group to join the church. I had second thoughts about that, but I figured I'd go through the religious training anyway just to see what it was all about. We got into some really good discussions. The minister was very understanding and did a fair job of saying, "It's complicated. Don't feel like you have to understand it all at once. You may not figure it out for a while, but stick with it." I graduated high school two years later, and I never really went to church after that. I didn't feel I had any specific reason to go. Nevertheless, it was nice to have that experience with such an open-minded minister, have the chance to

Klein family, just before David
graduated high school, 1945. Back,
L–R: David and Betty. Front, L–R: Dad,
Dick, Mom. COURTESY OF DAVID KLEIN.

explore those ideas, and discern my own beliefs versus those that I took from
my parents.

As I said, my father was a big influence on me when I was growing up, so
it was a blow to me when he died in 1946 from complications of diabetes.
He was only fifty-five years old. At age eighteen and away from home in
the Navy, I felt the loss deeply. I had wanted him to see me develop into a
full-fledged adult male. He was diagnosed with diabetes when he was in his
thirties. He was a very active guy, who was not obese and was in good health
before that. Fortunately, by this time, insulin had been discovered, so he was
able to give himself daily injections, but it still was difficult for diabetics in
those days to maintain a reasonable balance of blood sugar levels. Mom had

to cook things differently, and she did a good job of balancing a healthy diet for him while also keeping us kids happy, like she would bake a cake and frost it to look nice, but my dad wouldn't eat the frosting. We children got the frosting, although dad was charged with dividing it fairly among us. His health was declining when I was in high school, but he would never let on to us kids that he was suffering or in pain. He was always upbeat.

Fortunately, by the time my father passed away, us kids were all grown and out of the house, so my mother wasn't left alone to care for a houseful of children. But not having his income was a financial burden for her. To make ends meet, she took in boarders and worked small jobs as a typist or secretary. And, of course, my brother, sister, and I helped however we could. When I was away at college, I certainly enjoyed going home for her Sunday dinners or taking her for a drive. She continued to be a supportive influence throughout my life until she passed away in 1968 at age seventy-five when I was already in Alaska.

David and his high school friends after graduation in their military uniforms, 1945. Back, L–R: David Klein, Earl Modean, John Hansen (who is not in uniform because he skipped a grade so was a year younger than everyone else and not yet of draft age), Randy Toop, and Bill Grady. Front, L–R: Paul Marty, Ray Carmody, and Donald Kennedy. COURTESY OF DAVID KLEIN.

2
Time in the Woods

When I graduated from high school in 1945, the United States was still at war in the Pacific with the Japanese, and when reaching age eighteen, young men became 1A for the draft. I was not big on military service, but there was no question that there was a real threat to societies because of the Nazis and the war in Europe was very important to my family due to my parent's European background. Of course, the fact that my brother and sister were both doing good things for the war effort made me want to do what I could, too. My brother was a navigator and warrant officer in the Army Air Corps and my sister was a lieutenant in the Women's Army Corps (WAC). With the war being in the Pacific, I realized the Navy was going to play an important role, and it seemed pointless to wait to be drafted, since you could end up just being a crewmember on a ship someplace. I didn't particularly think that would be great. I thought being a pilot would mean interacting with a better bunch of people. I didn't necessarily want to be a pilot. It was mostly just the thought that if I was going to go into the military, the idea of going to the front lines and just being "cannon fodder" didn't appeal to me at all. If it was a cause I believed in, I figured I wanted to play a useful role.

I heard about a pilot training program in the Navy, so I went to their recruitment office. They said, "Sure, you can apply. But you have to take a special exam to see whether you did well enough in high school, and take a physical." I had done poorly in school, so I thought I would likely flunk this test, but I ended up passing it. But after the physical they said, "Now, you've got a problem. We don't think you can qualify. You have a heart murmur." I ended up doing a second physical where they did a more intensive EKG and they said, "Yes, you've got a heart murmur, but it's apparently the kind that you and the Navy don't have to worry about."

They let me go into the program, but you had to have the equivalent of about a year and half to two years of college with a heavy focus on math and trigonometry, plus English literature and composition. Since I had just finished high school and had not completed all these courses, I was sent to the University of Richmond in Virginia to take them. We lived in dorms and went to class, but had to wear Navy uniforms. It was not a bad deal at all, although I sometimes had to get help from my buddies on the math sections. I was with bright young guys, and we bonded well. That time together was a good time for all of us. We were just like other young people going to college right out of high school, when you are mentally unprepared to be a freshman, but we were different in that we were much more focused because we had a cause. We knew we were in military service and misbehavior was not tolerated. We didn't have a lot of supervision, but we were kept all together in one dorm and there were older guys whose job it was to keep us from acting too much like dumb freshmen. For example, every night there was a bed check, and although we weren't locked in, if you missed a bed check you were in serious trouble. Or if you went off campus, this meant you were leaving without authorization, and that could have gotten you kicked out of the whole program. Of course, we did get into some shenanigans and pulled pranks like most young guys do.

We started the second semester of the academic year at Duke University, and then the war was over because of the dropping of the atomic bombs on Nagasaki and Hiroshima. We had signed up for the duration of the war plus six months, thinking the war would go on for an extended period of time. And so here it was, three or four months into our training and the war was over. The Navy said, "You can continue with the training because we will need trained Navy pilots, but you have to stay through the training period plus another six years after you get your commission and your pilot wings." This meant about eight more years, which was reasonable pay back for the military expense of training you as a pilot, but once the war was over, I had no desire to stay in the military. I had pretty much decided that I was a pacifist and didn't want to get involved in wars in the future. Although I did stay in that pilot program, I still had to finish out my required Navy service, so I was assigned to the Great Lakes Naval Training Station on Lake Michigan, north of Chicago. I went through basic training there, which wasn't all that great for me psychologically because I didn't really want to be in the military. We got assigned to kitchen duty, which was mostly dishwashing, and did guard duty at the gates of the base. Boring stuff like that.

Sometimes if I'd get a weekend pass, I'd go in to Chicago for the day and go to the museums. They had an excellent museum of science and industry, a good planetarium, and an outstanding natural history museum with some of the best stuffed animals and painted scenery. I especially was fascinated with the mountain animals, like mountain sheep and mountain goats, and the depiction of the vegetation around them. I was an Easterner and I loved the mountains in New England, but we didn't have any of those beautiful mountain creatures there. Seeing all this was formative for my mountain curiosity. Or my buddy from Georgia, who was also the outdoor type, and I would hitchhike to a place in northern Illinois or southern Wisconsin where there was a lake or stream, and we'd rent the cheapest cabin we could find that had a rowboat. We would go swimming and rowing out on the water. Both of us liked to fish, but we couldn't afford to buy fishing gear. But we just liked this kind of camping out.

After we finished basic training, we were scheduled to go home for about a week before we were supposed to show up for regular duty. The morning we were supposed to head home, I noticed these spots on my chest. Then my buddy noticed he was breaking out in a red rash. We weren't feeling top-notch, but we were all excited about going home, so we dressed up in our full dress uniforms and went through the final inspection. But then we thought about it and wondered if we really had contagious diseases, was it a good idea to take them home with us? Finally, we went to the infirmary and I was diagnosed with German measles and he had scarlet fever. They put us in the local hospital and that was the end of our leave. I stayed in the hospital for about five days, and recovered fine.

Then there was a screwup with paperwork where the Navy said we had not completed basic training because going home on leave was part of the requirement. This meant we had to do the six weeks of basic training again. This time, however, we knew that if you always make the morning roll call then you can "disappear." That they never counted throughout the day. So we went to places like the library, or to the swimming pool and acted as if we were in a class. We weren't 100 percent successful, but we were pretty good at this. Also, we knew not to irritate any of the sergeants, and keep away enough so you don't give them a chance to recognize your face. I completed that second basic training, including going home on leave, and was discharged in 1946.

After I got out of the Navy, I went back to Connecticut, but I didn't really know what I wanted to do. It was a new world after the war was over. I had become an adult without really appreciating it. A main objective was getting a job. Of course, I needed money to pay for living expenses and gas for the big, black LaSalle sedan I bought, but money wasn't my main purpose in life. I was looking for something more meaningful. There were not many jobs at the time, because there were other veterans coming back, too, and most of them were more senior than I was. There was a servicemen's work compensation program for veterans that provided a small stipend until you got a job. A couple of my high school buddies figured, "Well, we did our service. We deserve this. Let's take it easy and get this free money." Like me, they hadn't seen any battle. That just didn't fit my standards. I didn't really know what I wanted to do, but didn't feel like I was ready for college yet. I was outdoor oriented, so I had thought about agriculture and farming, but I realized that I had broader interests than just living on a farm. I was interested in things that related to a farm, like a trout stream that ran through it or the deer that would come to eat his apples. I'd always liked working in the woods, so I thought a little bit about going into forestry. In retrospect, I now realize I was more interested in general ecology, but at the time the ecological concept was only in its earliest stage of development and I didn't know much about it.

Eventually, I ended up getting a job doing forestry work at Meshomasic State Forest, which was about forty miles south of Buckland. I got the job with the help of Betty Willard, who was a fifth and sixth grader teacher at the Buckland elementary school who was a boarder in our house. After my dad died, my mother rented out an extra room in the house in order to make a little money. Betty knew somebody that knew the forester at Meshomasic State Forest, who was a guy in his thirties who had been trained in forestry at the University of Connecticut. They had a woods crew that worked all winter long, and she thought that there might be a possible job for me there. This was fall time when there weren't many outdoor jobs available.

I talked to the chief forester in charge, and although he thought I was a bit young for the woods working crew and didn't have all the required skills, I appeared to be capable, so he offered me a job. He said, "You'll be working mostly with other young men thinning pine plantations. We have a bunkhouse and there's one bachelor that works in the field that is staying there, and you can probably bunk with him until we can make one of our cabins livable. Would that work out for you?" I said, "Oh, definitely." This offer seemed like nirvana for me. I never expected I could get a job like that in Connecticut. That was just the kind of work that I needed.

Most of the work we did with our hands using a heavy single-headed axe and a big Swede saw, which is a bow saw with a thin blade. It was hard work. You had to buy your own axe head in a hardware store, put a handle on it yourself, and learn how to use and sharpen it properly. You had to keep your axe super sharp, so you always carried a sharpening stone in your pocket. Back at camp headquarters, there was an old-fashioned peddle grindstone where you could work the blade back into good condition. There was a bachelor guy in his forties who had worked there for many years who was sort of the senior guy on the crew, and he gave me advice because I'd never used a grindstone like that before. He was good at training and explaining things. I had learned some of these woods skills as a boy living in a rural setting and on a farm, from working with my grandfather, and from having been a Boy Scout, but he showed me how to do a lot of things.

A lot of the state forest was managed under a policy of sustaining it as a natural ecosystem. Our work there mainly involved cleaning up trees that got blown down during winter storms and fell across roads. It was a mostly pristine area, however, there were areas of uniform red pine plantations scattered throughout that had been planted for use as poles for telephone lines and highway barrier fences. Mostly, we were thinning the red pines. The average size of the larger trees was about six or eight inches in diameter, but the foresters wanted them to be about twelve inches before harvesting them. Some of the smaller trees were used for firewood or paper production, while some of the bigger red pines were made into lumber at small mills in the area. We cut the smaller diameter trees into four-foot lengths for cordwood to be used as firewood and stacked them in piles to be retrieved later by a tractor and wagon.

A crew of three or four of us worked together in one pine plantation every weekday. When thinning the trees, we didn't want to be working so close that if a tree fell it would hit another person, so we were safely spaced out. We were frequently just far enough apart so we couldn't see one another, but you could hear the other guys. I don't think we yelled "Timber" or anything, because we always knew where each other was. You'd hear the crack as the tree was coming down, and then you heard it when it hit the ground. But if a tree got hung up in other trees, you heard cussing like hell. The worst-case scenario was if your saw got bound up and stuck in a tree. If it pinched the saw, then you needed another saw and another person to help get it out. We all did it occasionally, of course, but we didn't want it to happen to us too many times in the day. It slowed you down. Your pile of cordwood wouldn't get very big if you hung up a lot of trees. We got paid for the day of work rather than by the number of cords cut, but it still wasn't good to be slowed down.

The senior person, Knight Ferris, who was in his sixties, loved hunting, camping, and woods work. He was a retired machinist who had worked for a firearms company during World War II making rifles for the military. He was a fabulous guy and kind of a mentor to us younger guys. We admired him because he enjoyed what he did and was so good at it. There were two other guys, Ed and Mark, who were a couple of years older than me and were also veterans, although they had served in Europe. We also bonded over a mutual interest in forestry and a desire to work outdoors. This was in the wintertime, so when we'd break for lunch we would build a fire, sit around it to keep warm, eat sandwiches that we brought with us, and have a cup of coffee from a can we had boiled over the fire.

When I had a little free time in the woods, I would do a little grouse hunting. By this time, I considered myself pretty handy at woodworking, so made a new stock for that old shotgun that my brother had broken years earlier. I had a little trouble drilling a long hole through the stock to attach it to the barrel, because I just had a hand drill. Finally, to my surprise, I successfully drilled straight from both ends and got the hole to meet in the middle. I was really proud of myself. I got more fun out of doing that than

I did out of hunting. I was not a very good shot, and the ruffed grouse were so alert that you had to be fast. You would hear the fluttering of their wings, and by the time you recovered and got the shotgun up, they would be gone.

I loved that job. I enjoyed that kind of work and learning about trees and working in the woods. I also learned that when tackling a job, do it well and do it until it's done. We'd put in a hard day's work, but it was fun work, and I worked with great people.

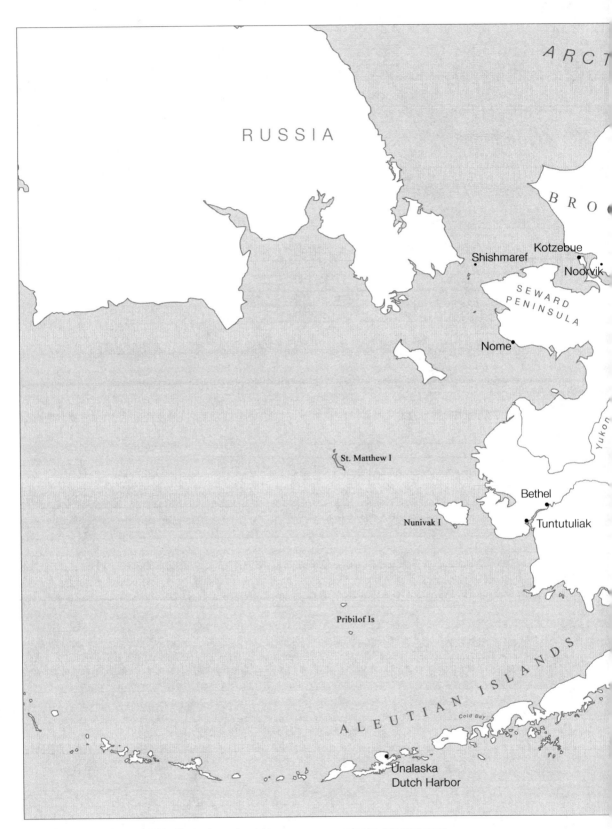

Places that David Klein visited in Alaska throughout his career as an ecologist. MAP BY UA PRESS.

David with his Model A Ford Roadster
arriving in Alaska, June 1947. COURTESY OF
DAVID KLEIN.

3
Discovering Alaska, Discovering Self

After working in the woods in the Meshomasic State Forest through the whole winter, the three of us veterans started talking about doing a trip together, and about how this highway to Alaska had just been built. Alaska was attractive because it was sort of the ultimate North American adventure. At that time, I thought there was no way I could even think about Alaska. It was so far away. Which it was! I didn't have the kind of money that you needed to go there. But the more we talked about how you could drive there, it started to sound feasible. The three of us sort of bought into this idea of "Well, we can do it." But I realized that we had to have a vehicle in better shape than my old junker Ford Model A Roadster. I thought this model would be ideal, because it was lightweight, easy to maintain, and had reasonable gas mileage. Plus it had a rumble seat that we could use as extra storage space.

I started looking around to buy a newer Model A Roadster, and, eventually, I spotted an ad for a 1931 one. The body condition was like new, but the previous owner had taken the engine apart to rebuild it and hadn't put it back together. From previously owning a Model A, I had basic knowledge of the engine and how everything worked, so I managed to put the thing back together again. After doing everything myself, it felt so good when it actually started. Of course, I still had to get a good battery, and tires, because I had to be sure that it was in good condition to go to Alaska.

In the spring of 1947, Ed Was and I quit the woods work and headed to Alaska. Mark had really wanted to come with us, but his wife said he couldn't go and leave her there alone with their new baby. Also, he had a steady job there at the forest and was already moving up through the ranks, so it made sense that he shouldn't lose that. Ed and I had everything we needed to rely on, including some food. We had to stop and get some occasionally, but we wanted to be as spartan as possible. We had camping equipment, including a small two-person tent and pots for cooking. We didn't have a Coleman stove or anything like that. We couldn't afford it. We figured we could just build a campfire. In retrospect, we did make a mistake, because we should have stayed in the US longer and gone up through Montana, but instead we drove through the Lake of the Woods country in northern Minnesota and then across the Canadian prairies. There was no main highway in that area. None of the roads were paved. They were all gravel. When it was dry, they were dusty. When it was wet, they were all muddy. There were frost heaves and chuckholes, so there were some places that you were lucky if you could go twenty-five miles an hour. This was in May, but it was still quite cold and frequently the wind was blowing on the prairies, and we had no side curtains on the car, so the wind would blow right through. To stay warm while we were driving, we would wear stocking hats and sometimes even gloves and a jacket. But that was okay, because at least it was fresh air. After coming out of the Lake of the Woods country, which was beautiful evergreen forest country, the prairie was a little more monotonous than we thought it would be.

Mostly, there were no official campgrounds along the way. It was all private land. Until we stopped in Manitoba at Riding Mountain National Park, which was an aspen forest. It was colder than hell and we could smell this aspen wood burning, but there was no way that you could get wood for your own campfire. They had these little cabins for rent there for like a buck fifty a night, and we decided, "Oh, we could afford that." So we got this cabin with a woodstove. And, oh man, that was nirvana to be nice and warm after all this cold wind blowing across us while driving.

The Alaska Highway was not officially open to civilians in 1947, so you were required to get a pass from the Canadian government. We had to be inspected in Edmonton by the Royal Canadian Mounted Police (RCMP) to get the permit, and in theory, we had to have an appointment to allow us to go over the highway. We lied. We said, "Yeah, we're going to be working up there. Doing fire control." They checked to make sure we had all these emergency supplies: extra fan belts, condenser coil, tools to do car repairs, a shovel and axe to fight fire in case there was a wildfire along the way, and at least ten gallons of water so if you were going to be camping you'd have water available. You also were required to carry fifteen gallons of extra gas, because there weren't many gas stations along the way, and you couldn't always be sure that they would have gas. Also, there was just not good gravel on the road, and rain would make things muddy, so you had to have chains in case you needed the extra traction. And, of course, you had to have two spare tires. In our case, the two spares were not good tires, but the four on the car were new ones. I had one flat tire from a nail. So that was pretty good.

There weren't many other vehicles on the road. There was some trucking, but not too much because the war was over and the military wasn't using the road as much. It was pretty good road surface, and sometimes you could average thirty miles per hour. If it was smooth, you could get up to about forty-five, and make good mileage per day. But there was a lot of dust. The trucks had to go pretty slow, so usually they weren't overtaking you, but if there was one coming toward you, you just pulled over and stopped because you couldn't see anything from all the dust. Plus, they threw a lot of rocks if they were going too fast. Mostly they would slow down. If you tried to overtake a truck that was going very slow, it was almost impossible because they were kicking up so much dust and you couldn't see if anybody was coming the other way. But that wasn't a problem very often.

At that time, flooding and washouts were not that unusual, and it was good we had chains with us. We came to the first culvert washout, and, oh man, there was this narrow four-feet-deep ditch right down the middle of the road. We put on the chains and managed to straddle the ditch and keep going. We sure felt good about dealing with that obstruction. The other place where we had to use the chains was when we got stuck after pulling off the road to camp. One time we came to this really nice place with mossy ground under the trees, but we had to go down a little slope to get to where we could set up our tent. Sure enough, it rained quite a bit that night and in the morning when we were ready to go we realized that this whole area had gotten soft. We had to put on the chains just to get back up onto the road. We also cut tree branches and laid them down for extra traction so the car wouldn't sink too far into the mud. Once we did that, we got back up on the road, took the chains off, and continued on our way.

We had one other serious incident, when suddenly there was a big bang, and the engine cut out. I thought, "Well, what the hell's going on?" I got out of the car and I could see flames inside the engine. I whipped around and opened up the side panels where you could access the engine, and here the whole carburetor was on fire. This car had no air filter and all the dust from the road clogged the jets that sprayed the fuel into the intake manifold, which caused the whole thing to overheat from the pressure. I thought, "What do I do?" I didn't have a fire extinguisher, and even though we had water, I knew that throwing water on a gas fire wouldn't do any good. I looked down and saw that there was mud in the ditch. I grabbed the shovel from the back of the car, scooped up this mud, and threw it right on top of the carburetor. I forced all this mud down in there, which stopped air from getting in and squelched the fire. Phew! But, now, all that mud was in the carburetor along with all the dust. It looked like a disaster. We took it all apart very carefully, washed everything out in gasoline, and blew through those clogged jets to be sure they were working. We put it all back together again, and it started up and ran fine the rest of the way. It was good that I'd put the whole thing together in the first place when I bought it, so I was very familiar with that engine and could handle these types of things.

It was a great adventure. It took us twenty-three days from Connecticut to Fairbanks. I had this little Brownie camera and took one or two pictures on the trip, but I should have taken more pictures. It was beautiful. Like when you went by Kluane Lake, I mean, you couldn't miss all the beauty there. The road was really winding there, but it was so spectacular. Ah, man, you realized, coming this long distance was all worth it.

We arrived in Fairbanks on June 10, 1947. Fairbanks itself had no paved streets, and some wood sidewalks. During the dry weather in the summer, it was pretty dusty. You'd get a hot spell and there'd just be a pall of dust over the city. And then, in the spring when everything was thawing, some of the streets were marginally useable and some not passable at all because of the mud. But the Model A Ford was great then. We could get around without any trouble. One big thing that struck us about Fairbanks was the "red light district" comprised of all these small, well-kept cabins around Fourth Avenue. They weren't allowed to do business from the front of the cabins, so they had a big picture window on the back that opened up onto a boardwalk.

The gals would be dressed all fancy, and early in the evening they would beckon you in. And, of course, there was still gold mining happening around Fairbanks, so that influenced the character of the place, too. The Fairbanks Exploration Company's dredges were operating out at Cripple Creek, Ester, and Chatanika. You could go and wander around the old tailing piles and find bones and teeth of bison, and other extinct species. Occasionally, if you were lucky you might find a mammoth tooth.

When we got to Fairbanks, the first thing we did was to find a cheap place to stay. We found a boardinghouse on Fourth Avenue, on the east side of Cushman Street, that had bunks in the basement. It wasn't a very good place, but it was like a buck and a half per bunk. But we couldn't afford to stay there too long unless we found jobs. We didn't have much money left from the trip, because even though we didn't have a lot of expenses, we did have to buy all that gas along the way. Ed had experience switching trains, so he got a job right away doing that kind of work at Ladd Field (now Fort Wainwright). It was pretty good pay, too. So he had a good job for the summer. I wasn't so fortunate. I wanted to find some job that would get me out into the country. I'd heard about geological survey work being done in the National Petroleum Reserve–Alaska, but by the time we arrived in Fairbanks, they'd already hired everybody for the summer season. And before we left home, we'd been told that you could always get a job in firefighting. But it had been a damp spring and there were no significant wildfires, so they were not hiring anybody.

By this time, I was getting kind of desperate. Then I met this guy in the boardinghouse, Tony Butler, who was a builder that was putting fireproof siding on houses. He needed some guys to work with him, so he hired me and another guy, Chris, who was from Oklahoma. Prior to this, Tony had overwintered in the Brooks Range at Wild Lake, and had fallen in love with the area and was talking about starting a hunting and fishing lodge there. He told us about his experience and that sounded like nirvana to me. He said, "If you guys work with me, and we save our money, by late summer we can go up to Wild Lake and build the first cabin for the lodge." From my limited experience with real wild country and wilderness in New England, I thought that sounded wonderful. I was in Alaska, and I felt really lucky. So Chris and I went to work for Tony.

Tony was kind of a ladies' man and he'd go to the bars at night and spend money, so that meant we weren't accumulating it very fast. Chris and I were beginning to feel like we'd been had. Both of us appreciated that we had a job, were making money, and were eating, but once we got started then it began looking like there was no future in it. We didn't want to be doing this work unless we knew the goal of going up to the Brooks Range was a real possibility. Tony had presented this whole thing as if we'd be partners in the hunting and fishing lodge, because we were contributing from the beginning. We questioned Tony a couple of times, "Well, are we on track for getting this trip to the Brooks Range?" He sort of would dodge the question and say, "We have to get more jobs and keep working hard." Well, it felt like that was what we already were doing. Finally, we laid down the law and said to Tony, "We're not going to keep doing this job unless you make a commitment that we're going to the Brooks Range and we start setting the money aside." After that, Tony knew we were serious. We didn't have to really go on a strike, but we were prepared to and he knew it. He bit the bullet and started curtailing his behavior.

We didn't quite make enough money to cover the full cost of the charter airplane, but we were able to go anyway. We had to work and pay off the last of the charter after we came back, but we paid enough up front so that the company knew that we were going to pay it off. We flew to Bettles in a Norseman, which is a large, single-engine freighting plane. Bettles Field had just been built. Before that, you landed on the river or on a gravel bar in front of Bettles. Once in Bettles, then we carried our gear down to the river, which was not too far, and they flew us up to Wild Lake in two small planes on floats. It was my responsibility to be sure we got all the gear and supplies into the planes. We had Coleman lanterns and a Coleman stove, and we had fuel for them in ten-gallon cans. We had an old-fashioned multipane glass window for the cabin we planned to build, and all of our food and stuff. Most of that went up with the first plane. They loaded up the passengers and fit in as much gear as they could. You couldn't overload an airplane on floats or you wouldn't be able to take off. I got in the last plane and had the window on my lap. We also had some gas for the airplanes, because they had to refuel out there in order to get back to Bettles. We tried to take off and there was no breeze, and we couldn't get off. The plane was just too loaded. So the

L–R: Doc, Chris, David, and Tony Butler in front of the cabin they built at Wild Lake, with a mountain sheep skin drying on the wall behind them, September 1947.
COURTESY OF DAVID KLEIN.

pilot said, "Take off ten gallons of gas. We'll just set it on the gravel bar and bring it to you in about a week or so when I have to fly up to Wild Lake for another reason." The pilot tried his takeoff again, and this time we got off.

This started our adventure, including building the cabin. It was a crude fourteen-by-sixteen-foot log cabin. The logs were only about five to six inches in diameter because we were pretty high in the Arctic and the growing conditions just aren't that good. We cut them and packed them down from a small stream valley to where we were camped at the lake. It was downhill, but it was hard on one's shoulders carrying those heavy green logs. We didn't peel the logs, so we got the cabin up in pretty short order. We used axes to split logs for the floor, used smaller poles for the roof frame, put some plastic down, and then put sod on top of that for a nice roof. It was hard work, but we got it done.

Besides Tony, Chris, and myself, there were two others that came along. One was a guy we called Doc that Tony had made friends with at the boardinghouse. He was really a nice guy, and was sharp and had a pretty good education, but he was bordering on alcoholism. He told Tony that he'd do all the cooking, but really he wanted to fish. He was a hard worker once we got up there. He was pretty philosophical, so he was sort of a little bit of a mentor to me in that regard. The other person was a Canadian woman named Barbara whom we met at the boarding house. Barbara talked Tony into letting her come along to Wild Lake, saying she would help with cooking. She worked hard and everybody really liked her. I was glad to get to know someone like her who was interested in seeing the world, but also could do work.

One time, Doc and I went mountain sheep hunting because we needed meat. He was a great guy to be in the field with. He just loved the country, and was a hard worker who was able to pack heavy loads. I remember it was getting close to freeze-up, and he and I were perched on a ledge on the side of a mountain and I was so cold in my flimsy army surplus sleeping bag, but the Northern Lights came out. It was the first time I'd seen them. Well, "Ahh." It was just ideal laying there in your sleeping bag with Northern Lights all around you. Seeing those Northern Lights made coming to Alaska worthwhile for me. They just went on and on, and changed shape, and it was just fantastic.

The next day, Doc and I finally spotted some rams. They were feeding out in a meadow opposite from our camp. It looked like there was no way we could get to them, but finally I said, "I think it would be possible to go behind the ridge and move around and go down this other ridge where they won't see me. Then I can get below them and crawl up the small drainage to where they are." He said he'd stay up on top because I probably would spook them before I got there, and he'd be ready for them when they came up. When I finally got down there, I was on my belly crawling with a rifle, and when the rams weren't looking in my direction, I'd inch a little farther over to where there was a hummock to hide behind. I finally got in range, and I shot one right through the heart. It turned out to be the largest one. This was a momentous experience for me. I had never shot a big game species. It was a difficult stalk and I had done everything right. It did wonders for my self-confidence. Plus, we were able to bring food back to the others.

Previously, I had done a little animal butchering with my grandfather, so started on that while Doc went up to see if those other two rams were still around. We already had more than we could carry, but Doc was an ardent hunter who really wanted to get his own sheep. He spotted a ram on a ledge, and when he shot it, it fell a long distance and bounced on the rocks, which pretty much destroyed most of the meat and busted one of the horns off. He cared about things like size and trophies, which I did not, so I gave him the horns from my ram. Doc took the trophy ram horns and head back to Virginia to have them mounted for hanging in his house.

We climbed down and recovered what meat we could salvage, and made a couple of trips to pack all of the meat from both sheep up to the top of the ridge where we camped for the night. The next day we carried a load down to our main camp, which probably took a little less than three hours. The rest of the guys helped carry the remaining meat, so we got it all packed down in one day. We had no way of keeping the meat, except hanging it, but if you left the hindquarters and things like that in single pieces, it kept pretty well. We ate a lot of sheep meat, which was great. Before that, we had been eating a lot of fish. There was good grayling and lake trout fishing. When Doc would cook one of those beautiful lake trout outdoors, man, was that good! Mostly, when we were all working on the cabin, Barbara would cook meals. For that many hardworking guys, there had to be big meals. After the sheep, Tony and Doc went out and got a bull moose. By the time the planes came to pick us up, we had consumed the mountain sheep and most of the moose. Luckily, we were able to take some of that moose meat back to Fairbanks.

We were up there about a month from late August to the end of September. We had to get out before Wild Lake froze. Coming back to Fairbanks was a bit of an adventure. The weather wasn't good. It was raining and overcast and the forecast was not too good, either. Bettles Field had radio contact with Fairbanks where the weather was clearing, so the pilot was eager to get back before the weather fouled up Fairbanks, too. It was tough in those days without a lot of navigational aids. He didn't have instruments for landing, so if he couldn't see the ground, he couldn't fly. He also wanted to get back before it got dark. We took off from Bettles and the visibility wasn't all that great and the pilot was having a hard time keeping track of where he was. We were flying in this stream valley, and he turned around and asked, "Can you see which way that water is flowing?" I was really concerned, because I figured if he doesn't know where he is, how does he know where he's going? I became really concerned, so glued my eyes on things. Finally, the pilot figured he had to go up through the clouds to get better visibility. I was relieved when we broke out into clear skies, because I couldn't see any mountains sticking up. We didn't go too much longer before it started to get dark, and then I started to get a little worried again. In the distance you could see the lights of Fairbanks, so then I felt more secure. By that time, he was fully oriented. I hadn't had a lot of flying experience at that point, so all of that was a little unnerving. It felt great to get back to Fairbanks.

After that experience at Wild Lake, I was living on a high. Alaska was better than I had imagined. I was very fortunate to have that kind of experience. Being out there in the Brooks Range was like nirvana. It was exciting and wonderful, and was like nothing I'd ever dreamed of when I was in Connecticut. I learned so much about the animals and the environment, became hooked on mountain terrain, and was fascinated with Alpine ungulates. Mountain sheep, in particular.

When we returned to Fairbanks, we still had a debt to pay on the air charter so Chris and I went back to work with Tony. It was early October now and temperatures were really getting cold, so it was not very comfortable working outdoors and putting on cedar shakes; you needed bare hands to pull the nails out of your pocket. I remember one time when it was down around ten below. Oh, that was really tough going! Although this scheme of a hunting and fishing lodge was tempting, by this time I realized it was not going to work. Tony was not a good businessman and because of my newfound interest in Alpine terrain and mammals, I had decided that I wanted to go to college and study wildlife biology and management, and there was a good program at the University of Connecticut. So as soon as we finished those two jobs and we paid our bills and Chris and Tony were getting ready to leave town, I said, "Well, I think I don't want to stick together on the idea of a partnership on the lodge. I think I need to go to school. That's what my calling is." Chris went back to Oklahoma for the winter, and Tony went to California. After they left, I lost touch with them,

The dairy cow herd that David worked with at the Fairbanks Experiment Farm on the campus of the University of Alaska, 1948. COURTESY OF DAVID KLEIN.

and Tony didn't end up building that lodge at Wild Lake. I also have never been back there.

At that point, I didn't have the money to drive all the way back to Connecticut, so I was going to have to find a job in Fairbanks for the winter. Because of my interest in agriculture and farming, I went out to the experiment farm at the University of Alaska. Fortunately, they had a position for a helper at the dairy. I would feed the cows in the dairy herd, help with the milking, and shovel manure. I loved working with cattle, so it was very enjoyable work for me. I was the assistant to the dairyman who was a really nice bachelor in his forties. I had to get up early for the morning milking, handling cleanup, and feeding the cows. And then I had to be there for the evening milking. I would put in about eight hours but still had the middle of the day available. This meant I was able to take a few college classes. I took some courses in dairy science and two or three animal science courses, and since I knew I was going to go back to school, I also took bonehead math because I wasn't very good at math. The animal husbandry man who was head of the animals at the farm, Lynn Hollis, was on the faculty and was a really nice guy. He sort of adopted me. He really wanted me to go into agriculture, but I told him I now was committed to wildlife studies.

The dairy job worked out well for me in other ways, too. Although the dairy didn't pay much, there was a small frame building with a little woodstove in it that had been used for workers in the summertime and I was able to live there. It was convenient, and it was not a bad way to spend the winter in interior Alaska. I had some sociality with the students in the classes I was taking, and the people that I was working with at the farm were good people. I enjoyed the work, and it was a healthy environment. I put the Model A up on blocks in the shed at the farm, and drained the radiator and took the battery out, and lived fine all winter without a car.

While in Alaska, I learned about game wardens and wildlife. But I realized that if you had a university degree, you could be more than a game warden, you could be a biologist working with the wildlife. After experiencing the Arctic-alpine environment in the Brooks Range, my focus shifted to ecology, the integrated relationship of plants and animals within an entire natural system, especially to mountain ecology and Arctic and northern ecology. I was beginning to recognize that for management of large herbivores in Alaska to be science based, it meant understanding the importance of plant ecology and habitat in relationship to animals and the natural foods on which they depended. I had considered attending the University of Alaska, but the university in Fairbanks was a small place with fewer than three hundred students at the time and only one biology teacher, so there was little offered in the biological sciences. I also was getting homesick and eager to go back to New England to see my family. I decided to go to the University of Connecticut where there was a well-established department of forestry, where I could study wildlife management and tuition would be moderate because I was a state resident.

The plan was to leave Fairbanks as soon as the spring semester was over, which was about the 1st of June 1948. I was going to take the long way home to Connecticut by driving through California to visit Yosemite, and go up through the south. I found two students who wanted to ride with me and share the cost of gas, which was a good deal. Eileen Mead was just finishing her junior year, and was going "Outside" to attend her sister's wedding. The other rider was a guy named Harry, whose last name I can't remember, but he was finishing his sophomore year and was returning home to Portland, Oregon for the summer.

We were delayed in leaving Fairbanks because it was a rapid spring melt-off and there was flooding. The highway was closed because it was washed out in several places between Delta Junction (also known as Delta) and Fairbanks, and bridges were washed out in the Yukon Territory. We were delayed about ten days before the water subsided enough and the road was repaired. We finally made it to Whitehorse and then the road was closed again, because they still hadn't repaired a major bridge south of there. We enjoyed being in Whitehorse. It was really interesting because we were there

L–R: Harry, Eileen Mead, and David at the Yukon River in Whitehorse, Canada, while waiting for bridge repair work to be completed on their journey out of Alaska, June 1948. COURTESY OF DAVID KLEIN.

when they launched the big sternwheelers on the Yukon River at the beginning of the season. They made a good splash and created a small wave. There was cheering and everything; it was like the whole town came out. The whole operation was really exciting to watch. Also, the weather was nice and we had tents, we could get food and water readily, and we camped there for two or three days.

The bridge wasn't getting repaired fast enough, and it was starting to look like if Eileen stayed with us she wasn't going to make it in time for the wedding. So she telegraphed her parents and they wired her some money to fly down from Whitehorse. I'll have to admit, I was getting more and more attracted to this gal, and she to me, I think. So I thought maybe in the long run, that was best, because our lives were going in different directions. Harry was a good guy. He was very quiet and we got along fine, so it was okay that it was just the two of us from then on.

I kept checking with the RCMP (Royal Canadian Mounted Police) about the road and they'd say, "Well, they're still working on it. They should have finished the pilings and now they're starting to lay the planking for the bridge. So we expect it'll be pretty close." We said, "Well, we want to get started on down the road." They said, "We don't advise it because there was still flooding in other spots." We took off anyway. We figured we could stop and camp wherever and wait. Then we hit this fairly level place where a culvert was blocked, and water was flowing over the road for about a hundred yards. We got out of the car and waded through the water to check it out. It was only three feet deep and looked like the part of the road that was left was wide enough for the car, so we started driving through. We didn't make it very far before the engine died from the water splashing up on the spark plugs. It probably would have worked if we'd taken the fan belt off or disengaged it, because it was pumping up and spraying water on the engine. Harry and I pushed the car and then opened the hood and wiped out all the water from the spark plugs and everything. We got the engine started again and took off. Then we had to wait an hour or two at the bridge for the last two or three planks to be put on. From then on, we didn't have any more problems with the road. It was just the car that acted up.

We were driving along and the car was running fine, then suddenly it stopped hitting on four cylinders. You're out there in the middle of the

David diagnosing car trouble along the Alaska Highway, June 1948. Note the water container on the ground in front of the car that was used for cooling off the overheating engine. COURTESY OF DAVID KLEIN.

wilderness with no facilities or services to speak of, but I knew this engine well so wasn't too worried. I did all the diagnoses, and finally I said, "Well, it must be a valve." We did some testing and Harry was able to tell that the valves were all going up and down, so that wasn't it. Then he said, "But the piston isn't going up and down." We took the engine head off and discovered that the aluminum top of the piston had broken off just above the rings. The rest of the piston was going up and down, but it was disconnected so it wouldn't take in the gas and wouldn't fire. We tried to fix it, but it wasn't too successful. Fortunately, we were still able to go on three cylinders.

The best bet for finding parts was Fort Nelson, which was down the highway quite a ways, where they had an airstrip, a post office, a trading post, and a good garage. Every five miles, some of the oil fumes from the crankcase mixing with the gas would ignite, and it would cause a backfire.

But the engine was still running and we didn't have any other alternatives, so we just kept going.

When we got to Fort Nelson, there was a sign on the gas station saying, "Closed." We went into the trading post and they said, "Well, the guy that runs the gas station is on a bender. Even though he's drunk, chances are you could use his ramp outside if you asked him, and he might even loan you tools if you need them. But probably your best bet is to telephone the Ford dealer in Edmonton and they can ship the replacement cylinder and rings for that Model A Ford on the next mail plane that is due in about three or four days." That was our only alternative, so we did that. Of course, we were already late getting out of Alaska, so this delay didn't help.

We used the outdoor ramp at the gas station to work on the car, but it was right at the peak of mosquito season, so it was terrible working outside. The only repellent we had wasn't very effective. When mosquitoes landed on you, you just rubbed them off, but our hands were all greasy, so we got covered in black grease spots. It was pretty rough, but we toughed it out. Harry wasn't too good of a mechanic, but he was a good guy and was handy to have as a helper when you needed two people. We got the engine apart, put it back together again, put the gasket back on, and it started up. What a good feeling that was!

We took off again and it was running fine, until a problem developed with the brakes. By the time we got into Bonners Ferry, Idaho, we had all these mountains and steep hills still to go through, and the brakes were so bad that we had to stop and get the brake irons welded back together. I didn't have all that much money to make it all the way back to Connecticut, but we stopped anyway. We found a repair shop that could do the welding, and we asked them to check out a knocking noise that had developed in the engine. They listened and said, "Well, you probably need some valve work, too. And then it might be the main bearing." I didn't have the kind of money needed for this level of repair, so the realistic thing was for me to sell the car and take a bus back home. It was disappointing because I was getting attached to this roadster. But I didn't have much of an option. We made it to Spokane, the closest big city, where Harry caught a bus home to Portland. It took me a couple of days to sell the car. It was still in good condition; the body was really top-notch. For some guy that wanted to work on the engine, it was a good deal. I sold it for about two hundred bucks.

I still wanted to stop at Yosemite National Park and Sequoia Kings Canyon in California, so I bought a Greyhound bus ticket that took me there and then back home through the south. Turns out that this wasn't the greatest idea, because the temperature in New Orleans was about a hundred and the humidity was terrible. You just sweat, you know. After about a month, I finally made it back to Connecticut.

David in the cedar swamp
in Connecticut where, as an
undergraduate, he did his first
ecological research project, circa
1950. COURTESY OF DAVID KLEIN.

4
Entrée into Ecological Fieldwork

In the fall of 1948, I went to the University of Connecticut in Storrs and I got a job at a small family diary in Bolton, about five miles from the university. The county agricultural agent was leasing this dairy farm with four or five milking cows, but also was working an eight-to-five job. He wanted to have someone live there to help out with the farm, and would provide room and board with his family. They had two young boys, and the mom was a very good cook. So it was kind of nice. They had a milking machine, and he would sometimes be available to help get the milking started in the morning before he left for work, but then I'd usually have to do the milking at around five in the afternoon as soon as I came home from the university. I also fed the cows, cleaned up, and washed the milking machine. I enjoyed that farm work. I also got to learn to use a horse team to haul wood for the wood furnace in the barn, and did some haying. The only problem with all this was the schedule. I had to get up really early in the morning and had to go to bed relatively early to get enough sleep, so getting homework done was a problem. I ended up doing a lot of homework between classes. This meant no socializing. But for me, who at age twenty-one was a bit older than the other freshmen, this wasn't too big of a deal. I was mature enough by then that I realized I had to study like hell and do well.

The wildlife program was in the Forestry and Wildlife Department, which was within the Plant Sciences College. The Forestry School had a good reputation, and the forestry and wildlife students were mixed together. This was good, because it was healthy for both of us to get forest ecology and management exposure along with the wildlife. Most wildlife management courses at the time focused on understanding animal population dynamics. Aldo Leopold wrote the first book on wildlife management that emphasized maintaining habitat for wildlife (Leopold 1933). Basic biology was important, but there was no course that was specifically ecology. My courses also were heavy on botany, including systematic botany; I almost had a minor in botany. Then in forestry, I took classes in forest ecology and tree identification. One of my electives was geology that was all about the landforms and dynamics of mountains, glaciers, and meandering rivers that I had just recently seen in Alaska. I could relate to and understand all those things, and was just fascinated by it. I got the highest grade in the class. I also had courses in horticulture, animal population dynamics, animal physiology, and comparative anatomy. At one point, I also was the president of the Forestry and Wildlife Club. I think I got a good education at the University of Connecticut, especially in retrospect when I realized what other schools offered.

Franklin McCamey was the only wildlife professor there. He earned his master's degree in forestry from Yale University and his PhD in ornithology from the University of Connecticut, and served on the faculty of the University of Connecticut's Forest and Wildlife Management department from 1948 to 1962. He was top-notch as far as I was concerned. He was a real mentor for me and a good advisor. He saw that I had interests and capabilities and talked me into doing an honors program for undergraduates where I had to do a research project. For this honor's thesis, I studied the ecology of a cedar swamp that was only about four miles from campus. White cedar is found sporadically in parts of New England, and they usually are in a very swampy area. This particular area probably had been an old lakebed during the post-glacial period that drained. But because there was such poor drainage, there was a lot of buildup of peat from the twelve thousand or so years since the glacier receded, so it had good quality soil, but was still sort of a swamp. That swamp was a fascinating place. It was a good project, and I learned a lot in the process. It was my first experience with fieldwork, and was good training for me in understanding ecological systems because it was broad.

Part of the project was to map the type of vegetation in the area. There was not a lot of vegetation, because it was such a dense canopy of white

Forestry Club, University of Connecticut, 1949. David is third from left in front row. His wildlife professor, Franklin McCamey, is the last on the right in the back row. COURTESY OF DAVID KLEIN.

cedar trees. That swamp had never been logged, so the cedars were all about ten inches in diameter. Around the edge of the swamp, it faded out into just shrubby areas where there were more willows. This was the transition into broadleaf forest, and then out to either agriculture or houses.

Another part of the ecological study included snaring hares and preparing study skins from them for the vertebrae anatomy class I was taking with a Dr. Whetsel. It was one of the few places in that part of Connecticut where there were snowshoe hares. There was not much sign of the hares in the swamp, but they were around the edge of it. It was a challenge for me, which was good, and I ended up catching a couple of hares. As a former Boy Scout, it was fascinating for me to be able to capture animals without using firearms. I also did studies on hares, tracking what areas they were using and why, and what they were eating. I also recorded the birds and other small mammal tracks, like fox, that I saw. There were deer there, but not very many. There was heavy poaching of deer in Connecticut.

My agronomy professor was interested in the history of the cedar swamp and said, "Well, it would be nice to find out how old that is and how deep the sediments are there." He suggested I probe it. The university machine shop made a long probe of small diameter steel rods cut into six-foot sections that I could screw together so it was easier to carry. I said, "I'd like your advice as to where to do this probing and how to do it correctly." So he came out to the swamp with me one weekend and we probed down about twenty feet. Mainly, the idea of the probing was to get an idea how much sediment there would be and how long it had been there. At the time, they weren't doing peat coring and dating, and my project was just an honor's thesis so this wasn't part of it. It was just sort of an aside.

I spent a lot of time in that swamp and knew it pretty well. I was out there alone, and even on weekends, because instead of going home to visit my family, I was working on this project. The swamp was so dense that it could be kind of eerie when there wasn't too much sunlight, and you could easily get lost unless you used a compass. I was out there one Saturday looking for my field notebook that I had lost earlier in the week. That notebook had all my data in it, so I was anxious to find it. I figured the odds weren't good, but I didn't have any other option. I was going through a marshy area where shallow sphagnum ponds were mixed in with the white cedar trees and there to my surprise and alarm was a human skeleton laying face up in the shallow water of a pool so that it appeared to be looking up at me. Nearby were a pair of big ol' army-type hiking boots, a long wool overcoat draped over a stump with a letter and glasses in the pockets, and part of a rope hanging from a tree. I decided I needed to report this, so I hiked back out, marking my trail with strips of my red bandana that I hung on branches. I drove out to the main road to a restaurant that had a telephone, called the police, and told them I found a skeleton in the cedar swamp. I said they would have to come out there for me to show them where it was because I couldn't really give them proper directions. I said, "They shouldn't come in their best clothes because it's rough getting through the swamp. They should have hip boots." An officer arrived about forty-five minutes later, and the coroner and a mortuary had been notified. At first, I think this officer didn't know whether to believe me, but I had the letter and the glasses as evidence.

As we were making our way through the swamp, someone said, "Oh, I think I found it." I thought it was too soon to find the skeleton. He came over and he had my field notebook. I was so damn lucky! Eventually, we found the skeleton and the coroner determined that it had been a suicide. That officer was a good sport; he did all this while still in his dress uniform and in hip boots. When the undertakers arrived, it was like Mutt and Jeff. They threw everything in a zippered plastic body bag they had, including the wet soggy overcoat, the wet boots, and all of these bones. They walked only a short distance and a sharp stick ripped that bag open and everything fell out. The language they used after that was not very good. The bag ended up breaking open three times before we got out of there. Word got around about that skeleton, so I got a little notoriety. And I impressed my agronomy professor by being able to find that same spot in the swamp again where the skeleton had been.

During college, the question was what to do in the summers to make money. I was so spoiled from spending time in Alaska that I just didn't want to take any old job. I got the idea to go to the lake country of northern Wisconsin where I had heard there were many fishing lodges that had summer jobs available. I talked an old high school friend into going with me, and we drove to Hayward, Wisconsin, where we found jobs but not at the same place. I worked at Lost Land Lake Lodge, which was on a nice fishing lake. It didn't pay a lot, and you had to do grunt work, but that didn't matter so much to me. I was able to be outdoors, which is what I enjoyed. Also, in my free time, I had access to a boat and could go out fishing on the lake. I enjoyed it up there so much that I went back the next summer.

I also learned a lot from the old man who helped run the place. He was probably in his seventies, which seemed pretty old to me at the time. He was from a Scottish family from Chicago who had started the lodge. He was mostly doing odd jobs around the place and was technically my boss, and he showed me how to do a lot of things with old tools that were new to me, like using a scythe to cut grass. I liked him because he was so knowledgeable about everything. For example, he would recite Robert Burns poetry, which inspired me to go to the library when I got back home to read more of it. I also was drawn to this old guy because he reminded me of my grandfather. The bond was mutual; he enjoyed helping me learn and appreciated having a young person listen to him.

I graduated from the University of Connecticut in the spring of 1951 with my undergraduate degree in Wildlife Management. I was only there three and a half years because I was able to take eighteen credits every semester, and I got a couple credits from the courses I took at the University of Alaska. And you had to have physical education and my military service automatically counted for that. The sooner that I got through college the better, because I had my heart set on coming back to Alaska. I knew what I wanted to do.

David doing fieldwork in the Kenai
Mountains for his master's thesis
on mountain goats, spring 1953.
COURTESY OF DAVID KLEIN.

5
Falling in Love with the Alpine

After I finished my undergraduate degree, I wanted to go on for a master's. I realized it was important to get a master's degree in order to compete for a wildlife research and/or management position. I really wanted to go back to Alaska, and I had several qualifications that I felt made me an appropriate candidate for UAF's master's program, like being interested in Alaskan subjects, having previous experience in Alaska, and my undergraduate record was good. After being in the Brooks Range, I was hooked on mountain ecology and mountain ungulates, like mountain sheep, mountain goats, and anything that was related to large herbivores. And from my training in botany, I was interested in the plant-animal relationships of these animals and how they could exist in the mountains of Alaska and the Arctic and Subarctic. This initial small interest of mine had to develop and grow more before I finally got into it later in life, but it was the start.

The head of the Alaska Cooperative Wildlife Research Unit, Neil Hosley, said they would be glad to accept me, but they didn't have enough funding to support me for the first year of the two-year program. It was a new Cooperative Wildlife Unit and so had very limited financial support. Neil Hosley was a senior professor who had done a lot of ecological research in the Upper Peninsula of Michigan on moose habitat relationships, so he understood my interests. He was only Alaska Co-op Unit leader for two years and then he became dean of students. Once I got that kind of response, I figured I would go to Alaska and find part-time work on campus to support myself until a stipend became available. I already knew the campus and figured it would be a good place for me.

I told Hosley that I would come to the University of Alaska but that I would have to find work, and asked if he knew of any work for the summer. Not long after, I received a telegram saying that he had lined up a job for me as a temporary field assistant for the summer at the Kenai National Moose Range (now the Kenai National Wildlife Refuge),[2] and I had to be there in five days. The job sounded great and just what I needed financially, so I took my final exams in Connecticut and left. I didn't stay for commencement. In order to get to Alaska in this short amount of time I was going to have to fly, so I had to borrow money from my mother to pay for the flight. I flew from Connecticut to Seattle, and then from Seattle in a DC-6 that landed at Annette Island to refuel and then continued on to Anchorage. My mother was, let's say, concerned, as a mother should be, that I was going so far away to a place where there would be so many adventures and risks. But she knew that as a young man I was attracted to this kind of adventure. She understood me well enough, because growing up I did adventurous things, too. Both she and my father were aware quite early on that I was oriented toward the outdoors and the natural environment.

There was no road to Kenai in 1951, so Dave Spencer, the refuge manager, flew up in a Fish and Wildlife Service (FWS) plane and picked me up in Anchorage. I didn't have direct contact with him, because he was busy flying all over the state for the Fish and Wildlife Service. At this time, it was obvious that the FWS had to have their own airplanes and their own pilots in order to do all the wildlife work that was needed around Alaska, so their aircraft division in Anchorage was just getting started. They didn't have enough pilots yet, so Dave Spencer was called on a lot to help out. It mainly included waterfowl work, which had been Dave's graduate education focus, but also included mountain sheep surveys. When I arrived, Dave was out on the Yukon-Kuskokwim Delta so I had to wait an extra day. I had a couple of nights in Anchorage, which wasn't the greatest. I didn't have much money since I'd spent all my money on the airline ticket. I found the cheapest place

---

2. The Kenai National Moose Range was established by Franklin D. Roosevelt on December 16, 1941. In 1980, the Alaska National Interest Lands Conservation Act (ANILCA) re-designated the Kenai National Moose Range as the Kenai National Wildlife Refuge and established 1.32 million acres as the Kenai Wilderness.

to stay, which was appropriately called the Rat's Nest. It had a bunch of army surplus double bunks all together in one large room.

Besides the refuge manager, the only other full-time employee at the refuge headquarters in Kenai was a maintenance man that kept vehicles running and did light maintenance on the buildings that previously had been part of military facilities associated with the adjacent airport. There was no money to hire a secretary, so Dave's wife, Eloise, who was well qualified, did that as a volunteer. Neither she nor he were at the refuge a lot of the time because he was flying so much, and while he was gone she didn't want to stay at the refuge alone so would stay with friends in Anchorage. I stayed in the bunkhouse, which was just a room in a big barn that functioned partly as a warehouse.

At that time, the railroad went from Anchorage to Seward and stopped at Moose Pass, where there was a gravel road to Kenai that went by Skilak Lake, a large glacial-fed lake on the Kenai River system that produced more commercially caught salmon at that time than any other river system in Alaska. There was a mile-and-a-half spur road that went out to Skilak Lake from the main road, and Dave wanted to build the first road-accessible public campground on the lake. Dave wanted to clean out all the tree and shrub debris that had been pushed up and left behind when a bulldozer made the road. He showed me what he planned on doing to make nice camping spots surrounded by trees, but he couldn't stay around very long. He said, "I want you to start working with a Swede saw and an axe to clear out this area." Since I had a lot of woods work experience, he knew that I knew how to do these things. I could see that there was much work to do to make nice campsites, and it was going to take a long time, but you have to start somewhere.

Dave Spencer also asked me to start a plant collection for a refuge herbarium. My resume had indicated that I had taken botany courses and knew plants pretty well, so his request made sense. He said I could use the skiff with a 15-horsepower outboard that he left there to travel around the lake, but cautioned me to only do that when the weather made it safe enough to be out on the water. Skilak Lake is a very dangerous lake. The wind blows like hell occasionally, coming down off the glacier at the head of the lake, and it's unsafe to be out on the water. He told me, "When it's not safe, stay off the water and work on the campsite." He seemed to put a higher priority on collecting plants, which pleased me. There was a trail located directly across the lake that he told me about that had been used in the early 1900s for guided hunts with horses for mountain sheep, moose, and grizzly bears. I could hike up there into the alpine area and collect plants. It was wonderful to get into the alpine habitat and start to get familiar with the alpine flora. And I quickly learned where to go for the best chance to see mountain goats and sheep in their summer habitat areas. I returned to the tent camp in the evening to label and put the plants in the plant press.

There was an old trapper and prospector who lived at the east end of the lake in the summer in a cabin he had built. Earlier in the summer, he had told Dave Spencer that he was not going to be there and we could use the cabin, but warned that there were a lot of grizzly bears around because it was not too far from a salmon stream. I went over there one day and spent the night. The bunk I was sleeping in was right close to the window. My mind was filled with stories about bears; animals with which I had virtually no experience. I suddenly awoke after hearing this horrible sound, like fingernails being dragged across a chalkboard. It sounded like *scrueeee, scrueee, scrueee.* I concluded that an animal was meticulously trying to claw its way into the cabin and it was right there outside the window only a few inches from my head. I felt around for my flashlight, but I questioned the wisdom of shining light directly into the face of a grizzly bear. I had been trying to imagine what a bear would sound like, and this sound just didn't seem right. But it was such a weird noise that I had to know what was there. I took the risk and turned on the flashlight. There I was face to face with a porcupine. It was trying to climb up the outside of the cabin, and was just slipping on the window glass. So that was pretty funny.

I did eventually run into one or two bears on the Kenai, but I never ran into that particular one that haunted the cabin. Mostly, my experience with bears down there was when I was in the alpine areas, where if they saw you, they ran away before you got close. But when I was working on that campground at Skilak Lake, I never had any trouble. Generally, the grizzly bears were in the mountains and would come down along the salmon streams, although black bears were more scattered out, given their opportunistic cosmopolitan diet, so they sometimes came around the lake and camping area I was clearing.

One of the Fish and Wildlife Service biologists based in Anchorage at that time was Robert (Bob) Scott. He had a master's from Oregon State University and was one of the first biologists hired in post-war Alaska. He had started a PhD at the University of British Columbia, but never finished because he was so focused on and challenged by his job in Alaska. He was a fascinating and brilliant guy. He was to become an important mentor for me. Much of his work was focused on mountain sheep, and he had been doing some work in the Kenai Mountains at the head of Tustumena Lake. When Dave Spencer had been flying mountain sheep surveys on the Kenai Peninsula, he took me along as an observer, so because of this experience I was assigned to assist Bob Scott. I got to spend about ten days in the mountains with the sheep. That was nirvana for me because of my interest in mountain ungulates and their ecology.

Dave flew me into a small lake near the head of Tustumena Lake, where he could land with the Widgeon on floats. I hiked from there up another thousand feet into the alpine zone to a tent frame hut with a woodstove in it that Scott and Spencer had built as a base camp for mountain sheep work. I took my camping gear and stuff, but we airdropped some food, so I didn't have too much to carry. Then when I got up there, I realized we forgot the plant press. Scott and Spencer both wanted me to collect plants while I was making sheep observations. Dave said that he would be able to fly over in a day or two and would drop me a plant press. That turned out to be an alarming experience for me as well as for Dave. The weather got too foggy, so Dave couldn't come when he said he would. The next day, I woke up in the morning and discovered that it had snowed during the night. There was an inch or so of snow all over the leafing-out low willow plants. The weather was lifting, and so, finally, I thought, "Well, he'll probably make it if the clouds lift enough." But even before the clouds had lifted, I heard the plane. He didn't have too much room between the clouds and where he was going to drop the plant press, but he knew the area. He was by himself in this Widgeon and he made this swoop, and I could see he was trying to push the plant press out of the pilot's window. Then the plane suddenly took a sharp dip toward the ground. The strap of the press had gotten caught around the flight stick. Luckily, Dave was able to straighten the plane out in time and regain altitude to make another loop. The second time, he successfully pushed the press out the window. He had it all rigged up with some cloth on it like a tail, so that when it hit the ground it wouldn't get lost in in the brush and be hard to find. He pushed all the cloth tail out first, and the wind just pulled the whole thing out and ripped the straps off the press that held the whole thing together. All of the twelve-by-sixteen-inch papers, blotters, and corrugated cardboard inserts fluttered down separately and scattered all over the area into this wet snow. Fortunately, it turned into a sunny day so the snow melted quickly and I could lay pieces of paper out to dry. But I didn't dry it all out completely. I ended up putting the blotters and the cardboards and stuff behind the stove in the cabin to dry. Later, Dave admitted that was a mistake on his part.

I was following up on some of Bob Scott's earlier mountain sheep studies. Mainly, after lambing they wanted me to count the number of lambs to ewes in the Indian Creek area. I had instructions on how to count the ewe to lamb ratios, and I was learning a lot about sheep by doing this. Bob was also interested in habitat and had already set up some enclosures that he made out of locally harvested alders where the sheep were doing a lot of heavy grazing to see what the effect would be on plants. By keeping the sheep away from certain areas, you could see a difference already with the plants. Then I knew if I hiked farther up, close to the glacier, there should be mountain goats. I went up there and spotted some goats and got a little familiar with goats and the kind of habitat they prefer. I was falling in love with working with alpine ungulates for sure. So I was definitely thinking strongly about that for my master's, but I still hadn't got to the university to start the program yet.

I realized that all of this was somewhat of a learning experience. And I realized that, in the case of sheep, I was collecting population data that was being used by Bob Scott for his larger study of mountain sheep ecology. That spoiled me from wanting to work with anything else. Scott was such a talented, brilliant guy, and was just top-notch with students. When John Buckley got appointed to a top position with the Fish and Wildlife Service in Washington, DC, as a sort of advisor to the president, Bob Scott was hired to be his replacement as the Cooperative Wildlife Unit leader. Dave Spencer was a mentor, too, but in a different way. I had a tremendous respect for him, and he went in the field with me a couple times when I was starting the mountain goat study. Having been trained in the mountain troops during World War II, he knew what you needed for a successful mountain expedition, including the proper climbing equipment and how to look at a mountainside and figure out a safe route, which were things I didn't have much experience with at the time.

Bob Scott was a good scientist; he understood wild nature ecology. Also, he understood me and I understood him. He had a lot of confidence in me and that I was capable of working on my own. In those days, you didn't have to have two people out doing fieldwork, and you didn't have to have a radio. I was insecure and lacked self-confidence, but I was always fascinated with exploration, especially polar exploration, and how these people managed to do it on their own. Pretty soon, I figured I could do it, too. I had been in Boy Scouts, which was all about outdoor life and being in rough, rustic conditions where you make do. And I had the woods work experience, so I was confident in using saws and axes, and building fires. You learned pretty fast to cook for yourself. And I had enough training in biology and wildlife ecology and was sharp enough to know that I could figure things out for myself. So I survived.

I had made good progress on plant collecting and clearing campsites, so I asked Dave Spencer about banding flightless young cormorants that were in nests on two rock islands near the northeast end of Skilak Lake. He said, "Sure, go ahead." He provided the bands and banding equipment and offered a few tips on how to do it properly. He cautioned that it would be a smelly process, because young cormorants either pooped or regurgitated semidigested fish in your lap while you were holding them. I quickly learned that wearing rain gear helped since it could readily be rinsed off in the lake. I banded about twenty young cormorants and figured there was little chance of any bands being returned since cormorants were not a preferred target of waterfowl hunters. About five years later, I received a letter from the FWS Bird Banding National Reporting Center in Patuxent, Maryland, reporting on the return of two bands that had been found on dead cormorants: one on the bank of the Kenai River downstream from Skilak Lake; and the other on a beach near Ketchikan, more than a thousand miles away.

As the end of summer approached, Dave told me that an annual narrative report was due. He was busy flying and had been gone a lot, so he said, "I want you to start the report." I thought, "Me?" I was a temporary, summer hire. I said, "I wasn't told I was going to do anything like this and I don't have that kind of experience. I don't know how to do it." He said, "I just do not have time to do it, so you're going to have to start it. Look at the previous reports, then go ahead and just start." At that stage, I never thought of myself as being a very good writer. I was always a poor speller, and, of course, they didn't have any spell-check back then. All you had was a pencil and a pad of lined yellow paper. Dave was long gone and I was there by myself, so I started. I roughed out the whole thing, and then he went over it. He said, "It looks like a good job. Let's get it typed up and then we can do more editing if we need to." I had never thought I'd be capable of writing a whole report like this. Well, that's how you learn. You may have abilities that sometimes you have to be pushed a little to bring out. I look at the report now and think it's not a bad report.

There was one activity that I did that summer on the Kenai that required working with others in a team effort. Managing for moose was the primary mission of the Kenai National Moose Range, especially given the abundance of large "trophy-size" moose on the western Kenai Peninsula. The whole concept of managing moose habitat at that time was based on the idea that good moose habitat was generated by the extent and frequency of wildfires. This led to the concept of using controlled burns to create better moose habitat.

At the time, there was little understanding of the biological history of the western Kenai Peninsula. About the turn of the century, it was thought there were no moose on the Kenai Peninsula. But Harold Lutz, a Yale University forester, interviewed Natives and old-time prospectors and trappers and showed that moose were present on the Kenai in the early 1800s, but there were so few that many people thought they did not exist (Lutz 1960). He speculated that the moose population was so low because there was a lack of quality moose habitat due to fires being extremely rare. At that time, summer temperatures on the Kenai Peninsula were too cool and foggy for lightning and thunderstorms to occur, a frequent cause of wildfires. But by the mid-1800s, the ecosystem was dramatically altered by the influx of mineral prospectors who are thought to have started extensive wildfires that destroyed old growth spruce and birch forests (Berg and Anderson 2006).

These were replaced by second-growth deciduous forests that produced ideal habitat for moose. This allowed the moose to shift from virtual obscurity to being the dominant large herbivore on the western Kenai (ibid.). Another consequence of the extensive wildfires and other associated human impacts was that caribou and wolves declined and finally died out. The first pack of wolves was not seen again until 1967.

Working in conjunction with the Bureau of Land Management (BLM), Dave Spencer planned to do an experimental controlled burn in the hills above Tustumena Lake in a shrub tundra kind of habitat that was mostly dwarf birch and not good moose browse. A team was put together of all the people they could gather from the BLM to join Dave Spencer and me from the Kenai Refuge. We moved into a tent camp near the proposed burn site. We cut a fire line in the brush and waited for the proper weather. If it was too dry or too windy, it was too great of a risk and they couldn't start the fire. If it was too wet, it wouldn't burn. So finding the right mix took a while. We were out there for about four days. Finally, we tried to start it when it wasn't quite as dry as we wanted but at least it was safe to try. With the breeze working in our favor, we walked along the fire line starting backfires with backpack flamethrowers. The fire would burn well where we had piled up brush, but it wouldn't carry. It died out when it hit the other vegetation. We made a major effort and we never could get the fire to take off, which meant that we couldn't really test the controlled burn theory. From our experience, though, we concluded that an unfavorable wind was likely to occur when it was dry enough to burn.

The use of controlled burns in the Kenai Moose Range was not without controversy. The fires did not always go where they wanted them to, and the growing environmental movement, largely among the Anchorage public, began to raise questions about the ecological wisdom of attempting to manage the Moose Range solely for moose in ignorance of the rich biodiversity in the recovering post-fire forests and the rest of the range. The Sterling Highway connecting Anchorage to the Kenai Peninsula was completed in 1951, which allowed more people to come visit and appreciate what a great and diverse area it was. They started to speak out about wanting a more balanced approach. It wasn't until passage of the Alaska National Interest Lands Conservation Act in 1980 that the Kenai National Moose Range

was renamed the Kenai National Wildlife Refuge, legally bringing its standards for management into compliance with basic principles of whole ecosystem management that were becoming accepted practice within the entire
National Wildlife Refuge System.

The Kenai National Moose Range couldn't have been a better place for
me to spend that summer before I started graduate school. The diversity of
opportunities I was given to learn about environmental management was
eye opening and gratifying for me. Having come directly from historically
conservative and urban New England to dynamic and as yet undeveloped
and wild Alaska was truly unique. I was convinced that I had made the right
decision in coming to Alaska for graduate education in wildlife conservation and management. I wouldn't have gotten that kind of experience if I
had gone someplace else. I look back sometimes and I'm just amazed that I
was so fortunate to have these experiences. You couldn't imagine how I felt
working with people like Dave Spencer and Bob Scott. And getting to do
things that in Connecticut I thought would not be possible, like being in
the mountains. From the first time I came to Alaska, I was hooked on the
mountains. New England was just too tame for me.

Jim King, who was employed on the Kenai Peninsula in the summer
of 1950 as a wildlife protection agent with FWS, was another influence
on me during my summer there. We shared the bunkhouse and cooked
meals together. Wildlife protection agents were responsible for enforcing
territorial game laws set by the Alaska Game Commission, and Jim was responsible for law enforcement at the mouth of the Kenai River with regard
to fishing. I got to know him well and appreciated learning about Alaska
and local wildlife management and enforcement from him. Later, he became a flyway biologist and played an important role in providing advice
and logistic support for some of my early students who were working on
waterfowl projects.

When I first came to the University of Alaska, I did not know that much
about what a master's degree entailed. At the University of Connecticut,
most students I knew didn't go on for a master's degree. You could get hired
with just a bachelor's degree and move up the career ladder pretty rapidly.
When I was accepted in the fall of 1951, I didn't really have a specific project in mind. I just felt lucky to be admitted into a graduate school at all. I

knew that I might not have free choice; that I might have to accept what was available. But on the other hand, I had become hooked on alpine ecology, and thought that the obvious plant-animal relationship that existed between alpine ungulates and the mountain flora would be interesting.

While understanding the relationship of the animals to their habitat was complicated, I nevertheless felt it was critical for successful management. At the time, the Fish and Wildlife Service and federal government had responsibility for the management of Alaska's wildlife as well as for the habitat that supported it. But the Fish and Wildlife Service tended to partition out research activities by species to their senior biologists, so one would be responsible for moose work throughout Alaska, another for caribou, and another for mountain sheep. Management, and subsequently research, was focused on the large species that were important for sport hunters. In those days, biologists were just starting to understand how important habitat really was.

The species-specific assignments of the FWS biologists had some effect on us graduate students in the Cooperative Wildlife Unit. We could not tackle anything as a thesis project that was one of the subject areas of the Fish and Wildlife Service biologists, unless it was a segment of a larger project. For example, with moose, you could look at them in interior Alaska and how mining affects winter browse activity and things like that, but you could not do a study of moose in the same way that the senior moose biologist was investigating them. While I would have been happy to work with mountain sheep for my master's thesis as a follow-up to what I already had been doing that summer on the Kenai, sheep research was already well covered by Bob Scott. I thought an open option for a master's project would be mountain goats and their alpine habitat relationships. They were another mountain ungulate and they weren't getting attention on the Kenai where I had been, or anywhere else in Alaska. However, I was naïve in thinking that a new graduate student would be able to select his or her own thesis project. In reality, it was usually the major advisors who got to make that determination based on their own area of interest and expertise and the likelihood of funding being available to cover logistical and other research costs essential for the project.

Neil Hosley had accepted me into the graduate program, so he presumably would have been my major advisor, except that he left the Cooperative

Wildlife Unit to become dean. John Buckley, a graduate of the State University of New York (SUNY) at Syracuse who had been teaching wildlife biology and management courses at UAF for two years, was selected to replace Hosley as Wildlife Unit leader. He then became my major advisor. Buckley's research focused on waterfowl and furbearer management in the Minto Flats area for which he had funding to support graduate student research. As his new graduate student, he expected my thesis research to be in this area. This was during a time when the Wildlife Unit did not have a lot of support money. Buckley was a good scientist and had a good record of advising graduate students, but doing research on furbearers and wetland habitat did not make good sense for me given my interest in alpine ungulates.

I think I was interested in the alpine and Arctic ungulates because, for one thing, they are charismatic species, but by this time I also had enough of an understanding that there was a relationship between herbivores and their food supply that I wanted to know more about. I think this notion partly came from working with dairy animals and realizing how much food drives the productivity of these herbivores. It was up to me to convince Buckley that I could do a thesis on mountain goats without close supervision. I argued that since Bob Scott was covering mountain sheep, mountain goats remained available as a subject for an MS thesis, that it would not be too costly because Dave Spencer had offered some support from the Kenai Moose Range, mostly flight time and use of a vehicle to get me in and out of the field, and that they both could serve as ad-hoc advisors. I had a hard time convincing Buckley that it would be okay for me to do this project and he could still be my advisor even though he wouldn't be able to spend any time in the field with me. I was persistent and John Buckley finally agreed to let me do the project and to serve as my major advisor.

Buckley was the only professor in the Wildlife Department when I started, but then he vacated the position when he became Unit leader and Jim Rearden was hired to teach the wildlife courses. I didn't take courses from Jim because I'd already taken those courses as an undergraduate, but I got to know him quite well and he was always helpful if you wanted any advice. By 1955, Jim decided academia was not for him and left the university. In 1959, he got a job as assistant area biologist with the Alaska Department of Fish and Game for the Homer region, later becoming area biologist and then a full-time outdoor writer. Neil Hosley continued to teach some wild-life courses after he became dean, and remained one of my advisors. I think he was on my graduate committee, as well as Brina Kessel.

After my wonderful summer on the Kenai, I arrived on campus for my first semester of graduate school raring to go. During my previous year in Fairbanks when I worked at the Experiment Farm, I had established a close friendship with Lynn Hollis. He was relatively new to Alaska, recently married and about to start a family, so he was building a house near the current Pump House Restaurant on land that they had homesteaded. It turned out that he needed some finish work done on kitchen cabinets and he knew I needed to earn some money, so he offered me the job. He drove me to the house one afternoon and dropped me off. I started working, and then I started not to feel well. I had a terrible upset stomach, and it got worse and worse. I finally just sat down on the floor and waited for him to come back at the end of the day. When he got there, I said, "I've got this problem." He took me to the university infirmary where there was a trained nurse, Miss Fish. She did a quick examination and said she didn't like the looks of things. She thought it could be appendicitis and told him to take me to St. Joseph's Hospital downtown by the Chena River.

Dr. Haggland examined me and agreed it was appendicitis. He did the operation and everything went well. But a couple of days later they discovered that I had peritonitis; paralysis of the lower digestive tract. They had to pump my stomach several times and put me back on intravenous fluids. I almost didn't make it. At first, I was feeling okay, but gradually it was getting worse and worse and I began to realize that it was turning into a very life-threatening situation. The doctor couldn't do anything because they couldn't operate again; it would be too great a risk. They just provided drugs and hoped for the best. I was in so much pain that they put me on morphine. Some of my fellow students and John Buckley came to visit me, but I was so sick and so drugged up that I didn't remember any of it. Eventually, the paralysis got so bad that they moved me into a private room, and a priest came in and wanted to know if I would appreciate having him say some things over me. I said, "No, thanks." He said, "How about a Protestant preacher?" I said, "No, I don't think so." Finally, it got so bad that I could no longer pee, which was very uncomfortable. They had to get a male nurse, which was hard to find in those days, to come in and put in a catheter to relieve the pressure in my bladder. That was a great relief, but I was still going downhill. I was in that private room for I think another three days. I did a lot of thinking about life during those days when I thought I was dying. I had always been philosophical about life and now that I was close to death I realized that in the past I should have valued my own life more highly. Then one morning, the nurse came in and said, "How are you doing?" I said, "I think I farted." She said, "Oh, that's wonderful." I knew enough to know that this was a good sign that things in the gut were starting to move. That was the turn around and it only took a few days before I was eating again.

Once I recovered enough to be out of the hospital, I was moved to the campus infirmary where Miss Fish could keep her eye on me. At first she was feeding me, but eventually she let me go to the cafeteria. They were having a special roast pork dinner that she let me go to, but she warned me not to eat too much. It was wise advice because my gut wasn't ready for all that fat. But it tasted so good to my nutritionally deprived and hungry body. I hadn't eaten much in weeks, so, of course, I ate too much. I came back and had horrible stomach pains. Miss Fish really scolded me badly for that. She said, "I told you not to eat so much." I had lost about thirty pounds total through all that. I was skin and bones. But I recovered very rapidly.

It was probably over a month that I had been sick and missed classes and was back on a regular class schedule. By this time, I had missed so much time from my classes that I wasn't sure if I was going to be able to finish the semester. Fortunately, I had teachers who loaned me their lecture notes and their course outline, and gave me extra reading assignments to help me catch up, which I did. In the end, I was able to finish the semester and did surprisingly well on the final exams.

After I got caught up in my courses, a job became available working with the dairy herd again. Charles Bunnell, the university president, had made a deal so that milk from the dairy and some produce and meat products could be used in the cafeteria on campus. The milk had to be pasteurized before it could be served, so they built a small building with modern pasteurization equipment in it. They needed somebody to do the pasteurizing. Since I had worked on dairy farms before and had taken a course in dairy husbandry that included training in pasteurization, I had enough experience to be hired. As soon as the milking was over in the morning, a truck would bring the milk cans over and drop them off in front of the pasteurization plant. I got up about 5:30 in the morning and ran the milk through the pasteurization process and then put it in containers in the cooler. A couple of students who worked in the cafeteria came over with a cart and picked up the containers of freshly pasteurized milk that fit right into the milk dispensers in the cafeteria. I then did a thorough cleaning of the pasteurization equipment and facility, and still had enough time to continue on with the rest of my academic day. The job paid well, but I had to learn to use my time efficiently.

When I first started my master's program, there were about six of us in the wildlife program funded through the Wildlife Unit. These included John Hakala, who studied beaver ecology and in 1952 was the first to graduate with an MS degree from the newly established Cooperative Wildlife Research Unit; Sal DeLeonartis, who studied rock and willow ptarmigan; Cal Lensink, who worked on marten in interior Alaska; Dave Hooper, who was researching waterfowl at Minto Lakes; Frank Wojcik, who was studying grayling in the Interior; Bert Libby, whose focus was beaver management in Alaska; and Jim Brooks, whose thesis was about the life history and ecology of Pacific walrus.

In the summer, most of the time I was in the field, either working for the Fish and Wildlife Service on wildlife-related studies or doing my own research. I worked on mountain sheep surveys for Bob Scott in the White Mountains and the Alaska Range, and was based on campus. And I worked in the Talkeetna, Chugach, and Kenai Mountains and based out of Anchorage. I didn't expect that I would be so lucky to be able to work over so much of the territory. It was like nirvana for me because of my fascination with alpine ecology.

I also worked as a field technician for the Fish and Wildlife Service on a team doing caribou sex and age composition counts on the Nelchina Caribou Herd. We were flown down to Clarence Lake, which is in an alpine plateau, and we hiked from there to where the caribou were. This was during the insect season, so during midday the caribou aggregated on top of a flattop hill where we would get pretty close without disturbing them. Then we'd wait for the weather to cool in the evening when they'd migrate down to greener vegetation, and using a spotting scope and binoculars we could do a count. We were mainly getting cow/calf ratios.

While we were at Clarence Lake, a plane came to move us to another lake that was closer to where the caribou were, and Starker Leopold and Frank Fraser Darling were on it. They were world experts on large wild herbivores who were traveling around Alaska with the Fish and Wildlife Service. I got to talk to them briefly, which was a momentous experience for me. I didn't fully appreciate it until I realized that they were going to publish a book (Leopold and Darling 1953). One of their conclusions about the caribou and the reason for a population decline wasn't an overgrazing problem as much as a loss of winter habitat through increased wildfires and the slow recovery rate of lichens, their main winter food.

In between these field trips, I came back to Fairbanks, but I didn't have too much time before I'd be out on another trip. In those in-between peri-ods, I lived with some friends in a place in the flats just below campus where the present power plant is located. The area was then called Vulture Flats. The building was a small frame cabin with a separate kitchen that was pretty run down and scheduled for demolition because the property was going to be sold. It was tilted at an angle because of melting of the underlying perma-frost. One student apparently had permission to use it, and so we'd all hang out down there when we were not doing fieldwork. We cooked our own food but were on a spartan diet, because we didn't have much money. Some of the others had some money from their research stipends, but I wasn't on a stipend yet. We'd buy the cheapest food we could get, which as meat eaters included buying horsemeat at the Piggly Wiggly grocery store. I don't know where the horsemeat came from, but it was marked fit for human consumption, although mostly dog mushers were buying it to feed their dogs. It was frozen and sold in large chunks. We chopped it up and put it in spaghetti sauce. It was great. We also sometimes bought frozen fish at the Piggly Wiggly. There was an old trapper who netted whitefish in the winter through the ice at Birch Lake, and a trucker who had befriended him brought gunnysacks of the fresh frozen fish to Fairbanks upon returning from his scheduled trip to Valdez. The frozen whole fish were inexpensive, and we learned that they were good when baked. We couldn't afford fresh milk, so we used powdered milk. It was something that we would use when going into the field that came in a big can, so we always had extra. We also harvested what we could from the wild. If somebody got something like grouse, ptarmigan, or fish, we shared it. It was a different world for us back then.

I never had a lot of money to go out and there was no place to go and spend it close by anyway. My friends and I did like an occasional beer, but downtown was the closest place to go out for a beer. We generally didn't have a vehicle available, so we had to walk into town, and it was kind of a long walk. We were concerned about some of the bars that were not safe places for students to go, but there were one or two that we thought were reasonable. We didn't want to get into brawls and we didn't want to get drunk. We couldn't afford it. But I remember making one or two excursions to the bar in Ester where you could get beer that had a slightly higher alcohol content. We could only afford to buy one beer each so that was a better deal. We did occasional things like that, but we did more of our socializing on campus, like being invited to dinners by the wives of our faculty members. They were really good about that for us grad students.

In terms of recreational activities on campus, it was not like it is today. I played some basketball with an intramural team, and evenings we often played Ping-Pong in a commons room in the Eielson Building, where Mary Zughaib, a young women recently hired to be dean of women, frequently joined us. She obviously appreciated socializing with us older male grad students, and we felt the same about her. Our group of single male wildlife grad students appreciated opportunities to socialize with females. Also, they had the standard kind of dances on campus, but we didn't get much involved in that. We were grad students, had served in the military, and were a bit older, so our focus was on learning and getting the degree, not so much on socializing. We were good students in that regard. We also knew a few senior female undergraduate students in biology and in anthropology who we often sat with when eating meals in the cafeteria, such as: Kay Morgan, who was studying anthropology and later married George Schaller; and Bella Gardiner, who was engaged to future governor Jay Hammond, who had graduated with a degree in biology a year before I got there. They were both nice women and we enjoyed their company.

In the wintertime, I would put on my army surplus snowshoes and go down into the flats east of campus, which were wetland areas that in the

David playing snowshoe softball
for the university team, playing
against the city team during the
Fairbanks Winter Carnival, March
1953. COURTESY OF DAVID KLEIN.

summertime you needed knee boots to walk around in. In the wintertime, of
course, everything was frozen so it was much easier to travel through. And it
was fun to read all the signs in the snow of the wildlife out there. There were
mink, marten, and snowshoe hares, plus smaller mammals and grouse. We
were encouraged to trap and hunt there by biology professor Brina Kessel to
secure specimens for the museum collections. This was during a time when
just seeing a new bird wasn't good enough; you had to shoot it and bring
it in, and they'd make a museum specimen out of it. I remember being excited to see a tiny, pure-white least weasel in the wintertime, and shooting
it for a study skin. The museum staff did a lot of patchwork to make the

specimen useable, because I had shot it with a shotgun and just filled the pelt with holes.

There was very limited cross-country skiing on campus at that time, and I wasn't a skier yet. The cross-country trails that existed were relics of those built by Ivar Skarland, a professor in the Anthropology Department who was originally from Norway, and some of his students in the 1930s. By the 1950s, the trails were not maintained, were grown over by brush, and were mostly forgotten. There was a little bit of recreational skiing on the trails and a few people used them for commuting to campus, but it was minimal. There was no trail grooming and no defined trail system like they have now. I finally got into cross-country skiing when I came back to Fairbanks in 1962 and joined the faculty at UAF, and even more after I spent a year in Norway on a Fulbright Grant in the early 1970s. After that, it became one of my favorite winter activities and I skied a lot both in Fairbanks and on trips into the backcountry.

Other than doing fieldwork in the summer, we didn't roam very far from Fairbanks. Most of us did not have cars, so if one of us was going out to do a project, there might be a chance for others to go along because a Wildlife Unit vehicle was being used and there was no extra transportation cost for the rest of us to join in. There was one graduate student who was working on a grayling project near the highway at Salcha and we would often go with him for the day. That was quite a trip on the gravel road back then. You didn't just whip up there and back again in a couple of hours like you can now on the good paved road. Or sometimes it was somebody working on the Taylor Highway, and we'd make it into a several-day trip. It might coincide with the hunting season, and if we were lucky we'd get a caribou or a moose. We were all pretty ardent hunters, and we always harvested small game. But mainly going out on these projects with other students was about exploring and seeing new country. That was part of being in Alaska.

I remember one November when I was camped out with some other graduate students on the Taylor Highway out in the Fortymile country. We had shot a couple of spruce grouse, skinned them, and put them in a pot to boil. We put some salt and pepper in there, and maybe we put onions with them. We probably didn't have a lot more than that to add anyway. We were sitting around the campfire cooking this, and a raven flew over. Cal

Lensink, who was a great waterfowl hunter and a good shot with birds, had his shotgun right beside him, which he proceeded to grab and just shot that raven right out of the air. It fell close by and Cal suggested we skin it and put it in the pot with the grouse. It turned out to be edible, although spruce grouse tend to taste pretty "sprucey" at that time of year when they are eating so many spruce needles to fatten up for winter. We were pretty hungry so would probably have eaten just about anything.

Then there was the wildlife club at the university, which was very popular among us wildlife students. Every year, we hosted a wild game dinner serving all kinds of wildlife that we had harvested. Also some trappers would turn in carcasses for us to examine in class for disease, parasites, and body condition, including lynx and wolves, and if the animal had been freshly killed and was free of disease, we would frequently dress it out and put it in the freezer to save for the game dinner. We usually offered a plate of some mystery meat and would ask people to guess what it was. One time we put raven out as the mystery meat. It had been cooked with spices and was served cold, and it came out okay. Another time we cooked up the back legs of a wolf. It smelled terrible when it was being cooked, but we put in bay leaf, some onions, and other spices to help flavor it and it wasn't bad. We then sliced it thin so you couldn't tell the difference between it and the other meats that were on the table. People liked the wolf and rated it really high in their taste testing. But we did cook it a long time to get rid of much of its odor. Nobody guessed what it was. We had to tell them after the fact that it was wolf.

Some key people who attended this annual game dinner were faculty members like Otto Geist, originally from Bavaria, who collected bones of extinct Pleistocene fauna exposed by gold-mining activities for the Frick Museum in New York, and Ivar Skarland. Some of us were taking Ivar's course about Alaska Natives because our advisors recognized the close connection between wildlife and the Native peoples of Alaska and recommended we take it. It took a week or two of class before I could fully understand his strong Norwegian-accented English. Ivar and Otto befriended us wildlife grad students, and we had a good relationship with them. We often hung out with them at the coffee shop that stayed open in the evenings, and they enjoyed telling stories of their working together on museum collecting

Wildlife game dinner held in the old main building at the University of Alaska, Fairbanks, October 1952. L–R: George Schaller (undergraduate student in wildlife), David Klein, Frank Wojcik (wildlife graduate student studying grayling), and Jim Brooks (wildlife graduate student working with walrus). COURTESY OF DAVID KLEIN.

trips. They also hosted a dinner for us wildlife grad students at the old cabin on campus where Ivar was living. This cabin is now known as the Rainey-Skarland Cabin, in honor of Ivar Skarland and Froelich Rainey, another well-known arctic anthropologist, who both lived in the cabin during their tenures in Fairbanks. When Otto and Ivar were together, they stimulated one another through their story telling, making that dinner one of the most memorable and interesting for us young wildlife biologists.

Also when I was a graduate student, Frank Glaser was another pioneering Alaskan who livened up our evenings on campus. After arriving in Alaska in 1915 and retiring from his adventurous life as a market hunter, trapper, dog musher, and predator control agent, Frank had moved to town from the Bush, married, and was working as a night watchman at the university. On summer evenings, many of us in Main Dorm would sit out on the front steps, enjoying the cool evening air after a warm day in the Interior. Frank would come by doing his watchman rounds and would join us long enough to tell a story or two from his amazing life where he learned from personal observation about the lives of moose, caribou, foxes, wolverines, mountain sheep, grizzly bears, and wolves. The stories he told often seemed farfetched to us "wildlifers," who thought we knew a lot about living in the wilderness. Because he was such a good storyteller, we thought he might be embellishing things and stretching the truth a bit. But we learned over time that, no, he was only telling you a little about all of these amazing things that happened in his life. Later, Jim Rearden published a book about Frank Glaser based on conversations he recorded with him that verified the validity of the tales Frank told us (Rearden 1998).

Another thing us wildlife students did to earn money was to work for the Fish and Wildlife Service at hunter check stations in the fall during caribou hunting season. In territorial days, FWS operated several of these stations around the state, mostly at the major hunting areas that were road accessible, where hunters would get instructions on where they could hunt legally and what the regulations were. They had big signs that said, "HUNTERS MUST STOP AT CHECKING STATIONS." I worked at one on the Steese Highway that was located just about where the road enters the alpine zone, about seventy-six miles from Fairbanks. I also operated a check station on the Taylor Highway up in caribou country close to Mount Fairplay.

Our job was to refresh the hunters' memory about hunting regulations. We had to check them as they went in and then check them when they came out to collect information about who was hunting and what they got. Even if they didn't get anything, you wanted them to stop and tell you because the agency wanted to know how many hunters were in an area and what their success rate was. It was mainly for caribou, but it also included moose and mountain sheep. We also collected lower jaws for aging the animals or stomach samples. Of course, that was voluntary on their part. Part of our job was education of the hunters, which included telling them about

David (top, right) looking at the scale while weighing a caribou at a hunter check station on the Steese Highway, circa 1951. COURTESY OF DAVID KLEIN.

the kind of wildlife studies that we were involved in and why we wanted to know the age of the animals harvested, what the sex ratio was, and what the success ratio of the hunters were. Going out and interacting with hunters like this was good training for us.

For the most part, the hunters cooperated. They didn't have to stop if they didn't want to, but it was presented to them as important and a requirement. But there were some that were probably potential violators of the law and didn't want to risk exposing themselves, so didn't participate. But we didn't make a big deal about it. As students, we didn't have law enforcement authority. If someone had a violation, all we could do was take down all the information and pass it on so that they could be checked again by the game warden. Of course, if there happened to be a game warden with us, well, they were the ones that handled those cases.

In my view, check stations were good because even though they were costly in terms of human hours to operate and not everybody was cooperative, they were informative to the public. To me, the lack of informing the public as to what is involved in wildlife management has been a shortcoming. That's where I've had problems with the Alaska Department of Fish and Game; there's not enough information going out as to what's being done to learn about wildlife and habitat relationships in relation to management. We need to be more effective in educating hunters about all this in order to get them to cooperate in management rather than just seeing us as game wardens.

Eventually, they discontinued using check stations. They did this for a lot of reasons. One was that by statehood there were more road systems and it cost money to set up check stations. So the question was how important were they for management and were they worth the price? And another reason was that in the period of early statehood, there was much more emphasis on management based upon harvest statistics because they gave you an indication of trends in populations. And using harvest statistics required only one or two technical people in the office in Anchorage putting this stuff together and summarizing it, instead of all those people at the stations.

After I finished my first year of grad school in May 1952, I had plans to go to the Kenai Peninsula for the summer to start work with mountain goats for my thesis project, but I didn't get any funding from the Wildlife Unit until the second year of graduate school. Luckily, I had earned a little bit of money by working through the school year and had been assured of receiving some free aircraft support from Dave Spencer and the Fish and Wildlife Service, so I was still able to go. I was dropped off in the mountains where most of the goats were located and spent four or five days by myself in a place before being picked up and moved to another location.

I was interested in the biology of these creatures and hoped I could get by without learning a lot of extra mountaineering skills. I didn't have any mountain experience before working for the Kenai Moose Range, but I learned the basics of mountaineering from Dave Spencer, who grew up in the Rockies, was a good mountain skier, and had received specific mountain training in the military during World War II. He showed me how to use crampons and ice axes, and how to read the snow and be safe, but I didn't have many opportunities to practice. For the most part, I just tried to minimize risk. Sometimes I'd feel challenged to go to the top of a mountain just because I was close. And then suddenly, I realized, oh, I was pushing myself beyond my capabilities. There were times when I may have gone up to the top anyway just to say I'd reached the top and to have a nice view, and then I'd come down. I never was interested in mountain climbing per se, because I'd lose interest in my surroundings as soon as I got beyond the vegetation and the animals.

I remember one incident when I was walking across an avalanche shoot that was loaded with snow. I didn't have crampons with me, and I slipped and went sliding down the steep slope toward a rocky area. I had to learn fast how to use the ice axe I was carrying to stop myself. It was pretty exciting, because I first tried putting the long sharp point of the axe into the snow, but it was grainy snow that just ended up flying over me so it didn't act as a brake. I flipped the axe over so the broad part was in the snow and put my weight on it. I quickly came to a stop. That was an unanticipated learning experience. I should have practiced that before I went into the mountains. But that's generally the way we were in those days.

Given my work with mountain sheep and goats, I was called in to help on a project where the Fish and Wildlife Service wanted to establish mountain goats on Kodiak Island. I was paid as a full-time field assistant and worked with two predator and rodent control agents, Buck Harris and Doyle Cisney. They were broadly experienced, middle-aged, and in good shape physically, and they were terrific to be out in the field with. The three of us were flown in an amphibious Grumman Goose airplane from Seward at the head of Resurrection Bay to Day Harbor, which is just east of Resurrection Bay. We set up a large canvas wall tent as a base camp on a narrow beach adjacent to a mountain known to have a mountain goat population. We were going to try to capture kid mountain goats using leg snares. It was a steep climb over rugged terrain up to the goat habitat above tree line, but once we got up there we could get around without too much trouble. We found places where there were goat trails suitable for setting leg snares, but those trails had been used in the spring and there was no sign of recent summer use. Eventually, we did find fresh droppings and tracks of ewes with kids at a slightly higher elevation where the alpine vegetation preferred by the goats was just greening up. We decided to move our camp up there to avoid climbing up and down to the beach every day.

The next day, we were able to approach two ewes with kids who were feeding close to a rock spire. Buck, who had considerable horse wrangling experience and was handy with a lasso, thought he might be able to lasso one of the kids. When the kid moved into range, Buck threw his lasso, but narrowly missed the target. Alarmed by this apparent attack on her kid, the nanny goat charged toward Buck rather than running away over the rocky slope as we had expected. Buck dodged the nanny by scrambling around the rock spire, and the goats all fled across a steep rocky slope. After this excitement, we concluded that live capture of kid goats was too risky for both humans and goats, at least at this location and time of year. We weren't going to be able to take a kid from a ewe, and we didn't want to shoot the ewe. So that was a failed operation. But for me it had been an opportunity to spend time with and broaden my understanding of mountain goats and their habitat, so that was great.

There was another funny story that involved me and capturing a mountain goat. I was flying with Dave Spencer in the twin-engine amphibious Widgeon pretty high over Cooper Lake, and I looked down and I saw what looked to be three swans swimming in the lake. It turned out to be three mountain goats. Dave quickly landed the plane, and was able to get between one of the goats and the shore to block its path. We slowly taxied up to the goat and Dave cut the engine, then he told me to crawl forward and try to get a piece of rope around the horns of the goat. It was just sheer luck that I succeeded and was able to gain control of the goat. Of course, it couldn't do much to fight or get away because it was swimming in the water. We headed toward shore where it was shallower and we could get in the water and wrestle the goat out onto the beach. However, as soon as that goat could get its feet on the bottom, it started to bounce and jump. Dave and I both leaped into the water, and together we were able to force it onto its side so that we could tie its feet together. It was a young male, about three years old, and it had solid five-inch horns. We put part of an old parka over its head to calm it down. Then we had to carry it back and put it in the plane. That goat certainly was not pleased with the experience.

The plan was to fly the goat to Kodiak as part of the mountain goat relocation project, but it was too late to fly to Kodiak that same day. So we flew to Kenai and put it in an old shed with some straw, food, and water, and untied its feet so it could move around. The next morning we had a little trouble capturing the goat again, but we did. We flew it to Kodiak to the base of a mountain where they wanted to try releasing goats. We put an ear tag in it and released it at the high tide line. Immediately, it went into the alders and started to climb up. That was a significant contribution to the future goat population, but it takes more than one male to get a new population started. Fish and Wildlife Service administrators finally concluded that the best way to acquire mountain goats for introduction to Kodiak was to offer local hunters who were very familiar with the goats and terrain $200 per live goat. However, it proved an insufficient incentive, so the price for a live goat was finally raised to $400, which was pretty good money back then. Both FWS and potential goat trappers agreed that yearling goats (those near one year of age) were the most desirable for capture, handling, transport, and release. In the end, the relocation project was successful. There are now mountain goats on Kodiak Island. Distribution is limited, but they are legally hunted.

My master's thesis was titled "A Reconnaissance Study of the Mountain Goat in Alaska" (Klein 1953). The idea was to learn as much as I could about the general behavior and ecology of mountain goats and their relationship to the habitat and vegetation. But it grew to be a little more than that. It was very interesting in many ways. I did most of the work in three study areas on the Kenai Peninsula where I could watch the goats from a distance and they weren't aware of me. One was in the mountains around Cooper Lake. Another was at Russian Mountain, near the head of Skilak Lake and Cooper Mountain. The third one was at Ptarmigan Lake. There was one other area I visited called Lost Lake that was close to Seward, but high up in the mountains. I had to hike a long way to get there, but it was on a good trail.

My whole project was based on an accumulated number of good observations, plus I did a lot of plant collecting so I could identify what was there and see what the goats had been eating. The ridge above Cooper Lake was an especially good place to watch goats feeding because I could watch them with binoculars from a ridge across the lake. I also had a spotting scope with which I could watch goats from a longer distance to see where they were feeding. I could identify areas with distinctive rocks and after the goats had moved out of that area I could go over and take notes on what was being eaten and determine from their fresh droppings how long they had been there.

I was able to make some good observations on interactions between mountain sheep and goats, and show that the habitat preferences of goats are different from sheep. Mountain goats and sheep are real specialists. Apparently, it is a terrain preference. Goats are almost always restricted to the real steep cliffs and heavy precipitation areas where their diet is comprised of shrubs if they are available, over-wintering fiddleheads of ferns, and other plants that grow on cliff faces. Mountain sheep, however, are restricted to drier slopes where the lighter snow more readily blows away and exposes the grasses, sedges, and other low-growing forage species they prefer. Sheep don't do well in the real cliffy areas, but while giving birth to lambs in spring females will occupy cliffs to be more secure from predation. But after that, they want better grazing so move into the lower areas where there is new green vegetation. There can be overlap areas where it is good habitat for both goats and sheep, but to my knowledge, no one has ever reported any aggressive behavior between the species

I remember watching an interesting interaction between mountain goats and mountain sheep on Russian Mountain. A group of three female mountain goats with three kids were feeding on a lush green shelf with a cliff on one side and rolling higher hills that were greening up on the other side. The group size was slightly larger than average for that sex and age group, and was about as large a group of mountain goats as I expected to see. The three nannies were maximizing their intake of the high-quality forage that was available there, while the three kids each seemed preoccupied with playing and having a good time, and were following behind their respective nanny waiting for an opportunity to nurse. Then, unexpectedly, a group of about thirty mountain sheep, mostly females with lambs, came pouring onto this same area and started grazing. The female sheep were indifferent to the goats, until they started foraging closer and closer toward the female mountain goats, at which time the ewes stopped briefly and watched the goats. Both goats and sheep were white and the sheep were used to large groups so were not disturbed by the goats. All the female sheep started feeding again, and the lambs started playing closer and closer to the goats. That's when the goats started moving away from the sheep. They just moved up and out of the area. I saw similar behavior once or twice again when sheep and goats encountered one another, but this was the most obvious example.

Another thing I observed was the effect of noise on the behavior of mountain goats. I was sitting on the south side of a slope looking across Ptarmigan Lake at the north-facing slope, where spring was delayed because it got less sun and warmth. But it was spring in the avalanche shoots, because things greened up faster in the places where the avalanches had wiped all the snow off. Many of the goats ventured down into these shoots to forage on all the really good green vegetation that was not yet growing anyplace else. You'd hear this *rumble, rumble* of an avalanche, but the goats would hardly notice it unless the sound was coming from above them. Then they bounded two or three times and quickly got out of the shoot and watched as the snow came crashing down. Once the avalanche passed, they went back to feeding. This showed that they related to the noise in a specific way. Their behavior was triggered by the noise only if it was coming from a certain spot, and they could tell the difference.

Throughout my life, I've always enjoyed fieldwork. It was about as satisfying as possible under the circumstances. When I was in grad school, it was pretty standard at that time to be on your own when doing fieldwork. It was sometimes exciting being in the field by myself. I learned a lot and gained a feeling of self-reliance. Normally, I had no radio contact as is generally required now and we had no cell phones or satellite radios. Even emergency locator beacons didn't come into play until much later. At some point, we did get some kind of a radio that in an emergency we could use to contact planes flying overhead. But I never used one. At the time, there was very little money to support the graduate programs at the university, or to support any kind of wildlife work, but we did have the advantage that aircraft in Alaska were beginning to play a major role in biological field research. This meant we could get into the field easier than walking, and we had a schedule to be picked up at a specific time, weather permitting. I felt confident because of my previous experiences in the field and as a Boy Scout. And my supervisors learned that I had the capability of working on my own and had the competence to do it. That was just the way most of the fieldwork was done in those days. This was why I came to Alaska. This way of life appealed to me.

When I was by myself, I never had problems that I thought were insurmountable. The problems were things like the plane didn't come on time and you didn't know why. It usually meant that the weather wasn't suitable for the plane to fly. You had to have reasonable weather, and frequently the pickup spots were where there were rivers or small lakes with challenging conditions and the pilot had to think about not only picking you up, but getting back out as well. I did have one problem in the Chugach Mountains on a trip where I was by myself. I hiked in and camped up high, so I went pretty light. I just had a tiny pup tent. Then I found a freshly dead lamb. I couldn't see any evidence that it had been attacked by a predator, so I wondered what had killed it. It was only a couple of days before I was going to be taken out, so I packed it back to my camp, put it in a plastic bag, and put it in a snow bank to keep it fresh.

The next day when I woke up I had an infection in my eye. And it got worse. It was kind of awkward because I was using a spotting scope and watching the sheep and doing counts. Luckily, it was only a couple of days with the eye infection before the helicopter arrived and was able to take me back to Anchorage. I went to a doctor right away since we thought maybe the lamb was the culprit. The doctor thought it was a type of eye infection that was common in animals, and that it was possible that I might have contracted it from touching that lamb. The doctor gave me some eye drops, which I used right away and it cleared up. The lamb was taken to the Public Health Service Lab for examination, which indicated that it had an eye infection, but they couldn't say for sure if that's what killed it. That was a little unnerving because I was by myself. Luckily, the infection was only in one of my eyes. If it had gone into the other eye, the outcome would likely have been worse.

For the mountain sheep work, mostly we had a base camp high up in the mountains. How we got there varied. Sometimes I had to hike in and carry everything all the way up. While in other places, like in the Chugach Mountains up above Eagle River, we talked the military into flying me in with a helicopter. One time, they sent a young enlisted man in with me as a field assistant. The military didn't like the idea of flying one person into the mountains and leaving him by himself. It turned out that we were in there on his birthday, so I decided to make a cake. Since we had been brought in by helicopter, there was some pancake mix that I used as the flour for the cake, and we had a few candles that we used as fire starters or at night if we needed them for a little light in the tent, so I put one of them in the center of the cake. We took a picture of him with his birthday cake that I later sent to him.

You always planned to go as light as possible, because you usually were packing stuff in. In terms of food in the field in the early days, we didn't have prepackaged dehydrated foods like they have today. You could get dehydrated peas, and peas and carrots, but you didn't get too fancy with taking extra things like dried vegetables. And to me, that freeze-dried stuff tasted pretty much like the package. You wanted things that were packed with calories and some nutrition in terms of protein, fat, and carbohydrates. Of course, we had basics like rice, which provided a lot of calories, but were not necessarily the best nutritionally. And you had a few other standard things like dried fruit or dried meat, which gave you good energy. Of course, salmon strips were great if you could get them. We also had things like powdered milk and powdered eggs that mixed together real well to make a sort of omelet. You could throw chunks of meat or bacon in with it, and it was quite edible. The flavor was there even if the texture wasn't quite right. You could get smoked and cured bacon that lasted forever that was good to take in the field. You can't get anything like that nowadays. You also could get ham or smoked sausage, but they were pretty expensive. And, of course, cheese was very important. There wasn't any bread that would keep in those days, but pilot crackers were okay. If you were out doing a lot of hiking, then you wanted to have real concentrated stuff for lunch, which included raisins, dates, or figs. Oh, and I used to take big chunks of semi-sweet chocolate. That was great stuff.

Sometimes when I was in remote places, if I needed more food than I could carry, they'd airdrop it. It is easy to lose stuff in an airdrop, but the pilots did this so much that they became pretty confident in how to do it successfully. One time we were at the headwaters of Dry Creek staying at a trapper's cabin and a resupply of food was dropped in a small burlap sack. We had done this enough times that we knew that it was better to put things like flour in cloth bags than to leave it in a cardboard box that might break. And canned goods were usually left loose so they were like a bean-bag. The pilot dropped the sack and it was a direct hit on a large rock and it just exploded. The flour busted open and filled the air so that it looked like smoke. Luckily, the flour was the only thing that was damaged.

In addition to the food, we generally had survival gear in case we needed to live off the land. Depending on where you were, that meant fishing line and tackle, and I carried a gun for bear protection, which I used to shoot small mammals or birds when I was running short of food. If you had a little bit of rice left, you could mix the fish or meat with that and make a reasonable meal. Lola Tilly taught home economics at the university and taught a course in outdoor cooking that she encouraged us wildlife grad students to take since so many of us were going out into the field and barely knew the basics of cooking. She was such a fine person, and she treated us grad students so well that she was like a mom to us. It was times like this when food was low that having taken this course really came in handy.

Although I didn't mind being alone, I also enjoyed doing fieldwork with other people. I appreciated having someone to share camp responsibilities with and to provide support for activities requiring more than one person. It was also nice sometimes to have someone to talk things over with. At times, it was essential to have someone else with you. For example, when observing caribou behavior in summertime when there are twenty-four hours of daylight, taking turns sleeping and working makes it possible to collect data over a full twenty-four-hour period. I did have some bad experiences working with other people in the field, but for the most part it worked out.

Most of the failures in fieldwork were related to bad weather. Obviously, you're frustrated if the clouds come down when you're supposed to be counting mountain goats and you can't see them. But, generally, I can't remember when it was totally fogged in for more than a day at a time. But I do remember a super storm when I was in the White Mountains in the middle of July. I had a little pup tent and fortunately it had a floor in it, because otherwise the tent would have blown away. It rained for hours, but I was relatively dry because I had the tent over me. The only thing you can do in a situation like that is just lie down and spread yourself out to keep the tent from flapping too much or blowing away. Other times bad weather delayed an airplane pickup, which could be worrisome because you didn't know when or if it might actually arrive, but it was not the end of the world. Although, sometimes just sitting around and waiting can be difficult. This was where you might have to start rationing your food or hunting or fishing to supplement what you had.

Of course, we were generally in bear country when we were doing fieldwork, but I never really had a problem with bears. I can recall one run-in I had with a bear when I doing sheep survey work in midsummer in the Talkeetna Mountains. I was hiking on a trail that had been used by hunters on horses to get into the high sheep country. It was in low hills with a lot of dwarf birch and some willows, where the vegetation was about four feet high. There was not good visibility too far ahead, so when I came around a bend in the trail all of a sudden there was a small grizzly bear coming up the trail. We saw one another at about the same time. I carried my rifle hooked over my Kelty backpack frame, so the first thing I did was take it off my shoulder and put a shell in the chamber. The next thing I wanted to do was grab my camera. But then the bear started coming closer and it was acting curious. I waved my arms a little bit and talked in a deep voice, but it kept coming. Then it stopped for a minute and was just standing there. There was a clump of sod by my feet and I reached down, picked that up, and threw it, thinking if it landed in front of the bear, it might frighten him a little bit. Instead, it landed right on his back. I could tell he felt it, but it was pretty soft sod so it didn't faze him at all, and he started coming toward me again. I thought how close should I let it come before it's too close and I have to shoot? I didn't want to shoot the bear, and I hadn't studied up much on bluff charges. By this time, I now had the gun up against my shoulder and was thinking, "When should I start to squeeze the trigger?" Finally, just when the bear was probably a little closer than I should have let it come to be totally safe, it stopped. It must have got my smell. It turned around and just ran back down the trail, off into the brush, and disappeared over the hill. I've had some other experiences similar to that, but that one was the most unnerving because I hadn't had much experience yet with bears.

Fourth Infantry Scouts on a training exercise in the
woods of Ladd Field having problems with the track
falling off their Weasel vehicle, 1953. PHOTO BY DAVID KLEIN.

I completed my master's degree in the spring of 1953, and this meant my
student deferment for drafted military service during the Korean War was
over. While I thought I had served my time in the Second World War, it
turned out that I only completed one year of active duty, and the draft law
now required two years in order to be exempt. So in 1953, I entered the
US Army in Alaska to complete my one year of required service, and was
sent to the 4th Infantry Intelligence and Reconnaissance Platoon based in
Fairbanks at Ladd Field. I went to basic training at Fort Richardson out
of Anchorage where I was quite a bit older and more educated than the

David running the gee pole on a dog sled on a mushing trip the Army group made from Tanana to Fairbanks via Old Minto, March 1954. David (in foreground) had the sled with the heaviest load and so had the biggest dogs. They flew people, gear, sleds, and dogs in a DC-3 to Tanana and mushed back to Fairbanks and had one airdrop that included dried fish as dog food. COURTESY OF DAVID KLEIN.

average draftee. All of these other guys were barely out of high school, so I was assigned to be a platoon leader and they immediately started calling me "Doc."

Once I was at Ladd Field, I was offered a wildlife law enforcement position where I would be assigned to the commanding officer to serve as his personal hunting guide. I declined the position and volunteered to be in a scouts platoon. Our lieutenant in charge realized that things were different for us older guys who had been in the military before, so he gave us a lot of freedom. He would say, "I want you guys to get out and be active, but I don't want to force you to do calisthenics, so when you're on base, don't be seen just sitting around, or I'm going to have to discipline you and have you picking up cigarette butts and stuff like that." He treated us well and would give us a pass to go off base on trips. Like we would take a jeep to drive out to Cleary Summit to go skiing or go skijoring behind the jeep. It wasn't the safest thing to do, but we did it anyway. And we did interesting trips that allowed me to see more of Alaska. We had a dog kennel with two dog teams, so we did dogsled trips, like one from Tanana to Fairbanks with stopovers at Tolovana and Old Minto. We also did river trips, like boating from Fort Yukon to Rampart on the Yukon River, where we participated in foot races on the 4th of July in Beaver and attended an old-time fiddling dance in Rampart. These experiences exposed me even more to the Native people and cultures of Alaska, which I developed a great appreciation for. It also helped teach me about traveling in rural Alaska, which is something I did a lot of later on.

Taking a break while traveling between the Alaska villages of Circle and Tanana on the Yukon River, 1953. PHOTO BY DAVID KLEIN.

Kids running a footrace on the Fourth of July when the boat trip made a stop in the village of Beaver, 1953. PHOTO BY DAVID KLEIN.

Also during this time, I built a twenty-by-twenty-four-foot log cabin on Linda Lane in the recently established Chena Small Tracts area. The idea was that once I had the cabin finished and got out of the military, I would live in it. I would get a weekend pass from the army and would go work on the cabin. I got some of my military buddies to come and help peel the logs, which was really helpful, but mostly I did the building myself by hand with a Swede saw and broad axe, a hand drill to drill holes, and a maul to drive all the pins down into the logs.

I was discharged from the army in the summer of 1954. I immediately got a job as a wildlife technician with the Fish and Wildlife Service, which was great because I had not earned much money while I was in the military. I was hired in the fall and early winter, so I joined teams that were mostly

David's finished cabin, winter, 1955. PHOTO BY DAVID KLEIN.

David's Army friend, Russell McGregor, peeling bark from logs for David's cabin, 1954. David constructed the tepee tent in the background from Army surplus tent material. He camped in the tepee when on a weekend pass so he didn't have to return to base every day. PHOTO BY DAVID KLEIN.

doing caribou work. I finished building the cabin when I was not out in the field. Unfortunately, I didn't end up living in that cabin, because I got an offer for a permanent position as a biologist in Petersburg. Up to that point, this type of job had been my goal in life, so I was excited for the opportunity.

David presenting deer harvest data
at a public meeting in Petersburg,
1956. COURTESY OF DAVID KLEIN.

6
Deer Ecology and Management in Southeast Rainforests

Starting in January 1955, I got a full-time job as a wildlife biologist with the Bureau of Sport Fisheries and Wildlife within the US Fish and Wildlife Service. I was based in Petersburg, working mainly with deer management and deer ecological studies for all of Southeast Alaska. Technically, you were working for both the Fish and Wildlife Service and the Territorial Game Commission. At the time, I was the only biologist strictly working with wildlife and its management in all of Southeast. My focus was understood to be primarily on the Sitka black-tailed deer because deer were the only readily available terrestrial wildlife species traditionally hunted for both its prime-quality venison and the sport and recreation associated with hunting. In order to extrapolate the sex and age of the entire population, I was required to do hunter surveys to find out what sex and age deer were being killed. A related responsibility was evaluation of deer habitat and how its status or quality affected the deer. Up until this time, my goal in life had been a permanent position as a biologist, so this was just what I'd been hoping for.

I was expected to do studies of the deer habitat and how that influenced individual deer as well as the structure of the deer population. I really enjoyed doing that and this is when I realized that science was my primary interest, rather than the management part. Management was interesting, because it tied the people to the resource and I had become fascinated with the people, both the Native cultures and the newcomers, but I soon became captivated by deer-habitat relationships. I initiated studies of both the winter and summer habitats used by deer and the vegetation that was important to them.

I also had other responsibilities related to hunting and fishing, game regulations, and management of wildlife. For example, I had to do an annual aerial survey of moose on the Stikine River, or if we were doing other aerial surveys on the mainland for deer, we also might check out mountain goat areas. Goats were only present on the mainland in Southeast, with the exception of Baranof Island, where at that time they were thought to have been introduced. Later, DNA analysis has shown that mountain goats survived the Wisconsin glacial period on Baranof Island. Since I had done my master's degree on mountain goats, I maintained a major fascination with their ecology.

Sigurd (Sig) T. Olson, the fellow that had been the biologist in Petersburg before me, was being transferred to Fairbanks where he was going to take over management of caribou for all of Alaska. His father was Sigurd F. Olson, a professor, wilderness guide, and outdoors writer living in Minnesota who played a major role in the development of the Wilderness Society and establishment of Voyageurs National Park and the Boundary Waters Canoe Area Wilderness in Minnesota (Backes 1997). Sig shared his father's love of wilderness and had done his master's degree on loons. He was sharp, knowledgeable, and had a wonderful sense of humor. He felt that when things got difficult that it was important to find the humor and keep things on the lighter side. He had a perpetual smile on his face, which he jokingly acknowledged was the result of shrapnel wounds he had received fighting in Italy during World War II. When I took the position, Sig stayed on for about a month and a half to help me get familiar with the job. I was still unmarried and he and his family treated me wonderfully. It was great to work with him; we had a lot in common. I could see what he had been doing, the limitations he faced, and what was the best way to go forward in the future. Sig was a real mentor to me.

Petersburg was a small town, and when I got into the community this group of women schoolteachers quickly adopted me. Many of them were wives of pilots who I knew pretty well, because with the deer management work, I was doing a lot of flying between towns checking with hunters, determining what they killed, and collecting jaws for age studies. Bill Stedman was one pilot who flew small planes for a charter company that I used a lot for deer or moose counts. I think these women felt sorry for me as a bachelor, so Bill's wife and one of the other pilot's wives arranged for me to meet a new teacher in town named Arlayne Brown who had recently arrived from Washington. Arlayne and I hit it off and got married in December of 1955. Our first two children, Martin and Peggy (who now goes by PeggyEllen) were born in the hospital in Petersburg.

With regard to deer hunting, there were plenty of deer to go around. Harvested venison was an important contribution to families' diets, but the total numbers of hunters in Southeast was low in relation to the numbers of deer available. Access was limited because there were virtually no roads outside of the communities. Most hunters went by boat to a location to hunt. The attitude for deer hunters was that you never went ashore to go hunting if there was another skiff anchored at the beach. Hunters didn't want to be

Klein family on a picnic in British Columbia, circa 1959. L–R: Arlayne, Martin, Peggy, and David. COURTESY OF DAVID KLEIN.

David in his office in Petersburg writing reports, 1956. COURTESY OF DAVID KLEIN.

in the same area with other hunters, and there were always plenty of other places to go hunting. One of the reasons was for safety. There were virtually no accidental shootings of other hunters in those days. Another reason was that deer were more alert and more difficult to hunt when other hunters were present. A third reason was because of competition. That maybe the other people were going to get the buck first. The attitude was that you were out there primarily for meat, and if you wounded an animal you stayed on it until you found it and were able to kill it. There was good sportsmanship in that regard, but it was hard to convince some of the longtime hunters to change practices that were no longer working in their favor.

There were still a few holdouts who believed that you shouldn't kill the females; that by not shooting antlerless females of reproductive age this would be the best way to have more deer. This was based on the Buck Law that was enacted to help keep deer populations high by protecting the reproducing females. But during the Second World War, in some communities most of the young men were off in the war and there wasn't much hunting, so deer numbers increased. This happened in Petersburg, so it no longer made sense to enforce the Buck Law. My job was to go to local meetings of the hunters to try to convince them of the need to reduce the deer population and that there was no point in protecting the antlerless deer because there already were too many deer in the environment. I did frequent slideshow presentations at meetings in Petersburg and Wrangell, as well as in Juneau and Ketchikan when I had opportunities to get there. Our studies had shown that after a series of mild winters deer numbers got so high that the deer over-browsed the winter forage species. There were too many deer for the available habitat, but you can't really convince a hunter that there's such a thing as too many deer. Antlerless hunting seasons were a desirable tool for deer management in order to bring the deer population down and allow for recovery of winter forage plants. However, this was something new that hunters were not used to. That's why I built fenced enclosures to demonstrate how quickly plant species recovered within the enclosures where deer could not get to them. Hunters who came across the enclosures and clearly saw the physical evidence were generally convinced of the impact that deer could have on plants and the habitat.

Sig Olson laid a lot of groundwork, because he was up against the same problems. I had instructions from him on how to proceed, and I'm a quick learner. First, I got to know people. I'd schedule public meetings about proposals for regulations in which I would explain what I was proposing and why. I had charts and tables that showed the average age of the deer that were killed by hunters, and the sex ratios and how this related to population growth pyramids. I showed that the deer population was growing vigorously and compared it to a slow-growing population. Also, I knew that hunters could be good sources of information, so I listened to them and tried to learn as much as possible. Like I'd ask, "How many deer did you see and did you see any females with young?" And they would let me measure the deer that they harvested. For example, I took measurements of the hind foot length, which I used to indicate growth rate in relation to age and body size.

The first technical publication I did was through the Fish and Wildlife Service, and it was based on some of this early work on deer management in Southeast Alaska (Klein 1957b). Sig Olson was a good artist, so he illustrated it for me with some cartoons. For example, there was a picture of an enclosure with a deer looking in and salivating accompanied by a sign

Cartoon illustration by Sig Olson of an exclosure that David was using in his research jokingly presented from the standpoint of the deer. USFWS FEDERAL AID IN WILDLIFE RESTORATION ALASKA, JOB COMPLETION REPORT, PROJECT W-3-R-11, ALASKA, JUNE 30, 1957, P. 4.

saying, "Keep Out! D. R. Klein." They even put those cartoons in the annual reports that were sent to Washington, DC. But somebody in Washington that outranked us biologists didn't particularly approve of this. I thought the cartoons would liven up the reports and make them more readable; that hunters and other people would start looking at them when they were amusing like that.

In addition to management and research duties, biologists like me had game law enforcement authority, but we were reluctant to exercise that authority because we wanted the hunters to cooperate with us. We believed they would be more willing to share information if they didn't feel like their hunting was being threatened. Also, we figured that was why we had game wardens. I did work closely with game wardens, such as Chuck Graham who was based in Petersburg, and frequently they helped me in the field,

Cartoon illustration by Sig Olson of David collecting hunter harvest data in Southeast Alaska. USFWS FEDERAL AID IN WILDLIFE RESTORATION ALASKA, JOB COMPLETION REPORT, PROJECT W-3-R-11, ALASKA, JUNE 30, 1957, P. 48.

if they had the time. Chuck had access to a fifty-foot gasoline-powered cruiser, the *Harlequin*, whose captain and cook was Joe Johnson, a wonderful and hardworking man in his late fifties or early sixties. I tried to do my research in conjunction with their work, so I could utilize the boat. For example, Chuck and I did annual spring deer mortality surveys throughout Southeast based off of the *Harlequin*.

During most of the five years that I was based in Petersburg, the deer population was in good shape, the deer hunting season was long, and the annual bag limit of four deer per hunter left the average hunter with little to complain about. As deer management biologist for the region, questions asked of me were usually about the biology of the deer, such as, "Where can I hunt for the largest deer?" or "Why are the large bucks that win the annual Wrangell deer derby almost always shot on Woronkofski Island or the mainland?" I had to reply that I didn't know the answer, but I had thought about that question a lot and had proposed a few hypotheses that had not as yet been tested and was initiating studies to address them. One of the studies looked at how deer shaped the vegetation within the habitat in which they lived, or stated more ecologically, what was the co-action between the deer and their habitat? The use of enclosures was a first step in showing how the deer shaped their habitat. Another study compared body size differences of deer between islands in an attempt to show that habitat shaped body size and probably the overall population size.

With hunting pressure not controlling the deer population, the high density of deer were having a pronounced effect on the vegetation and lowering the future carrying capacity of the habitat. Because of this, I was telling the hunters and the Territorial Game Commission that we should liberalize the hunting season in Southeast Alaska. There really were too many deer, especially around Petersburg. But it was hard to make the case. The hunters would say, "Well, the only time you see so many deer is when there's snow and they're all pushed down to the beach." This was true to some extent, but there was an awful lot of beach, and every beach was not the same. During mild winters, deer were widely dispersed and hunters had little difficulty in shooting them. But when the deer decreased, the hunters blamed the wolves and they wanted the wolves to be poisoned. In central Southeast, wolves were a factor influencing deer numbers, but in northern Southeast on Admiralty, Baranof, and Chichagof Islands, called the ABC Islands, there were no wolves. The deer population was more likely suppressed by starvation during a winter of extreme snow depths, not because of wolf predation. However, when conditions improved, the deer population was slow to recover. Frankly, we didn't know the deer-wolf relationship very well at that time. In response, we did follow-up studies where we counted the number of deer remains and carcasses of those that starved, and were able to differentiate between starved deer versus those killed by wolves.

Sig Olson had started to collect this information and I continued it, and we made it available through a paper we published on winter mortality of deer (Klein and Olson 1960). It was based somewhat on our aerial surveys along beach lines and then walking parallel to these beaches just back into the woods where starving deer went to die. We were able to show that in those places where we found dead deer, they weren't all being killed by wolves. Some of the deer were starving, some drowned in rough water while trying to escape from the wolves, and some died after being wounded by hunters.

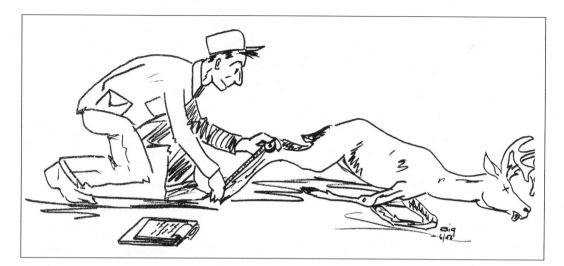

Cartoon illustration by Sig Olson of a biologist measuring the length of a deer leg, which was a way to determine lifetime nutritional status of a deer. USFWS FEDERAL AID IN WILDLIFE RESTORATION ALASKA, JOB COMPLETION REPORT, PROJECT W-3-R-11, ALASKA, JUNE 30, 1957, P. 26.

One of the purposes of our studies was to try to show whether there was really a need for the wolf bounty. By the late 1950s, change was happening within the Fish and Wildlife Service. More young, college-educated people were being hired and longtime old employees, especially game wardens, didn't like the idea of their agency being turned over to a few newly hired biologists. These guys had a lot more experience in the field and therefore thought they knew better than we did. We were trying to interact more with the animals in the habitat, whereas they had been interacting more with the hunters. We'd say, "Well, we're not so sure wolves are the problem." While the view of the game wardens was that hunters knew best. We didn't have hard data and that was a big problem. For example, if there's heavy winter mortality of deer by starvation, then you have to think about how many deer didn't starve, as well as how many did wolves kill? We didn't have that level of information. Eventually, some wolf studies were started by Paul Garceau, who was a young biologist employed by the Fish and Wildlife Service.

One of the big problems we faced was the difficulty of estimating numbers of deer so that we could determine population trends over time. It was important to know what the hunting pressure was and if it was reasonable in terms of the numbers of deer. It was very difficult to assess populations because it was a rainforest and you can't see the deer very readily. Even when the snows would get very deep and the deer were forced down on the beach, we didn't know how many were on the beach in relation to being in other places. Also, the deer population in Southeast Alaska fluctuated widely in relationship to winter conditions, snow depth, and severe storms. Deep snow at higher elevations made food unavailable to the deer, and they were forced down to the old-growth forests close to the beach where they had a wide variety of plants to choose from. However, in a severe winter, there could be snow right down to sea level and so they could not access forage at this last place they had gone for refuge. This could cause a big starvation and loss of deer.

One winter in the Wrangell area, it was a big snow year and there were lots of deer down on the beach. The people were concerned that the deer would starve, so the Wrangell hunters got the idea of, "Well, let's go up on the Stikine River and cut down willows and aspen, and bring them in to feed the deer." I wrote a long letter that was printed in the local newspaper explaining that this was not a good idea because the animals have a special complex of microorganisms in their rumen and can't respond rapidly to a sudden change in the type of food they are eating. I went over to Wrangell and talked to people about this. I told them that there was no need to feed the deer, and, in fact, that if they started feeding them, they had to start feeding them early in the season and continue to feed them all the time, because they would now be domestic animals. I explained that if deer starved because snows were so deep they could not reach the normally available winter forage, this was just part of the natural cycle. There was a school-teacher there who also was an ardent hunter and he told me that he appreciated that I had taken the time to come to Wrangell to explain to hunters what we were learning from our studies.

All of this encouraged me to investigate what was required for deer to survive tough winters. I knew plants were used differently and during different seasons, but wanted to know how they affected the nutrition and growth of the deer. Before this, we just hadn't paid much attention to what deer were eating. So I started some research projects looking at habitat relationships; what deer were eating and what effect they were having on the vegetation. One of the first things I did was to build ten-by-ten-foot-square fenced enclosures to keep the deer out and protect the vegetation inside to see what kind of plants and plant communities were most important for the deer. I put them in old-growth forested areas and in more open areas to compare the differences. One of the main reasons I chose this method was that as a young biologist I wanted quick solutions to problems. With the enclosures, in many cases, it only took one year, one winter, and then we saw a difference. We didn't realize that the deer were eating winter green plants on the forest floor, because when they ate these green leaves it didn't kill the plant. And then they didn't eat some of the shrubs at all, like devil's club and what was called buck's brush. After a few years, you could see in the enclosure that without the deer the forest would have been super brushy and hard to walk through, but instead it was open and park-like underneath the trees.

One of the challenges of my job as the wildlife management biologist in Petersburg was that I frequently was at odds with the Forest Service. Even though they were another federal agency, we had a lot of disagreements, because technically the Fish and Wildlife Service had responsibility for the well-being of the wildlife and the fish within the national forests. The Forest Service was supposedly a multiple-resource management agency and they talked about managing all the resources on the land rather than just focusing on one, but the whole attitude of the Forest Service in Alaska at that time was to log. The agency was staffed by foresters and didn't have any biologists. When there had been selective logging by hand loggers, they only took one tree here and there, so they did not have any significant impact environmentally on the forest or the deer or other wildlife. But then larger-scale logging started being pushed by the Forest Service and loggers, and pulp mills were established at Ketchikan in 1954 and Sitka in 1959. Clear-cut logging initially focused on logging the old-growth forest close to the beach, which meant they were harvesting the wintering habitat that was critical to the deer during severe winters. The Forest Service was pushing to get this forest into production and seemed to forget about forest resources other than timber. Everything else, including the salmon spawning streams and the deer, were ignored.

Salmon streams were on Forest Service land so technically they had responsibility for the streams and their sustained productivity, but the Fish and Wildlife Service and the Bureau of Commercial Fisheries wanted to be sure that salmon spawning streams were protected when logging occurred. The regional forester didn't think there was strong enough scientific data at the time regarding salmon spawning streams, but it was generally understood by fisheries biologists, fishermen, and locals that this type of logging was damaging spawning habitat for the pink salmon. Research was showing that logging close to streams resulted in an excessive increase in water temperatures in the spawning gravels. In addition, some Forest Service studies were beginning to show that bears were spending a lot of time on the banks of salmon streams and that the marine nutrients brought in by the decomposing salmon remains were important for sustaining the entire watershed and ecosystem.[3]

When I was in Petersburg, the Forest Service finally came through and we did some studies jointly with them to try to identify how many bears there were on a given salmon stream during the spawning time and see what effect they were having on the salmon population. One study in particular that I worked on was to estimate the numbers of bears on different drainages on Admiralty Island. The Forest Service claimed there weren't many bears and that they were moving between the streams so it looked like there were more bears than there actually were. On the other hand, we in the Fish and Wildlife Service claimed there were a lot of bears, and they were mostly staying on the streams when the salmon were running. But we really didn't know how much they moved.

Being in charge of this study was a challenge for me. I wondered how we were going to estimate numbers of bears in a rainforest. The only thing I could come up with was measuring paw imprints in the sand on salmon

---

3. Eventually in the 1990s, some studies were initiated through the Forestry Sciences Laboratory in Juneau, which was a subsidiary of the Pacific Northwest Forest and Range Research Station within the research branch of the Forest Service. This research showed a strong connection between salmon and the forest. The Lab's research biologist, Tom Hanley, and UAF PhD graduate student Merav Ben-David used stable isotope analysis to demonstrate the importance of spawning Pacific salmon in bringing marine nutrients to entire watersheds (Ben-David et al. 1997; Ben-David et al. 1998). Merav's seminal research showed that the Pacific salmon that died after spawning were keystone species in enriching entire terrestrial ecosystems with substantial benefits to all plants and animals within the system.

streams. We were supported by a Forest Service boat and aircraft, a Fish and Wildlife Service boat and aircraft, plus a chartered helicopter. The helicopter would fly a team of two people up to the head of a salmon stream and drop us off in the muskeg or on a gravel bar. One person carried a bear gun (a shotgun with slugs) and the other person had a clipboard and tape measure. We measured and recorded bear tracks in the sand as we walked down the stream to the sea. When we got down to the beach, the helicopter would move us over to an adjacent drainage, where we did the same thing all over again. One team could do maybe two or three drainages in a day, and

Joe Saloy flying one of the helicopters used to move research teams between drainages when conducting bear surveys with the US Forest Service on Admiralty Island, 1959. PHOTO BY DAVID KLEIN.

we had about eight teams. We stayed overnight on the boats and worked our way around the island.

That was pretty exciting work. Luckily, we didn't have any bear attacks, but we still had some scary moments. We walked directly in the salmon stream wearing hip boots because that's where the bear tracks were liable to be, but the running water in the stream made a lot of noise, so often we wouldn't hear bears, nor could they hear us. Then sometimes we couldn't walk in the stream, because it was too deep or there was thick brush, so we would walk on the bank and then when there was a sandbar we would jump down to the stream. One time we did that and surprised a sow with cubs. We sure backed off fast! Another exciting experience occurred when suddenly we came to a massive logjam across the stream. It was at least six or eight feet high in the highest part and more than a hundred feet wide. We were climbing over the logjam and were near the top, and then I saw a bear walking upstream toward us. It didn't see us because we were down amidst the logs with just our heads looking over. We thought, "This is interesting. What's this bear going to do?" The bear was close enough that we thought it would see us and run away, but then we realized all it could see was our heads, so we began to wave our arms and shout. The bear looked up and it still couldn't identify what we were so became curious and continued toward us for a better view. By that time, we had our bear gun ready, but I suggested that we climb up and expose our whole bodies so the bear could tell what we were. We climbed to the top of the logjam and shouted and waved our arms some more. The bear looked up and was surprised to see that these two small and strange creatures suddenly had turned into full-sized humans. It turned around and ran downstream as fast as it could.

This was a good project where the Fish and Wildlife Service and the Forest Service worked together well. We measured tracks and differentiated moderately well how many different bears were on salmon streams (Klein 1959b). We were able to make a strong case that there were a lot more bears than previously thought, that they were a unique resource, and that during the salmon runs they stayed on given streams and didn't move around between drainages. This showed that the bears were connected to the salmon and the salmon were connected to the bears. Admiralty Island was designated a National Monument in 1980 under the Alaska National Interest

Lands Conservation Act (ANILCA), largely because of the richness of both salmon and brown bears there.

I remember another situation related to bears and salmon spawning streams that came up at one of the first logging operations on southern Admiralty Island at Windfall Harbor. The Forest Service was ignoring concerns about bears, so the Fish and Wildlife Service started looking into it. It was at a temporary camp of small-scale operators that had moved to Alaska from Oregon and Washington with their families and mostly cut saw logs for the Wrangell saw mill. Immediately, there were complaints that the bears were coming into the camp where they had kids and they were worried about safety. They wanted those bears out! Well, we wondered why the bears were coming into the loggers' camps. When we visited the camps, the loggers admitted, "Well, yeah, we don't have any good garbage disposal situation. But we're here to log and the bears are preventing people from doing their jobs." As it turned out, their camp was located right at the mouth of a pink salmon spawning stream. Of course, bears aggregate at these streams during the spawning period, so obviously this meant there were going to be more bears around a logging camp located there. It wasn't just a matter of scaring a few bears away from camp because of garbage. That was obvious.

I went to the chief forester of the district to talk about this bear problem. I said, "The bears are there because the loggers are not taking care of the garbage around the camp. And the camp is located on a salmon spawning stream which attracts bears." He said, "Well, we're trying to get them to do a better job with the garbage." Finally, he got frustrated and said, "Let's face it, the future of this area is logging. The bears gotta go." At that time, the behind-closed-doors attitude of the chief forester was, "You wildlifers have to face up to the fact that bears are just not compatible with logging, which is our primary use of the forest." This was based on their perspective of what "primary use" meant. My job was to take care of wildlife, so I responded, "Well, look, wait a second, the bears have a place there. So are you saying that the fish will have to go, too?" That was the end of the meeting. I had said too much.

I contacted my supervisor in Juneau after this, and he said, "You know, this is Forest Service land, they call the shots." I said, "This is unreasonable. I want to send a strong memo to the regional forester about this." My boss said, "No. We have to work with those guys in the Forest Service. We have to find ways to get along." He said, "Remember, we could have a worse guy than him." After I kept pestering him, my boss finally agreed to arrange for us to talk to the regional forester in Juneau about this bear problem at Windfall Harbor. I told him about the situation and said, "This isn't working. The bears are a valuable resource." "Oh well," he said, "they're not all that valuable. The timber's much more valuable." After some back and forth, he finally agreed that they did in fact have a garbage disposal problem, but blamed the loggers for it. He was getting a little pissed off and frustrated and finally said, "You've got to face up to the reality of this thing. The future of this area is logging, and bears are just not compatible with humans!" We made a case for the economic benefits to the region of having guided bear hunts and all that, but it didn't matter. We parted ways and my supervisor said, "Go ahead and write your memo. At least get it on the record." So I did. I'm not sure it did anything overall to change the way the Forest Service was managing bears and logging, but it felt good to get my opinion in the written record.

While I was stationed full-time in Petersburg, in the summer I usually moved to Anchorage to help with other Fish and Wildlife Service projects throughout Southcentral Alaska. One of these projects was banding geese in the Copper River Delta based out of Cordova. We stayed at a FWS cabin in the tidal delta for about two weeks. I hired Bob Belsas, a Cordova gillnetter in his early twenties, as a field assistant and rented his large Cordova skiff and outboard motor. As a commercial fisherman, he was available during the time I needed him and he enjoyed doing the banding work. We were out there in the early summer when the adult geese were just regrowing their flight feathers after molting, so they couldn't fly, and the young geese were big enough so that you could band them at the same time. We had a target of four hundred geese to band, but if we could get two hundred banded that was considered a minimally adequate sample size. This was prior to the 1964 earthquake when the delta rose nine feet and resulted in the loss of the majority of the nesting habitat of the dusky Canada Goose. Consequently, their production dropped off to a fraction of what it had been.

We were under the supervision of the Fish and Wildlife Service waterfowl flyway biologist, Henry "Hank" Hanson, who was based out of Juneau.

Bob Belsas with two Canada geese he caught for banding, Copper River Delta near Cordova, 1954. PHOTO BY DAVID KLEIN.

He came out to visit us occasionally, but it was pretty much up to me and Bob to figure out ways to be most productive in catching the geese. At high tide, the sloughs would fill with water and flood into the intertidal wetlands where the geese would be grazing on the higher, dry ground where we could catch them in nets. Others had done this before us so we had an example to follow. Our success rate was dependent on hitting the tide cycle correctly, because if we were in the wrong place at the wrong time, got a late start, or the weather was terrible we might miss the high tide and only get four or five geese banded per day.

We did it the old-fashioned way. Bob ran the outboard as we snaked through the sloughs, and I stood on a platform in the front of the boat holding onto a rope, so I could look over the tall sedges and marsh grass to see where the geese were. I'd lean back against the tightened rope, so I had good balance in case the boat came to a sudden stop. The geese would hear the boat

Traveling by boat through
the sloughs of the Copper
River Delta in search of
geese to band, 1954.
COURTESY OF DAVID KLEIN.

coming, and they would pop their heads up and then pull them down quickly. When I saw these heads, I gave Bob the signal to head for shore. Then the
two of us jumped out of the boat and took off in hip boots running as fast as
we could toward the geese. After the young are hatched, two or three broods
of geese aggregate into groups where you might have twenty-five or thirty
geese together. We had salmon landing nets that we threw out into these
groups to try to capture as many birds as we could in one first chance before
they scattered and hid. Although the molting geese couldn't fly, they could
run like mad and they could hide. And, of course, if they got in the water,
we couldn't get to them. If we were lucky, each of us could get about three or
four geese, which was as much as we could carry in our nets. Usually, we had
the bands and the banding wire on a wire hung around our neck so we could
band the birds right where we caught them. We identified whether they were
young or adults and made general comments on their size and whether the
young ones were starting to grow their flight feathers. Then we would release
them and go back and try to capture some more.

We had to work fast, because we'd only have a short time while the tide
was high. It's a big tide that comes and goes fast; you can have plenty of
water for the boat and then half an hour later there's none. If we waited

too long, low tide prevented us from getting the boat back into the main drainage channel and returning to the cabin. We didn't prepare for being out for a long time. We only had our rain gear, hip boots, and a snack in the boat with us. There was one time I remember when we didn't time it right and got stuck out there. We came around a bend in a slough and there were geese swimming right in front of us. They split up with the majority heading to one shore, and I shouted to Bob, "Let's follow that group and go to shore!" He dropped me off, and for some reason he went to the other side of this fairly narrow deep channel to go after geese over there. I was pretty successful in catching geese, but when I came back to the boat, I discovered that it was on the other side of the channel. He tried to get the boat off, but the tide had dropped and now the boat was stuck. It was too late. He was stuck on one side of the channel and me on the other. And I had to let my geese go because he had the bands in the boat.

There wasn't enough water left in the slough for me to swim to the other side, but it was deep enough that I couldn't just wade across. We ended up staying there five or six hours waiting for the tide to come back. That was not the greatest for me, because I was just in a tee shirt and trousers, which was plenty warm when I was running around in hip boots, but now I had to literally keep walking to keep warm. This was okay, but eventually you get tired of walking. And, of course, we were hungry. Finally, when Bob could get over to me with the boat, he was pretty embarrassed; he hadn't even captured any geese. We went back to the cabin, had a big meal, and slept for a long time.

We also had a few mishaps when our supervisor came for a couple of days. First of all, even though Bob and I said that we had to move quickly to take advantage of the tide, that first morning we'd cooked up pancakes and Hank didn't want to rush through breakfast. So we got a late start. Then he wanted to stand up in the front of the boat with me. This meant we didn't have enough room to spread our legs far enough apart to get good balance and we shared holding the rope. The first time around a bend, I said, "Hank, you've got to be alert and brace yourself." The boat suddenly jerked, and he just went right overboard with all his clothes on. We immediately turned around to go back to the cabin, so he could change into dry clothes and warm up. Now it was too late in the day to get out, so we waited for the next tide. But at full tide, you can't see the narrow drainage ditches in the tidal flats. I told Hank to watch out for those. I said, "They're only about two feet wide, but they're sloping banks so you've got to know when to jump." We got to one spot where there were a lot of geese, and Bob, Hank, and I took off running in different directions. I could see that Hank was doing very well and then suddenly he just disappeared. He didn't see a ditch, and just went right down into the water; it was total immersion. Poor guy. He stuck it out for the rest of that high tide, until we could get back to the cabin where he got dry again. Fortunately, I never fell in the water like that. I fell down sometimes in the thick mud, and got a little muddy, but never total immersion.

I did the geese banding for two summers, and mostly we met our targets. It wasn't easy work to chase after all these geese while running in hip boots, at the same time keeping an eye out for places you could fall in, but I didn't think too much of it. I enjoyed that project. There was the excitement of the chase, as well as the satisfaction that came from obtaining band return data that was of importance in regulating hunter harvest of the geese on their wintering grounds in eastern Oregon. Later on, the Fish and Wildlife Service decided it was more efficient to hire a big crew, set up nets, and do a large bird drive than the way Bob and I did it. It used more labor and cost more money, but they usually could finish the work in one week. They also had air support and things like that, which we didn't have.

The goose banding effort was only a couple-week period, so the rest of those summers I was counting mountain sheep for Bob Scott on the Kenai Peninsula, in the Chugach Mountains, the Talkeetna Mountains, the Alaska Range, and the White Mountains. Every summer, I was gone for about a month and a half total, then I'd go back to Petersburg. I had to be back in time to prepare for the hunting season that started in August. This also meant I had some summer left to go out with the family picnicking on the beach and boating around the area.

In 1959, when Alaska statehood came, management of Alaska's terrestrial wildlife was transferred from the federal Fish and Wildlife Service to the state's new Department of Fish and Game (ADF&G). At this point, the jobs that we had as biologists with the Fish and Wildlife Service were eliminated. I had to make a decision. If I wanted to stay with the Fish and

Wildlife Service, I would have had to transfer out of Alaska. There were no available Fish and Wildlife jobs in Alaska because they were cutting back positions and I had only been there for five years, so I didn't have the seniority needed for a good assignment. My wife and I wanted to stay in Alaska, so the best option was to go work for ADF&G. They were eager to hire me. The first director of the Game Division (later the Division of Wildlife Conservation) was Jim Brooks, who had been a fellow student at the University of Alaska with me and I knew him well. A large percentage of the people being hired were graduates of the UAF wildlife program. It was a good transition for me to ADF&G. During this period, there was good cooperation between the state and federal government in terms of wildlife management. The federal government continued to take a lot of responsibility for studying both the habitat and the relationship of the animals to habitat, and ADF&G emphasized counting animals and studying population dynamics.

By this time, I knew that I wanted to go back to school and get a PhD because I thought ultimately I wanted to be at a university, but I also had a wife and two kids to support. So I agreed to work for ADF&G if they would let me stay in Petersburg and continue the deer studies, which would be part of my PhD dissertation. Then I would take leave without pay, called educational leave, to spend the required two academic years of residence time at the University of British Columbia (UBC) for the PhD degree. ADF&G couldn't save my existing job for me, but they said they would have some kind of job for me when I got back.

I chose UBC because they were doing the kind of studies with deer that I was interested in and that I already had started. I was fascinated by the fact that the deer were bigger on some islands than other islands. Was this because of forage or was it genetics? Another reason that I got involved with UBC was that I had made some earlier connections there regarding Sitka black-tailed deer. In 1957, I had proposed to my supervisor in Juneau that it would benefit my understanding of deer ecology and increase our effectiveness in deer management if I were able to make a trip to Vancouver Island, where there were black-tailed deer and clear-cut logging was becoming extensive. I was then getting started on studies of the effects of large-scale clear-cut logging on deer in Alaska. I made the trip there and visited with Don Robinson, the wildlife biologist for Vancouver Island. I also had been in contact with Dr. Ian McTaggart-Cowan at UBC when he was doing comparative behavioral and nutritional physiology research of the three coastal black-tailed deer subspecies, and wanted live "orphan" Sitka black-tailed deer fawns.

There was a problem around Petersburg with people picking up newborn fawns along the side of the road in the spring thinking they had been abandoned. They would bring them to me as the Fish and Wildlife guy. Not really knowing what to do with these so-called "orphaned" fawns, I would take them to the Alaska Experimental Fur Farm in Petersburg that was affiliated with the university[4] where they would have to bottle-feed them to keep them alive. Despite being a busy mom, my wife, Arlayne, even helped bottle-feed some of these fawns. Eventually, we would let the deer go back into the wild, but these fawns bonded with people, so their chances of survival were unclear. We just did not have a long-term and humane solution to this situation. So when Cowan asked my supervisor, Pete Nelson, if there were any fawns that he could get to use in his studies with captive deer, I got involved in shipping them to him.

Starting in 1959, I spent two winters in Vancouver during the academic years with Arlayne and my children joining me. In the summers, I came back to Alaska to continue the deer work out of Petersburg and they went to Walla Walla, Washington, where Arlayne's family lived. UBC was a good place for all of us. We lived in campus housing, where there were a lot of other married families with children that Arlayne made friends with, and there was a good play area for the kids. When I was gone, ADF&G filled my position by hiring Harry Merriam, who had just earned his MS degree

---

4. The University of Alaska operated the Alaska Experimental Fur Farm in Petersburg from 1937 to 1972 as one of its Agricultural Experiment Station projects. To start with, the farm had blue fox, silver fox, mink, and marten. One of the "early investigations revealed that an all-salmon diet was detrimental to mink" (Isto 2012:132). In 1941, James Leekley was hired to run the fur farm, replacing territorial veterinarian Jule B. Loftus. Leekley "continued to perform diet and breeding experiments with arctic foxes, marten, and mutation mink" (ibid.:170), and he retired when the farm was shut down in 1972. Also in Petersburg, Earl Ohmer owned and operated the private Yukon Fur Farm that in the early 1930s was known as the "territory's largest minkery" (ibid.:129). Yukon Fur Farm went out of business in the mid-1950s with Earl Ohmer dying in 1955 (ibid.:168–69).

in biology at UAF. In summer when I was back doing my research, Harry became my field assistant. This was helpful to me, but it also allowed Harry an opportunity to learn more about how to carry out his new job responsibilities. So it worked out real well for both of us.

My doctoral dissertation compared the growth, body size, and population response of Sitka black-tailed deer on two islands with different ecological conditions. The first study island was Woronkofski Island, which was a relatively small island located close to the mainland near the estuary of the Stikine River, had the more continental climate of the mainland with deep winter snow accumulation, and was close to the community of Wrangell. The island rose up precipitously into moderately high mountains with a lot

David weighing a deer in deep snow to determine body condition as part of his research comparing deer on two islands in Southeast Alaska, March 1956. COURTESY OF DAVID KLEIN.

of alpine summer habitat. The treeless alpine vegetation was loaded with lush deer forage in summer. The deer on Woronkofski Island were large, the population was high, and the deer weren't greatly impacted by wolves. The second study island was Coronation Island, which was nearly the same size as Woronkofski but didn't have as much alpine habitat, and was located on the outer coast where the stormy coastal maritime climate meant milder winters and less snow accumulation. Coronation Island had particularly small deer and no wolves or bears. It has subsequently been designated a wilderness area by the Forest Service. With the use of enclosures, I was able to compare the effect of deer grazing and browsing on the vegetation of the two islands. I also evaluated how the presence or absence of predation by wolves affected the deer. These two islands offered an ideal situation for doing this type of research, compared to deer studies that were being done elsewhere and were very popular in the 1950s and 1960s where deer populations were fluctuating in relationship to logging, fire, hunting, grazing, and agricultural conflicts without any variable controls to work with. These islands were fairly remote and had minimal human impacts, so people could be eliminated as significant causes of change. Later on, we did look at deliberate manipulation of the environment caused by logging and how it may have led to differential growth responses of the deer.

The results of my PhD research showed that the larger deer came from Woronkofski Island where the snows were deeper, but also where there was a lot of alpine range available for summer foraging. On Coronation Island where there were warmer winter temperatures and less snow, the deer were smaller but were more abundant and the group's age structure was older. I was able to show that these differences in body size were largely related to the quality of the forage, and that skeletal size was an indication of nutrition (Klein 1964). On Coronation Island, the high-quality forage plants had been eliminated by the long, heavy pressure of deer browsing without a lot of snow, so the deer were forced to live off poorer quality forage. Individual animals could never grow very big because they were not getting enough overall nutrition. In comparison, the trophy-sized deer on Woronkofski Island were able to develop such a large body size because enough good-quality forage remained available to them in the alpine habitat during the summer growth period. This indicated that the quality and

A field camp in alpine habitat of Woronkofski Island that David used as a base for some of his PhD research on deer and their habitat, circa 1958. On this particular trip, he was accompanied by parasitologist Ken Nieland from the Alaska Department of Fish and Game (right) and his assistant (left) who did autopsies and studied the parasites of the deer David harvested for his own research. PHOTO BY DAVID KLEIN.

availability of summer vegetation mainly controlled body size of an individual deer, whereas winter vegetation determined population level. Snow was a main controlling factor. For example, it was hard for the deer to move around in the deep snow of the alpine areas of Woronkofski Island and as the winter progressed most of the forage would get covered by snow. Therefore, the deer would gradually move down to the lower slopes and timberline forest where there was less snow and it was easier to find forage, especially blueberry shrubs, which were their main winter browse. In severe winters, the available food in these lower areas also was virtually covered by snow, making it more difficult to find quality forage. When both the alpine forage and the lower areas were not available to deer, you'd get big starvations. This population decline meant the remaining animals were able to get more of the good, lush alpine forage during the next spring, because there were fewer deer competing for the quality vegetation. This led to bigger individual deer, but an overall smaller population. In mild winters, these deer populations rebounded as they were able to access the high-quality alpine forage throughout the winter. In contrast, mild winters of little snow on Coronation Island would result in overall low deer mortality, leaving more deer available to reproduce and raise young the following summer.

We also had to factor in hunting pressure and predation by wolves, which made understanding the ecosystem relationships complicated. Woronkofski Island had wolves, but Coronation Island did not. Wolves were sometimes on Woronkofski Island because they could swim across a narrow channel to Etolin Island, but wolves had been unable to cross the narrow and dangerous channel between Coronation Island and nearby Kuiu Island to the north (Klein 1995). Because there was no predation of the deer on Coronation Island, these deer were less wary and easy to hunt, but there was very little human hunting there because it was difficult to get there. While there was the potential for wolf predation on Woronkofski, it did not appear to be a big factor. In the summertime, deer are at higher elevations and are more scattered, which makes it harder for wolves to prey on them. And the summer is when wolves are focused on raising their young, are staying at lower elevations where a greater diversity of prey is available, and is a time when they do not hunt in packs.

Southeast Alaska was a great place for me to study deer ecology and deer ecosystem relationships. A major reason was that the diversity that existed in deer habitat conditions between islands and between islands and the mainland enabled comparative studies of how the habitat variables of weather, landscape, plant community types, and wolf and bear predation affected the deer and their population size.

Although I was mostly focused on my deer research, I did get involved in some work with wolves. A litter of six wolf pups whose mother had been accidently shot on Kuiu Island were brought to the university's experimental fur farm in Petersburg. Harry Merriam and I designed a research project to study the growth of these wolves from pups to adulthood. The family who managed the farm agreed to house the wolf pups in one of their vacant fox cages and bottle-feed them.

Once they were weaned, the pups were fed the fishmeal-based diet that had been designed to meet the nutritional needs of the captive mink and arctic foxes. After I returned from fieldwork, Harry and I went once a week to weigh the pups, and I photographed each pup in front of a three-by-four-foot white board with a gridded background to visually show their size increase. Getting these actively growing and energetic pups to stand still for the photos was sometimes a challenging game that the pups liked to play with us. Finally, the wolves got too big for the fox cages, so we built a large, long, and narrow kennel so they could have running room. The two largest males got to be 125 pounds in less than a year. Wild wolves rarely exceeded 100 pounds. Obviously, the wolves were growing well on their fishmeal diet, which was not the type of food they would have eaten in the wild. However, this did show us the wolf's genetic potential for growth. It was also interesting to observe the behavioral differences in the six wolves as they grew.

Then the question was what to do with these wolves? One of the submissive males was accidentally killed when an ADF&G biologist gave it an overdose while testing an anesthetizing drug. The other submissive male was sent to a zoo in the Lower 48. A few senior ADF&G biologists suggested releasing the remaining two pairs onto wolf-free Coronation Island. This would be an experiment. First, to see if wolf predation could reduce and hold the deer population at a low enough level to allow the deer habitat to recover to a much higher carrying capacity. And, secondly, to see if wolves could sustain a population on a small and isolated island that might not tolerate more than one wolf pack territory. While ADF&G viewed this wolf introduction as a research study, they figured that the public might not see it that way; that the idea of a governmental agency transplanting wolves to an island full of deer wouldn't be popular. So the study was undertaken without alerting the public.

Then a strange and unexpected thing happened. During foul weather, a fisherman from Ketchikan seeking refuge in one of the bays on Coronation Island ended up shooting two wolves he saw running on the beach. The ear tags indicated that they were the original two females that had been released. Initially, he did not tell anyone about this incident, because he didn't know whether he had violated a law and might get in trouble. Finally, word leaked out that he had shot these wolves and everyone wondered why there were now wolves on Coronation Island, which didn't used to have wolves. Finally,

Jim Brooks, head of the Game Division at ADF&G, had to explain that this had been a research project and the island provided a perfect laboratory-like setting. By sharing data that I'd collected on the negative effects of the over-population of deer on the island, the public was able to see that introducing predators to reduce the deer population would help restore the habitat and eventually lead to larger deer as the forage quantity and quality improved.

Subsequent visits to Coronation by Harry Merriam indicated that the wolves had adapted quickly to their freedom, and that deer had become a major portion of their diet. He was able to show that the wolves had bred, produced a big litter, and that the population had leveled off at about fifteen animals. But it was mostly pups, because now there were only two males of the originally introduced group left. They did release another fe-male wolf onto the island, but no known additional litter was ever produced. Eventually, the deer population was greatly reduced, and the wolves were forced to feed on other things. For example, one time, Harry saw two wolves digging up and eating clams at low tide, or they killed seals that were hauled out in rocky places. Once the wolves had killed virtually all the deer and there wasn't enough other food to support a wolf population, they would start to starve. In fact, at one point, Harry found indications in wolf drop-pings that they were eating one another. It must've been nine or ten years from the time they were introduced until there were no more wolves on the island. I ended up publishing a paper about this wolf introduction experi-ment and what was learned from it (Klein 1995).

In 1961, when I finished the academic requirements and residency for my PhD and had essentially finished the fieldwork, ADF&G wanted me to come back to work and move to Juneau. By this time, they realized that I could take on more of an administrative leadership position instead of just being a field biologist. I was happy to do this, because I needed the time to finish up my dissertation and needed the extra income after those years of only working in the summers and having little financial support from UBC. This had been hard, because, at the time, our children were so small that Arlayne wasn't able to work. Later on, she did work as a substitute teacher.

My job with ADF&G was to be the administrator of the Pittman-Robertson funds that the state received from the Federal Aid in Wildlife Restoration Act. It was a federal program for wildlife research that gave money from a tax on the sale of firearms and ammunition used in hunting and distributed that money throughout the states to support wildlife conservation work. The proportion of Pittman-Robertson monies given to each state was in relationship to the number of hunting licenses sold in the state and the size of the state. At the time, that was the major support for wildlife management work and associated biological studies. There were specific ways you could use the money and ways you couldn't. For example, you couldn't use it for wildlife law enforcement, but you could use it for research on habitat improvement for wildlife species. My duties included budgeting and managing the funds and providing oversight of the projects throughout the state to make sure that the biologists who received this money were spending it according to the federal regulations. Technically, in addition to being in the office, I was supposed to spend a lot of time traveling to check on funded projects. I didn't want to travel too much because I had a family at home, and I had the thesis writing to do. Frankly, I liked traveling and I liked keeping in touch with the researchers, so it was just the right balance. My job was to provide guidance for the project set-up and the scientific approach to be used, and to be sure they understood how to work within the available budget. Or in some cases, it meant arguing for a bigger budget. It was a good experience and good training for me.

Getting to travel around Alaska to visit the various Pittman-Robertson-funded research projects was one of the most positive aspects of the job. It allowed me to get a good sense of what was going on around the state. And it was good training for me, whether I stayed with Fish and Game or not. I got to go to Kodiak and Afognak Islands, where elk studies were being done, and I learned a lot about elk habitat that I didn't know previously. I got to visit moose studies on the Kenai Peninsula and near Anchorage, and caribou research out of Fairbanks. Excellent people had been hired and I knew quite a few of them, because we had been students together at the University of Alaska in Fairbanks. The job also included paperwork and putting together quarterly and annual reports based upon project reports submitted by the field biologists. I also served as editor and advisor if they wrote any technical papers for publications, although not many of them did that.

Jim Brooks was thinking ahead and knew that I wouldn't want to stay in that particular administrative position forever, and that I would be willing to look at other options. Before he became head of the Game Division, Jim had lived on the Seward Peninsula, was a pilot, did marine mammal work in Bristol Bay and Prince William Sound, and married a Native woman, so he had a good understanding of Native interests, which were sort of ignored in the old territorial days before statehood when wildlife management was focused on the non-Native population of hunters and the guided sport hunters. Jim wanted to create a Subsistence Division at ADF&G, was going to lobby the legislature for funding, and wanted me to become the head of the new division. That was the kind of challenge I liked and I always had a keen interest in Alaska Native people and their cultures, so this appealed to me. I had a little previous experience working with the Native community, because when I was working in Petersburg I occasionally went to Native villages to assess their deer harvest numbers. I certainly had a concern that their interests were important and should be considered in management rather than just ignoring them.

In the long run, obviously, a job like this where I wasn't out in the field doing my own research wouldn't have been very satisfying to me, but at this point I still had to finish writing up my PhD thesis. Jim Brooks made it clear when I came back from Vancouver and said, "You've got a job to do for us and it's an important one, so I don't think it's going to work out to write your thesis on the job." So I worked at home in the evenings on my dissertation. While this meant I was busy, at least I was at home and had more time with my family than if I'd been away on fieldwork. I didn't get as much done on the dissertation as I had hoped, because of the lure of playtime with my young children. Nevertheless, I was making some progress in writing. Jim did try to take some of the pressure off me at work by creating an assistant position to help me. We hired a female biologist with some training in wildlife ecology. At that time, women were having a hard time getting jobs in wildlife. She took over writing and putting together some of the required reports, which helped me a lot.

While in Juneau, I was so busy that I had little time for social interaction with colleagues to discuss ethical and environmental philosophy issues that were pertinent to the development of both state and federal policy for the conservation and management of Alaska's renewable resources. I did have friends in ADF&G, FWS, and the Forest Service in Juneau who were also advancing into leadership positions in their respective agencies and were as challenged as I was by philosophical and ethical issues related to natural resource management in our young state. A few of them encouraged me to join the Juneau Toastmasters Club to enhance my public-speaking abilities, so I decided to give it a try. While it did help my self-confidence in this regard, it also provided an opportunity for discussion of current issues confronting government. One of the presentations I made was titled "On Being Objective," where I emphasized that doing well-designed ecological research required adhering to principals of objective science; there was no room for subjectivity (see chapter 21 for full text of this presentation). I felt that it was only in the application of knowledge gained through objective science that we could properly manage wildlife and their subsequent human uses. My wildlife colleagues argued that there had to be room for subjectivity in managing human use of renewable resources in order to accommodate the role of social welfare in wildlife management. Even that early in my career, I clearly was leaning more toward becoming a wildlife scientist at a university rather than a wildlife manager. I also was beginning to develop my views on the responsibility that we all have to be active and engaged citizens.

RESEARCH

The chapters in this section are based on the oral history interviews and cover David's professional career as the leader of the Alaska Cooperative Wildlife Research Unit at the University of Alaska Fairbanks, the research he engaged in through this position, and his work teaching and mentoring graduate students. The following stories demonstrate how David's early training and research built toward an understanding of ecological relationships and how these guided his major work with reindeer, caribou, muskoxen, and other species. David's years of focus on St. Matthew Island proved pivotal in his shifting views on animal-habitat relationships, and the long-term nature of the work has been a major contribution to biological studies in Alaska. The role he and his graduate students played in understanding caribou in northern Alaska, especially in relation to oil field development, has been critical for ensuring that such development has occurred with as minimal environmental impact as possible. It is clear how much satisfaction David got from his research and being out in the field, forming collaborative relationships and friendships with colleagues, as well as both learning from students and seeing them get excited by the natural environment.

Second-largest lake on St. Matthew Island, referred to as Middle Lake since it is located in the middle part of the island. This is where David camped on his trip to St. Matthew in 1966. The small white dot visible on the gravel beach at the far left end of the lake is their tent. Pinnacle Island is visible in the distance through the fog on the right. PHOTO BY DAVID KLEIN.

7
The St. Matthew Islands: Challenging Conventional Ecological Wisdom

The first major research project I undertook after my PhD was on St. Matthew Island, located in the middle of the Bering Sea off the southwestern coast of Alaska. After six trips to St. Matthew Island over the course of fifty-five years, it ended up being critical to the transformation of my ecological thinking on herbivore and habitat relationships.

Reindeer were introduced to St. Matthew Island by the Coast Guard in 1944 during the Second World War when there were nineteen men stationed there at a LORAN navigational station. Although isolated from the major war zone of the North Pacific Ocean, St. Matthew Island was of strategic importance to the US military forces fighting in the Aleutian Islands. In the early stages of the war, it was not known whether St. Matthew would be cut off by the Japanese, and might even be invaded, so an emergency food supply was needed in case the men stationed there became isolated from other American forces. The Coast Guard thought it would be a good idea to release reindeer for this purpose. Using a Coast Guard ship, twenty-nine reindeer (twenty-four females and five males) were moved from Nunivak Island to St. Matthew to establish a reindeer population (Burris and McKnight 1973; Rozell 2010). When the war ended precipitously in the Pacific in 1945, the Coast Guard shut down the LORAN station. They could not remove the reindeer, which had become feral, so they were left on the island where there were no natural predators and no people living within 250 miles to hunt them.

The island was a hard place to get to, since it was far away and had no harbors or airports, and, as part of the Bering Sea Natural Reserve established

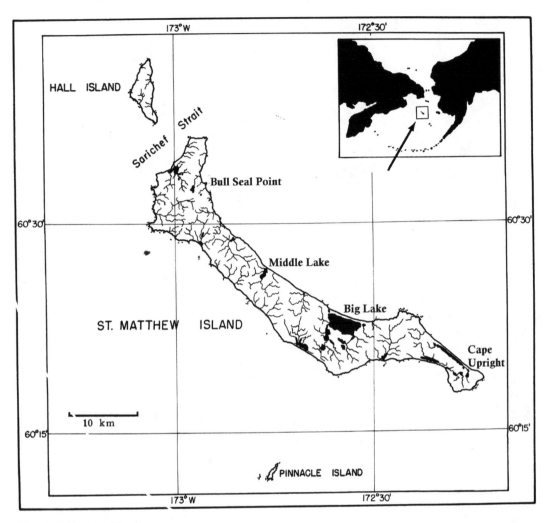

Map of St. Matthew Island.
COURTESY OF DAVID KLEIN.

in 1909 by President Teddy Roosevelt, hunting was prohibited on the island. The Bering Sea Natural Reserve was the first such reserve in Alaska and along with Pelican Island in Florida they were the first national biological reserves established in the US. The reserve protecting the St. Matthew Islands was established primarily to protect the nearly one million birds that are present there in summer for nesting. In addition, a diversity of marine mammals use the waters around the islands and walrus, sea lions, and hair seals regularly haul out on these islands. Today the islands are within the Alaska Maritime National Wildlife Refuge and were designated wilderness in 1980 under the Alaska National Interest Lands Conservation Act (ANILCA).

Fat bull reindeer on St. Matthew Island, 1957. COURTESY OF DAVID KLEIN.

Being within a biological reserve, the Fish and Wildlife Service was responsible for managing the wildlife on St. Matthew Island, but prior to the Second World War they knew little about the ecology of the animals present there, other than what was written in ship logs of Coast Guard boats and their precursors, the Revenue Cutters. There was interest and concern over the possible impact the introduced reindeer might have on the vegetation and rare plant species, and what impact there might be on the singing voles and ground-nesting birds, especially the McKay's bunting. For example, scientists did not know what competition there would be between reindeer and voles for the green vegetation that they both consumed, whether grazing by the reindeer might actually stimulate the green plants, or whether overgrazing by the reindeer would likely be detrimental to the voles. No one really knew to what level the reindeer population could increase until it started to crash. The availability of lichens, the reindeers' preferred winter forage, was thought to be one of the limiting factors.

The first scientist to do research on St. Matthew Island was Robert L. Rausch, a parasitologist and mammalogist with the Public Health Service, and his wife, Reggie, who went there in 1954. The Coast Guard transported them to the remote island by ship, where they camped in a driftwood hut

The driftwood hut originally built by
Robert Rausch on St. Matthew Island
where David and Jim Whisenhant stayed
in July 1957. PHOTO BY DAVID KLEIN.

that they built with help from the crew. Their objectives included studying
parasites and the genetics of the endemic vole species (*Microtus abbreviatus*), which generally is referred to as the singing vole due to its similarities with the mainland species, and the arctic fox (*Alopex lagopus*) (Rausch
and Rausch 1968). They were investigating a parasite that the arctic foxes
were thought to be carrying that posed a threat to humans, and collecting

Group of reindeer on St. Matthew Island, 1957. PHOTO BY DAVID KLEIN.

specimens for use in the first genetic work with chromosomes to try to determine whether the voles on the island were a true endemic species. At this time, the Rausches reported that the reindeer on St. Matthew Island were increasing and were having an impact on lichens. They estimated that there were at least a few hundred reindeer on the island with many new fawns.

In 1955, Clarence Rhode, regional director of the US Fish and Wildlife Service in Alaska, flew a twin-engine aircraft to St. Matthew Island and did a rough count of the reindeer they could see in the open tundra. He estimated there to be about 1,350 reindeer. This count stimulated the FWS to initiate a long-term ecological study of the unique situation of reindeer on an isolated island of virgin, natural habitat, free of natural predators. The main question was how to maintain St. Matthew Island's natural environment with an exotic herbivore species present. It was unrealistic to think of removal of the reindeer, because of the remoteness of the island and the logistical problems of getting and working there. Although, at one point, that had been suggested as a possible solution to the problem. And then, of course, there was the attitude that these reindeer should be harvested by or for people who could use the meat. St. Matthew had never been settled by Native people, and it was unrealistic for people to come from the closest communities on the Pribilof Islands because of the costly, complicated, and risky logistics. The cost of boating there with no harbor and no shore facilities would be many times the price of hunting elsewhere.

Bob Scott with the FWS was asked to design a project that would monitor the increase of the reindeer population and assess the consequences for the island's plant communities and other animal species. In the summer of 1956, while doing mountain sheep counts out of Anchorage for Bob, he asked if I was interested in being project leader of this potential long-term study. I envisioned research on reindeer that were introduced to a remote and uninhabited island in the absence of natural predators as a unique opportunity to carry out a classic scientific study of the role of food in the regulation of large herbivore populations. Such a study might well provide resolution to controversies among animal population ecologists over mechanisms of animal population regulation. Although St. Matthew Island was a long ways from Petersburg, where I was still living, I could not pass up this opportunity and agreed to lead the project.

The Six Expeditions to the St. Matthew Islands

1957 I went to the island in 1957 to spend about three weeks there to obtain a count of the reindeer, do an initial survey of the island's vegetation, and build three fenced enclosures in the plant communities where lichens constituted a major portion of the ground cover. Bob Scott had proposed the rough outline of what needed to be done to initiate the study, but once I got there and gained a feeling for the land-animal relationship I was on my own to follow through and decide where my priorities should be. Counting the animals was one goal, but also doing a vegetation reconnaissance, taking some quantitative measurements, building enclosures, and exploring the island all became part of my mission.

Jim Whisenhant, an undergraduate wildlife student at the university in Fairbanks was hired as my field assistant. We flew commercially to Kodiak, where we met a Coast Guard boat that Bob Scott had arranged to be our transportation to St. Matthew. It was a large training ship, the *Wachusett*, with over a hundred Coast Guard trainees and crewmembers on board. Jim and I got aboard with our gear and the ship cruised from Kodiak Island southwest along the Alaska Peninsula, then through Unimak Pass into the Bering Sea.

When we were still in the Pacific, a big storm came up and it was pretty rough going. In retrospect, it was amusing, and even a little bit funny while we were actually aboard, that neither Jim nor I were seasick. When we boarded, we were told, "Unfortunately, all the ship's bunks are full, but we have two bunks topside in the weather balloon release structure." It was like a small garage with a door where they released weather balloons. Our bunks were way up above the deck, and to get there we had to climb up through the superstructure of the ship. So as the ship was rolling in the storm, we were literally thrown through a greater arc than the crew down below deck. Fortunately, the bunks each had a steel bar that you could get your knee under to keep you from rolling out when conditions got rough. We got little sleep during that storm. There were a couple of locked metal filing cabinets in the room, and with each sway of the ship as we quartered into the storm something inside one of them repeatedly rolled back and forth making a tinny *bang, bang, bang*. Later we learned that it was a Japanese glass fishing float that one of the crew had previously picked up when beach combing and placed in one of the drawers for safekeeping.

When we got into the Bering Sea, the storm finally was over, and Jim and I climbed down to the galley for breakfast where we were allowed to eat with the officers. The only other person there was a young red-haired officer who announced that all the others were too seasick to eat. We sat there enjoying our bowls of oatmeal and were told that we were lucky to even get that, and that as the sea calmed and the cooks recovered, future meals would be better. They were.

After a delay to participate in a search operation for a missing fishing boat from Dillingham, where we discovered that after having engine problems the crewmembers figured that they weren't going to make it through the storm so had gotten seriously drunk, we were ultimately dropped off at St. Matthew Island with all of our gear. The Coast Guard got us from ship to shore using their wooden lifeboats with an inboard motor. They had a capacity of about twenty-five to thirty people, so if I remember correctly we could transport all of our gear in one load. The double prow lifeboats could handle the surf pretty well, but we had to be careful. If there was not too much wave action, hip boots were adequate for getting on the beach without getting too wet. If it was a little rough, then somebody had to get wet. Usually, those boats had about four crew members, so a couple of them could be holding the boat while we transferred gear and got in or out. Our gear included a radio so we could communicate with the Coast Guard boat and the Fish and Wildlife Service office in Bethel about 370 miles to the east. At that time, light-weight, shortwave radios for use in the field were not available, so FWS mechanics at the Aircraft Division in Anchorage rigged up a special radio for us using military surplus electronics, and built a four-by-four-by-one-foot wooden box to house it. We had a generator to recharge the car battery that ran the radio, and gasoline for the generator. All of this together made for a lot of weight just for the radio. It was difficult to unload all this from a lifeboat in moderate surf. It took four husky Coast Guard crewmembers wearing World War II–era splash suits to get the radio from ship to shore while maintaining it in an upright position and keeping it from being immersed by a breaking wave.

Just before the Coast Guard dropped us off on St. Matthew Island, they dropped me on Hall Island, one of the three islands in the St. Matthew group. St. Matthew is the largest one, at about thirty-two miles long by about three and a half miles wide on average. The smaller, rocky island about nine miles from the south end of St. Matthew is called Pinnacle Island. It is very steep sided, but has an abundance of nesting seabirds in the summer. Hall Island is only about three and a half miles north of St. Matthew, but the reindeer never got to it. It had vegetation types similar to those on St. Matthew with an abundance of lichens, so I wanted to get ashore to make comparisons between the lichens there that had not been impacted by reindeer versus those I was going to see on St. Matthew that had.

Once on St. Matthew, Jim and I stayed in the Rausch's driftwood hut, which was in pretty good shape, except we covered the roof with a large tarp to prevent leakage and to keep it dry inside. We put the generator outside of the hut and ran it only when recharging the radio battery. This was generally in the evening when light was low, and we used an extension cord and one light bulb to provide light in the windowless hut while we were cooking dinner and writing up field notes on rainy days. We also had a Coleman lantern and candles to provide light, so it all worked out pretty well. The radio required a long antenna that we had to reel out and we found several long poles among the driftwood that we tied together to make suitable poles from which to hang it. We had a prearranged schedule with the office in Bethel as to what time everyday we would radio in to tell them that we were okay, and were surprised that it functioned successfully on the first try. I asked them to relay our appreciation to the Aircraft Division for their effort in providing the "homemade" radio that us novices were able to set up.

The only way we could get around the island was by walking, but Jim and I were both in good shape, so this was not a problem. We hiked over the entire island, systematically counting the reindeer as we moved north from mountain ridge to mountain ridge and looked over broad areas to the lowlands. We found that most of the reindeer were in the southern one-third of the island, close to our camp. In retrospect, that was where most of the lichens were that provided the best winter forage. Whenever we found unique vegetation types, we would stop and use a long tape laid along the ground in a straight line to establish a line transect as a guide for sampling and measuring the distribution of individual species within the marked area. We put a small cairn at one end or the other, and at point intervals along the tape we recorded the vegetation by species. We established individual hundred-foot line transects in all of the major vegetation types on the island.

Then we selected places to build three enclosed vegetation plots that would exclude the reindeer. They are usually called enclosures because they protect vegetation plots from being grazed, but they are also referred to as exclosures, because they exclude herbivores from being able to graze the vegetation within. We erected each of the three enclosures in a different type of plant community that appeared to have been used by the reindeer and that had reasonable amounts of lichens remaining. We built two of them within close walking distance from our campsite, and the third one was at a location farther south where the cattle wire fencing, steel posts, and tools needed for construction had been dropped off by the Coast Guard so we didn't have to carry it so far. These materials were heavy so Jim and I appreciated having this help. It took the two of us to carry one roll of wire across the tundra, so having a shorter distance to carry it saved us valuable time that could be devoted to other activities. The fenced enclosures were

Jim Whisenhant putting up an enclosure near Big Lake on St. Matthew Island, 1957. PHOTO BY DAVID KLEIN.

three by five meters with a two-meter-square vegetation plot in the center and two plots as controls outside of each enclosure. We drove metal stakes into the ground with a specially designed hammer, and used heavy-weight steel wire to secure and guy all four corners because it is so windy there. We permanently marked the corners with ten-inch steel spikes, described the vegetation within each plot, mapped the ground cover of individual plant species, numbered each plot, and photographed it with a camera on an elevated tripod. We did a nice job under the circumstances.

We had a permit to take ten reindeer to get body composition measurements and collect other information from them, like age, sex, and general body condition, and look for parasites on them. So, of course, we ate a lot of reindeer. But we had to be careful with the reindeer because there were a lot of arctic foxes there and they were real scroungers. You could not put any food out unless you hung it from a pole or from the roof of the cabin so they couldn't get to it. Things kept well in the cool, moist, windy air, and there

David with a large bull reindeer that he harvested to weigh and take samples from in order to determine health and body condition of individual animals as part of his research on the reindeer population of St. Matthew Island, 1957 COURTESY OF DAVID KLEIN.

normally weren't flies to bother us unless it got calm. We also ate quite a bit of char that we caught in a small gill net while we were camped at Big Lake, the largest lake on the island. So we ate well.

When we did a long hike and were going to be gone from the hut for more than a day, we took a small tent and a little gas stove with us. We tried to camp on a beach where there was enough driftwood so we could build a campfire. In some places there was a great abundance of driftwood and in some places there was none, depending on the side of the island you were on. But we didn't know this at first. And there are no trees or shrubs on the island that are big enough to use for a fire, especially if it was raining with a strong wind blowing, so then we would use the gas stove. We often continued walking until we found driftwood and then pitched our tent there. By that time, we were usually pretty wet. Our sleeping bags were usually in plastic bags so they were dry and we had inflatable air mattresses that we blew up to sleep on, but at this point all effort was directed at trying to get a driftwood fire going. We carried a small axe or a big knife that we could use to cut shavings from the drier part of the wet driftwood, and we had coils of dry birch bark we had found on the beach that were helpful for starting fires. Stubs of candles were also good for starting fires. Once we got a large fire going, we would load it with wood and then it would dry out the other wood fast enough that we would get a lot of heat. Then we could take off our rain gear and get a little bit of exposure to the heat from the fire.

To do this, however, we needed to find a place where we were not in the full force of the wind, which was usually on the lee side of the island at the base of a cliff. Nevertheless, it was extremely turbulent and the winds would circle around and the smoke would go in all directions. We ended up breathing in a lot of smoke because we wanted to get close enough to the fire to feel its warmth. But we managed. We could rake out enough coals to make a small fire for cooking our meals, and we could get relatively dry before we went into our sleeping bags hoping that the weather would moderate by the next day. It often did.

We took pride in being prepared and being able to survive under those conditions, and we felt wonder in being in such a spectacular environment. There were always things to see that we did not know about or expect. I remember waking up one morning at a campsite on a small beach with a steep cliff behind us when suddenly to our surprise a gray whale surfaced and blew less than twenty-five feet away. It was after a storm, it had stopped raining, and the sea was fairly calm. What an exciting experience for both of us; to see a whale so close while kittiwakes and murres with small fish in their beaks were flying just above our heads on their way back to feeding their young in nests on the cliff ledges. St. Matthew Island was proving to be a fantastically dynamic place.

We were there from July 15 to August 9. The Coast Guard boat picked us up again, and took us back to Dutch Harbor, where we took a commercial flight home. This trip was intended as a reconnaissance study to collect some baseline information. At the time, there was no knowing when anybody would next get out there. But it turned out that my preliminary work and report that was published as a Fish and Wildlife Service series publication (Klein 1959a), was the beginning of a longer-range study to monitor the reindeer and vegetation on St. Matthew Island.

1963 The next time I went to St. Matthew Island was in 1963 for three weeks from mid-July to early August. By this time, it had become my project through the Co-op Unit, so I did all the planning, including contacting the Coast Guard, who again took us out and picked us up.

This time a large team went, because the 1957 expedition had stimulated a diversity of scientific interests in the island's flora and fauna. For instance, the Rausches had saved the stomach contents of char that they had caught in Big Lake in 1954 and sent them to Professor Wilimovski, a fisheries professor at the University of British Columbia (UBC). When Wilimovski looked through them, he found muscle tissue of another fish that could not initially be identified. It was finally identified as blackfish. This was interesting because blackfish are strictly a freshwater species and are unable to live in saltwater, whereas char can readily get into some of St. Matthew's lakes when outlet streams flow over the beach gravel to the sea. Old beach ridges had closed off Big Lake from the sea, but the char were breeding successfully. Because of all this, Gary Cowan, a fisheries graduate student from UBC joined our 1963 team primarily to collect blackfish specimens, as well as other fish from both the freshwater and in-shore marine habitats. The blackfish is presumably a relic from when St. Matthew was part of Beringia, some twelve thousand plus years earlier when sea levels were substantially lower. Other team members included Jack Manley, with the Bureau of Indian Affairs, who volunteered to join the expedition and help with the reindeer counting and other work, and Dr. Frances "Bud" Fay, a research scientist with the US Public Health Service and an affiliate at UAF, who came along to observe foxes and collect live voles for Dr. Rausch's genetic work and assist in the reindeer counts and autopsy work (Fay 1963).

While Bud and the two fisheries biologists usually stayed around Big Lake, the rest of us did hikes trying to count the reindeer. As anticipated, the reindeer were abundant, but it was so foggy that we were unable to make successful counts of their total numbers over the entire island. Occasionally, the fog would lift and we could get estimates of the population composition of groups that we could see, including sex and age ratios, and proportion of yearlings and calves, but when we would get in a position where we could see big areas, the fog was too dense for us to make accurate counts. In summer, most large males are separate from the females and calves, so we were unable to get reliable counts of sex ratios.

It was frustrating to not have sufficient visibility to complete a count of the reindeer or to collect the ten reindeer we had permits to shoot for research purposes. The fog also made it difficult to navigate as we hiked over the thirty-two-mile-long island. I had not remembered the fog being so persistent in 1957. In 1963, the weather was so uncooperative that we needed to use compasses a lot. GPS equipment was not available then, but we had some aerial photos showing residual snow patches of variable sizes and shapes that remained similar from year to year, which we could use as navigational aids. Sometimes it ended up that we did not take the easiest route when walking; we went over mountains in the fog that we could have avoided and gone around if the visibility had been better.

It also was rainy and windy. It wasn't really hard rain, but drizzle, and with the wind often blowing at twenty-five to thirty miles per hour it seemed much worse than it was. In these conditions, you have got to have super good rain gear or the water's going to get in. We had mostly wool clothing with rain gear that was always coming apart at the seams. And on a long hike, you were going to be pretty wet by the time you came back, especially if you were packing a heavy load and perspiring, too. So it was tough going, but you don't notice this if you've got a woodstove and a hut to come back to. We were able to use the same driftwood hut that we used in 1957, although the beach was gradually being eroded away and a portion of the hut had been undercut by a storm since we had been there. It was convenient to pick up pieces of driftwood on the nearby beach to make a fire in the woodstove we had installed. We cooked food on the stove and dried out our wet clothes easily, and were warm and dry while in the hut.

We were also able to visit the enclosures and plots that I had established in 1957 and look for any changes that may have taken place. Already in the six years since their establishment, I could see differences between inside and outside of the enclosures. An unanticipated problem with the enclosures was that the high salt in the air of the marine environment was causing rusting and erosion of the steel corner posts. The cattle wire fencing also was beginning to fracture at the enclosure corners due to the extreme force of the nearly constant high winds, especially in winter. At one enclosure, a bull reindeer had apparently gotten his antlers stuck in the fencing while thrashing around during the rut, and in his efforts to get away, he knocked down the fencing and heavily trampled the enclosed and adjacent vegetation. The two plots established as controls outside of the enclosure were not affected, but the study of lichen recovery rates at that enclosure was changed to a study of lichen recovery from excessive trampling.

By 1963, the lichens had been virtually eliminated as a winter food source for the reindeer. The reindeer population was still increasing, but not as fast, and the body size had declined. In 1957, the body sizes of the St. Matthew reindeer were much larger than the original reindeer that had been imported from Nunivak Island, but by 1963 they were back down to Nunivak Island size. The calf-to-cow ratio and the yearling-to-adult ratio had both dropped. Although there had been a decrease in body size, the St. Matthew reindeer were still reproductive and capable of expanding the population, but the rate of their increase was not as high as it had previously been. One of the questions we wanted to answer was why the rate of increase was on the decline.

The boat that dropped us off at St. Matthew was a Navy icebreaker. I think it was the *North Wind*. We kept contact with it either directly by radio or via the Fish and Wildlife Service office in Bethel, who could relay messages. Things were pretty much on schedule and gradually the time was coming when they were going to come back for us, but we had been totally frustrated by the persistent fog keeping us from obtaining a good count of the reindeer. Finally, the day they arrived, we had the best weather of our whole trip. It was still overcast, but it was high overcast, no fog. I knew the ship had two helicopters aboard, so when they came, I explained to the captain that we had completed most of the investigations and recognized that there were lots and lots of reindeer here, but because of the fog, we had not been able to get a count. I asked, "Is there any way we could use the helicopters to do a survey?" Within a couple of minutes, he responded with, "Yes, we can make both of the helicopters available." They flew the two helicopters over, picked up our gear and took it back to the boat. Then Bud Fay got in one helicopter and I got in the other, and we divided the island in half. He took the south half of the island and I took the northern half. Doing these surveys with the helicopters was ideal under the circumstances. The weather was good, except that in the bright sun the reindeer cast shadows, which makes it hard to estimate numbers when you see a group. But in conjunction

Using a Coast Guard helicopter to help count reindeer on St. Matthew Island, 1963. COURTESY OF DAVID KLEIN.

with the well-trained pilots, we were able to get relatively accurate estimates of the numbers in large groups by moving around so that the sun was behind us and animals that had been lying down had time to stand up and start to move. We stayed far enough away from the reindeer to avoid causing them to run, which would have made counting them more difficult.

When I finished counting the reindeer, I had one other thing to do at the northern end of the island. There was an apparent archaeological site that appeared to be an Eskimo-type house foundation. It had been mentioned by early explorers visiting the island in the mid-1800s, and I had seen and noted its location when on the island in 1957. Frederick Hadleigh West, a UAF archaeologist, had asked me, if there was time available, to dig a quick trench across the shallow sandy soil of the site to look for artifacts. It was the only evidence of prehistoric human presence that had been found on the island. I had permission to dig under Fred West's general archaeological reconnaissance permit from the State Office of Archaeology. When the helicopter landed next to the site, the pilot told me the battery was low so he could not risk shutting it down. He said, "I will keep it running on idle, but I can only do that for about twenty minutes to be sure that we have enough gas to get us back to the ship. So that's the only time you have."

I moved a lot of sand in that short period of time. I dug a trench across the foundation site, and fortunately hit the floor of the hut at less than a foot down. The pilot was sitting close by watching intently. His fascination increased markedly, as did mine, when I began to pick up several pottery shards, a polar bear tooth, and was finding charred oily rocks, indicating the former presence of a hearth.[5] As I started to stand up and pick up the shovel, the pilot said, "You can take five more minutes to complete the trench since you are finding such interesting things. I always factor in fuel contingency for important unexpected events." I finished the trench, and there were a couple of very large whale jawbones adjacent to the hut depression that were obviously used in its construction, and more whale bones nearby. I am not an archaeologist, but this suggested to me that the people who had lived there had killed a whale when hunting near the ice edge in the Bering Sea and got stuck on St. Matthew waiting for favorable ice and sea conditions to return to their home village.[6]

Back on the ship, Bud and I put together our rough survey notes and were able to announce that there were approximately six thousand reindeer on the island. And of equal and timely importance, we acknowledged the captain's willingness and effort to make the helicopters available to us, and praised the pilots for their skills and their eagerness and interest in collaborating with us. All of this enabled us to be successful in meeting essential goals of the project.

The Coast Guard visited St. Matthew briefly in the summer of 1965, when they stopped to let some of their crew go ashore and hunt reindeer. They had done this before when the reindeer were numerous, but this time

---

5. "The recovered material was later given to West who deposited the artifacts in the University of Alaska Fairbanks Museum (collection #UA-63-61)" (Griffin 2017; 90).
6. For more about the human history and archaeological sites on St. Matthew Island, see Griffin 2017.

David at a whale skull on St. Matthew Island in 1957 that was so far inland he believes it must have been moved by a large wave. Pinnacle Island is visible in the distance. COURTESY OF DAVID KLEIN.

they could not find any reindeer to shoot. They saw a few fresh tracks in one area, but other than that there were just skeletons scattered over the landscape. The Coast Guard notified me of the reindeer die-off, so I wanted to get out there to determine, if I could, what happened and why. I wondered if there were any reindeer left, what the conditions were if they were still there, when they died, and what the status of the vegetation was.

We later learned that in the winter of 1964 there was an extreme storm event with a record-breaking combination of extreme sixty-mile-per-hour winds and heavy snowfall. Normally, when it snows in these marine areas, the temperature goes up at least into the twenties. Instead, that winter the temperature was down around ten degrees Fahrenheit, I think, or even colder. And it stayed cold. So all this contributed to a big die-off of the reindeer in the late winter of 1964 (Klein 1968). Many years later, I asked

John Walsh, a climate scientist at UAF, if he could account for that extreme storm event. Using archived weather and climate data he found on the internet, John was able to demonstrate how an extreme low-pressure system associated with the Mount Agung eruption in Indonesia and an extreme high over Eurasia and the Russian Far East had converged directly over St. Matthew Island and caused the massive storm (Klein, Walsh, and Shulski 2009; Rozell 2010).

1966 It was not until the summer of 1966 that I was able to get to St. Matthew Island again. The team consisted of Vern Harms, a botanist with UAF; Detlef Eisfeld, a postdoc working with me from the University of Kiel, Germany; and myself. We flew to Dutch Harbor, where we were picked up by a Coast Guard buoy tender and went directly to St. Matthew. Vern and Detlef were seriously seasick, and did not feel well until they got their feet back on land. This time we had a lighter radio, nicknamed the "silver box," that used dry cell batteries and had been designed for stream guards in Alaska's coastal areas during the salmon fishing season. We had extra batteries, but we still had to be conservative about using the radio, especially for transmitting. As we did on the previous trips, we tried to keep in touch with the Coast Guard and the Fish and Wildlife Service office in Bethel. After they dropped us off, the Coast Guard ship was headed farther north through the Bering Strait up to Point Lay then turning around and coming back, and were scheduled to pick us up about the 20th of August on their return trip south.

Vern, Detlef, and I initially did long day hikes together looking for fresh sign of the remaining reindeer. Detlef and I took skeletal measurements from the remains of the starved reindeer we encountered to determine their sex and age, and Vern collected plants from unfamiliar plant communities from which species had not previously been collected. Detlef and I also stopped to check the enclosures I had built in 1957, but not enough time had passed to see much of a difference between vegetation inside and outside of the enclosures or for any of it to have rebounded. In 1957, lichens had been virtually eliminated by the reindeer from areas where the previously ungrazed lichen mats were three to four inches thick and had suppressed most of the nearby vascular plants. The arctic willow, a prostrate shrub found

Detlef Eisfeld measuring
antlers of the skeletal remains
of a reindeer that died during
the 1964 reindeer die-off
on St. Matthew Island, 1966.
PHOTO BY DAVID KLEIN.

on scattered raised hummocks among the lichens, was an exception to this, because it grew above the cold soils beneath the rootless lichens and its foliage shaded out any of the slow-growing lichens.

Eventually, Detlef and I also did multiday hikes until we found live reindeer. It took us a long time, until one day we hiked the seven miles down south to Big Lake, and as we came down the hill toward the lake, the fog lifted just enough that four reindeer became visible. We had a permit to take ten reindeer for research purposes, so we fired our guns. We shot three reindeer, which we quickly butchered, weighed, measured, and autopsied. They turned out to be two female reindeer and one male that looked like a female because it had reduced antlers and shrunken testis, but otherwise they all were in good physical condition. We collected ovaries from the females, lower jaws for aging, and any other tissues we needed for our research. Of course, we salvaged the meat from these three reindeer to bring back to camp as a supplemental food supply. The foxes quickly arrived to scavenge the carcasses.

Finding a few of the surviving reindeer was important because we then knew the general area where to look for others. Finally, Detlef and I went all the way down to the southernmost part of the island again, and spotted about forty reindeer in the same broad expanse of the valley where we had seen the first group. After watching them closely through binoculars and a spotting scope for over a half hour, we concluded that they were all females. There were no young animals, neither fawns nor yearlings. I was focused on getting our sample of ten reindeer, so I wiggled on my belly and got close enough to shoot seven of them. Now, we had seven reindeer lying on the ground, and it was late in the day, so we went to work. It was hard work and tiring for the back. First, we butchered them and cut them into fifty-pound chunks so we could weigh them piece by piece with the relatively small spring scale that I had. Again, we collected ovaries and lower jaws. We then salvaged as much of the meat as we could carry, including a lot of liver and heart and tongue. With all of the meat and specimens, Detlef's and my packs were loaded to what seemed like more than capacity as we started off to hike the ten miles back over hilly terrain. When we made it back to camp around midnight, we figured that we had covered twenty-two miles that day, most of it with heavy packs. But we had accomplished our primary objectives for the study. We counted what we were convinced were the last reindeer, and we got the scientific samples we needed. To verify that no other reindeer were present on the island, a couple of days later we hiked north of our camp at Beauty Lake to the northern part of the island, and found no fresh sign indicating that there were any reindeer in that area. We later figured there had been forty-two reindeer remaining on the island and we killed ten, meaning there were still thirty-two there. In the absence of any males, these remaining females would be unable to play a role in restoration of the St. Matthew reindeer population so the future of the herd did not look good.

Then the unexpected and frustrating challenge to leave the island began. When we got back from autopsying those last seven reindeer, we heard that the Coast Guard boat was going to be delayed longer than anticipated. We had already learned through our radio contact that the Coast Guard might be as much as a week late, but we felt that a week was not such a long time under the circumstances. We were, however, getting a little short on food, but we were camped on a lake near the midpoint of the island and we could catch char right next to our tent. (By this time, the driftwood hut we had used previously had long since been washed away by wave action.) The

Coast Guard now told us, "We will be delayed probably as much as a month. We can probably get you an airdrop of food if you need it."

A month or more delay would create major problems for all of us. Vern had classes to teach when the semester started at the beginning of September, and all three of us had families anxious for our return. So I started to look into possible alternative ways of getting off the island. First, we contacted the Coast Guard in Kodiak to see if they might be able to fly their big twin-engine, amphibious airplane to land in the sea and pick us up on the beach with inflatable rafts. They considered the request but eventually declined, explaining that their small inflatable boats were inadequate for getting through the surf at St. Matthew. I then contacted Theron Smith, head of the Fish and Wildlife Service's Aircraft Division in Anchorage to see if their amphibious, twin-engine Grumman Goose that was equipped for long-distance flights over open water might be available to come get us. While we were optimistically waiting for his response, the captain of the Coast Guard boat radioed us asking for a list of food we would need in an airdrop. I said, "Well, we don't need an airdrop now. We're looking into other possibilities for getting off the island." But the captain was pressuring me for a list in case the airdrop was needed. I was getting frustrated, because I didn't want to consider an airdrop as long as there was some hope for an alternative. A short time later we got a message from the FWS saying they would not fly out to St. Matthew. They didn't want to risk the new plane by flying such a long distance, and realistically, our lives as well. We now had been turned down twice, and we were understandably fairly dejected.

We were sitting in the tent, contemplating what our options were for getting off the island, when all of a sudden we heard what sounded like the engine of a small aircraft. We went outside and to our surprise we saw a Super Cub on floats coming down through a hole in the clouds. St. Matthew is 250 miles from the mainland, and most pilots would not fly a Super Cub that distance over the open ocean. The plane emerged through the broken clouds, flew low over our camp, dipped its wing, landed on the lake, and taxied up to our tent. A young red-headed pilot climbed out and began unloading ten gallon cans of gas, stating, "These are for refueling." He stepped onto the beach and said, "Hi, I'm Stu." I asked, "What brought you out here?" He said, "I have lived in Bethel for several years and I have heard that there were a lot of reindeer out here. I was not busy, so I thought it would be a nice opportunity to fly out here." He had flown from Bethel to Nunivak Island, where he refueled, and then continued on to St. Matthew. It was just luck that he ended up at our lake, which was one of several good lakes for landing a small plane.

We invited him into our wall tent to have a cup of coffee and told him our sad story about being stuck there. He said, "Well, I can try to contact an outfit in Dillingham on my way back. They have Grumman Gooses that they fly to the Pribilof Islands. I should be able to make arrangements for them to fly out here tomorrow. Weather permitting." Then he said, "But I can take one of you back now, because I'm going to have the backseat empty after we put all that gas into the plane." Vern, Detlef, and I discussed it, and I said, "Personally, I do not want to go with him in the Super Cub over so much open water." But Vern said, "Oh no, I want to go back. I have to be in Fairbanks to teach classes." So Vern went with him. The plan was that the first thing Stu would do after arriving in Bethel in about five hours was to call the Fish and Wildlife office to confirm the charter and they would relay the message to me over the radio. We waited and waited and still no radio call. It was way past when Stu and Vern should've landed in Bethel so I was starting to get worried. Finally, the FWS called us. It turned out that Vern and Stu were so hungry when they arrived that they stopped at a restaurant to have a hamburger before they called. Stu had arranged for a charter from Dillingham to come pick us up the next day. They would fly first to Bethel, refuel there, and then fly out to St. Matthew.

Since we were going to get flown out, I was about to notify the Coast Guard to call off the airdrop when we heard what sounded like a large airplane and suddenly a four-engine air force cargo plane appeared out of the clouds. The plane disappeared into the clouds, made a big circle, came out of the clouds again, and dropped a large bundle wrapped in a cargo net. A parachute opened and the emergency food neatly stacked on a four-by-eight-foot piece of plywood landed on the beach a short, but safe, distance from us and our tent. A large shipping tag was attached to the bundle with the large print notation: "THIS NET AND PARACHUTE MUST BE RETURNED TO EIELSON AIR FORCE BASE." The air force did the drop at the request of the Coast Guard and probably did it on that particular day to take advantage of good weather that was not likely to last. Even though we did not need the supplies, at least we knew they were concerned for our welfare. There were at least ten cases of C-rations, ten whole hams individually sealed in tin containers labeled "Keep Refrigerated," numerous large boxes of oatmeal and pancake flour. This was not the type of food we had asked for, but by this point, I was beginning to see some of the humor in this. Detlef was so hungry for meat that he said, "Let's cook one of those hams right away." I knew that just the two of us couldn't eat that whole ham and it probably wouldn't keep long once we opened it, but we had been eating lightly and sort of rationing our food since we didn't know how long we'd be on the island. As a young, active guy, Detlef sure ate a heck of a lot of ham.

The next morning we got up and it was still beautiful, clear weather and the pilot in Dillingham said he would probably be arriving at St. Matthew around 1:00 p.m. Well, you know how it goes. One o'clock came, two o'clock came, three o'clock came, and still no plane. Detlef tended to be a pessimist and repeatedly asked about what might have gone wrong. I am an optimist and had considerable more experience with aircraft support in the field, so kept reassuring him that I was confident that the plane would eventually arrive. Finally, to our gratification the Grumman Goose landed in the lake and taxied right up to the shore adjacent to our campsite where we could wade out to it in hip boots. The pilot unloaded three fifty-gallon drums of fuel that we pumped into the plane's fuel tanks to be sure we had enough gas for the return flight. We loaded all of our gear plus all of the food from the airdrop into the plane, as well as the cargo net and parachute, taxied out into the lake, and were finally off the island. Since it was perfectly clear weather, I asked the pilot if he could fly over the general area where the remaining thirty-two female reindeer were last seen. Sure enough they were there. Since we had not seen sign of reindeer in other places on the island, we had confirmed that these were the only remaining reindeer. It was nice to see them one last time from the air.

Since the weather was so exceptional, we flew directly to Dillingham, and the next day we were able to catch a flight to Anchorage and then on to Fairbanks. What a relief to be back home after such a complicated, suspenseful, and ultimately successful effort to get all three of us safely off of St. Matthew Island. The next day I felt it necessary to drive the cargo net and parachute the twenty-five miles to Eielson Air Force Base to return them as instructed. The officer I met seemed to appreciate my effort to deliver the items, although he did not have a clue about the airdrop. I figured that the air force and Coast Guard would not care about getting the food back, so I kept it to use on future student field projects.

I learned a lot about the reindeer on St. Matthew during the summer of 1966. By 1963, in the absence of natural predators and humans, the twenty-nine reindeer introduced to St. Matthew Island in 1944 had increased to six thousand, but only forty-two reindeer appeared to have survived the 1964 winter die-off, all females except for one male. An analysis of ovaries we collected in 1966 from nine females showed that they had ovulated normally in 1964 and 1965, but had not conceived. This was also suggested by the apparent absence of fawns and yearlings. This verified that the single surviving male was not viable. In addition, the forty-one females had been either yearlings or two-year olds in 1963, so were most likely not carrying an embryo going into that harsh winter of 1964. We examined bones of embryos found within female skeletal remains, and by knowing the pattern of growth of embryos of domestic reindeer during gestation we were able to estimate that the pregnant females died in March. The ones that survived were probably not pregnant and so were in good enough condition to survive the winter and withstand the extreme, long periods of deep snows, bad weather, and poor food availability.

To help answer the question of why the females on St. Matthew Island survived the unusual storm event in the late winter of 1964 better than the males, it is necessary to examine the breeding strategy of polygamous animals where a single male may breed more than one female. With caribou and reindeer, the highest genetic priority of the mature adult male is to pass on its genes to as many young as possible during the mating season, while winter survival is secondary. Males must expend much of their stored energy to hold a harem of pre-estrous females together, and keep other males away, if they are to successfully breed all these females as they come into estrous. Going into the breeding season in the fall, the big dominant males are super fat, but during the actual rutting period itself they do not eat very much because they are so focused on breeding the females. This means they end up losing a lot of their fat and go into the winter in poor condition.

In contrast, adult female caribou and reindeer must survive the winter in good condition if they are to pass on genes through a successful pregnancy, provide milk for a newborn calf, as well as live long enough to nurture, guide, and assist the young to learn adult behavior. Therefore, in the fall time, females in harem groups continue to feed intensively in order to store fat reserves necessary to ensure their winter survival and success of their likely pregnancy. The physiological demand on the female's body increases during the terminal stage of her gestation and the development of the embryo, but the greater physiological demand on the female occurs once she has to start producing milk. That new calf is going to be growing faster than it was when it was inside her, so after she gives birth, she has to feed on the highest-quality, quick-digesting food she can find. Literally, all the female does is eat and digest and produce milk for the first three weeks of the calf's life before it begins to graze.

Knowing this breeding and eating strategy helps explain why no viable male reindeer survived the harsh winter of 1964 on St. Matthew. They were more vulnerable to starvation because they had not been able to rebuild their body condition after the breeding season, so they lacked the necessary reserves of body fat that would enable them to withstand the extremely tough winter conditions they encountered. If it had been a relatively normal or mild winter, there still could have been a large die-off, but it would be unlikely that all the males would have died.

After the 1966 trip, we were not able to keep track of the numbers of reindeer on St. Matthew Island because no one was getting out there specifically to check on them, but we assumed that their numbers would be decreasing due to a lack of viable males. At one point, Art Sowls, a biologist for the Alaska Maritime National Wildlife Refuge, reported that one lame female still remained a couple of years after all the rest of the reindeer had disappeared. But by the next year she was gone, too. We estimated that she lived about twenty-one years. Female domestic reindeer tend to survive a maximum of twenty-one years, although twenty-nine years is the record lifespan for captive reindeer. With no males present, the surviving females on St. Matthew did not have the physiological stress of conceiving young, nurturing a developing embryo, or providing milk for a newborn fawn, so they might have lived longer than was typical.

Despite my conclusions about the precipitous end to the unique and accidentally initiated population ecology experiment of the reindeer on St. Matthew Island, there were deniers who focused on carrying capacity and possibility of food shortage (Hardin 1968, 1985). It is correct that in 1963, prior to the winter storm of 1964, the six thousand reindeer on St. Matthew had far exceeded the carrying capacity of their constrained island habitat, so already were headed for a major population reduction. The overgrazing and trampling by the high density of reindeer substantially altered plant communities, especially those where lichens previously dominated over vascular plants. Studies have shown that lichens could never recover to the level of abundance that existed prior to any reindeer being on the island (Scheffer 1951; Klein and Shulski 2009). Without an abundance of lichens on St. Matthew, it is likely there would only have been a few hundred reindeer that could survive, and as long as there were reindeer on the island this would prevent the recovery of the lichens as shown to be the case on the Pribilof Islands (ibid.). In addition, the singing vole and McKay's bunting (*Plectrophenax hyperboreus*), both species endemic to the St. Matthew Islands, also were likely negatively affected by the reindeer. Reindeer competed in summer with the voles for the highest-quality green vegetation, and the bunting nests located in the entrances of old vole runways were at risk of being stepped on by reindeer (Klein and Sowls 2015). After all of this, I was starting to look upon the St. Matthew study as an opportunity for me to maintain a focus on the importance of lichens in the annual nutritional/physiological cycle of caribou in their native habitats.

1985 My next trip to St. Matthew Island was in 1985. I was interested in returning to assess the rate of recovery of lichens that had been so badly overgrazed and in finding out how the vascular plant communities on the island had changed in the twenty-nine years since the reindeer die-off. By this point, I was leader of the Cooperative Wildlife Research Unit and preoccupied with raising money to support graduate students, so I did not have any surplus to pay for a trip for myself to St. Matthew Island.

St. Matthew Island was now part of the Alaska Maritime National Wildlife Refuge (AMNWR) that was established to protect the seabird colonies and marine mammal rookeries in coastal areas and islands in Southeast Alaska, Prince William Sound, the Aleutian Islands, the Pribilof Islands, and through the Bering Strait as far north as Point Lay. The challenge for AMNWR is huge in terms of managing, monitoring, and providing protection for these ecologically important components of Alaska's coastal ecosystems that are spread out over tremendously great distances. Obviously, they cannot get to all these places every year to do research, but refuge staff established a schedule to visit St. Matthew Island once every five to seven years.

In 1985, AMNWR wanted to do seabird counts and other investigations at St. Matthew Island, and I was eager to return to examine the vegetation plots I had established in 1957. I wanted to see how much recovery was occurring in the lichens after being overgrazed by the reindeer and to analyze changes in plant community composition. At this time, AMNWR did not yet have their own research vessel, so there were logistical problems in getting to St. Matthew. They chartered a crab fishing boat, and I flew to the Pribilof Islands to meet them. It was a stormy and fairly rough boat trip over to St. Matthew Island, especially for the majority aboard who suffered from seasickness. Not being prone to seasickness myself, I enjoyed sitting in the pilothouse watching the fulmars and kittiwakes as they rode the wind along the crests and troughs of the large waves in search of food brought to the surface by the turbulent sea.

Upon arrival, the crab boat dropped me off with camping gear on the southern part of the island close to most of the old vegetation plots and enclosures. Unlike previous years when our boat dropped us off and left, this time the boat stayed around the island while I and some of the bird biologists carried out our specific investigations on shore. I hiked to all three enclosures, and remapped and photographed the vegetation inside and outside of each. I had an idea what I would find in terms of which plant groups would be showing the greatest response to the previously heavy grazing. My assessment of the vegetation mainly focused on the differential recovery rates of different lichen species. It showed that the lichen species that were present in 1957 were no longer there after the overgrazing that occurred as the reindeer population approached its peak in 1963. There was no significant recovery of the climax lichen species, primarily *Cladina* and *Cetraria*, which are the reindeer's preferred winter forage and had been virtually eliminated by the overgrazing. In the few areas where lichens had reestablished in the twenty-two years since the reindeer die-off, it was the pioneering largely brown-colored lichen species of low palatability to reindeer.

The lichens were not as advanced in their recovery as anticipated. The main reason lichen were slow to come back was that there was no significant living lichen material left for new lichen to build on; they had to start from scratch with pioneering forms (Klein 1987). However, by greatly overgrazing the lichens, the reindeer had exposed a lot of bare ground, and green vascular plants, especially sedges and to a lesser extent grasses, soon established themselves in the exposed soil and were the first to show recovery. Most green plants do not do well in competition with lichens, partly because when lichens are dense or only lightly grazed they create an insulating layer and prevent the rays of the sun from reaching and warming the soil surface. Cold soils are not a problem for lichens because they are not rooted; they are dependent upon sunlight and they can photosynthesize in temperatures just even a few degrees below zero. But they dry out rapidly, and once they dry out they become dormant, so even on sunny days they do not grow.

Given the situation, it was pretty much accepted in my mind that it would take at least fifty years for the lichens to recover and probably longer. Most biologists familiar with caribou and reindeer range agreed with me. I suggested such a long period because at that time we did not know very much about growth rates of lichens on St. Matthew Island in comparison with other areas. We had a little bit of knowledge on this, since some of my students were studying growth rates of lichen on the Seward Peninsula that caribou ate (Joly et al. 2010). The lichens that were coming back on St. Matthew were a different kind, and we did not have knowledge of their growth rates. There was Russian literature on this that was helpful, but growth rates of lichens are highly variable among species, geographic locations, and the climatic regimes within which they grow, thereby making comparisons with St. Matthew Island problematic at best.

After finishing my investigations of the enclosures near Big Lake, I was picked up by the crab boat and dropped off again where we had camped in 1966 and seen a lot of reindeer skeletons, because I wanted to see what that area now looked like. Then I planned to walk ten miles to a camp at

Bull Seal Point to visit my daughter, PeggyEllen, and future son-in-law, Rich Roeleder. They were based there as part of a research team led by Ed Murphy, a biologist at UAF, that was studying the nesting ecology of several large colonies of auklets around the island. For me, the highlight of the 1985 visit to St. Matthew was walking into that camp on a foggy day and being greeted by my daughter. I was honored by the firing up of the sauna that evening, which they had constructed out of driftwood, Visqueen plastic sheeting, and a rusted-out oil barrel for the stove. The sauna provided exquisite and unexpected relaxation at the very edge of the Bering Sea. It was terrific to be out in the field with PeggyEllen in this place that she had heard a lot about from me and was now experiencing herself. She and Rich definitely fell in love with St. Matthew and the seabirds and the sea, all of which shaped their lives. It was wonderful to see them enjoying the experience. After a couple of days with PeggyEllen and Rich, the crab boat picked me up and I rejoined the rest of the team heading back to St. Paul Island to catch our flights home.

2005 In 2005, I visited St. Matthew Island again. It had been forty-one years since the reindeer die-off, so I wanted to assess the 1957 vegetation plots to see what changes had occurred. By this time, the Alaska Maritime National Wildlife Refuge had its own boat, the *Tiglax*, which was available to support this operation. The *Tiglax* was a well-equipped ship with a crew of about six based in Homer that was set up to handle scientists. Similar to the previous trip, a group of different biologists came to do research associated with the refuge's efforts to inventory and gain basic ecological knowledge of the biodiversity of the St. Matthew Islands. While I was looking at vegetation change, others worked with the auklet colonies at Hall Island and on the northern portion of St. Matthew, and Art Sowls, a biologist with the refuge, focused on the influence of red foxes that were suppressing the arctic foxes. Art was planning on retiring in 2006, and he was counting on me to take over responsibility for the fox project so it was key to have this time in the field together.

We established a main base camp at Bull Seal Point on the north end of the island, and used Zodiacs to travel to other parts of the island, such as the southern part where my old vegetation plots were. After waiting a

Red fox pups
on St. Matthew
Island, 2012.
PHOTO BY RICH
KLEINLEDER.

few days for the sea to calm down and wearing survival suits, Art, Karin
Holser (a volunteer on the project), Max Malavanski (a volunteer from St.
George Island), and I launched a Zodiac loaded with food and camping
gear in waterproof bags, and headed slowly down the coast. We established
a temporary camp at Big Lake that was only about a mile from the plots so
we could easily walk to them. Art and Karen did extensive reconnaissance
hikes, and Max and I remapped and photographed vegetation in the meter-
square plots at the three enclosures. We spent four days investigating the
vegetation plots as we had other projects that would occupy our time.

In my thorough assessment of plant regrowth, I found that lichens had
only partly recovered from the past heavy grazing by the reindeer. I expected
to see much more recovery. I already knew that the lichens would be slow
to come back, but the major question was why was the recovery so slow. It
turned out that it was a combination of factors. As I said before, there was
not much living tissue of lichens left after all that grazing, so they pretty
much had to start from scratch. In addition, St. Matthew's high winds, particularly in winter when the reindeer were eating the lichens, accelerated

lichen loss by blowing a large portion of the highly fractured lichens out to sea. The wind also caused some loss of the bare soils after lichens were gone, and that left a substrate that was hard for the lichens to get started in. Another thing I observed was a pronounced change in arctic willow, a prostrate willow species that had suffered from heavy summer grazing. It now was growing well on small hummocks that previously had been surrounded by lichens. With the lichens gone, the willows recovered more rapidly because they still had their root system and older stems from which regrowth could start.

Because regrowth of those lichen species had been so slow, I started looking for evidence to see if climate warming may have been a factor. By 2005, it was apparent that the weather had changed on St. Matthew Island. Some of the lakes that had no outlet to the sea were drying up or had much lower water levels and arctic willows were showing much more vigorous leaf and stem growth, all of which suggested warmer summer conditions. I subsequently developed the hypothesis that lichens on the Bering Sea islands were a relic of a colder climate in the more distant past (Klein and Shulski 2011). Lichen growth depends on having sufficient moisture in the air from rain, fog, or dew in order to keep the lichens moist and provide water for growth. Longer, warmer, and drier summers with less fog meant that lichens were more frequently in a dormant no-growth phase and meant slower growth (ibid.; Joly et al. 2011). Climate warming, with its associated longer summers, less fog, and more sun, generally is more favorable for growth of vascular plants.

Art Sowl's fox project was intended to monitor the status of the red and arctic foxes on St. Matthew Island and collect information on how many arctic foxes remained on the island and whether they were occupying maternal dens. By 1999, it was known that red foxes had arrived and were breeding (Matsuoka 2003), although it is not clear exactly how they got there. In 2005, we discovered a red fox den with eight young near our campsite at Bull Seal Point, and another one on the north end of the island, also with eight young. In both cases, the young were of uniform size and all in good condition. These large litters of healthy kits indicated that the parents were able to bring back sufficient food to support the whole family, whereas if food is limited the smaller kits do not survive. Both parents took turns

Young arctic fox on Hall Island, 1985. PHOTO BY DAVID KLEIN.

hunting for food and would return with eight to ten voles or six or eight least auklets hanging from their mouth.

You come to realize that the different types of foxes have a preference, but will eat whatever they can find or catch. It is not easy for either arctic or red foxes to capture auklets. The evolutionarily derived strategy of auklets for successful production of young includes nesting in crevices underneath large boulders where they are secure from being dug out by foxes. If foxes are to be successful in catching auklets, they have to be at the colonies in the brief period just as the birds are coming out and aggregating before they take off in this big black cloud of ten thousand birds to head out to sea to feed. The entire colony of birds emerging in synchrony results in their literally swamping the predators. The birds return from the sea in smaller groups and quickly go back into their nests, so there is no chance for the foxes to capture them. Adult murres and other cliff-nesting birds are less susceptible to fox predation because foxes are not such good climbers. However, arctic foxes are better climbers than the longer-legged red foxes, so may kill a murre occasionally. Given the choice, red foxes on St. Matthew prefer to hunt small mammals, which are a more reliable, year-round food source, but, in the summer, nesting birds, their eggs, and young are much more abundant than the voles and they are just too tempting to ignore.

By 2005, we found very few arctic foxes left on St. Matthew and could not find any dens where they were producing young. There is evidence that arctic foxes were on the island as early as 1912 (Hunt 1975), and they were prevalent on my previous visits; they often came to our camps in search of food. After the arrival of the red fox in the late 1980s or early 1990s (Matsuoka 2003), the composition of the fox population began to shift. Red foxes are more strongly territorial than arctic foxes, which makes it diffi-cult for arctic foxes to breed when red foxes are around (Klein and Sowls 2015). In combination with competition for food, this led to the red foxes out-competing the arctic foxes and a decline in arctic foxes and an increase in red foxes on St. Matthew Island (ibid.).

This trip proved to be pivotal in terms of what we learned about revege-tation and lichen growth, and about the relationship between red and arctic fox populations. As with all the research I did, this knowledge expanded my understanding of ecological relationships and led me to investigate new questions.

2012 | The next opportunity to get to St. Matthew was in 2012, and it was likely my last chance. By this time, I had "inherited" the fox project from Art Sowls, and I wanted to continue our work on the relative compatibility of red and arctic foxes on the island, as well as the differential effect the foxes had on the island's birds. Also, I was interested in focusing on what was going on in the coastal areas, because I had become involved in climate change research and its effects on wildlife throughout the Arctic and Subarctic.

The expedition team was fairly large because it included several refuge staff members, including the refuge manager, Steve Delehanty, who had never been out to St. Matthew Island, and two bird biologists who wanted to continue their study of auklets. There also was a large number of other scientists, including Derek Sikes, curator of insects at the University of Alaska Museum of the North, and his graduate student, Casey Bickford, who were conducting a survey of the island's insect fauna; another graduate student, Monte Garroute, who was a botanist working out of the Museum of the North under the herbarium curator, Stefanie Ickert; and archaeologist Dennis Griffin, from the Oregon State Historic Preservation Office, whom the refuge had invited to investigate sites of human habitation on the island (Rozell 2015; Griffin 2017) given that there had been limited archaeological work done in the past (Dixon 1999; Frink et al. 2001).

In terms of the fox project, after our research in 2005 indicated a rise in the red fox population and decline in the arctic fox population, we had no assurance that the red foxes were going to be dominant there permanently. We did not know how the red foxes would survive the winters compared to the arctic foxes, which seemed to be better adapted for winter on an island surrounded by sea ice. But in 2012, there were still no red foxes on Hall Island, although arctic foxes there were doing fine (Klein and Sowls 2015).

The larger focus of my work on this trip was to monitor the possible effects of coastal erosion on seabirds during the nesting season. Based upon my earlier observations, I was able to see that coastal erosion was occurring in some of the rocky coastal areas, and it seemed to be related in some ways to the colonial nesting birds, but I was not sure in what way. My curiosity was stimulated, and I became more cognizant of coastal erosion in relation to the local geology. That is when I started to focus on rock types and their vulnerability to erosion by rising sea level.

I did not have a very good understanding of the geological history of St. Matthew Island. When you are on the island, it is difficult to see the rock types in the coastal cliffs compared with viewing them from a ship. Unless you were at a point of land, it was hard to look back along the coastline. When we were hiking, we might walk along a beach below the cliffs where we could have looked up at the rock types, but we learned that sometimes the beach suddenly would end. We were forced to turn around and go all the way back and up over the hills and mountains bordering the coast. This was frustrating and time consuming, and, frankly, there were times when it was better footing and less tiring just climbing over the hills in the first place

Rocky coastline of Hall Island.
MARC D. ROMANO/USFWS.

rather than walking on a cobble beach. So we often just avoided the beaches, which meant less opportunity to observe exposed rock types. However, when we were down on a beach, we would look up with binoculars and identify different kinds of birds nesting in the cliffs. This gave us a feeling for what kind of rock formations were favored by specific bird species.

In 2012, we collected rock samples from coastal areas around St. Matthew, Hall, and Pinnacle Islands. I took them to the Geomorphology Lab in the Geology Department at UAF for identification. Graduate student Carla Tomisich helped identify rock types, their relative hardness, and their likely mode of volcanic origin, and Jeff Benowitz, research assistant professor at UAF's Geophysical Institute, measured the density of the rocks as an index to their hardness and therefore their resistance to coastal erosion. Understanding the diversity of rock types and their hardness and how they are the result of a history of active volcanism dating back sixty and seventy-nine million years ago helped explain the pattern of distribution of seabird nesting sites on St. Matthew, their vulnerability to coastal erosion, as well as the risk of fox predation to the nesting birds.

It became clear to me through all of this that seabird nesting relates very much to the geological history of the island, and I was able to observe differences in erosion in different parts of the island. There were places where the underlying rock was softer because it was derived from earlier pyroclastic volcanic explosions that left behind ash and tuff. That type of underlying volcanic layer can be fine-grained and may become a lubricant if water penetrates fractures in the harder surface rock. This is what led to the massive land slumps most apparent on the northwest coast of St. Matthew and southwest coast of Hall Islands. Some erosion is generated by the sea, but some of this slumpage over long periods of time is facilitated by the presence of particular types of rock. In other places, vertical cliffs of flow basalt rise directly from the sea and the rock is so hard that the power of the sea's waves rise up the cliff face without causing significant erosion. In some sections of coast, massive basalt flows that fractured when cooling have cracks where rain and melt water penetrate and contribute to continued frost action cracking. This makes them vulnerable to erosion by wave action at their base. In those spots, there were large piles of rocks building up from the resulting erosion. Of course, in mid to late winter when sea ice surrounds the island, there is very little coastal erosion due to the absence of wave action. Now, the presence of sea ice at St. Matthew in the winter is of shorter duration than in the past, so there is more open water in early winter, which is when storms are most intense. In recent years, the large waves generated in these early winter storms have been eroding some of the more erodible coastal areas at a higher rate than in the past, but this is usually not at the cliffs where kittiwakes, murres, and fulmars are the dominate nesters in summer.

Coastal erosion is slowest where the rocks are hardest and cliff-nesting birds like murres and kittiwakes prefer to nest on this hard rock, so their successful nesting is not being threatened. In addition, although there are more early winter storms with higher waves than there used to be, these birds are gone by then so are not affected by this change. In comparison, the small auklets dig nesting cavities under large boulders and rocks in areas of volcanic soils that are generally more susceptible to erosion and associated

Murres and kittiwakes nesting
on "Pinhole Rock" at St. Matthew
Island, 2012. PHOTO BY RICH KLEINLEDER.

with large coastal earth slumps. Viewed from a geological time perspective, St. Matthew and Hall Islands are slowly eroding and getting smaller. They eventually will be lost to the sea, but at the present time the rate of erosion is not causing a problem for auklet nesting or for cliff-nesting seabirds (Klein and Kleinleder 2015).

Shortly after our return from the 2012 expedition, I discovered an excellent geological reconnaissance map of St. Matthew Island that had been published years ago by W. W. Patton, a geology professor at the University of Washington (Patton et al. 1975). It was an exquisite geological map of the entire coast focusing on the various volcanic rock types and the origins of those that were exposed. Although finding Patton's map was quite unexpected, it immediately stimulated me to begin work on what proved to be a fascinating bio-geological paper where I made the connection between rock types, coastal erosion, and nesting seabirds (Klein and Kleinleder 2015). In the process, I broadened my understanding of geology as a component of the ecology of the St. Matthew Islands with help from geology graduate students who acted as my teachers.

Even though I am not a geologist, one of the reasons I was focusing on geology relates to the fact that I had been trying to understand the paleo-history of the St. Matthew Islands during the middle and early Holocene, including the distribution of mammals. We already know that there were mammoths that lived on the Pribilof Islands until about 5,000 to 5,500 years ago (Veltre et al. 2008), that polar bears were summer residents on St. Paul Island as recent as about 3,500 BP (ibid.) and on St. Matthew Island until the last were shot in the 1890s (Klein and Sowls 2011), and that analysis of pollen profiles from lake sediment cores obtained on St. Paul Island have enabled reconstruction of past plant communities (Rozell 2014; Wang et al. 2017). However, no sediment cores had been obtained from St. Matthew, so there was keen interest in getting a core for pollen and plant tissue analysis of past plant community structure. There were two main reasons why there were no lake sediment cores from St. Matthew Island. First, winter is the best time of year to do this type of coring and trips to St. Matthew had only occurred in the summer. Second, in order to assess paleo-history from lake sediment, the cores must be from lakes that have not been encroached upon by the sea and none of the lakes on St. Matthew Island appeared to qualify.

As an alternative to lake sediment coring, I discussed the use of peat and marsh coring with Miriam Jones, a postdoc at UAF who had experience with marsh coring for paleo-ecological plant community reconstruction on Alaska's Seward Peninsula. The advantage of peat coring was that you did not need to do it in the middle of a lake. Since Miriam was a specialist in peat coring, I planned that she would join the 2012 expedition and I would assist her. Unfortunately, after planning all this, Miriam received and accepted an offer of a full-time research position with the US Geological Survey in Reston, Virginia, and was no longer available to join the expedition. However, she remained interested in doing the pollen and other paleo-environmental assessment on any cores we secured.

After an unsuccessful search for someone else with coring expertise that could help us, I was left with having to do it myself. I couldn't do it alone, so I asked my son-in-law, Rich Kleinleder, in Homer to come as a refuge volunteer. We ended up having to buy a peat corer, because there were only a couple of peat corers in Alaska at that time and none of them were available. The plan was that we would get the new corer with enough time before the trip so Rich could learn how to use it with guidance and assistance from Ed Berg, a recently retired biologist from the Kenai National Wildlife Refuge who had used a marsh corer extensively. Miriam had already cautioned us that it was tricky when you got too deep. When field-testing the corer, Rich and Ed got it stuck almost immediately in dense marsh sediment. Obviously, it was not designed very well and fortunately Rich was able to modify it so we could take it on our trip. I very much appreciate all that Rich did. Without his help, the marsh sediment coring project would not have been able to proceed.

Examination of 1948 US Navy aerial photos of St. Matthew Island showed that the most desirable place to do the coring was in a marshy area at the northern end of the island. It was a three-mile hike to the coring spot from our campsite on the east side of the island. However, we had previously delivered the heavy coring equipment to the coring site when the *Tiglax* had been able to get ashore at a closer spot, so we didn't have to carry it such a long distance. At first, we could not even core through the annual frost layer because it had not thawed enough yet, but we finally found a place where enough water had seeped through and thawed the marsh. We were successful in getting a couple of suitable cores (Rozell 2012a & 2012b). We got down a little over a meter before we hit mud and gravel. This was discouraging, because in order for gravel to get there it meant that this place had been washed over by the sea at some point in the past, which could affect the accuracy of the paleo-ecological information we were seeking. Miriam had told us that getting even a meter of sediment would be good, because it would provide so much information from this island where we had nothing before. This made us feel better that all of our hard work was worth something. We placed the cores in plastic tubes and kept them horizontal, as Miriam had instructed, because you did not want water to drain through and carry anything from one level of the core to the other. Back in Fairbanks, we placed the cores in the freezer and then shipped them to Miriam for analysis. While she has not yet completed a full analysis, preliminary results indicate a date from the bottom of a core that was about 4,500

Rich Kleinleder and David Klein with the peat corer on St. Matthew Island, 2012.
PHOTO BY NED ROZELL.

years BP. We had hoped it would include the full Holocene, which would have been about 12,000 years. It is possible that coring at a different location could produce older material and better information. The Alaska Maritime Refuge is eager to support coring efforts to better understand the Holocene history of St. Matthew Island, so hopefully there will be another expedition to do this in the future.

The final thing I wanted to do on this trip was to get onto Pinnacle Island in order to collect rock samples for comparison with St. Matthew and Hall Islands. Pinnacle remained foggier than the other islands most of our time there, and we were all busy with other projects, so the effort to get me ashore on Pinnacle Island was left for the very end of the day we left. It was late in the day and it was getting dark, but when we were about a quarter mile away we got a faint view through the fog of the island's steep basalt cliffs. The skipper edged the *Tiglax* to within a safe distance from shore where there was a short, narrow, and steep-rising beach on which a Zodiac could land in order to get Rich and me ashore to collect rocks. I wanted to try to get ashore if it could be done with low risk to us and the crew, but I was also aware that most of the other expedition members were already in their

View of Pinnacle Island as seen
from St. Matthew Island through a
telephoto lens. PHOTO BY DAVID KLEIN.

bunks after a busy day and were not particularly supportive of delaying our
departure just so I could pick up rocks for reasons of little interest to them.
But we gave it a shot and made it ashore, and I had just enough time to
collect a few key samples. We then headed to St. Paul in order to catch our
scheduled flight to Anchorage the next day.

Finally getting to go to Pinnacle after all those years of going to the St.
Matthew Islands was a fabulous experience. It was incredible to have murres
and kittiwakes come out of the fog at high speed and look down at us as they
passed overhead, apparently trying to figure out what we were and whether
we posed a threat to their eggs or young. The thick fog and semi-darkness
seemed to have little effect on their flight capabilities and curiosity. I also
was impressed that murres and kittiwakes nested down to the wave splash
zone, but this was because there were no foxes present on Pinnacle Island.
This absence of mammalian predators on Pinnacle had not always been

the case. There is evidence of polar bears climbing on the cliffs of Pinnacle Island and feeding on the eggs of nesting seabirds (Dawson 1894), as well as accounts of summer resident polar bears on St. Matthew Island (Elliott 1875; Elliott 1882; Healy 1889; Merriam 1901–1910; Hanna 1920). After a lot of library research, I came to the conclusion that the Revenue Cutters and the Canadian and American sealers on the Pribilof Islands most likely and collectively finished off the population of summer resident polar bears that had existed on the St. Matthew Islands (Klein and Sowls 2011). It is ironic that the Revenue Cutters that played a positive role in the conservation of fur seals in the late 1800s had such a negative impact on the polar bears of St. Matthew Island through their thoughtless and wanton killing of a major portion of this meta-population of the Bering Sea polar bears.

Implications of Long-Term Change

I was fortunate that my connection with St. Matthew Island enabled me to keep going back over time to conduct a long-term study and effectively monitor change. A lot of scientists do not have such an opportunity to repeatedly return to the same place. While we had some information about St. Matthew dating from 1875 when Henry Elliott was there to 1954 when Bob Rausch spent time there working with the voles, foxes, and their parasites, nobody had done a comprehensive or quantitative assessment of the flora and fauna and documented change through time. Through my comprehensive research from 1957 to 2012, I was able to monitor change of the vegetation on St. Matthew, as well as the change in the reindeer, including their body weight, and the sex and age ratios of the population. Studies by Scheffer (1951) on St. Paul and St. George Islands were particularly helpful for comparative purposes. From my own perspective, change on St. Matthew Island was initiated by the introduction of reindeer toward the end of the Second World War.

It was such a unique experience to be able to keep going back to St. Matthew Island. There was no way I could observe everything of interest on the island in one trip. My perspective on the ecological issues on St. Matthew Island, of course, changed over time as well. Each time I returned to the island, I began to change my focus as I observed that things were changing there. During most of the time I had been looking at environmental change, there was little focus on climate change within the scientific community. The significant change associated with global climate warming in Alaska occurred in the Bering Sea area about 1976 when there was a steep rise toward warmer conditions as reflected by a longer period without sea ice each year (Luchin et al. 2002). Although my research had not focused on climate change per se, with the newfound interest in the subject I began to realize that after so many trips to St. Matthew I had noticed some overall changes. For example, I observed how the size of the vole population related to how the arctic foxes preyed on them versus on birds. If the voles were at a peak in their population, that reduced the predation pressure on the birds because both arctic and red foxes ate more voles. And having walked over the entire island, primarily from south to north, I saw different types of terrain, different vegetation, different habitats, and different types of rock strata and how they may have varied over the years. We did do rough mapping of vegetation types to try to cover everything that existed on the island, although the general vegetation type is Arctic low shrub tundra. This was not only doing something new for science, but it was good training for me in applying textbook knowledge and in learning to record information on vegetation in a systematic, scientific manner.

There is not any single way that St. Matthew Island has been important to me. It was such a dynamic and exciting place that was fascinating to study and where, from my perspective, everything was relatively new. I started simply by investigating the reindeer population, its growth rate, and growth of individual animals by sex and age, which then shifted into studying the vegetation that was the source of food for the reindeer, and eventually my curiosity was stimulated and influenced by being at the interface of the sea and land where the birds and mammals have adapted to these special conditions. In the process, I learned much more about marine birds than I anticipated (Klein and Kleinleder 2015), which has only added to my understanding and appreciation of the entire St. Matthew Island ecosystem. There were no other biologists doing similar work there, and certainly I had the advantage over other scientists in that I had acquired all this background knowledge over the years of my previous visits. A lot of the knowledge I had accumulated was in my head, and by returning time and again I was able to write reports, publish papers, and build a corpus of scientific work on the place (Klein 1959a; Klein 1968, 1970a; 1973–1974).

In addition to what I wrote about St. Matthew Island, there have been some exciting science education products developed by others as a result of my work. For example, my former graduate student Sue Quinlan, who had studied breeding biology of storm petrels at Wooded Islands in Prince William Sound, wrote up my St. Matthew reindeer story in a science outreach book for children (Quinlan 1995). In 2007, this was included in the grade K–6 textbook *Reading Street* (Scott Foresman Company 2007). Sue did an excellent job on the chapter called "The Mystery of St. Matthew Island" that included maps, figures, and photographs to make it fascinating reading for the student audience (Quinlan 2007). I was gratified that Sue had been able to use my St. Matthew reindeer study so effectively to explain the role of science in answering complex biological questions. Stuart McMillen, a science education advocate, was another person who accepted my conclusions and utilized my St. Matthew work, although in an unusual way. He compared the St. Matthew situation to "peak oil" and global overdependence on oil production, and created a cleverly designed comic as a means of science outreach (McMillen 2017). Other material related to St. Matthew Island that appears on the Internet is a video *St. Matthew Island Integrated Science Expedition of 2012* sponsored by the Alaska Maritime National Wildlife Refuge (Burn 2012) It is gratifying to learn that our St. Matthew reindeer study has stimulated such broad and unanticipated science and educational outreach via the Internet. I strongly believe in the importance of fostering science education for young people.

David giving a lecture at the
University of Alaska Fairbanks, date
unknown. COURTESY OF DAVID KLEIN.

8

Leading the Alaska Cooperative Wildlife Research Unit and Mentoring Graduate Students

At the end 1961, while I was coordinator for the Federal Aid in Wildlife Restoration program with ADF&G in Juneau, I was offered the position to head up the Cooperative Wildlife Research Unit at the University of Alaska in Fairbanks. This position provided contact with many people in state and federal agencies around Alaska, which then connected me with a wealth of possibilities for fascinating research.

The concept of the Cooperative Wildlife Research Unit program in the United States was developed in the early 1930s through the efforts of J. N. "Ding" Darling, a conservationist and political cartoonist for a newspaper in Des Moines, Iowa. He understood the need for information to be used "for managing wildlife populations and habitats for sustained production and a means to educate a cadre of individuals to understand and to use the information properly" (Goforth 2006:5). The first Cooperative Wildlife Research Unit was established in Iowa in 1932. The basis for Cooperative Units was collaboration between the federal government, a state government, a university, and the newly established Wildlife Management Institute. The Fish and Wildlife Service paid salaries for the unit leader and assistant unit leader, the university provided office facilities and secretarial support, the state's Department of Fish and Game provided financial support for graduate student research, and the Wildlife Management Institute lobbied Congress for funding and fostered appreciation for fish and wildlife resources and their sustainable use by the American public.

The Alaska Cooperative Wildlife Research Unit was established in 1950 at the University of Alaska in Fairbanks (UAF) to support graduate training for people to become wildlife managers.[7] At the time, the University of Alaska also was establishing a graduate program in wildlife ecology and management through the Department of Biology and Wildlife. The university hired a professor of wildlife to teach the wildlife courses, and the new Unit leader became another faculty member helping them build a program; they now had two faculty members while only having to pay the salary of one. The Co-op Unit's graduate program was the first organized graduate program at the university. A couple PhDs had been awarded through the Geophysical Institute, but it was not an organized and systematic graduate-level educational program. At the time, none of the university's departmental faculty members were expected to do graduate-level teaching.

Those who served as Unit leader prior to my taking the job created a strong foundation for me to build upon. Neil Hosley was the first leader of the Alaska Wildlife Research Unit. He had been with the state wildlife department in Michigan, and his research on moose ecology and food habits was pioneering. In 1951, Hosley became dean of students, and John Buckley, who was a wildlife professor, became the new Unit leader. He had a PhD from the University of New York at Syracuse, and had extensive experience working with wetland wildlife. The next Unit leader was Robert F. (Bob) Scott, the FWS biologist whom I had assisted on mountain sheep studies and was a mentor on my MS thesis study on mountain goats. He was perhaps one of the best qualified in terms of education, training, experience, and interest. When given the opportunity for advancement within the Fish and Wildlife Service, Bob took it, and eventually became manager of the entire National Wildlife Refuge System. As a result of Bob's departure, the Alaska Wildlife Unit leader position became vacant, and Bob Scott and Neil Hosley recommended me for the position.

This offer to head the Alaska Wildlife Unit came out of the blue. When I was a graduate student, it never occurred to me that I would some day

---

7. In this chapter, the Alaska Cooperative Wildlife Research is referred to in multiple abbreviated forms: the Wildlife Unit; the Unit; or the Co-op. In later years, the name was officially changed to the Alaska Cooperative Fish and Wildlife Research Unit, when the previously separate fisheries and wildlife units were combined, but the shorthand names of Unit or Co-op continued to be used.

come back as Unit leader. It certainly was something that fit with my long-term goals, but I was modest enough to know that those things didn't just happen. I thought moving into a position like that could be a possibility in the future, but down the road many years after I had gained more experience. But in Alaska things happened fast, especially with statehood bringing about new positions to fill without enough people with the right education and experience to do the work. The Co-op Unit position required someone with more education and I was in the process of finishing my PhD, so that worked out. At first, I said I couldn't accept the position, because I had only been with ADF&G less than a year and felt I couldn't just walk out on that responsibility; they were depending on me. Plus, I hadn't finished writing my PhD dissertation yet. However, it was actually the ideal position for me, so I decided to talk with my boss, Jim Brooks. He said he appreciated my loyalty, but he thought Wildlife Unit leader would be the best thing for me. He said, "Personally, I'd rather have you stay, but if I was in your position, I'd go. You should take the job. It'll be in your best interest and you'll be working closely with us anyway." I agreed to stay until the end of June, the end of the state's fiscal year. So I became the Cooperative Wildlife Unit leader in July 1962.

When I first started, I didn't have the self-confidence as a new faculty member until I finished writing my PhD dissertation and defended in 1963. And there was some question of whether I could handle the job as a married man with two young children and a third one soon to follow, so I wondered, "Can I rise to the challenge?" But I had support from other faculty members, so that helped.

As the Unit leader, I was technically a member of the university faculty with regular faculty member responsibilities for teaching and advising students, but I was getting my salary from the Fish and Wildlife Service, so I was a federal employee. This meant I had two bosses. I had the boss in Washington, DC, heading up the thirty-nine Cooperative Wildlife Units throughout the country, and I reported to and worked under the university administration. This also meant having to work through two systems when it came to advancement. There was the federal government's merit system that required formal periodic review before moving up in position with subsequent salary increases. And at the university, I had the opportunity to advance from assistant professor to associate professor to full professor by following the whole peer review process, but the promotion came without a salary increase or access to tenure or sabbatical leave.

Some of the regular university faculty resented the fact that I had a year-round salary, whereas they only had a nine-month contract that just supported their responsibility as teachers of specific courses during the academic year. However, it was often overlooked that my commitments to manage the Wildlife Unit, raise funds, and provide advice and guidance to graduate students were year-round responsibilities. At that time, faculty were not expected to do research, many were not taking on graduate students as advisees because they weren't being paid to do that, and unless they were doing research of some kind and had a grant paying their salary in the summer they didn't work. This was a sore point with the faculty and justifiably so. The university president had a difficult time getting enough money in the university's budget to enable teaching of the basic courses, let alone pay faculty in the summer. Summer was when most of the biology and wildlife students were in the field and departmental professors would assist their student advisees prior to their field season, but then most were not available to do anything else for the student throughout the summer. Some faculty who were conscientious about advising volunteered their time in the summer to help their students, but more often than not the responsibility was left to the Unit leader, even if they were not Co-op Unit students.

One of the key changes that occurred within the whole university system after I got there was in terms of research and teaching, and I was able to play a supportive role in changing things. Beginning in the 1950s, increased research in the sciences and establishment of the Geophysical Institute and the Institute of Arctic Biology (IAB) research institutes ultimately led to the employment of research faculty. The research institutes were not tied to the academic departments, so research faculty would only do limited teaching, and rarely did it include graduate-level or specialty courses. While if you were a departmental faculty member, your job was just to teach and you didn't have to do research. This led to polarization between research and teaching faculty. Research faculty were often viewed as elitists because they had money to pay for their research and they didn't have to teach, while in comparison those faculty that did teach were underpaid. There was gradually pressure on the research institutes about how it was that they were doing all this good research, yet the university's teaching wasn't benefiting from it. The administration wanted to make better use of the research people and get them split appointments that included both research and teaching. Of course, there are some people who are good researchers but not good teachers and vice versa, and there is the question of whether a person could be a good teacher without doing any research. In my view, that's why both teaching and research are important components in evaluation and advancement in academia. In the biological sciences, we were the first to really do this split appointment between a research institute and an academic department and make it work. Partly, this worked because biology was one of the required core courses that had to be taught, so all of the department's faculty had to teach.

When I started as Unit leader, the faculty didn't have a voice in governance of the university. The faculty had no union, there was no tenure, and no standardized review process for advancement. When there was an arbitrary dismissal, there was no grievance committee or anything like that. Several faculty members felt there was a need to establish a chapter of the American Association of University Professors (AAUP) to help with faculty representation. Even though my position as Unit leader was complicated and was not salaried by the university, I tried to behave as a faculty member, was committed to working to increase the role of the faculty in the governance of the university, and believed that the success of the Wildlife Unit could best be assured by a more democratic system within the university. So I joined the AAUP and participated as a faculty member on issues of academic governance, professional ethics, and academic freedom of expression. I also was elected to the Faculty Council, which was comprised of elected faculty members and was directed to address governance issues. But it was only advisory to the president and had no direct influence. University President William "Bill" Wood would come to our meetings and explain his vision for the future of the university and then suggest we talk about his plans and provide feedback to him. We sometimes made a strong case for an alternative way of doing things, often suggesting a more democratic process than he had laid out. Wood's response would be, "Thank you, that's helpful." Then he'd go on and do his own thing. I think the university president and top administration just considered us to be young firebrands. They thought of the council as a sandbox for us faculty members to play in just to keep us busy. But we did get into some complicated issues, such as when the council didn't agree that faculty, let alone students, should be required to attend religious ceremonies at graduation. It was not enforced, but it was implied that not attending might affect your advancement. We said, "This is a state-run university and even the private universities don't force students and faculty to attend chapel." After a lot of debate, we finally won and got rid of that requirement.

Most of the faculty wanted to have more voice in governance of the university, so the Faculty Council came out with a strong statement that said if we were not going to be listened to then we were just wasting our time. We wanted a Faculty Senate that would have real authority, and we eventually made that happen. AAUP also dealt with disputes involving what we considered to be unfair treatment of faculty, and both AAUP and the Faculty Council were involved with getting the tenure system established.

It turned out that I almost got myself in hot water because of some things with AAUP. Brina Kessel, who was my department head at the time, told me that when she was at a meeting with President Wood he had wanted to look into "getting Klein transferred because he's a trouble maker." Technically, the university couldn't touch me, but Wood could report to FWS that I wasn't doing my job well from the university standpoint and request that I be replaced. Brina was very supportive of me, and she told Wood, "Klein has been doing a wonderful job as the Unit leader and as a faculty member through the Unit. But you don't have to worry about him. He's going on sabbatical to Norway for a year under a Fulbright Grant, so he's going to be totally out of campus politics." I appreciated her speaking up in my defense. When I came back from Norway, the offending issue had died down, of course, and she put my name forward for advancement to associate professor. She didn't dare do it before that. It went through without any trouble, and President Wood became civil with me after that.

At the time when Brina Kessel was head of the Department of Biology and Wildlife, male faculty weren't used to women being department heads in the sciences. In fact, in the early days of the Cooperative Wildlife Unit, only men applied for graduate work in wildlife. Eventually, women started applying and were accepted, but that was not until much later. In the post–World War II years before the Alaska Wildlife Unit was established, Druska Schaible was the only female full-time faculty member teaching biology at the University of Alaska. She eventually became dean of women at the university, but died tragically in an apartment fire in downtown Fairbanks in 1957. Brina Kessel, who had a PhD from Cornell University in ornithology, was hired in 1951 to teach both biology and wildlife courses. When Druska Schaible died, Brina became head of the Department of Biological Sciences, was named dean of the College of Biological Sciences and Renewable Resources in 1962, and in 1980 started to develop the ornithology collection at the University of Alaska Museum of the North.[8] I think the first woman faculty member hired directly by the Alaska Cooperative Unit program was Jackie D. La Perriere, who was assistant Unit leader for the Fisheries Unit, which was established as a separate entity in 1978. For me, I adapted well to working with women in the sciences. From the beginning, I always had a lot of respect for Brina. She was a good teacher and was doing excellent investigative bird research. Some of the male faculty who accepted Brina as a reasonably good department head and would acknowledge her doing good work still said, "I don't like the idea of working for a woman." It was that kind of a mentality. I never had this problem because all of the women I got to know well or married were feminists. So apparently, I was a feminist fairly early on. I was influenced by my parents who believed in equality, and the Second World War kind of broke down a lot of those barriers of men being the breadwinners and women only working in the home.

When I started as the Wildlife Unit leader, I was the only faculty member in the unit, and there was one secretary. As time went on, assistant Unit leader positions were approved nationwide for the Cooperative Research Unit System, and I ended up having three different assistant leaders. Peter Lent was the first one. He had been a student at UAF and did caribou investigations during the Cape Thompson studies associated with Project Chariot (Lent 1962; Wilimovsky 1966), and completed his PhD on caribou

8. For more about Brina Kessel and her role at the University of Alaska Fairbanks, especially with Project Chariot, see Daniel T. O'Neill. 1994. *Firecracker Boys.* New York: St. Martin's Press.

at the University of Alberta. We worked well together, sharing some of the administrative burden of the Wildlife Unit, but he also advised a moderate to heavy load of graduate students, spent extensive time in the field assisting student research projects, and doing his own research on caribou, reindeer, and muskoxen behavior and ecology. I was fortunate to have such a broadly experienced, adaptable, and capable assistant Unit leader who contributed substantially to the productivity and quality of the work of the Unit while maintaining his own professional advancement as a scientist. It also gave me the opportunity to focus more on students, my own research, or take time off if I needed to. I felt it was good for me to do these things and in the long run would make me a more effective Unit leader.

When the Alaska Cooperative Fishery Research Unit was established separately from the Wildlife Unit, this meant there was now a Fishery Unit leader and a Fishery assistant Unit leader, in addition to the Wildlife Unit leader and assistant leader. Eventually, there was pressure from Washington to merge the Wildlife and Fisheries Units. It made sense in terms of funding and administration, because it reduced the number of people required to operate the Units. Only one leader and one assistant leader would be needed at a merged Unit, instead of the previous two for each. The joint Cooperative Fish and Wildlife Research Unit was established in 1991, and all the administration and budgets and proposals were being handled through the university's Institute of Arctic Biology (IAB), and there were some advantages to that. I was offered the position of Unit leader for the merged units, however, I didn't want to take on additional administrative responsibilities. I wanted to continue to focus on my research on wildlife in the Arctic who were experiencing rapid change as a consequence of the changing climate and continued emphasis on oil and resource development in Alaska's Arctic. I appreciated that my Washington supervisors felt, as I did, that I could best serve the Cooperative Research Unit program in the special position of senior scientist where I would continue to be involved in research activities and advisement of graduate students but have less administrative responsibility. Jim Reynolds, a fisheries biologist, became the overall joint Unit leader. The most recent Unit leader has been Brad Griffith, who just retired in 2018, and who had expertise in wildlife population modeling.

David's graduate students Olav Hjeljord (front) and Spencer Linderman skiing at Denali National Park while doing fieldwork, circa 1970.
PHOTO BY DAVID KLEIN.

I have a lot of pride in the Biology and Wildlife Departments and the Institute of Arctic Biology at UAF and how they have worked together. The relationship between the regular Biology and Wildlife faculty and the Wildlife Unit sometimes was a problem, especially early on. But it got better. Some of it related to salaries; they weren't always in synchrony. However, IAB was great for collaboration. The faculty would gather daily for a coffee break where we talked to one another about our work or items of daily interest. Sometimes faculty members would argue and disagree strongly, but we generally respected one another. We collaborated frequently and coauthored papers, and put on conferences together. We were all part of a team and that was what gained the Cooperative Wildlife Unit here in Alaska recognition for being one of the most effective Wildlife Research Units in the United

States. Some of the others were good units, but on their campuses they were thought of as the Feds because they were not as good at including others.

The longer I served as Unit leader and interacted with others in the university administration, the more I became convinced of the value of the Wildlife Unit and tried to instill it in others. I think it is a great concept and I believed that the main reason we existed was to train young people at the graduate level for positions with state and federal agencies. I thought this was a wonderful way to do it, because students would easily get exposure to agencies and sometimes the agencies would be providing in-kind support with aircraft or assistance with fieldwork. The Wildlife Unit students were meeting biologists and other agency personnel that were potential future employers. These contacts increased their chances of finding jobs after graduation. In the 1970s, I became curious about what other Wildlife Units around the country were doing in terms of how they were educating their students about the basics of biology and ecology. I was pretty biased toward the kinds of academic arrangements that we had in Alaska, both from my own experience and from visiting some of the other Wildlife Units and seeing how they did things. I always lobbied for having biology and wildlife together in a single academic department, because I felt understanding basic biology and ecology were essential for being a successful wildlife manager. So I sent a questionnaire to each Unit leader asking the following questions:

1. Is your Wildlife Unit affiliated with a university academic department that puts primary emphasis on wildlife courses and secondary emphasis on basic biology courses or a university academic department that puts primary emphasis on basic biology courses and secondary emphasis on wildlife courses?

2. Which of the two options would you prefer at your unit: primary emphasis on basic biology courses or primary emphasis on wildlife courses?

Results of the survey of the thirty-nine Wildlife Units indicated there was about an equal split between emphasizing basic biology courses versus wildlife courses. More surprising to me was that unit leaders were essentially satisfied with the existing course emphasis at their units.

Part of the job of both the unit leader and assistant leader was to advise and guide graduate students through the program and to seek additional funding if necessary to support their students. Before statehood, the Alaska Wildlife Unit might get in-kind support for students doing thesis projects, but there was limited direct support. This changed with statehood when the newly established Alaska Department of Fish and Game (ADF&G) started providing a fixed amount per year to the Co-op Unit for graduate student stipends from Pittman-Robertson Federal Aid in Wildlife Restoration Act funds. Even though this was a small amount, it was critically important support for Wildlife Unit students. When I became Unit leader, my efforts were split between securing funds before accepting new students for a project, and raising supplemental funds to help existing students with projects that had exceeded initially estimated costs. Graduate students always had to be on the lookout for supplemental funding because stipend money from the Unit was usually insufficient to cover all the costs of their research and thesis completion.

Since the Wildlife Unit started, it had been broadening the type of research it was doing because the wildlife issues in Alaska that needed to be better understood for management purposes were becoming more varied and complicated, and of increasing interest to the public. It was becoming obvious that studies were needed by the Territory of Alaska and later the ADF&G that went beyond management of traditional hunting of large terrestrial wildlife, trapping of furs, and management of migratory waterfowl, to obtaining a better understanding of the broad ecology of species and specific habitats. Students frequently had a greater potential for additional funding if they worked on studies that were of interest to the territory or state. And if the students could get more of their own money and didn't need as much from the Unit, the Unit could support more students overall. Nevertheless, I still often had to lobby federal agencies for additional funding, even if a student may have already received partial support from them. I had to keep my ear to what would be available and build up relationships with all of them. And I did. For example, I had a good relationship with Tom Hanley at the Forest Research Laboratory in Juneau, which is a subsidiary of the Pacific Northwest Forest and Range Research Station in Portland, Oregon. Tom often approached me when there was a need for new studies that would be appropriate for Wildlife Unit investigations and suitable for master's or PhD projects. And if a student had been funded by an agency, then often I would have someone from that agency serve on the thesis committee. I had a similar, but less personal, relationship with the Bureau of Land Management, the National Park Service, the Forest Service, and the Fish and Wildlife Service. It was important to maintain diversity in funding of Unit research. I was always trying to establish good contacts for the future. And I enjoyed those connections because I was working with well-qualified people that I respected. Some of them I'd known for a long time, and some not at all previously.

One of my main strategies was to jointly get funding from multiple sources. All of the federal and state organizations and agencies did not always have the greatest working relationship, but by having worked with each of them I had a clear understanding of how they functioned internally. When they could do it through the Unit and both contribute some funding, this helped to avoid polarization and encouraged them to cooperate. Usually, the amount of money that each component was able to contribute was not great, but put together it made for a successful project. We also had to take into consideration the fact that both at the state and federal level, budgets change politically, seasonally, and with the changes in the economy, so they did not always have a lot of money in their budgets for research. It sometimes was easier to get smaller amounts. The real advantage was that by state and federal agencies working together, the students got better training and experience. The student was always the primary consideration: that they finish their project in a reasonable time frame, do it satisfactorily from the student's standpoint, and earn their degree.

By funding student thesis research through the Co-op Units, we could assure these agencies that the greatest proportion of their grant money was used directly for student support and not for overhead or other administrative costs. We could go to the Fish and Wildlife Service, ADF&G, the Forest Service, the National Park Service, or the Bureau of Land Management and say you've indicated an interest in some area and if you support a student to do the study with a grant of ten to fifteen thousand dollars your money will

Graduate student Lisa Saperstein (left) and botanist Joan Foote (right) looking at post-fire recovery of rooted plants versus lichens in the Selawik Flats, circa 1990. PHOTO BY DAVID KLEIN.

go a lot further than if you did the project yourself or contracted with the university. Or sometimes their staff wouldn't necessarily have the expertise or the time available to focus on a project and then they would have to hire additional people whose salaries would have cost them megabucks compared to having a student do the work. So it was often a better deal for these agencies. For example, there were a lot of research questions that related to management of marine mammals who were preying on salmon, halibut, and other valuable commercially harvested fish, and, at the time, there were no Fish and Wildlife Service biologists that were trained to work on this, so it made sense to let students do the research.

While research through the Wildlife Unit often enabled agencies to get studies done, it was particularly valuable for the students. Frequently, it led to their getting jobs after they finished their degrees. After statehood, both state and federal agencies were growing organizations with increasing responsibilities, and funding for federal aid and wildlife restoration work was increasing. More and more, they were in need of well-trained and educated wildlife biologists and managers. So the Unit almost was like an apprenticeship program for our students.

By finding money to fund research projects and getting students involved in those research projects, I was sort of setting a research agenda for the Unit. We were sort of like a contractor for federal agency research projects. The projects were all within my interest from the standpoint of understanding ecological systems and their management, so it fit with my research, but I also realized that it tied in with all of the teaching and my interaction with the students. I did have a salary and a small budget that covered mostly travel expenses to do my job, but then I was free to do research if I could fund it. Sometimes I would do research in association with a student and getting a student started on a project, but I also was able to apply to agencies and organizations for funding of my own projects as well. It was a good arrangement in many ways.

I enjoyed the complexity of my job as Unit leader, but it was challenging. In addition to advising my own students and teaching at minimum one course a year at the graduate level, I also served on committees of other students in Biology and Wildlife, and had the responsibility associated with supporting my students as well as others in the program whose major professors might be faculty in the Biology and Wildlife Department. I also had commitments as a faculty member to attend departmental faculty meetings, as well as university administration meetings. I sat on panels that were made up of institute directors that were time consuming and sometimes seemingly not too productive, but it was important to maintain a presence and recognition of the Cooperative Unit program within the university system. I definitely preferred to spend the majority of my time involved in the research of my student advisees and my own research in the field, rather than be in my office working on administrative items. However, I soon became aware that my time spent in administration and searching for funding was essential for the success of my students and the long-term well-being of the Alaska Unit as a whole. The real challenge for me was how to keep focused on the most enjoyable aspects of my work and maintain my own psychological well-being. That included balancing my job with a home life where I had a growing young family, along with time spent with students, whether that was doing research with them in the field, advising them regarding their education, or being in the classroom with them.

Although I didn't have to teach as much as regular faculty, when I did teach, it usually was a graduate-level course. But I only taught one or two courses a year. My teaching usually involved a graduate-level field course or a combination of classroom and field lab. However, there was no money in the department to support going into the field, so I would try to get money through the Co-op Unit. Sometimes, the ten-day field courses went to Southeast Alaska and other times to the Kenai Peninsula. The trips in Southeast involved boat trips where the students had to pay for their ferry ticket, but I was able to negotiate the use of smaller boats for specific site visits at no cost to us. Because I had appropriate connections from

Members of the spring field course on a trip to the Kenai Peninsula observing mountain sheep on a slope above Kenai Lake near Cooper Landing, 1980s. David is on the far right wearing the patterned sweater and leaning against the front of the station wagon. PHOTO BY DAVID KLEIN.

the past, I frequently could shame the Fish and Wildlife Service agency heads into supporting the course by making their boat available. The cost of one boat charter would have greatly exceeded university funds available for the course. I explained that the students should know what the Fish and Wildlife Service does, and there's no better way than to go out and work with them directly. When the field course went to the Kenai Peninsula, we toured the Kenai National Wildlife Refuge, visiting its diverse wildlife habitats while learning about its associated wildlife management practices. In the early days at the unit, we had our own vehicle for a while, a station wagon, which I used to transport students, so that was a good deal. But then the university wanted all vehicles to be under their system, which became problematic, because it meant we now had to pay for use of a vehicle. I was able to keep the cost of the field course low for the students in other ways by obtaining free use of agency bunkhouses or facilities, and we prepared our own food as much as possible.

All of this took a lot of coordination on my part and a lot of leaning on people that I had known for a long time. But once they came through, then it was great, and, of course, that made these trips wonderful. It was wonderful for all of us. If I could get the agency to pay for it, then I could get some of their biologists to go out with us so I was not the only one along with appropriate expertise or experience. Of course, the students were the major beneficiaries, but I also was building contacts that strengthened the relationship between the Unit and these agencies. These field trips were usually the most popular courses offered at the university. I enjoyed doing these trips and being out with and getting to know the students, and in seeing the complexity of the planned trip become reality.

The one course I would teach every other year was called grazing ecology. It was all about the winter ecology of herbivorous wildlife, be it the large mammals like moose and caribou, those intermediate in size like hares and porcupines, and small ones like lemmings and voles. It also included the resident herbivorous birds like ptarmigan and grouse that through evolution have collectively shaped plant forms and consequently have altered seasonal landscapes. I usually would ask at least two other faculty members who I respected to join me in team-teaching the course. These were primarily Steve Maclean, who taught ecology courses, Bob White, who did extensive

Bob White (standing) with a graduate student investigating the possibility of doing PhD research on muskoxen on Nunivak Island, circa 1980. PHOTO BY DAVID KLEIN.

research on the ecophysiology of caribou and other ruminants, and Terry Chapin, who taught and did extensive research on plant community ecology and physiology. We all gave talks about our areas of expertise and then sat in on the student presentations that covered the variety of topics we had discussed in class.

A highlight of the field course was a weekend in April where we based at the IAB log cabin near Cantwell along the Alaska Highway. Jack Luick had arranged for the cabin to be built at the reindeer research station where earlier he had been funded by the Atomic Energy Commission through IAB to study the effects on reindeer and caribou feeding on lichens contaminated by radioactive fallout from US and Soviet atmospheric testing of atomic bombs, and later built a sauna adjacent to the clear-water stream that flowed behind the cabin. I led the students on excursions on skis or snowshoes into the surrounding landscape where caribou, moose, snowshoe hares, and all three species of Alaska's ptarmigan were wintering. Generally, we were able to observe some of these herbivores while they were feeding, but students also learned through their observations how herbivores differentially affect the plant species that they depend upon for their winter survival. The evolutionary interaction between the herbivores and their primary plant forage species was a primary interest of mine, as well as being the focus of thesis research by several of my graduate advisees. The field trip was fun for both students and faculty involved, and we had excellent discussions and debates in the cabin during morning and evening meals or in the sauna after a long day of skiing.

These field courses were also so enjoyable for me because being outdoors and camping were important things in my life. I did a lot of it, both with my family and my students. In addition to the official course, I also organized a lot of field trips for students, both in the summer and the winter. Even if the trip did not involve direct teaching, it was always related to the responsibility I felt in helping students learn how to live safely in the wild and in the Arctic. Some of their thesis field research was going to take them out to unfamiliar places and extreme conditions that they might not be fully prepared to deal with, and I wanted them to have some experience before they went out on their own. One of the things we tried to do regularly, which I really appreciated, were recreational ski trips on weekends in the late winter based out of the IAB cabin at Cantwell.

My family and I also did ski trips in the wintertime, and went on camping trips together in the summer. By the time my three kids were preteens and teens, they were busy with school and scouting activities, so it was harder to get the whole family together, but when we could all go on camping trips it was great fun. One place that became very special to me was Quartz Lake, because in 1973, after returning from sabbatical in Norway, we bought a lot there and built an eighteen-by-twenty-four-foot log cabin on a bluff overlooking the lake. This became a family project. While I used a bow saw and axe to cut the logs in the spruce forest above the cabin site, Arlayne, PeggyEllen, and Laura stripped the bark from the freshly cut logs. My son, Martin, played a major role in helping me drag the dry logs to the cabin site in early winter, and then with the actual construction the following spring. After we finished the cabin, we spent a lot of time there. In the summertime, it was swimming in the lake and hiking, and in the wintertime, we enjoyed cross-country skiing. I sold the cabin to a friend in 2016.

In 1987, I built another remote recreational cabin. It was a five-by-eight-foot stone hut with a metal roof located in the hills east of Fairbanks along the North Fork of the Chena River. It was a beautiful spot high on a ridge top with a beautiful view. Building it was quite a project because it was about five miles to ski or hike in and we had to carry in all of the building supplies. I built the hut up against an embankment of a cliff, so the back wall was the natural rock and then built up the other walls from rocks collected in the area. We had a woodstove in that hut, so despite some cold spots and frost build-up on the inside, it made for a cozy and warm shelter during a winter or spring ski trip. Although, the snow drifted in so much that we had to dig out the place when we arrived, including down to the roof so the stovepipe could be put up. We used the hut for several years, but eventually Mother Nature took its toll. Porcupines got into the cabin, causing significant damage, and a big wildfire in 2006 came through the area and burnt the trail and the surroundings. Eventually, porcupine chewing destabilized the roof and a section blew off in a big storm. That was the end of using the stone hut.

I really liked working with students and teaching them about the natural world. When we were doing ski trips or going hiking, you could rationalize that you were training the students, but the students and I were all just having a wonderful time in life. I loved getting out in the field where we were communing with nature, and where you could read all the information that was out there about wildlife that we were all interested in.

While my own research focus was on ungulates primarily and their plant and habitat relationships, one of the reasons I liked the Cooperative Unit was it forced you to be broader and to work with other people. Being a broad ecologist like this was a bit unusual within the field of wildlife biology where you gained recognition as a specialist. Now, there's more of a tendency to recognize that we should be broader in our understanding of the ecosystems that we're working within, especially from the standpoint of applied management. While being broad in my research and approach is not typical, there are others that have done the same thing, but perhaps not as broad as I have been. I think collaborating with colleagues forced all of us to think more broadly, do better science, and provide a broader education to our students. Also, when helping students get started, you have to become broader and broader in your thinking. I loved this part where I learned as much from the students as they learned from me.

One biologist in particular at IAB who I bonded with as a friend and collaborated with was Bob White. After I'd been here a couple years as the Wildlife Unit leader, he came as a postdoc from Australia. He was an animal physiologist and was interested in how the function of the rumen of sheep and cows worked in relationship to horses, which have a different kind of a system. Although Bob had not yet completed his PhD, he was encouraged to accept a position developing a program in IAB focusing on rumen physiology under Professor Jack Luick. I liked Bob and realized that his training and research in the physiology of domestic animals would likely enable him to transition into wildlife ecophysiology. I provided several opportunities for him to see much of Alaska and gain experience in the ecophysiology of Alaska wild ruminants, especially moose and caribou.

For example, I brought Bob White along when I was working with reindeer in the Aleutian Islands with Robert Moss, an IAB and Wildlife Unit postdoc, and a brilliant young scientist from Scotland who had done research on land management practices to facilitate red grouse production and was familiar with the moorlands of northern Scotland, which had been deforested for lumber and sustained grazing pressure by sheep and other livestock. Prior to this, L. J. Palmer, who was one of the early wildlife biologists in Alaska, had started studies of lichens on the reindeer ranges in the Aleutians back in the 1920s and early '30s when there were a lot more reindeer out there (Palmer 1926; Palmer and Rouse 1945). He set up vegetation plots to see what the impact was on the lichen from all the grazing. Sort of as a follow-up, I was funded by the Bureau of Land Management to investigate the foraging dynamics of less than a thousand free-ranging introduced reindeer on Umnak Island, where there also were more than ten thousand domestic sheep. The sheep were being ranched largely for wool production by one family who lived out there throughout the year and used limited fencing or herding. I had a permit to kill a couple of Aleutian reindeer to determine their body condition and to look for parasites and diseases. This meant that Bob White could work with fresh-killed animals to collect data.

He was able to do some quick observations in the field to see what kind of organisms were in their stomachs, and collect rumen samples for later research on the fermentation processes.

I did not appreciate at the time how fortunate I was to have both Bobs with me on Umnak Island at that time. They both had insight about the role of sheep in altering the vegetative landscape, although in two quite distinct and widely separated parts of the global landscape, and here we were all together in the Aleutians sharing this connection in this so-called wilderness landscape altered by a domestic herbivore. We all gained from that mentally stimulating time together and returned to the university each with new ideas for the direction of our own future research. Bob Moss went on to do some interesting research on ptarmigan and digestion of their winter food (Moss 1973). Bob White ultimately became internationally recognized for the quality and extent of his research on the ecophysiology of northern ungulates, and he and I continued to collaborate in many ways during our joint tenure at UAF. We served as members of each other's graduate student committees with each bringing our own perspective. Bob and I gained reputations for challenging one another, but both agreed that disagreement and arguments among scientists created a healthy learning environment for students. In fact, both Bob and I were viewed as good scientist role models for students because of our argumentativeness. However, Bob and I also were always kidding one another. Like when we were together in the Aleutian Islands and observed sheep ranching there, I enjoyed teasing him that as an Australian he was happiest when he could jump into a corral with a bunch of sheep. We also gave joint seminars and coauthored papers together, like in 1985 when we presented a joint paper on comparative foraging strategies of northern herbivores at the Fourth International Theriological Conference in Edmonton, Canada (White and Klein 1985). And finally, we organized conferences and symposia together, such as in 1972 when we jointly organized the First International Reindeer and Caribou Symposium with Jack Luick and Peter Lent (Luick et al. 1975), or in 1977 when we co-organized a symposium and workshop on caribou population ecology in Alaska and co-edited the proceedings (Klein and White 1978).

I also teamed up with faculty members in other disciplines. The university was small enough then that we had more interaction with those from other disciplines, like anthropology, geology, or the physical sciences, although, doing interdisciplinary collaboration was not always common or easy. One of my earliest collaborations was with Dale Guthrie, who was educated in paleontology at the University of Chicago. As a paleontologist, he had good training in biology, but not much in general ecology. Dale became focused on ecology because he was trying to explain what the environment for mammoths, muskoxen, and horses had been like during full glaciation more than fifteen thousand years ago. We knew there weren't many trees around then, so the question was what were these herbivores eating. There were other people doing studies on vegetation and looking for relics of the past, and through some of his own research Dale had shown it was a different environment than in modern times. While he wanted to know what plants were there, I was more interested in animal adaptation and food limitation and in the ecology of the present complex of wildlife species within the Alaska environment. Despite our differences, there was a remarkable overlap of our interests and I enjoyed my discussions with Dale. We both were linear thinkers and built on one another's differing knowledge through debate and mutual exchange of knowledge, though not without argument and rejection of hypotheses poorly supported. We also were both hunters who primarily enjoyed the excitement and challenge of the stalk and the chase, but also the satisfaction hunting brought as a food gatherer feeding the family. So Dale and I became close friends.

Another important nonbiology collaboration for me was when I initiated a discussion group on environmental philosophy jointly with philosophy professor Rudy Krejci. I wanted to have more discussion with graduate students about environmental philosophy and the world we live in, including management of resources in a responsible way so you don't destroy them, but environmental philosophy was not then a course offered in a biology/wildlife program. It seemed a better fit with the philosophy program, but there was no graduate program in the Philosophy Department at that time, nor was there interest in the topic. So Rudy and I decided to try it in the Biology and Wildlife program. There were problems fitting it into the department's teaching schedule, so it ended up being just Rudy and me hosting a noncredit discussion group with about five or six grad students from biology and wildlife, most being Wildlife Unit students. I usually would pick the topic, for example, the ethics of trapping, or a major conservation issue like the proposed construction of the Rampart Dam, trying to keep it on the philosophical level rather than being branded as an environmentalist. I relied on Rudy to show how classic philosophers dealt with similar topics in the past, and he was an important contributor to the discussions. Finally, these environmental philosophy discussion sessions boiled down to meeting informally about every two weeks in the evening at my home and I would suggest a specific reading be done in advance to get the discussion started.

Another benefit enjoyed by the Unit was that if a wildlife-related issue was controversial and the state and federal governments were at odds with one another, a solution was to have the Cooperative Unit do the study because we were within the sanctuary of the university and not government controlled. For example, Alaska had many challenges associated with resource development, especially with oil development on the North Slope in the 1970s. The pro-development interests and the related industries didn't have enough knowledge of how to proceed nor were there specific directions of how to do things in the natural environment from the responsible agencies, and the scientific community didn't have enough knowledge about wildlife and wildlife habitat relationships and how wildlife populations might respond under both short-term and long-term development. That meant the university and the Co-op Unit were in a position to get better funding to research these issues, but we also realized that any research we'd do would be highly scrutinized, especially in cases where the results were not pleasing to the oil industry or other development interests. Although the oil industry was contributing money to our research, we had the advantage of serving state and federal interests at the same time, so that helped with working toward compromise.

As the Cooperative Wildlife Unit leader, I was often in the middle of the controversy over assessing the impact of oil development. I remember an encounter at a meeting with the dean of Engineering and Science at UAF who, as an engineer, found it difficult to understand and accept why biologists were being funded to do studies in the North Slope oil fields. My recollection of his frustrated outburst was, "Why do these damn biologists have to be involved in planning for the pipeline? I mean, it's the engineers that are involved and necessary here. The oil industry is far more capable of designing a pipeline that will work where caribou are moving than a bunch of biologists that go up there and are being paid big bucks and it's like a vacation for them." I spoke with him afterward and said, "Well, that was an engineer's perspective. Now do you want to hear the biologist's perspective?" He realized that he shouldn't have said what he did.

While I might fight for something I believed in, like the fairness of firing someone without cause or the pipeline issues, on the other hand I had to be super careful because of my position with both the Fish and Wildlife Service and the university. My goal was to try to maintain credibility, as well as not add to the polarizing arguments over issues. It was critical to stick to findings of basic science and emphasize the fact that our studies were done according to strict scientific principles that were subject to peer review and criticism. I nevertheless had responsibility to speak out as a scientist when we clearly distrusted what the oil industry was trying to do. For instance, it was ethically wrong for consulting firms to take money from the oil industry and do so-called "research" that then would yield results prescribed by the oil industry.

University president William Wood didn't like my challenging the Trans-Alaska Pipeline design from the standpoint of its potential obstruction to movements of caribou. He felt that I was obstructing progress. I gave a talk once where two or three of us spoke about some of these problems and Wood was in the audience. There were questions from the audience, and I remember he asked me, "Well, I can't understand why the caribou don't go under the pipeline." There was certainly phony information coming out in the media about how a pipeline wasn't going to obstruct anything. I replied to Dr. Wood by saying, "Well, that's a good question, and if caribou could communicate with us I could probably provide you with an answer." He appreciated my resorting to humor to emphasize my humility regarding his question. Then I told him about the research we were planning to do to study how caribou would respond to various obstructions. I explained, "Yeah, if you get a caribou running fast enough, it might be able to jump over the pipeline. But they're not jumpers, usually. If they were antelope, yeah, they could handle it, but we just didn't know enough yet about what the caribou would do."

Exchanges with Other Cooperative Wildlife Units

My experience working overseas, where I had so many wonderful experiences with foreign colleagues that expanded my understanding of varied scientific approaches, as well of different environments, people, and cultures, inspired my idea that we ought to have an exchange program within the Cooperative Wildlife Unit program to try to bring the Co-op Units around the country closer together. I realized how beneficial such educational and scientific exchanges were for all those involved. So I made the suggestion to Reid Goforth, the national supervisor for the wildlife units, that short-term reciprocal visits between Unit leaders would be beneficial for the program. He was supportive, but pointed out that given the associated costs for travel and per diem to visit another Unit would likely make it a hard sell. I emphasized that the exchanges would only be for a couple of weeks, would be strictly voluntary, organizing them would be the sole responsibility of the two units involved, and that costs could be kept low if the visiting partner stayed as a guest in the host's own home. Staying with your colleague and their family was not only convenient, but also enjoyable. The idea also was that those who came on these exchanges would have time to interact with students and get out in the field to visit Unit projects.

I did the first exchange by visiting the Ohio Unit. Some of the other Unit leaders said, "Why would the Unit Leader in Alaska want to go and do an exchange with Ohio?" I said, "I wanted to go there to see how they carried out their program." Right away, I established a close friendship with Ted Bookhout, the Ohio Unit Leader. He was a top-notch guy. They did a lot of waterfowl work, so we looked at a lot of marshes and I learned about major problems they were facing and possible solutions. It was fascinating.

Then Ted visited Alaska. We knew that he was not going to be able to see all of Alaska in a week or ten days' time, so we tied him in with my spring field course, which that year was a road trip to the Kenai Peninsula. He had a wonderful sense of humor, which we all enjoyed, and he was a real asset for the field course. Ted also joined me and graduate student, Bob Summerfield, for a three-day trip to look for wintering mountain sheep along the proposed route of the Trans-Alaska Oil Pipeline. Ted and Bob snowshoed and hiked through Atigun Canyon searching for sheep, while Ken Whitten, an ADF&G biologist, and I skied a more challenging and longer route over a

5,000 foot pass between the headwaters of the Sagavanirktok and Atigun Rivers. The weather was clear and ideal for our search for the wintering sheep and the mountain landscape was particularly beautiful in the rapidly returning sunlight of a northern spring. It was, however, colder than expected for late April with daytime temperatures dropping from minus 10°F to minus 35°F at night. In view of Ted's inexperience in sleeping out in the extreme cold of the Arctic, I had advised Bob that they should excavate a large snow cave for them to spend the night in. At the slightly higher elevation where Ken and I spent the night, there were no snowdrifts deep enough for digging a snow cave so we used a small tent. To keep our packs light for skiing and not anticipating the extreme temperature drop at night, we had not brought warm enough sleeping bags. We knew we would have to do everything right in order to make it through the night and get going again the next day. Late the next morning, Ken and I met up with Bob and Ted and they were equally excited about having weathered the cold night successfully. All in all, Ted appreciated the experience and it turned out that he and Bob saw many more mountain sheep than Ken and I did. Because of this trip, I was able to share with Ted the unique nature of our Co-op Unit work in Alaska, as well as teach him about the unique adaptations of mountain sheep and other arctic ungulates that enable them to survive the harsh cold of arctic winter.

The next Wildlife Unit exchange was between Norm Smith, the assistant Unit leader at the Arizona Unit and myself. Norm, an ardent wildlife photographer, hosted my visit to the Arizona Unit, which I found fascinating largely because of the focus on desert ecology. I've always been interested in desert habitat because of the adaptations plants and animals have to make to survive in a hot and dry environment. Plant defenses against herbivory had become an interesting focus for me, so it was intriguing to see that while spines generally protect cacti from being eaten by herbivores, desert mountain sheep learned to stomp the small barrel cactus open with their hooves to obtain the stored water inside and eat the succulent internal tissues. I also was able to observe firsthand how the physiological adaptations of desert wildlife parallels, in many ways, those of Arctic and Subarctic wildlife, where animals are adapted to extreme seasonality in availability of liquid water. When Norm visited the Alaska Unit, we again timed it to coincide with my spring field course. This time it was to Southeast Alaska, where there were excellent opportunities for photography. He interacted well with the students and contributed substantially to the field course, as well as appreciating the chance to become familiar with a diversity of Alaska's habitat types.

A third Unit exchange took place with Mike Vaughan, the assistant leader at the Virginia Cooperative Wildlife Research Units based at Virginia Polytechnic Institute (VPI) in Blacksburg. He showed me several areas where Unit projects were under way, including attempts at wildlife habitat recovery where surface mining of coal had left acid-polluted streams and soils; coastal sand dune stabilization to protect coastal wetlands on the Virginia and North Carolina coasts; and investigation of the distribution and status of endangered freshwater clam populations affected by stream pollution. Mike was beginning a study of black bear in Virginia, which required live capture and monitoring of bears though radio collaring, so when he came on his reciprocal visit to Alaska, I arranged for him to join black bear studies being conducted by ADF&G biologists near Fairbanks. The connection with Mike continued through a collaboration with my PhD student, Merav Ben-David, who was working in Southeast Alaska investigating the role of brown bears in spreading nutrients brought by spawning salmon (Ben-David et al. 1998). I considered this collaboration to be the major benefit resulting from the exchange between the two units.

Graduate Student Diversity

Being an educator and working with students is one of the things I really enjoyed about working at the Co-op Unit. But when I first began, I didn't have any experience as a professor advising graduate students, and I took on students working on projects whose topic was not in my field because there was nobody else to do it. I should point out, though, that most of the young people wanted someone who understood the ecology of animal populations and could deal with management conservation. Those kind of were challenges, but they were good for me because they forced me to broaden my understanding. Like if I was advising a student on a subject I was not familiar with, such as a study of sea lions in Prince William Sound, I wanted to learn as much as I could, especially when I was going out in the field with them. If I didn't know at least a little something about their topic, how could

David's graduate student, Peggy Kuropat (in the foreground), and Tata Ringberg, a Norwegian physiologist visiting the Institute of Arctic Biology, observing the Western Arctic Caribou Herd as part of Peggy's study on the timing of forage selection by caribou at their calving grounds, circa 1983. PHOTO BY DAVID KLEIN.

I advise them if they came to me with questions about what they were finding? Everybody should have the humility to be in a learning environment. I've always felt that I've always been a student myself and I want to learn as much as I can about the world I live in. I'm just ecologically curious. In addition, working with other members of these graduate committees who were knowledgeable about other specialties taught me things that I could apply to my own research.

I advised so many graduate students that I cannot talk about all of them. But I am proud of how many continued on to do interesting wildlife work within a professional or academic setting. At the moment, however, there are a number that come to mind. One of the early students I had was Steve Young, who was really committed to understanding vegetation and blueberries. I had good botanical training, but nothing to understand the community relationships of blueberries. He came from a smaller college in Vermont where he'd had a lot of focus on botany, so had a good background. I was his major professor because there wasn't anybody else on campus to do it. It turned out to be fun. It forced me to draw heavily on my previous training in botany, and to build on and strengthen it. I used to kid him that he got into blueberries because he loved blueberry pie. He was a top-notch student, and turned out to be a leader in Arctic vegetation research, including some classic work on the vegetation of St. Lawrence Island. After he completed his master's, he went on and did a PhD, and then went back to Vermont and became a faculty member at Middlebury College. I never realized he would go in this direction, and it made me feel good to know that this student of mine did so well.

Another student I remember was Finn Sandegren from Sweden who wanted to study the behavior of sea lions. Finn had an outgoing personality, had excellent grades, and was a highly motivated young person. The Alaska Department of Fisheries funded his thesis research at a large sea lion colony on Wooded Islands off the southwest coast of Montague Island in Prince William Sound. Finn was a good photographer, so he took a series of 35-millimeter color slides illustrating breeding and maternal-young behavior of the sea lions. However, he really wanted his thesis to include black-and-white illustrations of the behavior positions. So I asked my neighbor, Bill Berry, who was an outstanding wildlife artist, if he could help. Bill was modest, explaining that he was not familiar with marine mammals, but agreed to give it a try. The line drawings turned out to be an important part of Finn's thesis (Sandegren 1969). We were lucky that there were people that could help out like this. Ultimately, Finn returned to Sweden where he became director of Sweden's major wildlife research institute.

Another grad student that I took on as major advisor was Tom Compton, who was actually a student in the School of Agriculture and Land Resources Management (currently the School of Natural Resources and Extension). His proposed thesis research was on summer grazing of domestic livestock on natural vegetation in an alpine habitat in Southcentral Alaska. Funding was through the Department of Agriculture and the university's Agricultural and Forestry Experiment Station in Palmer (currently the Matanuska Experiment Farm and Extension Center). None of the faculty in that program felt qualified to serve as Tom's major advisor because they had no experience with alpine vegetation, so they asked if I would be willing to do it, given my experience with grazing ruminants in relationship to alpine vegetation. I talked with Tom, who was already employed as a herder of cattle being grazed on natural habitat in the Talkeetna Mountains, and was impressed by his general understanding of the nature and feasibility of the proposed research. From my perspective and wildlife bias, Tom's thesis was quite acceptable. Tom was able to show that if cows are put out to graze on a natural mountain pasture when plants are starting to grow in early summer, they select forage that is of the highest nutritive quality, and they learn to avoid eating plants that are toxic to them, such as false hellebore (*Veratrum viride*) and lupine (*Lupinus Arcticus*). Wildlife does this same sort of thing, with young animals learning which plants are good for them and which they should avoid. So this project related well to studies that were being done with wildlife, and it was great to have this crossover into applied agriculture.

Another Land Resources Management student that I took on was Bob Ritchie, who was working on a degree in land use and recreation, but they didn't have any faculty at the time who wanted to take on the responsibility of being his major advisor. Bob had thought things out well, was dedicated to the goals he had set for himself, and had a good academic record, so I agreed to be his major advisor. The focus for his thesis research was the Yukon-Charley Rivers National Preserve, so we were able to obtain funding from the National Park Service. Part of his research was focused on the Yukon River, and I joined him on a canoe trip from Eagle to Circle in a homemade canoe I had. We camped out along the way, and I got to know Bob well and enjoyed his company. We shared a common sense of humor and it was a fun trip. I felt he was going to be an outstanding graduate student that I would enjoy working with. And that turned out to be the case. Working with Bob was very satisfying for me because I felt that I played a real part in his career development. In 1976, Bob and another graduate student of mine, Jim Curatolo, started ABR (Alaska Biological Research), a science-based environmental consulting firm in Fairbanks. Eventually, the company expanded, and through the years ABR has hired a lot of our graduates. In 2018, Bob retired from running the company.

David's graduate student Martha Robus at her winter field camp, used during her study of muskoxen habitat use in the Sadlerochit River drainage, circa 1980. PHOTO BY DAVID KLEIN.

In the 1960s, only males were applying for graduate studies in wildlife and taking wildlife courses at the undergraduate level, which was not surprising, because there was no cultural tradition of women being wildlife biologists in Alaska. The general attitude was that wildlife management was a man's profession and that women shouldn't be out in the field, especially in Alaska where remote conditions were challenging. This was clearly a male gender bias common throughout white-dominated society at the time. The first female graduate student that I recall to get her master's degree through our program was Sandy Kogl. After she graduated, in the mid-1970s she got a permanent position with the National Park Service as the dog handler at Denali National Park where she took responsibility for the care and training of the sled dogs used by park rangers for winter patrols. She gained a reputation for her expertise in training sled dogs and in managing the associated interpretive visitor program.

David's graduate student Maria Berger explaining lichen
status and grazing pressure to a group of students tasked
with recording lichen composition and response to caribou
winter grazing during a field class near Cantwell, 2002. Tatyana
Vlasova (on left in cap) was visiting from Russia and joined the
group. PHOTO BY DAVID KLEIN.

Eventually, the gender of wildlife graduate students changed over time
from predominantly males to predominately females. Cheryl Boice who
completed her MS degree in 1977 on the breeding of sandhill cranes in the
Yukon-Kuskokwim Delta was my first female graduate student advisee. In
later years, I ended up having more female students as advisees than other
faculty. I accepted the best applicants no matter their gender, and this often
turned out to be more females than males. At the beginning, some of the
other male faculty members were not quite ready for female students. Like
one remarked, "I don't know how to work in the field with a female." I replied, "It shouldn't be any different than with a male student. Why not give
it a try?" Some did and learned that times were changing.

One female graduate student advisee that stands out is Maria Berger,
who did a master's on summer grazing by bison and related habitat selection

and use by the bison herd south of Delta. It was focused on vegetation, and Maria had a good background in plants, so she had the right qualifications. She was originally from Ontario, Canada, where she did an undergraduate degree, and then took a job in northern Labrador with the Newfoundland government working with caribou being affected by hydro development in Quebec and iron mining in Labrador. In order to best study the bison and do the vegetative work on the grass-covered gravel bars where the bison were spending the summer, Maria and another female student who was her assistant had to cross the Delta River. It's tricky crossing that river, but they soon became accomplished at handling it safely. Maria certainly proved herself both with her research and her outdoor and leadership skills. After she graduated, Maria did work for a while with ADF&G assessing possible locations for introduction of wood bison, and then was a naturalist guide at Camp Denali, a wilderness lodge located ninety miles inside Denali National Park. It was gratifying to see her put her degree to good use.

Of course, during all this time I was still carrying on my own caribou research, so often I had students working on caribou ecology projects that were tied closely to my work. All of this research built on itself to create deeper understanding of broad ecological topics, such as caribou behavior, where students looked at the movements of caribou in relation to insects, timing of migration, food availability during migration and how that determined their migration route, or how insect harassment related to the nutritional well-being of caribou. An example of one of these types of MS projects was by Canadian grad student, Wendy Nixon, who did her MS thesis on insect harassment of the Porcupine Caribou Herd, which in different parts of its annual cycle lives in both Alaska and Canadian ecosystems. Most of her investigations were in Canada, but we had a good understanding with immigration and custom services in both Canada and the United States, so we were readily able to work across the border while out in the field. I was her major advisor, one of her committee members was with the Canadian Wildlife Service, and the others were on the faculty at UAF, including Bob White.

One example of a grad student of mine whose caribou research contributed to our overall understanding of caribou behavior in relationship to oil field development was Dan Roby. He studied caribou avoidance of the road

Simulated cloud cover research on the growth and productivity
of several species of willow at the head of the Wood River in
the Alaska Range, circa 1990. Pat Valkenberg (right), a former
graduate student of David's working for the Alaska Department
of Fish and Game and a pilot, and a visiting Swedish student (left)
volunteered to help David with this project. She is measuring
precipitation levels, and the box on the ground in front of her
recorded weather data. PHOTO BY DAVID KLEIN.

and the pipeline (Roby 1978). (For more details on Dan's research on the
North Slope, see chapter 9: "Wildlife Reactions to Oil Development.") Dan
and I became close friends, and he even joined me on moose hunts I did on
the north side of the Nenana River, where we camped on a gravel bar opposite the Reindeer Hills. After he completed his master's degree, Dan spent
six months working in West Greenland with Henning Thing, a Danish biologist who I had collaborated with while he was doing his PhD on caribou
habitat relationships. It was tough work, carrying big packs and hiking long
distances, sometimes carrying caribou that they had shot to get information from, but they had a lot in common and worked well together. They
also flew to the northernmost part of Greenland, near Thule, where they
searched for evidence of caribou where they might have come across from

David's graduate student, Dan Roby, doing fieldwork, circa 1972. PHOTO BY DAVID KLEIN.

adjacent Ellesmere Island, Canada. They found no evidence that caribou had come to Greenland from Canada in recent years. After that expedition, Dan returned to the US and did a PhD at the University of Pennsylvania on seabirds along the coast of Labrador. He got a faculty position at Western Illinois University, was assistant Unit leader at UAF for a number of years, and then transferred to the Oregon Cooperative Wildlife Research Unit where he just retired as the Unit leader. Dan is another example of one of my graduate students who obtained a good education and gained excellent experience through the Wildlife Unit, and applied what he or she learned to a successful career in wildlife studies and wildlife management. I am proud of all of my students, but gain extra pleasure from those that have gone on to make important contributions in the field of wildlife management.

Henning Thing came to Alaska to research the energy costs for caribou of their foraging behavior. Like, how much energy was involved from a mechanistic standpoint of digging a feeding crater in the snow? He was looking at how the caribou use their feet for cratering down into the snow for forage, and how leg length was related to how deep the snow was. I had another master's student who was doing similar research related to the Western Arctic Caribou Herd, so it made sense for them to work together because they were getting similar information through observation of the caribou, but they were using it differently. I spent some time out in the field with them in the late winter in the Waring Mountains, just north of Kotzebue near the village of Noorvik. We were camped in a little narrow valley right at the edge of the hills where we were out of the major wind and there was a good source for wood. We lived in a big white wall tent with a woodstove in it, which was wonderful since temperatures would drop down to thirty below at night. It was all really very comfortable and warm, and all three of us just loved being out there.

We did a lot of skiing around there, but it could be brutal because of the wind. It could be ten below and the wind blowing, so to stay warm we'd wear down trousers and down parkas, facemasks, and goggles. Sometimes the wind was so strong, it made for tricky skiing. I remember one time when we had to go uphill and the wind was behind us, man, it was just blowing us up the hill. Then you had to be careful in some places where the snow was really hard packed. Fortunately, we had backcountry skis with metal edges, which really helped give us good traction in these conditions. The wind sometimes also affected our ability to observe the caribou. The wind would frequently blow the snow along the ground, obscuring the visibility and making the caribou hard to see. Sometimes, if you just lay down on the ground the wind wouldn't be blowing quite so strong down there and you could see things better. Other times, it was easy to see caribou and we could just watch them busily digging down into the snow for food.

Henning did a lot of measurements on skeletal material and compared reindeer to caribou in this regard. He showed how reindeer are more efficient at feeding in the absence of snow than are caribou, because caribou are more long-legged so have to reach their head further down and then pick it up higher when they are chewing and swallowing (Thing 1977). It is also

David's graduate student, Henning Thing, in West Greenland when David joined him on a research project, circa 1981. PHOTO BY DAVID KLEIN.

interesting to note that social hierarchy of the group plays a role in feeding and energy use. Having expended a certain amount of energy to dig a hole in the snow, the caribou wants to protect it from other caribou. This is where pecking order and antlers make a difference. If you don't have antlers, you're more readily going to get kicked out from an existing cratered feeding hole. It generally is accepted now that the breeding females retain their antlers later in a season because it gives them an advantage in keeping other caribou out of their cratered hole. This allows the female to have better access to forage since she needs to eat more to maintain the embryo. The only other caribou a pregnant female will allow to feed in the crater is her own calf of the previous spring.

Another graduate student who contributed a lot to his particular area of study was Bob Jones. He had an amazing career in the Aleutian Islands starting in 1947 when he was hired by the Fish and Wildlife Service as the first resident manager of the Aleutian Islands National Wildlife Refuge (now the Alaska Maritime National Wildlife Refuge). He studied sea otters (thus his nickname "Sea Otter Jones"), as well as the Pacific black brant, emperor and Taverner's Canada geese, and Steller's eider ducks that migrated through or wintered there, and he worked hard to remove introduced foxes from Amchitka Island. Although Bob loved his work in the Aleutians, he felt an intellectual isolation being stationed at Cold Bay, and he ultimately obtained educational leave to do a master's degree through the Wildlife Unit under my supervision. Bob did an excellent master's project where he investigated the timing of when brant geese took off from Izembek Lagoon and headed south to their wintering grounds in the Gulf of California. This was important for air traffic, because tens of thousands of birds would all take off from Cold Bay, and there was concern that huge flocks of migrating birds might be a problem if they intersected with flying aircraft. Bob was able to determine what kind of weather instigated the birds to fly, and worked with the military, the FAA, and radar at the Cold Bay airport to show how they could monitor and predict when the birds were about to take off. Bob interacted well with the other, much-younger graduate students, who looked upon him as a role model and mentor, and both the students and I enjoyed his presence and the many fascinating discussions he stimulated.

That is by no means all of the graduate students that I advised, appreciated, or admired. It is just a small sample to show the diversity of the graduate students and projects that I had. I enjoyed working with students and learned a lot from advising so many. And these were people that I had selected just based on what they had written on their applications. In the early days, there was no way of meeting the students before you accepted them, unless they happened to be coming up through the undergraduate program here, but mostly they didn't. It was all done through correspondence. You had their CV and three letters of recommendations. So you made the decision sometimes just hoping for the best.

I ended up with some top-notch students, but I also ended up with some students where it didn't work out. There were some brilliant young people who just had a hard time. Some of them didn't know what they wanted to do and couldn't focus in very well on a specific thesis project. Some went out in the field for the first time and realized that this wasn't the right fit for them, despite having done excellent in their coursework. And I had one who was not able to pass her comprehensive exams. It was disappointing to me to have a student fail like this. I like teaching and like to see people learn, but I believe strongly in having standards. So not every student selected for the program was successful.

Over the years I served as major advisor for sixty-seven MS and PhD degree recipients. The major focus of thesis topics of my advisees had been on the biology and habitat of the ungulate species—(caribou, muskoxen, moose, deer, mountain sheep, and mountain goats) upon which my own research had focused. The work I did with students is important to me, and I think they appreciated me as an advisor. It was a relationship beneficial to all of us. I tried hard to pay attention and stay connected with my student advisees, including going out in the field with them if I could. I wanted to provide the best advice and support I could to guide them through the program and into a successful career. I liked interacting with students in a social setting, not just in the classroom. It gave us a chance to get to know each other better. So I would host potlucks at my house for any of the grad students who wanted to come. I favor use of the term *filial* to explain the close bonding I experienced with my graduate student advisees: father-son and father-daughter. In many cases we developed close friendships, and I have stayed in contact with former students and know what's happened to them and their families.

I think the kind of education graduate students got in our program was broad and helped make them good citizens. I believe that we should not just be scientists who are so focused on what we're doing that we're not aware of how it relates to the society and the world in general. Training students as good citizens and to think more globally than just nationally prepares them for seeing the big picture and for handling controversy they may come upon in their lives and careers. In my advanced years, I've begun to feel more and more that understanding ecology and understanding ecosystems and understanding humans in relationship to ecology and ecosystems means understanding ourselves as a biological entity. It all ties together. I think it's important to understand ourselves, and understand ourselves in relationship to the environment in which we live. If the living world is changing, then we should know more about how it's changing and how we can adapt more

Karen Max working as a field assistant and collecting vegetation samples for Stephen Lewis, who was doing a master's study on deer and vegetation on Coronation Island in Southeast Alaska, circa 1990. PHOTO BY DAVID KLEIN.

effectively to the changes, no matter whether they're human caused changes or just natural changes.

I believe that as scientists it is important to be responsible citizens and share our scientific understandings in order to inform better decision making when it comes to regulating human use of the environment. I was involved in this type of science outreach in a number of ways. First, in 1975, I was selected by Governor Jay Hammond (1974–1982) to be one of twelve members of his Alaska Growth Policy Council. Some other council members included Vic Fischer, a member of the Alaska Constitutional Convention and professor of political science at the University of Alaska; Emil Notti, an Athabascan from the village of Koyukuk in interior Alaska who served as the first president of the Alaska Federation of Natives; and Fran Ulmer, a member of Hammond's staff with a strong background in economics and political science who later served as a state representative and was lieutenant governor from 1994 to 2002 under Governor Tony Knowles, thereby becoming the first woman elected to statewide office. According to Lowell Thomas Jr., chairman of the Growth Policy Council, the basic purpose "was to involve Alaskans in formulating state policies. The method was to inform people as to the critical issues facing the state, stimulate discussions on those issues, and carry citizen recommendations to the governor and the legislature" (Elliot 1978:ii).

The Growth Policy Council established the Alaska Public Forum as a way to inform the public about issues facing the state and to stimulate discussions via workshops in communities throughout the state. Results of these workshops showed how people in different regions had varying views on issues. I participated in the 1978 forums in Fairbanks and Anchorage and helped with workshops in Emmonak, Nunapitchuk, and Chalkyitsik where subsistence issues dominated the discussions. An observer from the White House who traveled with the Forum during its 1977 workshops in Southeast Alaska commented: "The people should have more influence over long-range policy than merely pulling a lever on election day. To make government accountable and efficient is the issue of the '70s and '80s. If the process of involving citizens in policy-making decisions is kept honest and continues, it could be a radical change in our country" (ibid.). The experiences I had working with the Growth Policy Council and the Alaska Public Forum greatly enriched my understanding of the role of state government in serving the diverse interests of all Alaskans, and it likely had a similar effect on other council members.

Another product of Jay Hammond's forthright thinking was the Scientist in Residence program, which I quite willingly supported. It was a great way to do science outreach and share a love of the natural world with a whole new group of young students. I volunteered for a ten-day trip to share science with schools in the Yukon River villages of Saint Mary's, Mountain Village, and Pilot Station. Saint Mary's had a Catholic boarding school, whereas the schools in the other villages were state funded. At Saint Mary's Catholic boarding school, I was favorably impressed by the advance science lesson given to the students by their teacher, Kate Doran, who had just recently obtained a bachelor's of science degree from the University of Oregon. I focused my presentation on plant-animal relationships, using the example of moose and snowshoe hares that both rely upon willows as their primary winter forage. I collected willow twigs from just outside the school and brought them into the classroom to show examples of those cut by hares versus those nibbled on by moose. These samples proved to be of keen interest to the students. Then the next day I led a walk to a willow thicket to show them the direct effects that the snowshoe hares had on the willow plants on a larger scale. I was impressed with how interested the kids were.

In Mountain Village, the teacher explained how difficult it was teaching science there. The small homes in the village had just recently gotten television and people would stay up late watching it, which kept the kids from getting their homework done or getting enough sleep. As predicted, the seventh and eighth grade students in the science class went to sleep during my talk and slide presentation. You could see how frustrated the teachers were by this situation.

The final school visit was to the small village of Pilot Point and showed another extreme in the rural school system at that time. The state-funded school had only recently been built and was well equipped, but there were so few students that all eight grades were taught in one room by two teachers. The teachers were a young couple with no children who seemed to be doing a good job under the circumstances, but the amount of time they could spend daily with students in each of the eight grades was minimal.

It is interesting to note that Judith Kleinfeld, a psychology professor at UAF, later did a sociological study showing higher achievement levels of students at regional boarding schools than students attending the state-funded elementary schools in the villages (Kleinfeld 1985). One factor could be that in the boarding school the students were monitored closely, and the staff had control over what the students did outside of the classroom.

My other volunteer efforts at science outreach included twenty-four years of service (1994–2018) to The Nature Conservancy (TNC) as a member of their Alaska Board of Trustees. I have shown such strong loyalty to TNC because I believe in and support their work, and I am able to play a role in assuring that science underlies their efforts. Because I worked professionally throughout most of Alaska and was familiar with the biodiversity and the dynamics of the region's natural ecosystems, I was looked upon by TNC staff as a readily available reference source on ecological issues throughout the state. During the past five years, I also have served in a somewhat similar capacity as a member of the Citizens Advisory Board for the Northern District of Alaska State Parks.

Caribou, mostly bulls, are not bothered by noise from a stationary oil drill rig on the North Slope of Alaska. PHOTO BY DAVID KLEIN.

9
Wildlife Reactions to Oil Development

I was not specifically trained as an environmental scientist, but I became one through both training and experience, and it has been important to me that I be recognized as a legitimate scientist, not labeled an environmental activist. Nevertheless, I was frequently on the side of environmentalists, but I was not deliberately on their side. I just happened to be there because I was doing the science that enabled me to take a stand that was often in agreement with environmentalist's concerns. As the Wildlife Unit leader, I was working with both the federal and state governments, as well as with the university, and I wanted to remain neutral regarding environmental issues. I was trying to be a good role model, do good science, and be objective as a teacher and science advisor. I had to be careful about my role in environmental work because I could have lost my government job, but I thought that what these groups were doing was important. If the Wildlife Unit had research findings or data that were relevant to environmental issues, I would make that available to environmental organizations to go public with, if they wished. Some of my own research funding came from the oil industry and I didn't want them to see me as being against them. But the Co-op Unit also accepted a contract from the Sierra Club Foundation, where we did one of the first studies using satellite imagery to map the wintering range of the Western Arctic Caribou Herd, which was an important first step in the future management of that herd.

While I didn't want to appear to be taking sides on an issue, there were times when I might speak out or at least drag my feet a bit. For example, after oil was discovered at Prudhoe Bay in 1968, I was an outspoken critic

A trench left open for several days during construction of the
Trans-Alaska Pipeline when the pipe was supposed to be laid
quickly and these trenches reclosed. An open trench like this
would deflect caribou moving through the area, especially if
it filled with water, which made it more difficult for wildlife to
cross. The engineers did not like this, but they were
supposed to abide by the rules. PHOTO BY DAVID KLEIN.

of the oil industry's ability and willingness to build the proposed eight-
hundred-mile Trans Alaska Oil Pipeline with minimal impact on wildlife
and their habitats. I openly emphasized that the oil industry lacked the
knowledge and experience needed for oil field development in the permanently frozen tundra of the Arctic without major environmental impacts on
caribou, waterfowl, and other wildlife and their habitats. Equally, scientists
didn't know fully how caribou would react and what type of pipeline would
have the least impact on them, so I argued for a delay in order to first carry
out studies necessary to do a better design for the pipeline and oil fields. Of

course, environmental organizations were critical, too, but they were viewed as trying to stop the pipeline from being built at all, while as scientists, we were trying to slow things down until studies could be done.

Then the oil industry was forced to wait, as a moratorium on construction of the pipeline was imposed by Secretary of the Interior Stewart Udall while Congress settled land claims of Alaska Natives to clarify who owned the land the pipeline was going to go over and how the Natives would be compensated if the pipeline went over their lands. These Native land claims were settled in 1971 by passage of the Alaska Native Claims Settlement Act (ANCSA), which paid $963 million to thirteen newly formed Alaska Native corporations around the state, who also received title to 44 million acres of land (Mitchell 2001). This debate allowed time for environmental studies to be done and for the oil industry to consider design options to facilitate movement of animals across the pipeline. A major concern was the potential impact on caribou, because as migratory animals their free movement could be obstructed by pipelines and oil field infrastructure. Once ANCSA was passed, development of the vast oil fields at Prudhoe Bay could proceed. After a four-year delay, the oil industry was honest enough to admit that it would've been a mess if they had started to build a pipeline right away. It would have cost them much more and they would have made more mistakes, including engineering mistakes and mistakes that would have negatively affected wildlife.

I had opportunities to work with most of the large oil companies during oil field development and pipeline construction. We had good relations with some of the companies, like ConocoPhillips (at the time it was still just Conoco), which as a smaller company was easy to work with. For example, they provided some logistics support for graduate student Jim Dau when he was doing a study for them. On the other hand, we had problems with ExxonMobil. First of all, they were known for spending millions on studies by disreputable consulting firms just to discredit good science. And then we had trouble with them about academic freedom related to research results.

ExxonMobil was concerned about bad publicity resulting from my criticism of the oil industry for their close-mindedness in addressing the problem of how to design pipeline crossings that would be used by caribou. We challenged and criticized them about not knowing how to build a pipeline to accommodate movements of caribou. At this stage, they were proposing to bury the pipeline in sections with gravel ramps built so that caribou could go over it, and then having the pipeline elevated in other places where the caribou could walk under it. But we did not know how to deal with caribou movement in the oil field, and needed to do research to find answers to what would work best. ExxonMobil then challenged us at the Wildlife Unit by saying that they would provide money to build a simulated pipeline in the oil field that we could use as a study site and to support a PhD-level student to see how the caribou would respond. They would use culverts and snow fences that the animals couldn't see through and build two types of crossings: ramps over the pipeline and an elevated pipeline that the caribou could walk under. I don't think they believed that we could put together a reasonable study. But my assistant Unit leader, Peter Lent, had recently been involved in a project where they tested pipeline crossings for reindeer using a simulated pipeline on the Seward Peninsula. The results showed that reindeer could be more readily herded over a gravel ramp to cross a pipeline than under an elevated pipeline (Child and Lent 1973). Child and Lent's experiment was interesting and informative, but, of course, herded reindeer are not the same as free-ranging caribou, although it gave us a workable model to follow for Prudhoe Bay.

We had problems negotiating the contract with ExxonMobil for the pipeline height study where they were going to construct a two-mile long simulated pipeline and provide the Co-op Unit from $80,000 to $100,000 to cover the cost of a graduate student doing the research. ExxonMobil insisted on having total control over the data. They wanted the contract to state that we couldn't release any data to the public without their approval. This meant that if we had any findings of significance we couldn't even publish anything as simple as a report without going through them. Of course, this was unacceptable to have an agency or funder controlling the data when you were doing science through the university. The standard practice is that as your project advances, you give papers at technical conferences and write up small publications about some of the findings along the way. A complete report with full results is not provided until the project has been concluded. So I said, "No, we can't agree to that kind of a contract. If the data and information can't be made available to the public without your approval, then

Caribou crossing a gravel ramp built over a simulated pipeline at Prudhoe Bay to test whether caribou were more likely to go over or under a raised pipeline, 1973. Caribou preferred the gravel ramp because they like to be higher up where they can see whether there are predators around, and do not like to go through an underpass, which is a visual obstruction they cannot see through to the other end. COURTESY OF DAVID KLEIN.

I don't think we can do this." I mean, how could we have a student work up there and not be able to publish the data he collected?

I didn't want to lose the project. It was good funding from the oil industry. So I figured the best way to get them to agree was to go to the Fish and Wildlife Service. I reminded my supervisors in Washington, DC, that if federal funds are used for research then any information that comes from the project is in the public domain, so even if they provided a minimal amount of money to the project that would mean that the data could not be controlled exclusively by ExxonMobil. So FWS provided around $10,000 to make this happen. This put Exxon in an awkward position. They didn't want it to get out to the media that they were rejecting research on caribou and pipeline crossings solely on the basis of wanting to control the data. In the end, my strategy worked and we both agreed that while we were collecting the data there would be no release of information by either party.

ExxonMobil built the simulated pipeline and an observation tower from which my PhD student, Ken Child, used binoculars and a spotting scope to count the caribou as they approached. He counted how many went over a gravel ramp versus under the elevated pipeline versus how many were being deflected by the pipeline itself. There were many variables that could affect whether caribou used a given type of crossing or were deflected in their movements without using a crossing at all. It often depended on how the caribou were approaching the pipeline, as well as on group size, sex and age ratio of the group, and whether insects were or were not harassing the caribou as they approached. Ken observed and measured all of these variables.

I was naïve in assuming that ExxonMobil could be trusted to abide by the terms of the contract, and it wasn't very long before they broke their own rule about not sharing information with the public. Early in the study, when an ExxonMobil employee was guiding a group of news reporters through the oil field, the group stopped to view and photograph the simulated pipeline. At the time, a large group of about one thousand caribou approached the pipeline and Ken Child up in the observation tower overheard the ExxonMobil guide tell the reporters, "We're already seeing that most of the caribou are going over the pipeline fine. These crossings are working, because 25 percent of the caribou are going over the ramp and 15 percent are going under the pipeline." Well, he didn't have any basis for saying that. We had all the data and were still doing the observations. Of course, the guide didn't mention the caribou that were deflected by the pipeline. He was just jumping to conclusions. Ken had a much broader view of the area from the observation tower and could see that the majority of caribou that failed to use the special crossings were being deflected upon first seeing the pipeline. They weren't even seeing the crossings as options and just turned away from the pipeline in general. Of course, their story got top coverage in the Alaska and Seattle newspapers, including photos of caribou using a gravel ramp and a quote from ExxonMobil saying our research was showing that industry could readily design pipeline crossings that would assure free movement of caribou within the oil field.

I complained vigorously that ExxonMobil had seriously violated the agreed-upon terms of our research contract where we wouldn't release any information while we were still collecting the data. Their response was to try to put the blame on the reporters, but they did agree to subsequently make the research area off-limits to anyone without prior approval from all parties. However, the information was already published that gave the impression that gravel ramps were going to work best, even though our studies didn't indicate that at all. It seemed that the industry didn't want information released to the public about animals being deflected and not effectively using the ramps.

After the fieldwork had been completed and Ken was back at the university working up the data, he planned to present a scientific paper on the caribou-pipeline studies at an international conference on animal behavior at the University of Calgary. Ken completed the summary report and a draft of the paper for the conference and submitted copies of both to ExxonMobil as required by the contract. They acknowledged receipt of the report, but threatened to take Ken to court if he presented the paper, claiming that he had not cleared it with them first. I responded by saying, "This is the student just presenting his information. It's not the final publication that will be available to the public. Plus, you already violated the rules earlier when you shared information with the media." We also took the threatening letter to university lawyers who responded directly to ExxonMobil, defending the wording in the contract and stating that there were university regulations and state laws that protected students. ExxonMobil then gave up their efforts to sequester the results. In the end, Ken presented the analyzed data that showed that caribou weren't going under overhead pipelines very well, that more caribou were being deflected by the pipeline than were using crossings, and if they were using crossings they used the gravel ramps (Child 1973). We also learned that caribou didn't like to go across roads or over pipelines if they could not see the other side. This is because female caribou have evolved to be cautious when not being able to see far ahead of them, since that is where predators could be hiding. I like to think that because of all this we helped educate the oil industry a bit about dealing with scientific information.

There was a lot of variability between oil companies as to how conscientious they were in dealing with environmental problems such as caribou
movements. Not all of the major oil companies were as unethical as Exxon
and its affiliates. Other companies have been relatively good at working
with biologists and funding research, although some seemed to be doing it
more for the window dressing that comes from saying they are supporting
research. For instance, British Petroleum (BP) was generally proactive in
bringing issues related to movements of caribou through the oil field to our
attention and in seeking advice in resolution of problems, and the employees that we worked with were generally polite, mutually understanding, and
respectful of our efforts to minimize the overall impact of oil development
on caribou.

Given my involvement with oil field research projects in the early days
of construction of the Trans-Alaska Pipeline, environmentalists would ask
me to talk about what we knew about caribou and pipelines and then what
was needed to cause less environmental impact in Alaska. My previous
knowledge about caribou reacting to development was based mainly on
work I had done in Scandinavia where pipelines for hydro development
and a road and railroad built between Oslo and Bergen in Norway inter-
fered with movement of both wild and domestic reindeer, and knowledge
I had about what the Soviets were doing with a natural gas pipeline in
the Taimyr region where the largest caribou herd in Eurasia was located.
Despite knowing about what was happening in other places, I explained
that caribou are the most complex of all the members of the deer family,
Cervidae (Geist 1998), and that you can not extrapolate too much about
the behavior and movements of a single caribou herd to other herds. I was
careful to emphasize that there was a limit to my knowledge, and that I was
responding as a scientist and an ecologist. I said that if we could do more
research studies then maybe we could better answer questions related to the
Alaska pipeline.

I did one of these types of studies in conjunction with one of my graduate
students related to how snow conditions affected the caribou's movements
through the Brooks Range to and from their calving grounds on the North
Slope. Caribou have long legs that help them walk better across long distances, and their broad flexible hooves spread out when they're walking to

support them across boggy areas or in snow. In the fall, caribou start aggregating and getting ready to migrate. The cows usually come into estrus during fall migration or when they're just arriving into the wintering areas. Caribou need to constantly eat to sustain their energy levels and body condition, to be strong enough to undertake their long seasonal migrations, and to have built up enough reserves to get them through the winter. This means having to move around the landscape a lot to find the best forage (Joly et al. 2010), although once caribou get into a wintering area and the snow is accumulating, they tend to stay in those generalized areas.

In the springtime when caribou are migrating to the calving grounds, they try to move at night when the temperatures are cooler and the snow hardens up to create walking conditions that require less energy than when sinking through soft snow. Interestingly, caribou tend to walk single file if they're migrating through deep snow so that only the lead animal and the first few animals are breaking trail and compacting the snow so it is easier walking for those that follow. When the lead animal gets tired, it just steps aside and the rest of the group moves by and it goes to the back of the group where it now has a packed trail to walk on. They rotate the lead position, the same as you would if you were in a group of skiers or snowshoers breaking trail. Of course, the caribou still have to feed when they're migrating, because they don't want to draw down all their fat reserves. Females still have to bear a calf when they get to the calving grounds and then they have to produce milk for it, so they select for optimal food along the way to maintain body condition even though staying on schedule for timely arrival at the calving grounds is top priority. A pregnant female feeds almost twenty-four hours a day during the migration, so she doesn't sleep much.

A lot of people think the greatest stress on the female caribou is getting through the winter. The female going into winter continues to put on weight up until the conditions get really extreme, and then she must draw on fat reserves for her own well-being. So the caribou are still feeding heavily on lichens at this time of year. Actually, the last trimester of a caribou's pregnancy is when there is a higher physiological demand on her because the fetus is getting large (Geist 1998), and then the greatest physiological demand on the female is during peak lactation, which is in the first ten days or two weeks after calving. Caribou calves grow faster than any other large herbivore and the milk that a caribou cow produces has the highest butterfat content of any of the deer family. When the caribou calves are born, they're totally dependent on their mother's milk, but within a few days, once they're up and walking and can follow their mom around, they start nibbling on green plants and lichens. Although, the calves still continue to nurse several times a day until they get larger and their rumens develop enough to where they can digest the vegetation consumed.

In our studies, we also learned about the need for timing the migration so that the females are able to get to the calving grounds in time to have their calves, and then once they got there take advantage of optimal snow and vegetation conditions. At the beginning of the migration when there is still deep snow, it's usually females and young animals going together to get to the calving grounds in time to give birth. The motivation of pregnant females to get there in time keeps them going. The males wait and go to the summer feeding areas later. The female caribou go back to the same general area to calve each year and there are a number of reasons why. One thing we can see is that the timing of the green-up of vegetation is important. They want to be in a place where green plants are just starting to grow when they arrive, so they have access to the highest-quality forage, but also still have remaining patches of snow. The caribou feel safer from predators if it's a patchy landscape with a mixture of snow and bare ground, because it is harder for predators to see the caribou in such a landscape, unless the caribou are standing on a snow patch where they are clearly visible from a distance. Of course, with calves this is especially good protection. In our study, at the time of calving we observed that there weren't very many wolves in the area, but bears were a major predator. They were just out of hibernation and were killing newborn calves that couldn't run fast enough yet to escape a short charge by a bear.

One thing we haven't figured out completely yet is how caribou navigate to get to the calving grounds. We know that they use a lot of subtle clues that we don't necessarily understand, because while they go the same general direction, they don't always follow the same route. Young animals that haven't given birth yet or a female who is giving birth for the first time travel in a group with older females who are more inclined to already know the route. In this way, we think they probably learn repeated routes.

Overall, I don't feel like the development that has occurred on the North Slope has all been done in the best way for the caribou. I think a lot of what I recommended for the pipeline and reducing impacts to caribou was listened to and applied, but how it was applied varied with the companies. They went along with a lot of things, but also there was compromise in what they did. There are some fortunate things that happened with regard to oil development that perhaps eliminated major impact on caribou herds in Alaska. One was that Prudhoe Bay and the pipeline were constructed in areas that were between the ranges of the two largest caribou herds in Alaska—the Western Arctic Herd and the Porcupine Herd. The Central Arctic Herd, which is in the area of Prudhoe Bay, has increased slowly since oil development, but it is hard to say why (Roby 1978). We do know that at the time of construction there was a high wolf population that had previously been protected and was rather rapidly eliminated after protection was removed. This reduced wolf predation, along with limited hunting pressure, are probably factors that contributed to the increase of the Central Arctic caribou. There are some behavioral modifications of the caribou that are the result of oil field development and the pipeline that we would assume would be detrimental on a long-term basis, but we have not seen any response to these detrimental effects in terms of changes to things like lowered productivity. Changes are mainly in the caribou's avoidance of the oil fields, pipeline, and Haul Road corridor, particularly females with young, which means that these animals have less range available to utilize and they have less free access to calving grounds and insect-relief areas (Cameron and Whitten 1980).

We did some studies to measure the effects of limiting access to coastal insect-relief areas in the oil field and if this would result in less effective foraging or feeding by animals during the summer. Part of the caribou's development of good body condition for going into the winter is related to the degree of eating success during the summertime. Mosquitoes come out around the end of June and are major harassing insects, and if the caribou can't get away from them the mosquitoes take the blood around their face, mouth, and on the legs where the hair isn't very thick. This blood loss not only reduces the caribou's body condition, but the constant harassment from insects keeps a caribou moving, which reduces their ability to forage as successfully. Warble and nose bot flies are two other insects that create problems for caribou, but in different ways than mosquitoes. Warble flies appear by late July and disturb the caribou by burrowing into the skin of the caribou's legs and lower body to lay eggs. Nose bot flies harass caribou mostly in the fall when they swarm around the caribou's face trying to inject live larvae into the caribou's nostrils.

Our research showed that early in summer before insects started harassing them, the caribou were located inland from the roads and pipelines. One of my students did a study that showed that these were places where the highest-quality green vegetation was present. At that time of year, this was what the caribou needed to eat for optimal growth and development. When temperatures were warm enough for mosquitoes to be flying, the caribou started milling around and trying to get away from them. Caribou react to the mosquitoes by bunching up and moving toward the coast where there is a breeze coming off the Arctic Ocean and the coastal temperature will be too cold for mosquitoes. When it's cooler, the mosquitoes go down into the vegetation and become quiescent until the temperature rises again, usually into the sixties. But the tradeoff is that these coastal locations are not the best grazing areas. While temperatures are low and the mosquitoes are less fierce, the animals move back inland, where there is better vegetation growth. Or if it is breezy and foggy inland then the mosquitoes are down in the grass and the caribou do not need to move to the coast but can stay around to forage in their better-quality range. Alternatively, if the caribou are in the mountains and too far from the coast, they seek relief from insect harassment by going up high onto ridgetops where there's usually a breeze. When caribou try to move to the coast, they mass up because this reduces the number of mosquitoes per animal, but they can't feed when they're all bunched up like this. So if caribou are prevented from moving back and forth to get to the better grazing areas, this will be reflected in poor survival and poor productivity.

You can point to positive aspects of development in regard to insect relief, especially warble flies. Caribou tend to use the gravel pads for insect relief or will stand on gravel roadways if there is no traffic. In fact, when being severely harassed by insects, caribou are much less disturbed by other kinds of activities, such as traffic. So when they are under insect harassment, it is not uncommon to see caribou crossing over or standing on a roadway,

Part of the Porcupine Caribou Herd seeking relief from insect harrassment on a windy ridge in the Northern Yukon Territory.
COURTESY OF DAVID KLEIN.

passing under a pipeline, or walking through the oil fields on their way to the coastal insect-relief areas. There is a bigger problem, though. When the coastal winds die down, caribou are motivated to go back inland to the better feeding conditions, and when they pass through oil fields or cross roads and pipelines, this is when there is a lot of deflection and delay in their movements.

When the Kuparuk oil field was being developed in the early 1980s, it turned out that the main transportation corridor between it and Prudhoe Bay went directly across the route the caribou used to get relief at the coast when insect harassment was bad. An earlier study had been done using aerial photography where you could see old trails going through certain corridors that made it possible to map the routes the caribou used. There was a lot of traffic and big trucks on the Kuparuk road, and sometimes when it was dry there would be a lot of dust flying. So this was a problem. Caribou

Bull caribou on the North Slope seeking
insect relief on an elevated access road
where there are fewer insects than on
the tundra. COURTESY OF DAVID KLEIN.

in big groups don't move readily across roads, partly because they are waiting
for the more adventurous ones to start moving first. Once they start moving
in small groups, then the rest will generally go across the road, but if a large
truck comes down the road that's the end of it. The caribou get frightened
and turn back, and it can take a long time for them to settle down and try
again. In the meantime, they are being attacked and harassed by mosquitoes,
and later in the season by biting flies and parasitic flies.

The joint recommendation from all of us working with caribou was that
there was no simple solution for the road to Kuparuk, but the best solution
seemed to be to convoy the trucks and traffic with most of the vehicle travel
done at night when it was too cool for the mosquitoes. But, if you had traffic
that had to go through during the daytime, all the trucks had to go together and there had to be a period of a couple of hours when no trucks were
allowed through at all. This was especially the case if there were groups of
caribou that were obviously waiting to get across the road. If the caribou were

in the distance, it wouldn't make too much difference if ten trucks went by versus one, whereas if no trucks went by then the caribou could successfully get across the road. The oil industry responded and said, "It's inconvenient and costly for us, but, yeah, we'll do it." They didn't actually say it that way. What they really said was, "Yeah, we'll do this. It's for the well-being of the caribou."

When Conoco wanted to build a twelve-mile road out to Milne Point to their new combined living and production center, they were designing everything to have minimal environmental impact, so they wanted to know where the best place would be to build a road. Some areas were pretty good insect-relief areas for caribou while others were not. There was a need to know the relative insect density so the road could be constructed to minimize disturbance to the caribou's movement and efforts to reach their all-important coastal insect-relief habitat. Wildlife Unit graduate student Jim Dau was selected to do this challenging study about insects in the area. It was a difficult project because he had to deal with both mosquitoes and parasitic flies. He first had to map the entire area and divide it into workable-sized units marked by flagging. To measure and map mosquito density, Jim used a sweep net while walking transects through each numbered unit. There was a vial in the bottom of the net where the caught insects were collected. He would quickly count the mosquitoes that he got each time, but would do the more detailed identification of insect types and species and accurate counting later on when he got back to where he was staying. He had to do these over and over again under different weather conditions to determine the effects of different temperature, humidity, and wind conditions on when mosquito and flies would be most active and therefore most harassing to caribou. Jim needed to walk through the area at about the same time as when the insects were most harassing to the caribou, so that was tough. That wet coastal tundra environment gets thick with flying insects when there is no wind and the temperature and humidity are just right. He determined the high-density insect locations within the various transects and produced a map of relative harassment for the entire study area (Dau 1986; Dau and Cameron 1986). This harassment map then was used by the road engineers to plan the routing of the Milne Point Road so that it would have the least effect on the movement of caribou to insect-relief areas.

Shortly after Conoco received a copy of Jim's thesis, they announced to the media that they were honoring him and the Wildlife Unit with their conservation award that covered all of the areas in the world where they had conservation projects. They said that Jim did the best study related to the environment and helped them build a more environmentally safe road that was compatible with caribou movement patterns. It was a $5,000 award that was given to the Wildlife Unit, but some people were saying that the student should get the money since he did all the research and the Unit was only getting the award because of the student's work. We appreciated all the work that Jim had done and acknowledged his major effort in designing and carrying out the project, but I decided that it was best if the Unit used the money to support students in the future. We felt quite honored to have this recognition from the oil industry and for them to be able to provide future student educational support.

There is a lot of variation in how effective oil field development can be in minimizing the impact on caribou. I think Prudhoe Bay is such a mass of pipelines, roads, and facilities that were put together without good planning for caribou that the area is now largely lost to use by caribou. Some caribou move through there, especially the bulls, which adapt more readily than cows, but they still have difficulty because of these obstructions. The Kuparuk field was built later and was built with more consideration for caribou movement, so there has been less direct impact on caribou there. Nevertheless, a major problem with oil field development has been that it happens to be right along the coast, so gradually a zone of development has occurred, which is perhaps the worst location from the standpoint of caribou gaining access to insect-relief areas.

The oil industry saw animals right in the middle of the oil field and would say that everything was going so well, that there was no evidence of impact to caribou. This made for some nice pictures for the oil industry to release to the media, but it is a lot more complex than many people think. Why? Because what they were seeing were mostly all big bulls with big antlers. The question was why were the bulls there, and not so many cows and calves? The answer is because it is too risky for the cows and the calves to be close to the oil fields; they don't want to be in places where things can sneak up on them like grizzly bears and wolves. They don't have a lot of wolves there close to the coast, but there has been some increase. Bears were on the rise because they were getting food from improperly disposed garbage, and if you have an increased number of bears that means increased predation on newborn caribou calves.

The effect of predation versus limitation of food sources on controlling population size of caribou herds was a question under debate at this time, as well (Bergerud 1969, 1974). My students and I did some research and were able to show that predators were the main limitation (Klein 1970b, 1973a, 1973b, 1979, 1980; Weeden and Klein 1971; Klein and Hemming 1977; Bliss and Klein 1981). In my mind, again, it was a result of not paying enough attention to habitat (Klein 1991). In terms of wolf predation, my graduate student, Dan Roby, noticed that wolves along the Haul Road (Dalton Highway) were killing more animals close to the road than away from it, which shows the wolves were not disturbed by the vehicles. In places where the Haul Road was elevated, especially if it was where there was a slight hill, if you were on the tundra you couldn't see across the road to the other side. So if there were animals on one side, they couldn't see the animals on the other side. Dan's research showed that the wolves would not hunt on the road surface itself, necessarily, but would use the road as a platform to hide behind. They could sneak up very cautiously and look over to see if there were any caribou on the other side. For killing caribou, if a wolf can make a rush and get them when they don't see it coming or they're just getting up from resting, the wolf has a better chance of catching one. If caribou have an opportunity to run and get a head start, a wolf has a lower chance of success.

The whole predator avoidance strategy of caribou is to be in groups so that when they are feeding some individuals have their heads down while others have their heads up, to be in open terrain to better see predators coming, and then move out before wolves can get close enough to actually make an attack. If some of the caribou start running, often the rest of the group will follow. Their long legs give caribou an advantage in that they can sustain running fast across the tundra better than their predators, and when a whole group of caribou takes off running there are too many animals spread too far apart for a predator to maintain focus on an individual caribou (Geist 1998). So the wolves learned that the road gave them an advantage and would use it whenever they could.

Caribou avoidance behavior has been studied enough that we know that cows with calves do not like to cross rivers with a lot of tall willows along their banks. They do not like using a corridor where their visibility is blocked. The bulls usually go right through without much bother, but females with young calves are cautious. None of them want to be the leader going through that brush. Finally, the whole group wants to get across and they will suddenly move rapidly through, much more rapidly than the males. They will not even stop to feed on the new leaves of willows, which are good forage. They know that something could be hiding in the bushes. Once they get through, then the cows and calves settle down on the other side. Observations have been made of caribou behaving similarly in their avoidance of roads and pipelines. However, Alaska Biological Research (ABR) did a study and found that the pipeline is not as bad as roads, because roads have traffic. The caribou are more frightened by the movement of the vehicles than by the stationary thing (pipeline).

How caribou reacted to noise was another impact of oil development that was investigated. For example, a consulting firm did some tests for a potential gas pipeline in the hills of the Arctic National Wildlife Refuge (ANWR) where they simulated compressor sounds that a gas pipeline might make. They wanted to see what reaction the caribou might have to the sound. They had a box with the sound coming out of it, and installed cameras to record what happened. The videos showed caribou just marching along in migration. They heard this noise and it got louder and louder and louder, but they walked right by and away from it. It was a continuous sound like rapids in a river with no movement associated with it, so they didn't pay attention to it and just went on through the area. Similarly on the oil field, we saw that even though they might be drilling an oil well and making a loud noise with the big diesel engine running, as long as there was no movement on the pad, caribou wouldn't pay attention to this. They wouldn't avoid the sound. They would continue to feed through the area or lie down and rest. If there was any visible movement though, like people or vehicles moving around the pad, then the caribou would avoid it. In general, we found that it was activity of people that made a difference. If the noise is stable and not related to something moving, the caribou are less bothered by it. I mean, what do they do when there is thunder and lightning? How do they react to that extreme noise of the thunder?

Another aspect of disturbance when building the pipeline had to do with whether to bury it or build it raised. People predicted that the Nelchina Caribou Herd near Glennallen were more likely to be disturbed by an above-ground pipeline going through forest habitat than the caribou on the tundra because in the forest their view of the pipeline would be obstructed until they got right up to it by which time it was too late for them to react. In reality, behavioral studies showed that the Nelchina caribou didn't seem to mind the pipeline so much because when they were going through a forest area they are already accustomed to going under branches so they would go under an elevated section of the pipeline in a similar way. Biologists working in Anchorage made these conclusions, but I probably would have made the same assumptions. The oil companies wanted to bury the pipeline in that region, if at all possible, but there was permafrost and they didn't want to have to build a refrigeration system, so the idea of an elevated pipeline was appealing to them. It turned out that they did bury a couple miles of it, and they have a refrigeration unit with pipes going down into the soil and motors running all the time to keep it frozen. It's questionable whether that was justified or not. The good part of it being buried is that nothing looks any different to the animals above ground, except the clearing, so it is just like walking across the road with no traffic.

Although not directly related to caribou, questions about changes in other biological relationships from the impact oil development began to develop. Like what was the effect of foxes on nesting birds around the oil fields? The fox population around the oil fields was higher than normal because it was almost impossible to keep food away from them. Foxes learn that there are more birds nesting close to roads because the snow is gone from there earlier, so they prey heavily on the eggs or young birds at these nests. But there are other potential biological impacts that people should be measuring, like what about carbon in the atmosphere and fall out on the land? Does this affect the snow and the quality of the melt water? And what other contaminants might be there? Fortunately, most of the pollution from the compressor stations and all the gas that they're burning off are blown out to sea. But we don't ask the question of what effect it has on polar bears and seals that use the sea ice, as well as on the sea ice itself. What's the effect on the marine environment? Another cumulative effect that is important to think about is what is happening to the Native people that used to use that area? Well, it is horribly complicated, and the only way you can really show the cumulative impact is to address the system as a whole. Eventually, a study was initiated to begin to understand the importance of looking at the cumulative effects of oil development (Committee on Cumulative Environmental Effects 2003).

I guess I did a good job of being a neutral scientist through all these studies about caribou and the possible impact from oil development, because once I was offered a job by the oil industry. I'd been doing some research with an Englishman at BP where the results might help minimize impact of oil field development on caribou, and he approached me and said, "The oil industry has a biologist position coming open, and we think you would be a good person for the job. You work well with us, etc., etc." He implied a much larger salary than I was getting at the Wildlife Unit. I said, "Education plays a major role in my job satisfaction and I'm still able to be a good scientist, so I want to stick with that. I don't see any long-term career goal that would be favorable to me in the oil industry."

I am glad I was involved in this research on the caribou in the oil fields, even though there were a lot of politics, because it was fascinating. If it hadn't happened, I would not have missed it, you might say, but I learned a lot about the oil industry and drilling and their engineering capabilities and limitations. I wanted to know as much as I could. I wanted to better understand the oil industry's perspective and what they were capable of. They were good about explaining things and I was always interested. There were a lot of things the oil industry was pretty good about, such as building ramps over pipelines, grouping smaller diameter pipes together to create less of a hindrance to caribou movement, modifying construction to provide for easier passage by caribou, reducing road traffic during periods of high caribou migration, and locating airfields so they could minimize animal conflicts. However, there also were negative impacts on the wildlife from the pipeline, infrastructure, roads, and construction-related activities. One example

A truck driver throwing a piece of ham to a wolf on the Haul Road near Toolik Lake, 1975. PHOTO BY DAN ROBY.

is how disturbing helicopters can be for caribou when they fly too low and get too close, which causes the caribou to start running. This was especially a problem in the winter. They didn't realize that if you run caribou hard at thirty degrees below zero, they're liable to get emphysema from bringing the cold air into their lungs so fast.

Another problem early on was not having adequate garbage disposal at the oil field camps, and foxes, bears, and other scavengers got attracted to the garbage. Then there was the problem of how the oil field workers interacted with wildlife. One time Dan Roby was cruising along the Haul Road and he saw all these young oil field workers standing in a line along the road looking at a big grizzly bear. One young worker was walking toward the bear with an out-stretched hand holding a sandwich. It was macho to be out there doing that with such a big, dangerous animal, but it also was stupid because that worker didn't understand the potential problem he was creating. By feeding the bear, he was getting it addicted to human food, but also it might take his hand off as it grabbed the sandwich. Another time, Dan saw a truck driving by a wolf when suddenly an arm came out of the window throwing a sandwich in the air, and the wolf grabbed it before it hit the ground. Of course, we reported these incidents. But it was not only the oil field workers who were a problem this way. The public, and even some biologists I took up there on a tour, forget that the animals they see along the Haul Road are wild and should not be fed.

I generally believe in the protection or the conservation of nature and wild places, but, in some cases, if there are big projects that need to be done for the economy and the country and to produce fossil fuels, which we are dependent on, then I don't necessarily want to stop them, but I want to be sure that they are done in the best way possible. An example was during the fight over the Alaska National Interest Lands Conservation Act and this question of whether the coastal plain of the Arctic National Wildlife Refuge would be available for development or even be part of the refuge (Kaye 2006). If you were going to consider developing an area like this, then you had to know the consequences for the animals and the environment (Klein 2001b). Our research showed that this coastal plain was critical habitat essential for caribou herds, migratory birds, and other species. Because of all this, the final legislation that passed was a compromise where the coastal plain was included in the refuge, but not given wilderness status, and left open the possibility for future development. In addition, time and money were appropriated to the Fish and Wildlife Service to study the status of the wildlife and how development might affect them, and to do botanical studies to identify critical habitat components for caribou and muskoxen.

One such study was to learn about how some caribou were able to stay up on the North Slope in the wintertime where there are fewer lichens available to eat, compared with the quantity of better forage available in the wintering grounds farther south and in open spruce forest (Joly et al. 2010). The reasons why are both simple and complex. The simple part is that there are fewer wolves on the North Slope in the winter, which makes it a safer place for caribou. The more complex piece has to do with availability of forage and energy costs of movement. Caribou that spend the winter on the North Slope conserve energy by not migrating, but there are fewer lichens

A cow of the Western Arctic Caribou Herd sharing a feeding crater with her yearling calf, Waring Mountains, circa 1976. PHOTO BY DAVID KLEIN.

so these caribou do not get as much food and nutrition per unit of effort when they're feeding compared to those who travel south. In addition, the snow on the North Slope is usually wind-blown and hard-packed, so it takes a lot of energy to dig down to find the lichens that are there. In comparison, caribou farther south in the forest have to deal with deeper and softer snow that takes a lot more energy to travel through, but takes less energy to dig down to ground level for lichens. This easier access to forage in their southern wintering range saves enough energy to justify that spent during long spring and fall migrations. So there's a tradeoff between energy spent digging versus migrating that must be considered when looking at where caribou herds spend the winter and why.

At the Co-op Unit, we were involved in a lot of these types of studies so I was frequently called to go to Washington, DC, to testify before Congressional subcommittees who were holding hearings about opening up ANWR for oil development. Once I was there, I was expected to be a good scientist and not offer my personal feelings. It was difficult at times, because we had people on these committees like Alaska's Congressman Don Young and Senator Ted Stevens who were trying to discredit you as a scientist. They tried to do everything possible to make your presentation appear questionable, because while there were some committee members who supported development, there were others who supported conservation interests. Their positions were usually related to party politics. You had to boil everything down, including charts and maps, to a twenty-five-minute presentation. That was a challenge.

But the bigger challenge, which I ended up enjoying, was answering the questions from the committee members. For example, some of Don Young's questions often did not seem well thought out. Like when they were considering laying the pipeline on the ground, he said, "Well, look, if caribou can go over the Brooks Range with mountains so high, why can't they go over a pipeline?" I pointed out that we had a study with reindeer out on the Seward Peninsula that showed they did not go over the pipelines. Then Don Young asked, "Well, why do they have to go to this particular area anyway?" He just opened himself wide open with that one. I said, "Well, this is their winter range. Their winter diet is mostly lichens, and that area is where the lichens are." And he said, "Well, why do they have to eat lichens?" I said, "Well, they're especially adapted to it. They have built up microorganisms in their gut that are especially designed to digest lichens." He must have seen some literature someplace that talked about how caribou in some places, like the reindeer out in the Aleutian Islands, can live without lichens. I replied that, yes, they can get by fine without lichens if they are in places where it is warm enough so there is green vegetation available all winter, but that is not the situation in most of northern Alaska. Then he realized I was lecturing him, and he said, "Oh, I know all that!" I felt like saying, "Then why did you ask the question in the first place?" But it was obvious to others that he had put himself in that awkward position. When he realized he was just embarrassing himself, he said, "Well, no more questions." This is all in the Congressional Record, which is nice.

When asked how I felt personally about it, I said, "My personal feeling is I want to see the public well informed because they are the ones that should be making this decision, not me. And if you're representing the public and your constituents, I want them to be well informed, too." I believe if it looks like your emotional feelings are guiding your science, then you lose credibility immediately. I wanted to be respected as a scientist who happened to do studies that ended up supporting environmentalists' positions. The studies I did related to understanding the caribou and the Arctic National Wildlife Refuge were based on wanting to understand the caribou and their behavior and possible impacts from oil development (Klein 2001b). To me, that was informing the public. This is a nationally protected public area, not just an Alaska protected area. I'd be willing to say, yeah, it's a wildlife refuge and if you're going there to do something like development then you've got to have special consideration.

The worst-case scenario I faced was when the Alaska Coalition of conservation groups contacted me and asked if I would be willing to go and testify on the importance of the coastal plain of the Arctic National Wildlife Refuge for caribou and muskoxen at a congressional hearing in Washington, DC. They wanted me as a scientist and because of my work for the Fish and Wildlife Service. I said, "Yes, I would, but as Wildlife Unit leader, technically, I had to get approval for travel from the federal government even though the Alaska Coalition was paying for it." The only way I could do it without approval was if I took a leave of absence from work, which would not make the people at the top of the Fish and Wildlife Service very happy. Finally, my immediate supervisor said, "Go ahead and put in a travel request and it's up to the FWS whether they approve it or not." They denied the request. The Director of the Fish and Wildlife Service was a Republican political appointee and his attitude was, "Well, we want good people working for us, and they're supposed to be outside of politics, so just lie low on these things and don't get too involved."

When I told the Alaska Coalition that I couldn't come, they replied, "Well, what about if we have you subpoenaed? Would you be willing to go?" I hemmed and hawed, and finally said, "Yeah, I would. I believe in the research I've done, and I think the results should get out there. I don't care whether it's you or the Fish and Wildlife Service that pays my way." They contacted the Director of the Fish and Wildlife Service and said, "We're going to subpoena Dave Klein, and if you won't authorize his travel that's going to be a problem." So the Fish and Wildlife Service Director caved in on that. He didn't want to be accused of muzzling me.

I think it is important to have humility, especially when being presented as the "scientific expert." Scientists frequently don't have this, which can be a problem with some young scientists that are called to testify or are interviewed. They don't know the answers, but they think they do. The interviewers say, "Well, you're an expert on this, therefore you should know the answer." And the question they ask them is not what they were studying, but it's a broader ecological question. Well, an ecological question is so complex and you have to do a lot of studies before you can answer any question. You cannot say you know the environment, unless you've done adequate research. I think it is important to know the limitations of your knowledge and not being afraid to say, "Well, I'm sorry I can't answer that question. This is going beyond the limits of our knowledge." There's a limit to what humans can know about some other organism's ability to think. In effect, we don't have enough scientific research done yet to be able to answer a lot of these questions.

Besides testifying before Congress or giving public presentations, I utilized my scientific understanding of the biological and ecological complexity of caribou and their ecosystem dynamics within the Arctic National Wildlife Refuge in other ways. For example, in 2001, Hank Lentfer was putting together a booklet of essays titled *Arctic Refuge: A Circle of Testimony* espousing the biological and aesthetic richness of the Arctic National Wildlife Refuge (Lentfer and Servid 2001), and he asked if I would contribute a biologist's perspective on caribou in the Porcupine Caribou Herd. I wrote "The Conundrum of Caribou Complexity" as an attempt to explain the complexity of the biology and ecology of caribou and why they present such a unique management challenge in today's world (Klein 2001b).

David measuring horn growth
in relation to age on a muskox
skull, Blåsø Lake, Greenland, 1987.
COURTESY OF DAVID KLEIN.

10
Ungulate Research Across the Circumarctic

Throughout my years of doing research, I understood the importance of gaining a broader perspective on wildlife and their habitat, so it was obvious to me that Alaska should be more international in how it operates in terms of biological and environmental studies. As Co-op Unit leader, I sought out and was provided opportunities to do comparative studies in other countries of the world, especially on arctic ecology issues. We can learn a lot by collaborating with others in ecologically similar areas all across the Circumarctic where ecosystems and ecosystem dynamics are similar in many ways, as well as in other countries where we can make comparisons with different ecosystems. The more international research work I did, the more I enjoyed it and the more opportunities came my way. Learning from and engaging with others in intellectual discovery is the basis of doing good science, and forming connections with people is a basic foundation of who I am. In addition to being fascinated by northern species and their habitat, I had a deep interest in other cultures and how they related to their environment. So while working in foreign countries, I was as eager to learn about the people and their lifestyles as I was to do science. I developed close relationships, and in some cases, lifelong friendships with some of the scientists I worked with. These international collaborations were enriching and fulfilling to me both professionally and personally. For these reasons, I believe discussion of the people and work we did together deserves significant attention in the retelling of my life and career.

I have chosen to discuss my international research according to country or global region, instead of presenting it in direct chronological order, because the accomplishment of science is a cumulative and collaborative, naturalistic and fluid process, where your understandings build on ideas that came before (both from your own work and that of predecessors), as well as what you learn from your colleagues via publications, personal networking, and discussions at professional conferences. I have tried to present the countries in the general order of when I first started going there, although I continued to work in some of them over the course of many years. Within discussion of each country, I describe events chronologically in keeping with the presentation of previous parts of my life.

Canada

When I began my employment in Southeast Alaska in 1955, there was little understanding of deer ecology in the rainforest of the Pacific Northwest. One of the earliest major human influences on the habitat for the native Sitka black-tailed deer in the coastal rainforest of Southeast Alaska was extensive clear-cut logging that began with the construction of the first pulp mill in Ketchikan in 1954. At that time, US Forest Service policy within the Tongass National Forest emphasized logging over sustainability of habitat for fish and wildlife. I had misgivings about clear-cut logging, but knowledge about the effects of extensive clear-cut logging on deer habitat in Alaska was lacking. As a new wildlife biologist, I had a little bit of experience ecologically, but not a lot, so I looked to Canada, Alaska's closest neighbor, for professional assistance in deer management. I corresponded with Don Robinson, a wildlife biologist with the British Columbia Fish and Wildlife Branch based in Nanaimo on Vancouver Island, who had several years of experience investigating the effects of clear-cut logging on deer habitat there and subsequent involvement in management of the deer. In hopes of developing better wildlife management practices in Alaska, I visited him at Nanaimo in 1957 to see the changes in deer habitat associated with clear-cut logging and trends in the nature and rate of post-logging recovery (Klein 1957a). One of the things I learned on this trip is that deer increased rapidly in the slash-and-burn areas following logging; deer production being greatest two to three years following clear-cutting. Production drops gradually after that period for about twenty to thirty years when density of the second-growth forest discourages hunters and supports few deer.

I also learned that patch logging appeared to be the most beneficial from the standpoint of deer management. Under this system, sufficient mature timber is left standing, which offers cover for the deer during severe winters. I predicted that these effects of logging would be more pronounced under Alaska winter conditions.

The trip to BC more than met my expectations and convinced me that the similarities between coastal British Columbia and Southeast Alaska in wildlife species, their habitats, and history of the people called for close collaboration in management of our fish and wildlife resources. Canada after all was our closest neighbor because of Alaska's geographical isolation from the rest of the United States. I maintained close connections with Canadians throughout my professional career. In addition, for a long time, the University of Alaska waived the non-resident tuition fee for Canadians from Yukon Territory and Northwest Territories, which made it financially easier for many Canadians to do wildlife graduate degrees. Later, an agreement between the University of Northern British Columbia and the University of Alaska enabled exchanges at the postdoctoral level and among faculty.

In later years, some of my research took me to Eastern Canada. For example, in the 1990s, I served as a consultant alongside a Norwegian colleague, Eigil Reimers, on projects studying the potential impact of hydroelectric projects on caribou in Manitoba and Newfoundland. In Manitoba, a river coming into Hudson Bay was going to be dammed with power lines running all the way down to Winnipeg. It was complex, because in addition to the direct problems of the dam and flooding, there were peripheral problems like putting in a power line through the caribou's area and not knowing the impacts of any of this, as well as what the cumulative impacts on the caribou might be. It was quite a different situation with regard to the caribou up north near Hudson Bay, because one of the big migratory herds was wintering in that area. You didn't want this development to interfere with the migration, whereas in the south where the woodland caribou were, the Native people were concerned that a cleared right-of-way would mean more non-Natives would come in with snow machines and hunt along the right-of-way and the caribou would be overharvested. Traditionally, only the Natives had been harvesting those woodland caribou. In Newfoundland, they were diverting streams and creating deep canals, and we raised concerns about whether a caribou got into the canal, could it get out. The other issue was the building of roads associated with the project and how this might affect the movement of caribou and their use of seasonal habitats. And, of course, you have to realize that once there are roads, people will use them as an easier way to come in for hunting. Our job was not to draw conclusions about the project, but to point out all of these potential problems that had to be addressed. The idea was to help the consulting firm doing the environmental impact assessment know where to put emphasis. Also, we were able to recommend things that needed to be done, like more studies on bears and how their predation might be impacted. In both Manitoba and Newfoundland, they built the projects, but they did a lot of modification to minimize the impacts. So that felt good to have played a role in reducing possible impacts to caribou, their migration, and their habitat.

The Fennoscandian Countries

Fennoscandia is a geographical term that acknowledges the shared geographical proximity of Norway, Sweden, Denmark, Finland, Iceland, and Greenland. Although there are well-defined differences in culture, language, and national origins of these countries, it is the commonality of the shared Nordic environment with its pronounced seasonality that has shaped lifestyles and accounted for their somewhat parallel historical, cultural, and nationalistic ties to Europe. Bioclimatic life zones characteristic of the Fennoscandian countries are, for the most part, also present in Alaska, along with similar plant communities and some of the key animal species. These biological, ecological, and cultural similarities through the circumpolar region may help to explain why I have been able to find opportunities to work professionally in all eight of these countries.

The Nordic countries, for the most part, have modeled their versions of modern wildlife management differently from North America. Aldo Leopold acknowledged that wildlife was a crop of the land and should be managed as such to maintain the health of the land. In North America, ownership of the wildlife remains with the state; however, in Europe wildlife is legally the property of the landowner and oversight of management and harvest allocation remains with the state. Despite these differences, the development of wildlife management techniques in the Nordic countries have drawn heavily on English-language publications in American and Canadian books and technical journals, and from international meetings and conferences.

Norway, Sweden, Denmark

My first trip to Europe was in 1965 when the Bureau of Land Management (BLM) funded me to travel to Sweden and Norway to learn about reindeer grazing on rangelands there. I had been doing some studies for BLM on feral reindeer on Atka and Umnak Islands in the Aleutians, and was trying to figure out why they hadn't gone through a big population explosion when they were introduced into a new environment without predators. I had begun to think I was pretty narrow in my understanding, and I realized that there was some work being done in Europe and some of their observations were quite different. I thought it would be healthy for me to learn more about these. The BLM directed me to observe the reindeer range research methodology being employed in these countries and to assess potential applicability for managing grazing lands used by introduced domestic reindeer and wild caribou in Alaska. As Wildlife Unit leader, I didn't get a sabbatical like a regular university professor, so I had to get outside support to do work like this. In order to take full advantage of this unique opportunity, I planned an itinerary to visit a wide variety of reindeer range types, range study areas, reindeer research stations, and reindeer administrative headquarters.

It is important at this point to recognize and acknowledge that reindeer and caribou are one and the same species, *Rangifer tarandus*. *Caribou* is a North American term for the wild form of *Rangifer tarandus*, which as such have never been domesticated in North America, as was the case in Eurasia. In Eurasia, the wild and semidomesticated forms are referred to either as wild reindeer for those that are not being herded and are managed as other wildlife, and simply reindeer for those under direct human control.

In Sweden, I made contacts with some of the reindeer biologists at the University of Uppsala who were doing studies on reindeer ranges, and I worked mainly in areas in northern Sweden that were grazed by the semidomestic reindeer herds controlled by Saami people (referred to as Laplanders at the time). The Saami are reindeer herding people in portions

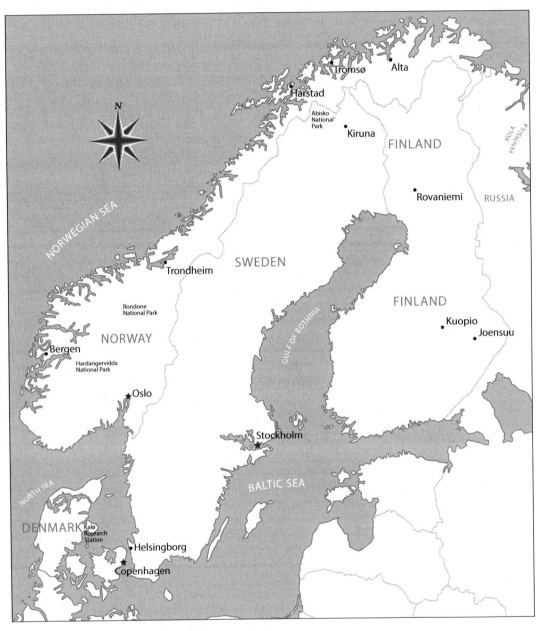

Places that David Klein visited in Scandinavia throughout
his career as an ecologist. MAP BY PAULA ELMES.

of northern Norway, Sweden, Finland, and the Kola Peninsula of Russia. In the past, the Saami people considered their traditional grazing areas to be their homelands irrespective of national boundaries and governmental regulations. However, nationalization of the Saami people over the past two centuries made them citizens of the countries in which they resided, brought schooling and health care to their villages, and provided some protection of their grazing lands.

In Helsingborg, Sweden, I met with Folke Skuncke, a senior forester in his early eighties who was recognized throughout Sweden and Norway for his accumulated knowledge of the ecology of lichens, and had spent much of his professional career investigating logging practices in the northern forest areas of Sweden and their influence on the traditional grazing patterns of reindeer owned by the Saami. At that time, botanists and foresters throughout Scandinavia had largely ignored lichens as important components in the dynamics of northern forest ecosystems. Lichens are the primary component of the winter diet of the reindeer, and they grow luxuriously in northern conifer forests, so the Saami reindeer herders in both Finland and Sweden traditionally used these forests as their winter grazing areas. These forests were generally on state lands where priority was placed on sustained yield harvesting through highly mechanized, clear-cut patch logging that can have substantial impact on lichens. By depleting their key winter forage, the reindeer population was then also impacted by these forest practices. Skuncke had recently published a book in Swedish reporting on his observational and investigative knowledge of lichen ecology, which challenged existing assumptions of foresters on the overall effects of clear-cut logging in forest areas important for winter grazing by reindeer (Skuncke 1958). After returning to Alaska, I was able to secure funding from BLM to translate and publish Skuncke's book into English (Skuncke 1969). It was gratifying to help share his observations and results with a wider audience.

Accompanied by two or three people, I visited reindeer research stations around Sweden that were set up through the university and I was able to collect a lot of baseline data. One research station that we hiked into was sort of like a model facility. Saami were running it, and Swedish researchers periodically would come to do botanical studies and then go back to the university where they had teaching jobs. At another station, they were doing research on the effective feeding of reindeer during the insect season. They compared what happened when they herded reindeer to places above the tree line where a breeze blowing kept the insects down while burning shelf fungus collected from the trunks of dead trees to create smoke was used to keep the mosquitoes away. They'd have these fires right at the entrance to these lean-to shelters that they built so the animals could go inside or stand just outside in the smoke. When the insects were so bad that the reindeer couldn't feed anyway, the smoke at least made it so they were harassed less or not bitten as badly. When it cooled off at night, enough of the mosquitoes went down that the reindeer could go out and graze, but they knew where to come back to for refuge.

Another one of the areas I visited was Abisko National Park in northern Sweden. The Swedish biological and botanical research station had been there for many years and continues to be an important place for studies of alpine Subarctic flora and fauna. Being able to visit there with one of the Swedish biologists was a great opportunity for me to experience the place from the perspective of the people doing actual research work. This led to later studies that I did in northern Sweden with another senior lichen specialist. That was really a great experience to hike through the range areas, to stay at these research stations, and get to eat Swedish food and reindeer. But I didn't realize at the time how fortunate I was.

One of the most unique and enriching experiences that I had in Sweden was on another trip in the 1970s with Olof Eriksson when I joined him in a visit to winter grazing areas used by the Saami reindeer herders in the pine forests of northern Sweden. Olof was affiliated with the University of Uppsala, had training in botany and forest ecology, and was considered Sweden's expert on the differential responses of ground lichens to grazing pressure by reindeer. He worked directly with the Saami herders in a government-sponsored position aimed at minimizing the effects of clear-cut logging on the lichen-dominated winter reindeer ranges for which the Saami had traditional grazing rights. When preparing for a two-day field excursion, Olof announced that we would be staying the night in a remote cabin. Upon arriving at the so-called "cabin," which was a giant culvert covered with gravel and equipped with a stove and bunks, Olof explained that we were in a fall-out zone for rockets that were fired at night from the launching facility near Kiruna (now the Esrange Space Center operated by the Swedish Space Corporation). This was one of several safe shelters that Saami reindeer herders had insisted be built throughout their grazing range before they would permit the area to be used as a fall-out zone. Actually, Olof jokingly then confirmed that no errant rocket would disturb our ptarmigan dinner or our secure slumber the rest of the night, because we would be spending the night in a different cabin that was just outside of the rocket fall-out zone that a friend of his had made available to us.

A couple of years after this, I was fortunate to host Olof on a visit to Alaska where we could exploit some of his extensive knowledge of winter grazing ecology of reindeer during a weekend field trip at Cantwell that was part of the course I taught on grazing ecology with an emphasis on the role of snow in winter feeding by caribou. Once the class was on skis, Olof, who obviously was an expert skier, trailed behind the slowest students. He claimed he was slow because of the narrow and relatively short fiberglass skis we provided him, preferring the wide, eight-foot-long, wooden skis that he used in Sweden. That evening back at the cabin, Olof admitted with a smile that he had been last not because he was a slow skier, but so that he could assist a female student just ahead of him who fell repeatedly and needed his help getting up out of the soft snow and back on the trail. Olof was sincere in his interest in helping others, and Bob White and I were surprised when later we each received a package from Sweden that contained a pair of the eight-foot-long forester's skis. We sure had a good laugh.

At the end of my 1965 trip, I attended the International Congress of Game Biologists in Stockholm (National Swedish Environmental Protection Board 1974). There I met this young Norwegian student, Eigil Reimers, who was starting his PhD studies on caribou. He invited me to visit his study area that was a place in Norway where I was already looking at the impact of roads and linear obstructions like water pipelines interfering with the seasonal movements of caribou (Klein 1971). For hydro development in Norway, they would dam and divert streams and destroy suitable mountain grazing habitat for the caribou, so they were beginning to be concerned. And when they built the railroad (and later a road) between Oslo and Trondheim, it went through an alpine area within a national park and prevented the caribou from migrating across the railroad. This meant the

David (left) and Eigil Reimers (right) in
Norway, 1972. COURTESY OF DAVID KLEIN.

one side where there was no grazing was lush with lichens, while the other
side was overgrazed (Reimers and Klein 1979). This began a long collaboration with Eigil on the effects of regional climate variability on the ecology
of wild reindeer in the mountains of southern Norway (Reimers, Klein, and
Sorumgard 1983), as well as a deep and lasting friendship.

This entire Scandinavian trip far exceeded my expectations. I saw both
winter and summer reindeer ranges that enabled me to broaden my knowledge of the ecology of northern grazing lands, associated research being
undertaken, and management practices being used. I made many contacts
with reindeer range ecologists that assisted in the exchange of knowledge
relevant to reindeer and caribou range ecology, its management, and the
associated human cultural dependencies that were helpful in subsequent research I did in both Fennoscandia and Alaska. Visiting reindeer and wildlife research stations provided an opportunity to discuss and plan for future
collaborative research on ungulate forage selection and related nutrition and
physiology. These included investigating the role of lichens in the seasonal
nutrition of reindeer with Sven Skjenneberg at the reindeer research station

at Harstad, Norway, and developing methods for assessing relative importance of lichens in the winter diet of reindeer and caribou with Dr. Eldor Gaare and Eigil Reimers from Trondheim, Norway.

Given my previous work on deer ecology and food availability (Klein 1956, 1957b, 1963, 1964, 1965; Klein and Olson 1960), when I was in Scandinavia in 1965 I had a discussion with Professor H. M. Thamdrup at Denmark's Game Biology Station at Kalø regarding a proposed visit to do research on factors influencing body size in roe deer. They had done a classic study dealing with roe deer, the small European deer, where they learned that fencing and feeding them was not a good thing to do. This led to me going to the Kalø Research Station in Rønde, Denmark, in 1967 for six months to study the roe deer. I took the whole family and we lived in a village adjacent to the research station. We put our kids in school, but the teachers in that rural school had very little understanding of English, so they didn't learn much. They didn't really learn much Danish either, because they weren't in school for any length of time and there were not many kids in the neighborhood for them to play with and learn from.

I did research on roe deer habitat relationships in collaboration with a young biologist in his thirties, Helmuth Strandgaard, who was beginning to work with radio collars to monitor movements of animals and was collecting good data. He was working on population dynamics and doing some early work with reflecting collars so that you could go out at night and count the deer with a spotlight. I focused on habitat in relationship to body size of the roe deer that were hunted in different areas. I studied vegetation that was available for the deer to eat and then compared the growth and body size of the deer. During the hunting season, when they were being harvested, we easily could get animals to work with to take measurements and determine body weights, and it also gave us the chance to get stomach samples to see what they were eating.

We had four primary study areas. One was on the grounds of a famous castle called Egeskov, and another was at a private manor house. All these places had game managers who lived on the estates, did counts of the animals, and managed the areas to protect crops from being destroyed by the deer. The roe deer were valuable for hunting; game meat was very popular and could be sold, and these estates made money by charging hunters for the

Kalø game biology station in
Denmark where David did roe deer
research, 1965. PHOTO BY DAVID KLEIN.

privilege to hunt roe deer on their land. Even though the deer were on estate lands, they were still wild, so the game manager was like a wildlife manager.

My study was mainly to look at the deer population in relationship to the history of how they cropped the land. For instance, at the Kalø station, there were forested areas where they made money by growing trees. It was pretty open where you could see between the trees and around the understory, but the deer avoided those places, especially when there was a hunt. They went into brushier areas or sometimes into fields with tall grains growing where there was better cover to hide in. In the wintertime, outside of the hunting season, they were frequently in the fields. Or in another study area along the Atlantic Ocean on the west coast of Denmark where sand dunes were encroaching on and destroying croplands, beach grasses were used to stabilize the dunes and exotic evergreen trees were planted to try to control the sand dunes' movement. In keeping the sand under control, they made a lot more land available for agriculture, but the soil had high sand content so it had to be fertilized heavily in order to grow any significant crops. Herders preferred to graze their animals in areas that didn't have to be fertilized so heavily, so they tended to stay away. There were roe deer out there in both the sand dunes and the cropland, but mainly they preferred the shrubby pine forest area where there was better cover.

What I found out was that animals with the largest body size were from areas with the poorest soils. It seemed counterintuitive. But I was able to show that where the deer had a larger territory in which to range, the density was low. If the soils were poor and they had a large home range, they could be much more selective in feeding than when there was a high population and they were all confined to a much smaller area of good soils. Yes, you could produce more deer under those conditions, but body growth was more limited due to the deer being dependent on selecting the best-quality forage, for which there was more competition.

What I learned in these studies about deer in Denmark was challenging a lot of European attitudes toward roe deer and deer management (Klein and Strandgaard 1972). The old German tradition was you fenced the whole area, but that doesn't work because if you fence them, productivity goes down and body size goes down. It was better to let them disperse. There is a difference in quality depending on the type of forage plants consumed. Different species initiate growth in the deer at different rates and during different seasons, so it is better if the deer can move around and eat different plants and different plant parts depending on when and where they're growing (Klein 1990). In addition, when you have "captive" animals then you have to feed them, and Strandgaard and I showed that supplemental feeding was not a viable approach. Feeding the deer attracts them into one area and they just crop the vegetation to the point where it won't regrow. So now you have overgrazing and a lack of food that can lead to population decline. A lot of what I learned in Denmark provided knowledge that I was able to apply when I started working with caribou and muskoxen and moose in northern Alaska.

The visits I made with wildlife professionals in Norway in 1965 were instrumental in leading to a Fulbright grant that assisted me and the whole family to get to Norway for the sabbatical year of 1971–1972. That was kind of tough financially because I had a family with three young children and the Co-op Unit didn't have any sabbatical program, so I had to accumulate annual leave. We were fortunate to be able to rent out our home while we were gone, and the Fulbright grant covered the travel costs for the whole family. I was a visiting professor in ecology at the University of Oslo where I gave weekly lectures in wildlife ecology and management and environmental sciences, and did research on wild reindeer ecology. I also spent time working on a paper on environmental philosophy, started in Alaska and further stimulated by discussions with philosophy professor Arne Næss and his graduate students, primarily Sigmond Kvaløy. I later presented that paper at the Tømte Gård workshop. (For more on this, see chapter 19: "Environmental Philosophy: People and the Environment.")

Professors, instructors, and interested graduate students with a focus on wildlife ecology, especially Ivar Mysterud, Eivind Østbye, and Eigil Reimers, gathered for lunch, coffee, and discussion on nearly a daily basis. I enjoyed the collegial environment that prevailed, and I greatly looked forward to these sessions. Ivar and Eivind were the primary professorial sponsors for my Fulbright year. Ivar was extremely sociable, was a deep thinker, and a prolific writer on theoretical aspects of ecosystem management. By contrast, Eivind was more at home in the field with his students and was recognized as an outstanding teacher of ecology. And Eigil was a key player in making my sabbatical year possible by getting the funding necessary to include me in joint research where we compared the body condition of feral reindeer and wild reindeer (caribou) in wet versus dry habitats. This provided me the direct connection with the Norwegian natural environment that I had hoped for.

Prior to this, Eigil and his young family had spent a couple of years at the University of Alaska in Fairbanks as a young visiting scientist in training affiliated with and funded through the Institute of Arctic Biology (IAB) and the Cooperative Wildlife Research Unit. He collaborated with Dr. Bob White on investigations of the physiology of caribou and reindeer using captive animals, and assisted me with my investigations of impacts of oil development and associated pipeline and road building on the ecology of caribou and other wildlife. Bob, Eigil, and I came from different cultures, training, and experiences, and all benefited greatly from our collaborative

Ski trip in Norway, 1972. David (left) and Eigel Reimers (middle) had been out on a reindeer research project and they skied from their base camp cabin to meet Eigel's wife, Sidsel (right), who took the train to join them for a three-day ski trip in the high country. COURTESY OF DAVID KLEIN.

and multidisciplinary efforts. My friendship with Eigil and his family grew during my sabbatical year, and their continuing kindness and generous hospitality on subsequent visits provided a pillar of growth for our friendship and working relationship. An outgrowth of this interfamily bond was the year my daughter, PeggyEllen, spent in Norway attending high school and serving as an *au pair* for Eigil and his wife, Sidsil's, two preschool children.

A highlight of my sabbatical year in Norway was my involvement in the winter field expeditions (January and April) of Eigil's research team. We shared a common interest in the winter ecology of *Rangifer* species, as well as the enjoyment of being afield on skis in the beautiful snow-covered alpine landscape. In Alaska, I was considered a top-notch backcountry skier, however, I was humbled in comparison to the Norwegians, especially after I had to borrow a plastic replacement tip upon breaking the tip of my new skis on the wind-sculptured "barcan" snow.[9]

My connections with Norway were initially tied to the University of Oslo, but they expanded over time to include the Norwegian College of Agriculture (later to become the Norwegian University of Life Sciences [NMBU]). Olav Hjeljord, who had received a master's degree at the University of Alaska Fairbanks doing his thesis project on mountain goat habitat relationships, played an important role in my connection with NMBU. Perhaps he was stimulated to focus on mountain goats because of a proposal by Professor Olav Gjærevoll, a botanist at Trondheim University, to introduce Alaska mountain goats to the rocky, mountainous coastal terrain of southwest Norway in order to increase Norway's low mammalian biodiversity, especially lacking large mountain herbivores, and perhaps for aesthetic reasons as well. Gjærevoll was in Fairbanks in the summer of 1953 on a plant-collecting trip to Alaska, and given my master's research on mountain goats, he asked my opinion about the likelihood of goats doing well in the Norwegian coastal environment. I told him that it might work given the similarities in habitat, however, it was important to consider what effect Norway's lack of major predators might have on goat behavior and population growth, and that when you introduce a species, you also have to think about the larger effects on the ecosystem. Olav Hjeljord had been my graduate student at UAF and we continued our connection after he became a faculty member at NMBU, where he initiated an academic program in wildlife management, and wrote a textbook in Norwegian for use in courses where aspects of Norwegian-style wildlife management were being taught as part of general environmental studies.

---

9. David is applying the term *barcan*, which is a type of sand dune, to the snow conditions. A barcan dune is a "large, crescent-shaped dune lying at right angles to the prevailing wind and having a steep, concave leeward side with the crescent tips pointing downwind. Barcan dunes form on flat, hard surfaces where the sand supply is limited. They can reach heights of up to 30m (98ft) and widths of 350m (1,148ft)" (*American Heritage® Science Dictionary*, Houghton Mifflin Company, accessed April 14, 2017, www.dictionary.com). These are challenging conditions for skiing, where ski tips are inclined to go under the crests of the much smaller ridges of hard snow that are formed by a prevailing wind when temperatures are close to freezing.

A field trip in Norway with Eigel Reimers in 1972 to observe feral reindeer in their winter range in Rondone National Park. They skied and drove a snowmachine to this mountaintop to get close to the reindeer on the other side. They needed the snowmachine because they had a permit to take ten animals to collect samples and the meat had to be salvaged and given to a game warden to distribute to those who needed it. PHOTO BY DAVID KLEIN.

I also visited a research station that was run by Sven Sjenneberg who did classic work showing that reindeer didn't do well on a diet of pure lichens. In a controlled experiment, they offered reindeer as much lichen as they could eat, but they weren't able to maintain their body weight on pure lichens. Sjenneberg narrowed it down to being the need for nitrogen, which the low-nitrogen lichen could not provide enough of. The reindeer needed to have some green vegetation to give them enough nitrogen. It turned out that the nitrogen was not so much needed initially by the caribou (reindeer), but by the digesting microorganisms. The microorganism population needed to build up sufficiently to handle large quantities of lichens. Sjenneberg's research showed that the reindeer would eat more lichens and put on weight once they started eating nitrogen-rich urea-soaked pellets along with the lichens. These reindeer were much healthier and had much better body condition than the ones that were eating just straight lichens and nothing else (Klein and Schønheyder 1970; Klein 1990). It was great for me to get exposed to all this stuff and think about ways to apply it back to my research in Alaska.

The strength and breadth of my research in Norway also increased and expanded over many years. My initial focus was on habitat relationships of ungulates, specifically caribou, in alpine habitats, where I did research on the wild reindeer in southern Norway, specifically in the Hardangervidda area, a plateau between Oslo, Bergen, and Trondheim. It expanded to include the relative importance of lichens in the seasonal diet of reindeer and caribou from the southern alpine habitats through the winter grazing lands of reindeer in north Norway, to the extreme situation of the Svalbard reindeer (caribou) that have adapted morphologically and physiologically to life in the high Arctic where predators are absent and where lichens are not a significant component of their winter diet. This coincided with increasing recognition of the influence of human activities on caribou/reindeer habitat loss and disruption of annual movement patterns, especially through hydropower, petroleum, and mining development and associated pipeline, railroad, road, and power line construction (Nellemann and Cameron 1998; Reimers et al. 2000). I also was involved in projects related to increasing public concern over the impact of industrial development on the natural environment of the Arctic, its wildlife, and its people (Reimers and Klein 1979; Anker 2007; Kvaløy 1974).

Having these opportunities in Scandinavia was important to me for a number of reasons. First, I felt it was really good for the family to be in places like Norway and Denmark. It was especially good in Norway for the children, who went to Norwegian schools and learned Norwegian. Also, I developed strong bonds of friendship with Norwegian colleagues that extended mutually to our families and helped to make us Alaskans feel welcome. For example, my family and I were often beneficiaries of recreational cabin or rural farmstead visits with the Reimer, Hjeljord, and Staaland families. I also became friends with Hans Staaland, a faculty member with Olav at NMBU, who had spent a sabbatical year at UAF associated with the Institute of Arctic Biology and the Department of Biology and Wildlife. Our families became close friends when they were in Fairbanks, and one

Svalbard reindeer, 1981. Svalbard reindeer have shorter legs compared with other caribou and wild reindeer of the Arctic, because the snow in Svalbard is not as deep and they migrate over shorter distances than in other regions. PHOTO BY DAVID KLEIN.

of the Staalands' daughters later became a graduate student in our wildlife program at UAF. In 1979, I spent three weeks with Hans in Svalbard (Spitzbergen) in association with his research on the physiological adaptation and extreme fat storage of the Svalbard wild reindeer that enabled them to exist at 79°N that was funded through the Norwegian Man and the Biosphere program. While there, we collected the persistent winter feces of reindeer and muskoxen where they occurred together in alpine habitats, even though the last muskox on Svalbard had died two years earlier. Analysis of plant remains in the feces showed diet overlap, suggesting that the muskoxen had died out through competitive exclusion following an increase of reindeer, a consequence of their protection from hunting in 1927 (Klein and Staaland 1984).

Second, this time in Norway provided an excellent introduction to the peoples, cultures, and ecology of northern Scandinavia. It stimulated a growing interest in human cultures endemic to Arctic and alpine environments that has persisted throughout my professional career. This has included a curiosity about the adaptations of Arctic- and alpine-dwelling peoples that have enabled them to develop their unique cultures, while making sustainable use of the resources upon which they have depended.

And third, having these experiences led to more and more connections and changes in my career. Through the years, I was invited to give talks at the Universities of Lund, Stockholm, Uppsala, and Umeå in Sweden. These were generally in association with my presenting a paper at a wildlife-related conference or workshop at the specific university, or through the European Fulbright program while I was at the University of Oslo. I was invited to the University of Umeå by Kjell Danell, professor and head of the Department of Environmental Sciences, under a faculty exchange agreement where I gave lectures, served as external examiner for a PhD thesis defense, and provided advice to grad students. I also was fortunate to accompany Professor Danell and other faculty on a field excursion to Abisko National Park, where we visited adjacent moose and reindeer habitats. At the Abisko Botanical Research Station, we participated in a workshop focused on northern ungulates and their ecology that was organized by Professor Terry Callaghan, director of the station. Abisko provided an excellent setting for the workshop, which likely stimulated the excellent discussion sessions around the technical papers presented. There was extended discussion about the paper that I presented on adaptations of caribou/reindeer that enabled them to occupy the northernmost land areas, which assisted in my being able to provide a more detailed explanation of the plant-animal interactions and improve the final published paper (Klein 1999). And in 1995, because of my involvement with an ecosystem research project about the Porcupine Caribou Herd in Alaska and Canada (Kruse et al. 2004), I was asked to be part of a committee reviewing the Swedish whole-system modeling project titled *Towards Harmony between Man and Nature in the Mountain Region* that was funded through the Swedish National Foundation for Strategic Environmental Research (Mistra). This review group was chaired by Anders Karlqvist with the Swedish Polar Center and included four senior professors who were internationally recognized for their focus on ecology (three were from universities in the UK, and me from the University of Alaska). We were charged with an objective review of the proposed project and the need to recommend for or against continued funding for implementation of the project. Through this experience I also was able to greatly expand my understanding of how environmental science was funded in Sweden, which I found more generally favorable to the scientists involved in comparison to the United States.

Greenland

Because of these exchanges I did and international conferences I attended, I started meeting people doing similar work in other countries. Either they'd invite you to come, or you'd say something like, "Well, it'd be great if we could get together and get out in the field in Greenland with you." I had built these connections for a long time, starting from the sabbatical year with the Norwegians, and I had started doing research in Greenland in 1977 because some of the same Danish people I had done the early work with had graduated to working in Greenland. I went back to Greenland in 1982, 1987, 1991, and 1999, doing research on the ecology of caribou and muskoxen, and Arctic herbivory.

By the 1980s, the Kalø Game Biology Station had assumed responsibility for research on caribou ecology in West Greenland and I was invited to join Henning Thing, who was from Denmark, as an advisor on his doctoral dissertation work where he was initiating long-term research focused on the foraging dynamics of the West Greenland caribou population. I knew Henning, because as I mentioned previously, he had come to UAF to do some research on the energy costs for caribou of their winter foraging behavior. Henning had broad ecological interests and had by this time developed into an outstanding investigative Arctic ecologist. My focus while collaborating with Henning was largely on the ecology of caribou in west Greenland in comparison to the ecology of muskoxen in east Greenland prior to their introduction to west Greenland. Henning got some money to partly pay for me to spend a couple of weeks with him based at this airfield called Søndre Strømfjord that during World War II had been a US military base. Gradually, it became Danish and was given the Greenlandic name

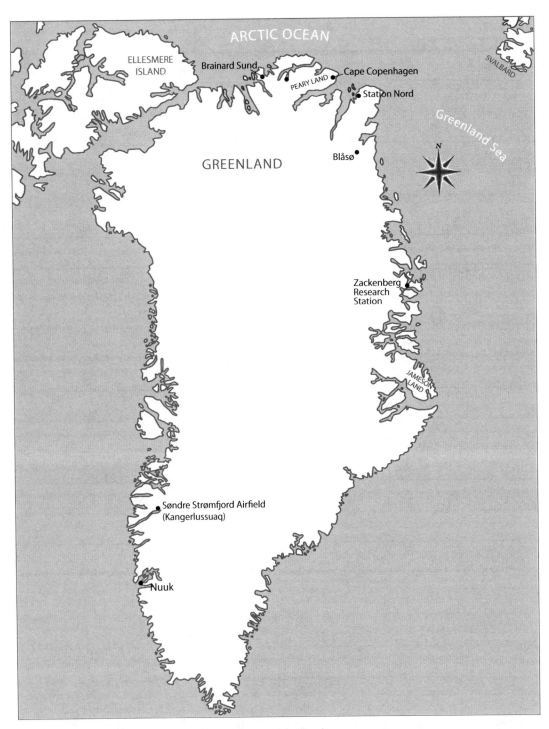

Places that David Klein visited in Northern Greenland and Svalbard
throughout his career as an ecologist. MAP BY PAULA ELMES.

Kangerlussuaq. I appreciated and enjoyed working with Henning and his Danish colleagues, and I always felt at the time that I was not giving enough to Henning in exchange for their paying to get me over there. We developed a really strong relationship. Sometimes it's not just about the science, but it's the connections you build with each other that then foster ideas and collaborations. You learn things from each other.

What I learned about the caribou in west Greenland is that they moved seasonally from the coast inland to the mountains in search of the best food for them. Out on the coast, closer to the sea, there was more precipitation so lichens grew well out there, as did a lot of other vegetation that made for good summer range, like sedges, grasses, and dwarf willows. But in the winter the snow would be deeper at the coast, so frequently it would be too deep for the caribou to dig through to get lichens. When they were close to the inland ice, there were not many lichens because it was so dry that they would grow slowly and caribou would eat them faster than they could grow. So there was this gradual increase in lichens as you went to the coast, but the availability to the caribou was dependent on seasonal conditions.

I was in Greenland again in 1982 for work with muskoxen to investigate possible disturbance effects from seismic work related to proposed oil exploration by Amoco Oil Company in Jameson Land in eastern Greenland. As the other major Arctic ungulate, muskoxen are quite unique and very different from caribou. In comparison to caribou, muskoxen don't migrate long distances or move around as much so they have lower physiological energy demands. And muskoxen are big animals with short legs that just kind of plow through the snow and are not as well adapted for movement in snow compared to caribou with their long legs. Also, their small hooves do a poor job of supporting the weight of such a large animal, so with every step taken muskoxen sink down more in the snow. It is easier for muskoxen living in windy areas, such as some places in Greenland, where much of the land gets blown snow-free, so the muskoxen can more easily wander around without having to deal with deep snow. But some of the best food is under the snowdrifts that form in the wind, so often muskoxen winter along the edge of those drifts in order to gain access to this good-quality forage as soon as it is exposed during the spring thaw. Finally, muskoxen differ from caribou in that they have a bigger rumen with a slower rate of passage of forage through the gut. This means muskoxen can eat poorer-quality food, and they spend a longer time ruminating and rechewing it and digesting it.

Because muskoxen do not have to run very much or very far, overheating is less of a problem so they can be better insulated than caribou. And because they are fairly stationary animals, they require more insulation to keep themselves warm in the cold winter months. Therefore, adult muskoxen have a lot of fat internally and under their skin over their whole body, and they have an outer coat made of long guard hairs and a thick, wool-like underlayer called *qiviut*. Muskoxen are so well insulated that they can't cool off rapidly, which makes them very vulnerable to heat stroke, even in the winter.

Given their physiological differences, muskoxen and caribou also have distinct predator avoidance strategies. Since muskoxen are not good runners, they utilize a "stand their ground" strategy and defend themselves with their sharp upturned horns. When they feel threatened, a group of muskoxen forms a nice tight circle of animals with all of the adults facing out and the calves shielded behind them inside the circle. They like to be on top of a little knoll when they do this, so they have a better chance of seeing incoming predators. If a calf makes a mistake and starts to break out, a large adult will butt the calf pretty hard to get it back to where it is protected. Of course, the group size needs to be sufficient enough for this technique to be effective, so they tend to congregate into large groups.

The sharp horns of the muskoxen are particularly effective when defending against wolves. Wolves will run around the encircled group of muskoxen, and when one of them charges in one of the adult muskoxen charges out and tries to hook the wolf with its horn and throw it through the air. This usually results in ripping open the gut of the wolf, which is really lethal for a wolf. So wolves learn that the best strategy for killing muskoxen, especially calves, is to sneak up close to them when they're feeding and somewhat dispersed, and then rush in before the cows can rejoin into a group. Sometimes, if a wolf is fast enough, he can pick off a calf before all the muskoxen rush back together into a protective group.

In Greenland in the early 1980s, Amoco had negotiated with the Danish government to do some seismic work where they would drill a shallow hole and put an explosion in it and instruments on the surface would tell you a bit about the structure underneath. This was relatively low, hilly country

Female muskoxen grazing in lush green sedge meadows, while a large bull takes a break from foraging and rests in the snow, Cape Copenhagen, July 1987. Compared with the males, female muskoxen are aggressive foragers who have to rebuild energy after giving birth and maintain it for feeding their calves, so they are eating nearly constantly during this period. Green plants thrive in the moist areas created by drainage from melting snowbanks, so these sedge meadows provide primary forage for muskoxen in an otherwise rocky landscape. PHOTO BY DAVID KLEIN.

and sort of rocky terrain in an area that was unglaciated and where there were a lot of muskoxen in the summer. There would be a big bang from the explosion and a big cloud of dust afterward, and they wanted to know how the muskoxen would respond to these explosions. Like if the muskoxen were close to the explosions and they broke up into groups, was there mixing between groups? Or how frequently did they mix with other groups and how frequently was the exchange? Well, how do you figure that out? Henning and I decided to put numbers on the animals so we could distinguish individual animals and watch where they went and see how they were mixing. To do this, we needed to live capture the animals by darting them and put on ear tags marked with a big plastic number that you could read with binoculars or a spotting scope from a distance (Thing et al. 1987).

I brought one of my grad students with me, Kent Jingfors, who was a Swede who'd done some work as an undergraduate student in the Canadian Arctic on muskoxen, so he had a lot of knowledge that I thought would be helpful. And we had a veterinarian with us, because when darting animals with a drug you want to make sure it is being done correctly to ensure minimum mortality. The question was how do you get close enough to safely shoot the muskoxen with a dart? They can be very dangerous, especially if a large bull is chasing you. There are no trees to climb, and you can't rely on just shooting them. So they hired a Native man from the nearby village who had muskox hunting experience to help shoot and capture them. The Natives in Greenland had learned that it's bad to kill a large muskox in a group because they're going to bunch up in their protective stance, and then how do you get to this animal that's lying on the ground in the middle of the group. It was better to hunt small groups and kill all of the animals in a group, and they found that the best way to hold the animals and get close was with trained hunting dogs that would run around and bark at the muskoxen in their defensive circle. This made it safe for the hunter to get fairly close, because the muskoxen would be focused on the dogs rather then the hunter.

The research team decided to use this technique for darting and tagging the animals being studied. We'd hike across the terrain with the Native guy's two dogs on chain leashes until we saw a group of muskoxen we thought we could work with. When we got as close as we could get, or if the muskoxen started moving because they saw us, we released the dogs who would run to catch up to the muskoxen. Once the muskoxen had formed into their protective circle, we would go in carefully, and then call off the dogs and put them back on their leash. Since we were shooting a dart, we couldn't be too far away, because you want it to have enough power to penetrate the muskoxen's thick fur and hide. The fur is thinner over their rump, where there is a lot of muscle tissue and not a bone close to the surface, so you wanted to hit there. The Native hunter was a good shot, and he knew to use a bigger syringe with a greater amount of drug in it for a large muskox versus when it was a smaller animal requiring a lower-charged dart. We didn't dart the calves. With the muskoxen in a group like this, we had to be really careful, because as soon as he would dart the adults, they would go down sequentially, but the calves that were not darted wouldn't go away because these animals always stayed together. As soon as the animals were down, we rushed in and the vet would get blood samples, we would collect a little bit of *qiviut*, and we put on the ear tags. We had to be fast because you shouldn't have ruminants like this down for very long.

While I was there, we marked thirty animals. We did kill one female by accident. The first dart went in and we thought it had hit a bone because the animal didn't go down. So the Native hunter gave it another charge. Maybe that first one eventually worked its way out of the bone and released the drugs so that it got too much of the drug, an overdose, and it died. But it didn't go to waste. We learned a lot from it because we skinned it and could see how the fat was distributed at that time of the year. Plus, we ate it and gave some to the dogs, too.

After we had the muskoxen marked, then we did some observations of them from ridges and areas where they couldn't see us, and observed how the muskoxen reacted to the noise when they set the explosions off, firing them remotely. A puff of dirt went flying in the air and from a distance we could hear the *boom*. We looked at the muskoxen and they hardly moved, even though the explosion was only a couple hundred yards away from them. Sometimes the muskoxen would look in that direction, but a lot of times they didn't even look up. They just went on feeding. The noise didn't seem to bother them. They wouldn't run, and the groups didn't fracture. We determined that because muskoxen don't move into their protective groups until they see something moving in the distance, like a wolf, just the noise without movement didn't trigger the grouping response. Also, if they were in places close to where there were glaciers, they would be used to loud noises of big icebergs cracking and crashing. It was just part of the sounds of the environment.

This was just sort of the beginning of my experiences in Greenland. I was becoming fascinated by the ecology of the high Arctic, especially in northeast Greenland where there were complete guilds of herbivores and other mammals and birds. Specifically, I was getting interested in the complex relationship of the muskoxen to their environment and how they were highly adapted for life in the high Arctic, which is a polar desert in terms of precipitation. How did these vegetation-dependent mammals possibly survive when the place was so dry? Earlier in my career, I was focusing heavily on big ungulates and Arctic adaptions, but it was the low Arctic. The number of vascular plant species on the North Slope, I think, is around three thousand. In north Greenland, in the high Arctic, we couldn't quite crack one hundred species. And there were four or five basic plant species that were essential for the herbivores. Subsequently, my research interests broadened to seek better understanding of how vertebrate herbivores in the high Arctic of Greenland, the northernmost land area, had co-adapted with the relatively few plant species seasonally available to them as forage. It seemed to me that in the high Arctic, where ecosystems lack the complexity common at lower latitudes, investigations of plant-animal relationships were easier to assess from both the plant and animal perspective. For example, it was easier to make comparisons within the ecosystem where there were only five species of plants that were primarily important for the muskoxen year round. This assumption underlaid my choice of the high Arctic of Greenland as a preferred locale for research on Arctic herbivores.

With encouragement and recommendation from Henning Thing, who was now working with the Danish Polar Center, I established collaboration with Christian Bay, a botanist with the Botanical Museum at the University of Copenhagen, who was involved in describing and mapping the flora of north Greenland for his doctorate on the vegetation of north Greenland. We first worked together in 1987, and by collaborating and joining our field investigations we were able to assist one another as needed. We established a close friendship that made our joint time in the field particularly enjoyable. His help and experience in herbivore habitat mapping and biomass measurement were invaluable to the success of the project, as well as his handling of the somewhat complicated outfitting and travel logistics to get us, our supplies, and field equipment from Copenhagen to and from north Greenland.

To work up there is a real expedition and the travel was fairly expensive because we had to fly in a Twin Otter from northern Iceland. Christian had a slim budget and I only had support from the National Science Foundation (NSF) to pay for my travel, so we shared that cost for the Twin Otter with another expedition of Danes and one Greenlandic guy who were explorers and historians. During the first half of the expedition, we were at about 82°

Christian Bay assessing prostrate willow (*salix arctica*) density in relation to muskox forage, Cape Copenhagen, Greenland, 1987. PHOTO BY DAVID KLEIN.

north in a different place than where the other group was, and then we went back to the Station Nord, which was the base for the Twin Otter. Then we joined up with the other team and went to a lake called Blåsø, which is a little bit farther south, around 79°north.

We were out about three weeks in the national park area of Greenland, and were trying to get an idea of things like how could there be two hundred muskoxen in this big valley area, but scattered out into various groups that didn't seem to be connected to each other? We were doing observations on feeding behavior and group dynamics in relation to feeding, plus did a lot of vegetation clipping and had small plots to measure the biomass of forage types. Then we were able to dry and weigh the plant samples and take them back for chemical analysis. There wasn't much vegetation there, and what was there was patchy, therefore we assumed the groups would be smaller than someplace else with better vegetation for foraging. This led me to focus on the effect of patch dynamics on muskox feeding and behavior.

During that first year in North Greenland, we had some funding to put three satellite radio collars on muskoxen in order to mark where they went. We wanted to get radio collars on animals so that in the wintertime when it's so cold and dark that you can't fly, you can still see where they go. We didn't have a clue where they went or how active they were during the long, dark winter. Well, this meant we had to be able to dart three animals. But this time, we wouldn't have dogs to help us. We naïvely thought we could maybe knock one cow down, but after watching the animals for a while, we realized there was no way we could knock a cow down out of the group and handle it to get a collar on. We didn't want this to be a major operation; we couldn't drug them all. The way the darts worked was that you had a shell that you fired like a .22 that propelled the dart. When it hit something, there was this little charge inside the dart that went off and it squeezed the drug into the animal. Well, that charge part was in a package that got left behind. And that was my fault because I hadn't checked everything before we left. So I had to figure out if there was any way we could still use these darts. I had read up on these darts a bit, and figured that when it hit the animal, the weight in back slid like a syringe and the weight forced the dart in. Well, I thought, I could possibly make something like that because I had a coil of soldering lead. I cut chunks of that off with pliers and made a weight that would fit inside, and then squeezed it because the lead was somewhat malleable. We hoped it would work. We also decided that we would have to settle for bulls, instead of cows, because there were some solitary bulls around who would be easier to target.

We loaded the gun with one of the modified darts and shot, but the animal didn't go down. And it didn't go down. Fortunately, we were able to get another dart in and we began to see a little bit of effect of the drug. My conclusion was that only a small charge was getting into the animal. So, I put a little heavier weight in and we tried to get closer, and then finally the animal went down. When we looked at the previously shot darts, we could see they hadn't fully discharged. We were lucky that it worked. We then were able to get a second muskox in a similar fashion. We felt good about getting collars on two muskoxen, and we had one more collar that we really wanted to use, but finding another single animal was not easy.

Previously, I had done a long hike by myself to the highest mountain in the area that was like a thousand or fifteen hundred feet above the surrounding terrain and had seen a shed caribou antler. Now, I went back to retrieve it to give it to the Copenhagen zoo so they could determine when

David and Ulf Marquard-Petersen loading a tranquilizer dart for muskoxen at Cape Copenhagen, North Greenland, 1987. COURTESY OF DAVID KLEIN.

that particular caribou had been alive. There I was by myself without the dart gun, and as I came over the top suddenly there was a large bull muskoxen lying down in front of me. I thought to myself, "I want to get that antler, but how can I get it without him seeing me? And if he does see me, then what do I do?" Well, there was a huge boulder that had been left by a receding glacier that I figured I could jump up on and be safe, figuring that the muskoxen probably wouldn't try to get up on it. Mostly, they just bluff charge anyway, but you don't want to risk it. So I tried sneaking over to the antler and just when I was almost there, he looked around and got up. I grabbed the antler and ran and jumped up on that rock. Well, this muskox was not happy. It came and made all these bluffs where it puts its foot down on a tussock or a rock and puts his head down and rubbed, and even butted the rock. There were a couple of smaller stones up on top that I thought about dropping down onto the muskox, but I figured that probably would just make it more angry. So I figured, well, I'll try to get over on the blind side of the rock so it couldn't see me and see what happens. I did that, but

Ulf Marquard-Petersen checking on the recovery of
a muskox after attaching a satellite collar and the
tranquilizer antidote had been administered, Cape
Copenhagen, North Greenland, 1987. PHOTO BY DAVID KLEIN.

the muskox just stayed right there. I was eager to get off and head back, so I finally slid down on the backside of the rock, quietly went over the edge of the flat top, and walked away very slowly. At last glance, I could see the muskox lying there by the rock looking in the other direction. When I got back to camp, I said to the other guys, "Let's go back up there and see if we can get that bull for the third collar." It was about a three-mile hike, and before we went up to the top, I said, "You better load up here." It was then that we discovered that the bolt had fallen out of the gun, so we had no way of firing anything. We didn't have any alternative way to dart the animals, so we only ended up collaring the two animals. Under the circumstances, though, that was pretty good.

The collars had batteries that were supposed to last for about two years. One of them lasted about eight months, and the other one functioned longer. We were able to download data showing where the muskoxen had wintered. By this time, Christian also had been able to get some satellite imagery of vegetation, and made a map of the vegetation in the study area showing that where the muskoxen were going was one of the richest places for willows in the whole north area of Greenland. It didn't tell us whether the females and young were doing the same thing, which was likely, but at least we had this information that these animals had to feed all winter long in order to survive up there (Klein and Bay 1990, 1991, 1994).

In 1991, the International Arctic Ungulate Conference was held in Nuuk, Greenland, and I was able to get several of my students over to that, which was terrific, and I stayed to do some more research. Now I was deep into the ecology of high Arctic vertebrate ecosystems, including hares, lemmings, ptarmigan, and migratory birds, which are all feeding on many of the same plants that muskoxen rely on (Klein and Bay 1994). Analyzing feces was a useful way to determine what animals ate, so I collected feces of hares and lemmings to confirm what we assumed they were feeding on. Earlier, I had been interested in doing the same with muskox fecal pellets for research

Christian Bay (left) processing plant samples to put in a plant press and David processing hare and lemming feces to determine what these animals were eating, inside Sirius Hut in Nansenland, North Greenland, circa 1992. COURTESY OF DAVID KLEIN.

I was doing (Klein and Thing 1989), so I told Dan Roby who was over in Greenland with Henning that I wanted some muskox feces. They dried them under high temperature to kill any organisms, eggs and things like that, and put them in a package for me. Technically, you have to have a permit to ship something like that overseas, which we didn't have. So I get this package that was labeled, "Contents: bull shit." Customs never bothered with it. We had a big laugh over that one.

Then the Danish Polar Center started a research station in Zackenberg at 75° North in northeastern Greenland (Meltofte et al. 2008). I went there in 1997 and was working mainly with the muskoxen, lemmings, and vegetation. My focus was on secondary chemicals and how these plants survive when they are primary food for herbivores. One species of prostrate willows is all-important for the lemmings, the hares, and the muskoxen, but during different seasons. I learned that for hares and muskoxen, the primary value they gained from willows was when the plants were just leafing out in the spring, but in the winter they would also eat the twigs that had grown in the previous summer and were exposed and not covered with deep drifted snow. If the willows were under the snow, then it was the lemmings that ate them.

In summer 2000, Christian Bay and I were both based at the Zackenberg Research Station and were able to continue our cooperative research on plant defenses against herbivores, and he could continue his vegetation mapping work. We were also caught up in the broader interest of climate change that related to all of the ongoing research at Zackenberg. Fiona Danks, a grad student beginning an MS thesis project involving remote sensing of muskoxen habitat in Alaska, accompanied me and gained valuable experience. Christian, Fiona, and I were primarily occupied in my investigations of secondary chemicals in arctic willow and their influence on selective feeding by herbivores. We picked willow leaves in order to compare male plants versus female plants. There had been a little research in Canada on this, and we were able to build on that to show that the male and the female plants were different. The female plants were more robust and maintained the secondary chemicals, but they grew much faster than the male plants. Male plants tended to be located and germinate on little bumps on the high-centered polygons, where it tends to suffer from summer drought, but was the first place where plants could start to grow in the springtime after the snow

Researchers and staff sitting oustide on a nice day in front of the mess hall at Zackenberg Research Station, Greenland, circa 1997. The net is for playing badminton, which is one of the things they did for entertainment, and the building on the left is the toilet facility. PHOTO BY DAVID KLEIN.

melted, whereas the females were down a little lower on the terrain, and were located right next to each other. We were able to demonstrate differential foraging pressure by muskoxen on male versus female plants of the dioecious arctic willow (*Salix arctica*) (Klein et al. 2008).

Also when we were at Zackenberg, Thomas Berg, a graduate student, was involved in initiating research that would become the meat of his PhD dissertation on aspects of the ecology of the collared lemming. Lemmings were numerous, and Fiona and I easily captured a couple. We housed the lemmings in a laboratory cage designed for mice, and provided them with water, a nest box, and fresh-picked willow leaves, which they seemed to prefer over other plant parts. I suggested that Thomas take over care of the lemmings and offered to help him design feeding trials to assess lemming preference for leaves of male versus female plants as correlated with differences in their secondary chemical levels. Thomas enjoyed working with the lemmings and after some improvements in research design and replacement of a few escapees he was able to collect sufficient data for use in his dissertation.

Iceland

In 1981, I received an invitation to go to Iceland to visit the grazing area of their only reindeer, a feral and hunted population of about 3,500 animals left over from introductions from Norway in 1771–1787. My initial curiosity about how Iceland's unique history and dynamic landscape shaped the culture of the Icelandic people was stimulated by Halldór Laxness's writings about the Icelandic people, their lives, and culture, for which he received the 1955 Nobel Prize for literature. So I was eager to go there and learn more firsthand.

The purpose of my visit was to assist the Icelandic government in assessing the possible consequences of a proposed massive hydroelectric project that would result in flooding of a large portion of the grazing area used by the reindeer. During my career, I had focused heavily on vegetation and the plant-animal relationship and was considered sort of an expert on this in terms of reindeer and caribou, and that fit well into what they wanted to find out about in Iceland. It was the question of plants supporting the grazing sheep and the reindeer. The location for the proposed project was north of Vatnajökull, Iceland's largest ice cap, where melt-waters flowing from the northern edge of this giant ice field were to be dammed and would destroy a lot of biologically rich habitat that was good for the reindeer, as well as sheep. I worked with two young biologists, Skarphédinn Thórisson, a wildlife biologist, and Kristbjorn Eigilsson, a botanist, who were employed through the Icelandic Museum of Natural History in Reykjavik to develop the portion of the environmental impact assessment relating to the effects of the proposed project on the reindeer.

My particular role in Iceland was working mostly as an advisor for a couple of months with these two young biologists. The main thing that I did was size up the situation and then figure out the best way to do studies. Essentially, I suggested doing some line transects and have study plots to identify the vegetation types and the seasonality of the quality of the forage for grazing animals. Lichens were not as big a factor as in other areas because the winter season was shorter there and they had a lot of rain. Plus, some of it is lava fields, which are pretty sterile. The only thing growing there would be a little bit of one kind of moss, which animals don't usually eat, a few lichens on the rocks, and little patches of grass where soil had built up. The volcanic ash had gradually built up over thousands of years and had a nice mat of vegetation on top that was about a meter and a half thick. But if that was grazed too heavily, that mat got broken, and all the rain and melting snow and wind would wash away the soil and vegetation. Animals would graze and move between these places eating a blade of grass here, a blade of grass there, but if they could get those areas back into production, it would give them more grazing land.

The entire study area was not road accessible, presenting a real challenge for getting us there to do fieldwork. First, we flew a circuitous three-hundred-mile route from Reykjavik along the south and east coasts of Iceland to avoid the vast Vatnajökull ice field, which was known by Icelandic pilots to "generate its own weather," to Egilsstadir, a road junction community with little worthy of note except having the only airfield in northeast Iceland and a small restaurant with two menu options, both lamb with boiled potatoes. I generally favor trying local foods that provide insight into the local culture and therefore chose the "half of lamb's head." This may sound repulsive to some, however, I had tried lamb's head in Norway as a Christmas delicacy and enjoyed it. In Norway, the lamb's head was admittedly more eloquently presented than in spartan and remote Iceland, where consuming the single eye of the unfortunate sheep was necessary before the succulent meat beneath it could be consumed. At Eigilsstadir, we rented a four-wheel drive surplus Russian military vehicle that was like a big jeep. All I can say for this vehicle is that it was tough. It was well worn and rugged, and functioned relatively well on the rough terrain of historic lava flows, course volcanic ash, and boulders through which we traveled.

Kristbjorn drove me and Skarphédinn to the edge of an alpine plateau that extended to the Vatnajökull Icefield, which constituted the grazing area for the reindeer, and the remainder of the day we walked transects across the tundra. This enabled me to become familiar with the dominant plant communities and to query Skarphédinn about seasonal patterns of use by the reindeer. By day's end, I had gained a good perspective on the eastern portion of the reindeer grazing area and Skarphédinn and I had covered a lot of terrain. As we were getting close to the end of our hike, we came over a low ridge to a spectacular view where we could see the miniscule sheepherder's hut where we had permission to spend the night located less than a mile ahead on the edge of a deep canyon cut through the basalt of an ancient lava flow by one of the major out-wash rivers from the giant ice field. The massive amount of water rushing over the rocks at the bottom of the narrow canyon created a spectacular spray of water and foam that rose well over fifty feet above the top of the canyon, obscuring the river below. The dynamic and spectacular view, certainly one of the most impressive in my lifetime, was quite unexpected. Skarphédinn, like most Icelandic people, was modest about the dynamic beauty of the landscape within which he lived and worked. However, when I expressed appreciation for the beauty of the scene he agreed and said that was a major satisfaction of his work in this remote part of Iceland.

For me, the unexpected was not over. As we approached the hut, I noticed that adjacent to it there was a hot springs with a pool of sufficient depth and size to accommodate several bathers in water up to about 90°F. While Skarphédinn and I were hiking, Kristbjorn had driven back a ways to where he could then drive on a rough and very circuitous route to within a few hundred yards of the hut so that we didn't have to carry food, sleeping bags, etc., so he had already enjoyed relaxing in the hot pool. While Kristbjorn prepared the evening meal, Skarphédinn and I soaked our tired bodies, which felt very luxurious. It certainly had been a most memorable day for me, partly through enrichment of my knowledge of this unique portion of Icelandic reindeer habitat with limited plant species diversity.

We spent the following day hiking close to the cabin identifying plant types that had been grazed by the reindeer versus those selected by the sheep, which also grazed this alpine habitat in low density during the summer. Late the next day, we drove back down to a sheep ranch at a lower elevation where we could walk into the western portion of the reindeer range. We stayed at the ranch for a few days, paying room and board, while we explored the higher portion of the rancher's summer sheep grazing area that overlapped with the year-round habitat of the reindeer. On several occasions, one or more of the family and their well-trained dog accompanied us as volunteer guides, helped run vegetation line transects, or assisted us in other ways. It was great to live with this sheep-ranching family for a few days, as it offered me the opportunity to gain unique insight into the life and culture of rural Iceland. It also enabled me to gain insight into the complexity of environmental, economic, and social issues at stake if the proposed hydroelectric project were to go forward. You could really see how they were so dependent upon what they could grow themselves because it was so costly to buy stuff, and they had fields where they could produce hay for feeding the sheep, and they had a couple of cows for milking.

Kristbjorn was an excellent botanist, and he was doing research for his doctoral degree on the *nunataks* that stick up through the ice with the vegetation on them. Skarphédinn was also an excellent biologist. They were a good team and got along really well together. It was fun working with young people that were so good and talented and eager to learn. I felt good about being able to work with them. Since I wasn't involved in the research directly, I didn't publish anything, but those guys wrote reports about what they did, and presented papers at the International Reindeer Caribou Symposium (Skarphédinn 2010).

In the end, that hydro project did not go forward. It is not clear whether it was because of economic concerns associated with aluminum production for whom the electricity was being generated, concerns over potential environmental impacts of the project, or concerns from the Icelandic people over threats to their aesthetic, psychological, and culturally based valuation of the natural landscape.

I made subsequent visits to Iceland to participate in erosion control, land restoration, and grazing ecology workshops and symposia, and to attend an Arctic Council conference on the Arctic Climate Impact Assessment project (ACIA 2005). It was, however, through my 1982 experience living and working with locals that I gained an in-depth understanding of the rural Icelandic people and their culture, and deep appreciation for the beauty of their landscape.

Finland

My early visits to Finland in the 1960s and '70s were largely associated with participation in international symposia and conferences, such as the

International Reindeer Caribou Symposium. Those of us in Alaska and Canada doing investigative research with caribou made important contacts with Finnish scientists doing similar work with reindeer biology and related management issues. These gatherings, where scientific papers were presented and formal and informal discussions took place, were a stimulus for subsequent exchange agreements.

One Finnish student who came on one of these exchanges and contributed to the international mix of the graduate student body at UAF was Leo Salo. He was working on a master's degree in wildlife management under my supervision, and was accompanied by his wife, Armi, who was trained in research methodology in medical sciences. Leo had been an officer in the Finnish Army Reserve assigned to United Nations peacekeeping forces in the Balkans and the Middle East, and served as a positive role model for younger American graduate students who tended to view service in the US military negatively because they only saw it as an inevitable consequence of war.

Another UAF graduate student, John Bryant, who was doing PhD research on the possible causes of the ten-year snowshoe hare cycles that were common throughout the boreal Subarctic of North America, played a major role in broadening my Finnish connections. There were many hypotheses for the periodicity of the cycle, but none had withstood the scrutiny of science at that time. In discussion with me, John suggested that looking at secondary chemicals in plants as defenses against herbivory and a possible tie to the periodicity of the snowshoe hare cycles was of interest to him as a topic for his PhD. Prior to this, during a snowshoe hare population high in interior Alaska, I had conducted research on food preferences of the hares in the woods behind my house. Among the most preferred species, aspen, birch, and cottonwood, there was a difference in preference between twigs available to the hares and those that otherwise would be higher in trees and shrubs out of their reach. This suggested that secondary chemicals might be involved in the difference in the hare's preference in plant parts (Klein 1977a). So I was thrilled with the idea that my backyard research had been instrumental in influencing John's decision on a thesis topic. John proved to be an outstanding scientist, and he developed collaborative relationships with faculty in the Chemistry Department at UAF, with researchers investigating secondary chemicals in relation to herbivory in Fennoscandia, especially those affiliated with the Forestry Department at the University of Joensuu, Finland, and he published prolifically.

John connected me with the Finnish scientists with whom he collaborated, and through them in 1993 I was invited by the Finnish Education Ministry to join an international panel to evaluate the biology department at the University of Joensuu. Other members of the committee included senior professors from Sweden, Germany, and England, and it turned out that I was the only one who had ever visited the University of Joensuu. The review process, although intense, included visits to forest research plots with the involved scientists. On the first day of the review at the forest research station, we enjoyed a relaxing sauna in the Finnish tradition in an attractively designed log cabin at the edge of a lake. Of course, the sauna included a cooling dip in the lake where new ice at the end of the dock had to be broken before we could dive in. At the end of the two-day review process, the panel presented a report synthesizing our joint overall evaluation, comments, and recommendations.

Later in 1993, I was asked to do a similar one-person assessment of the environmental biology program at the much smaller and younger University of Kuopio, about sixty miles north of Joensuu. The University of Kuopio's primary education focus was premedical and was associated with a regional hospital located there. It also offered veterinary training with a focus on a regional economy dependent on fur farming of foxes, raccoon dogs, and other furbearers. I readily accepted the evaluation request, realizing that it would further enlighten me about the Finnish education system while nurturing my growing fascination with the Finnish culture. My report for the review at Kuopio acknowledged that the department was inadequately funded. The infrastructure was modern and well equipped, but the few faculty employed were barely able to teach the core courses needed to meet country-wide minimal standards for the biology degree and were left with insufficient time to conduct research expected of them on applied forest and fisheries ecology of the region. I recently learned that in 2010 the University of Eastern Finland was established in Savonlinna, sixty miles south of Joensuu, through the merger of Joensuu and Kuopio Universities. In retrospect, it is gratifying that many of the recommendations by our external evaluations were adopted in creating the University of Eastern Finland.

Another Fennoscandian event, nearly four decades after my first visit, that influenced and contributed to the broadening and shaping of my global perspective was a course developed by the Circumpolar PhD Network in Arctic Environmental Studies (CAES). I was honored and pleased to be invited as one of the instructors. A team of senior faculty from Finnish, Swedish, and Norwegian universities, several of whom I knew as colleagues and friends, was primarily responsible for organizing the course that was based at the Arctic Center, University of Lapland, Rovaniemi, Finland. The course was titled "Reindeer as a Keystone Species in the North—Biological, Cultural, and Socio-Economic Aspects," and was focused on actual research questions in reindeer husbandry and related environmental, social, and cultural issues. There were eighteen students from Russia, Sweden, Finland, Canada, Norway, and the United Kingdom taking the course, and eight faculty instructors from Sweden, Finland, Norway, Denmark, and the US. A major attraction of the course for me was the international and cultural diversity among both students and faculty. Adding to my enjoyment was that my partner at the time, Heather McIntyre, was able to join the course support staff. She had a master's in horticulture from UAF and worked in the university's greenhouse. Heather had similar experience in Alaska working with faculty-student teams mapping plant community structure in reindeer and caribou grazing areas on the Seward Peninsula in northwestern Alaska.

From September 1 to 15, 2000, the group traveled by bus through northern Finland, adjacent northern Norway, and the Kola Peninsula of Russia, visiting different sites where important aspects of the course topics were studied in real-life situations. We got to see a lot of stuff firsthand, which was great for the students. For example, in Finland, we learned about research that was being done on insect harassment of reindeer and modern techniques they were using to deal with it. It was some of the best work being done at the time on the subject. They injected the animals with a drug that helped fight off mosquitoes, get rid of parasitic flies, and even helped stop internal gut parasites. In the Kola, we went to a village where reindeer herders lived and had their herds close by. These people had held out and didn't collectivize under the Soviet regime so had not been treated well. We were there after liberalization and the Russian government was trying to make up for the past and treat them better, which wasn't particularly well. In another place, a Russian researcher showed us how she was using study plots to look at different effects from open-pit mines and pollution on vegetation in different conditions, like wetlands versus uplands. It was really interesting going through this part of Russia; I could explain and show different levels of grazing pressure, and we got a feeling for the whole culture there, which is so different. Then we went through northern Sweden and Norway down to Alta, which is a little bit north of Tromsø, Norway. We got into the reindeer grazing area and went to a small town that was all reindeer herders where we interacted with the people. We went out and visited some of the grazing areas, and Bruce Forbes, a professor at the University of Lapland in Rovaniemi, Finland, and I, who were considered experts on lichen growth and the effects of grazing, were able to really talk about this in context. It was good that we could get outdoors and really see things like this.

Each student was assigned a faculty mentor who was expected to provide guidance in the student's preparation of a semitechnical paper as a result of the trip. As an advisor and mentor, we had some role in interacting with the students and helping them define their topic in a general way. So, one of the things we did when we'd stop someplace for the evening was we'd have a gathering where the students would make short presentations on what their objectives were and what they expected to find. I mentored Dina Judina from the Petrozavodsk State University in Karelia, Russia, who had a little bit of experience with forest reindeer and management. Unfortunately, Dina's lack of proficiency in English impeded her full participation in the course and limited my ability to serve effectively as a mentor. Although, the other Russian students helped her as best they could to enable her to understand and participate in at least a portion of the learning process.

I also mentored Robert Weladji who was an outstanding student in the course. Originally from Cameroon in West Africa, where he had been trained and worked in forestry, he was on a Norwegian scholarship at the Norwegian College of Agriculture. Robert and I shared a common interest in reindeer/caribou ecology and I knew and respected several of his PhD committee members whom I had worked with previously. We developed a close bond of friendship during the field course that has persisted through his completion of the PhD, two postdoctoral years in Norway, and his present faculty appointment at Concordia University, Montreal, Canada. Subsequent to the field course, I coauthored a paper with Robert dealing with climate change influences on caribou (Weladji et al. 2002), and in 2013, we found ourselves serving together as experts in caribou ecology on a panel of the National Sciences and Engineering Research Council of Canada reviewing a proposal for research in northern Saskatchewan. It was, of course, chance that brought Robert and me together in Saskatoon so far from our countries of origin, but it was Fennoscandia that initially stimulated our joint pursuit of ecological knowledge about caribou and reindeer and their relationship to humans (Klein 1999; Weladji et al. 2003).

Overall, it was a very stimulating trip for me, but also I think for everybody that was on the trip, especially the grad students. I felt good that the students responded really positively to this whole concept of mixing students up from so many different countries and different training. Among the faculty, the common friendships and commitment to advancing understanding of Arctic ungulate ecology, as well as the associated human cultures, were strengthened by our joint participation in the course. It led to further collaborations and connections. For example, Bruce Forbes and I later served together for several years as board members of the Arctic Research Consortium of the United States. I crossed paths several times with Rasmus Rasmussen, a social scientist and professor at the Danish Roskilde University. We were both involved in a 2002 workshop on social and environmental impacts in the North as a consequence of mining and energy production that took place in Apatity on the Russian Kola Peninsula (Rasmussen and Koroleva 2003; Klein and Magomedova 2003), and in November 2005 we both attended the Second International Conference on Arctic Research Planning (ICARP) in Copenhagen, which brought together scientists, policy makers, research managers, indigenous peoples, and others interested in and concerned about the future of arctic research (ACIA 2005).

David Klein (fourth from right) and Pat Webber (second from left) and their Russian hosts visit the greenhouse complex in Norilsk, Soviet Union, 1976.
COURTESY OF DAVID KLEIN.

11
Soviet–US Détente Exchanges in Arctic Ecology

As a boy, I had seen world globes in rare visits to a city library and wanted one in my own home so I could put countries I "discovered" through stamp collecting in a global perspective. It wasn't until I was about thirteen that my parents, who were recovering financially from the Depression, were able to purchase a world globe as a family Christmas present. Eventually, my global perspective shifted northward, somewhat stimulated by my curiosity with how people were able to live and enjoy life in the Arctic, be it indigenous cultures, traders, missionaries, or exploiters of mineral or biological resources. Even though the Soviet Arctic remained largely unknown under Stalin's closed-door policy, once in college where libraries were available, I continued my pursuit of geographical information about the Russian North. Unfortunately at that time, library sources were largely historical and outdated. As my career studying arctic ungulates developed, looking at the species in the Russian North was a logical extension of the other Arctic research I had been doing.

Starting in the 1970s, I was involved with a science exchange program between the United States and the Soviet Union that came out of the Agreement on Exchanges and Cooperation in Scientific, Technical, Educational, Cultural, and Other Fields made between President Nixon and Soviet Premier Leonid Brezhnev in 1972 (United States–USSR 1972). Part of their détente agreements included creation of a US-Soviet Joint Commission on Scientific and Technical Cooperation to establish and promote cooperative programs in the fields of science and technology and make possible exchange visits of scientists between the two countries

Places that David Klein visited in Russia throughout his career as an ecologist. MAP BY PAULA ELMES.

(Nixon 1972). My first scientific exchange to the Soviet Union was in 1974, the second one was 1976, and the third one was 1989. The length of these exchanges varied. I think the longest one was just short of a month, which was the first one.

Of immense interest to me was the fact that in 1974 and '75 under Brezhnev, there was some liberalization in the Soviet Union and recognition that science exchanges shouldn't be curtailed. This was a good move on the parts of both Brezhnev and Nixon to be able to bring about that breakdown of the Cold War/Iron Curtain. It was all very official. The exchanges had to be done through the State Department, and, of course, there had to be proper visas, with everybody on both sides going through inspections to be sure they were qualified to represent their countries. Officially, you had to be a scientist of some respect and recognition. But unofficially, there was the question of what can we learn about other components of the government. The Soviets were wary that we might be spies, and in the US there was some worry that we were not going to represent the country properly, or that we would be asked to represent the interests of the FBI or CIA.

For the exchanges I participated in, there was general agreement they would be about caribou/reindeer. Both sides felt that there was a lot we could learn from each other. Three of us were recommended to go to Siberia to visit reindeer ranges and meet with Soviet biologists to discuss common interests in the management and ecology of domestic and wild reindeer (caribou). The trip was also envisioned as leading to longer-term and more comprehensive exchanges in the future. All of us were excited, enthusiastic, and honored to be involved in this effort to decrease tensions between the US and the USSR through increased exchange of scientists, although we each may have held varying degrees of curiosity and skepticism about its likely success.

1974 Dr. Jack Luick at the Institute of Arctic Biology and Department of Biology and Wildlife was the first contact. He was doing a lot of research on caribou and stable isotopes and fallout of radionuclides from atmospheric testing of bombs, both in the US and Russia. He was studying this relationship of caribou to the lichens, which would absorb the radioactive cesium. Jack recommended that I go, and then we recommended that someone representing the caribou work being done by the Alaska Department of Fish and Game also should go. This turned out to be Jim Hemming, who was a biologist with the US Bureau of Land Management, at that time assigned to the Alaska Pipeline Office, but formerly had been in charge of caribou research for the Alaska Department of Fish and Game and had worked a lot with the Nelchina Caribou Herd.

The three of us went over from August 20 to September 5, 1974. It was not without a lot of frustrations because everything that was supposed to be done and organized by the Soviets wasn't ready, so we sat around in Moscow waiting for visas to be processed, and so on. We left Moscow on the morning of August 21 and flew to Norilsk, a city of 300,000 people at 69° North on the Taimyr Peninsula (also spelled as *Taymyr*), which is about the same latitude as Umiat, Alaska. We were accompanied by Yurie Feigin from the Central Laboratory for Nature Conservation, who acted as an excellent interpreter and guide throughout our entire stay in the Soviet

Union. He played an important role in keeping the focus of our visit on reindeer-related science. We were met by a welcoming party of five Russian men in black suits, including Dr. V. A. Zabrodin, Director of the Extreme North Agricultural Research Institute (IENAR), and three of his professional staff who headed up the institute's research and management of domestic and wild reindeer on the Taimyr. The unaccounted-for man introduced by name only was the token person appointed by the Communist Party to be an observer at all official meetings associated with the exchange agreement. This was presumably to verify that we were biological scientists and not spies for the US.

The Norilsk area is where they have the world's largest nickel mining and processing industry. After discovery of the ores in the 1930s, a huge metallurgical complex and large city was built. It had been part of the Gulag Archipelago, so a lot of the building of the city and operation of the mines was done by political dissidents who were exiled to Siberia and used as slave labor. The Russians we interacted with were embarrassed to talk about this darker period of their past, but during the official meetings we had together they told us all about the city and the wonderful construction and what a wonderful place it was. We spent a few days around Norilsk that were devoted to showing us areas where the tundra vegetation had been severely impacted by air pollution generated by the ore smelting. Fallout in the downwind pollution plume from the mine's processing plant had totally eliminated lichens, which included previously important winter grazing areas for reindeer.

We also saw how their gas pipeline, which was about the same diameter as the Trans-Alaska Pipeline, proved to be a major obstacle to the movement of wild reindeer along their traditional migration route (Klein and Magomedova 2003). At that time, the herd was a couple hundred thousand, so it was a big migration in the fall when they were traveling back to their winter ranges. The pipeline had been laid on the ground on top of railroad ties, and there were only a few places where the wild reindeer could get over or under the pipeline. They tried to get the caribou past the pipeline by raising it fairly high so that they could walk under it, but the caribou stayed away from it. Then they tried making gravel ramps over the pipeline by building wooden bridges with gravel on the approaches in places where there was already gravel on the soil so it would look and feel the same to the reindeer. None of these things were very successful; they failed to encourage more than 25 percent of the reindeer to cross the pipeline. In the worst-case scenarios, reindeer would just mill around the pipeline and trample and overgraze areas, so they weren't getting enough food. In other cases, reindeer moved long distances laterally along the pipeline and would end up in new wintering areas. The best success they had was building lead fences that would direct the wild reindeer away at an angle into new wintering grounds that actually were good places for them to go. It was an area that was adequate for the population to continue to grow and increase, but it was sort of by accident.

We were told that we could not take pictures of any of this pollution damage, although the next morning Jim and I were up early and went out and took pictures of things we probably were not supposed to. For example, I was interested in how the pollution affected the vegetation, especially the lichens and trees. It didn't have so much effect on sedges, but it did on broadleaf plants like willows and larch, which were the only forest trees there. They were skeletons that mostly had all been killed over a few years from this pollution. Of course, if they were with you on a walking tour around the city and you wanted to take a picture of the statue of Lenin or one of these new big apartment complexes, they would let you take these pictures, but they didn't want you to take other pictures. One time I tried to take a picture of a horse pulling a two-wheeled cart with one guy on it. I thought it was rather strange, that here's this horse pulling a cart in the Arctic at 69° North, and they didn't want me to take a picture of it. Admittedly, the mine and smelter smokestacks were in the background. They would let me take pictures of modern things like automobiles and buses, but not older things like that.

Then they took us out into the field to spend a few days at a camp where the institute's model reindeer herd was being grazed. We traveled in a party of ten, using two large tracked military vehicles that supposedly were suitable for going over the tundra, except they damaged it badly. The trip to the reindeer camp normally took about a half day, but it took us almost two days, due to getting lost. Dr. Borozdin, head of the institute's domestic reindeer program, sat up front in the lead vehicle and provided directions for the driver. At first, they didn't want to acknowledge that they were lost,

A tarp rigged up between two tracked vehicles to make a
temporary overnight camp when the group got lost on their
way to the model reindeer herd camp, Taimyr Peninsula,
Soviet Union, 1974. L–R: Jack Luick, Jim Hemming, Yurie
Feigin (interpreter), and Dr. Borozdin. PHOTO BY DAVID KLEIN.

but finally they did and Borozdin showed us the crude maps he had to work
with. It turned out that Borozdin had not laid out a route on the maps in
advance because he thought he knew the way, and the compass he had was
useless without known reference points.

Since we didn't get to the camp that evening as planned, we had to camp
out. Fortunately, we were well equipped. They rigged up a tarp and had
some folding cots for us and they had sleeping bags made out of some kind
of animal skins with sparse amounts of hair still on that weren't as warm as
they should have been. The sleeping part of that night was short. We had a
nice fire and they had food. Although trained as a biologist, Borozdin's wife
had volunteered to be the cook for the group. Having a woman there livened
things up a bit. Of course, there was plenty of vodka available to facilitate
the evening's unexpected social gathering and lubricate the post-dinner
party around the campfire. Although unplanned, it was an excellent way to

Enjoying an improvised dinner made from the limited supplies on hand when the group unexpectantly spent the night on the tunrda when they got lost traveling to the model reindeer herd, Taimyr Peninsula, Soviet Union. 1974. COURTESY OF DAVID KLEIN.

start the field experience and to get to know one another, far away from both the Kremlin and Washington, DC.

We spent most of the next day going in some directions and not finding anything and going in another direction and not finding anything. Finally, it was getting late and we thought we were going to have to spend another night out. Fortunately, when it got dark enough, we saw a fire in the distance that the people at the reindeer camp had set to show us where they were. We stayed there for several days. They'd set up some big tents with tables inside where we all had dinner together. These dinners were one of the really nice parts of the whole experience. Most of the Nenet reindeer herders would join us, and Yurie and the other interpreters were kept busy facilitating the Russian/English conversation. We talked about everything, but generally focused on reindeer well-being, herding practices in relation to grazing in different plant communities, and seasonal changes in forage quality. The Native herders were interested in us and how we lived in Alaska, and we wanted to talk about their whole operation and how it compared to what

Dr. A. D. Mukhachev, head of Taiga Reindeer Research (left) and Dr. E. K. Borozdin, head of Tundra Reindeer Research (right), on a break while en route to visiting the model reindeer herd about thirty miles from Norilsk, Soviet Union, 1974. PHOTO BY DAVID KLEIN.

we did. There was no political talk at all; frankly, none of us really wanted to talk about politics. So it was productive.

The herders were accompanied by two veterinarians working with the reindeer and one wild caribou biologist. We spent time in groups talking about reindeer and caribou, we examined animals, and they talked a lot about veterinarian handling, including how they castrated some animals and how they treated animals for possible brucellosis. Also they were experimenting with ways to reduce the warble and botfly parasites, which they later made good progress on along with the Scandinavians. I learned a lot and there were some good exchanges of information and knowledge (Klein and Kuzyakin 1982; Syroechkovskii 1995).

There was plenty of good food at the camp, plus our group had brought more. The woman who was cook did a great job of making Russian-type food, like boiled cabbage and potatoes. They put out a gill net in a small lake and caught twelve- to fourteen-inch arctic char and whitefish, and they even slaughtered one of the reindeer. And, of course, there was plenty of alcohol. We had brought a few bottles of American whiskey to share, which were quickly drained, but they had plenty of vodka. They would serve vodka at every meal first thing as you'd sit down, except at breakfast. We'd have toasts with a small glass of vodka, and, of course, you were supposed to drink it all at once. If you only drank half of it, then they would fill it up. Their tradition was that with each toast you drank the whole glassful. This was limited to the men of the group. The women were served juice or something else.

The plan was for us to be picked up by a large helicopter and returned directly to Norilsk. However, thick fog moved in the day the helicopter was due, delaying its arrival for two days. While there was plenty of food for us for the extra days, the supply of vodka being used to toast the success of our international cooperation ran out. The Russians said, "Nyet, nyet. No problem." It was no problem, because they had plenty of 100-percent-proof lab alcohol for veterinary specimens, but it was in unlabeled old vodka bottles, as was the cooking fuel. They would pull these bottles out and they couldn't tell for sure whether it was the alcohol or the gasoline. They'd pull the cork off and smell it, "Nyet." Put the cork on, get another one out, and "Nyet." Sometimes there'd be a disagreement about the contents, so they'd pour some on the ground and light it with a match. If the flame was blue, it was the lab alcohol they were looking for and they'd say, "Da, da." They'd put about half of this alcohol into an empty vodka bottle and dilute it with 50 percent water to make the vodka replacement. It wasn't the greatest stuff, but we had our vodka. But you had to wait for the alcohol and water to mix, so this procedure delayed the start of our meal since we couldn't eat until vodka had been drunk. We survived. But that was one of the humorous things on that trip.

When the helicopter finally arrived, we were hurried aboard to get back to Norilsk while flying conditions were still suitable. To our surprise there were several nicely dressed Russian women from the institute on board who greeted our "rescue" with bottles of champagne, smoked fish, cheese, and fresh-baked Russian brown bread that we enjoyed during the flight back. This was the women's idea. They wanted time with the "interesting Alaskans," the first foreigners permitted to visit Norilsk under the Soviet system.

Ultimately, we were going to fly to Yakutsk for a visit hosted by Professor Andreev, who was a senior specialist on lichens. But our flight was diverted to Irkutsk where all flights had been grounded until morning to avoid violent thunderstorms. All hotel rooms were already booked by other grounded passengers, but Aeroflot got permission for us to stay in an orphanage that had recently closed. However, we found that the beds were designed for children about four and a half feet tall, so trying to sleep in an extreme fetal position made for a cramped body and an uncomfortable night. We were relieved when the storms had subsided by morning and we made it to Yakutsk.

Our time in Yakutsk was reduced to three days because of our weather-related delays, but Professor Andreev was an excellent host. On one beautiful fall day, we were picked up at the hotel and driven to the larch-lichen forests in the Vilyui River drainage and to bluffs overlooking the Lena River Valley where semi-steppe vegetation predominated. There was a lot of traffic on the gravel roads, each small auto was packed with people. It turned out that this was the last weekend before snowfall that it would be possible to pick berries and gather mushrooms. Those few people who owned cars filled them with neighbor families and they all headed out of town. In fact, when we stopped to do a hike through a larch forest, Andreev took along a plastic bucket specifically to collect edible mushrooms that we might happen across. Being out in the field with Andreev was an excellent opportunity to learn from him about effects of forest-cutting practices and increases in wildfires on the recovery of lichens. In addition, we had the privilege of visiting his *dacha*, a small old house on the outskirts of the city with a garden, where he and his wife lived mostly in summer. Normally, on these exchanges you never got to see where people lived; he was not allowed to bring us to his apartment in Yakutsk. Being at their *dacha*, eating a meal of food they had gathered or grown, and seeing how they lived was the highlight of our visit there.

Originally, the Soviets had wanted us to return to Moscow before retracing our steps through New York to Alaska. Jack, Jim, and I protested because we had almost circumnavigated the world to get to Yakutsk and it would therefore be much less expensive for both the Soviet Union and the United States if we flew from the Russian Far East to Japan and then

A young Nenets man with his herding dog driving a handmade wooden sled pulled by reindeer, Taimyr Peninsula, Soviet Union, 1974. He keeps his dog on a leash until he needs the dog to run and bark at loose reindeer to push them back into the herd. The sled is outfitted with steel runners in the summer for going over rocks and rough tundra that are then removed in the winter when bare wood slides better over snow. PHOTO BY DAVID KLEIN.

directly to Anchorage. Frankly, in addition to the large reduction in flying time, we had had enough of the buxom Aeroflot stewardesses who never cracked a smile and provided no service except on extra-long flights when half of a boiled chicken (the infamous Aeroflot rubber chicken) unceremoniously arrived on your fold-down tray. They finally agreed to let us go to Komsomolsk, which is on the Amur River, then to Niigata, Japan, on Japan Airlines, where we would catch a flight to Anchorage.

Getting out of the Soviet Union was difficult. It was a slow and drawn-out process with multiple passport checks and opening of baggage. They were strict on things you weren't supposed to take out, so when we got to the airport there were so many soldiers all over the place. Despite the restrictions, I had things I wanted to bring home. One was part of an old reindeer saddle made out of wood that I found high and dry up in the driftwood on a big, beautiful lake that had been a wintering area for indigenous reindeer herding before it was "collectivized." The Soviets with me said, "I doubt they will let you take that out." There were just some rusty nails that held it together, so I pulled it apart and put the pieces flat on the bottom of my suitcase and I was able to get it out. Also, I was given several things as gifts that were made out of bone, and two beautiful caribou bulls, a ptarmigan, and a few other small animals carved out of marine mammal ivory. This was after passage of the CITES legislation (Convention on International Trade in Endangered Species of Wild Fauna and Flora) that regulates international trade to prevent species from becoming endangered or extinct. I didn't even think about that. I was able to leave the Soviet Union with all these items without a problem. They didn't seem to care, or they didn't know about them. And then in the Taimyr region, I had collected some twigs of willows, dwarf birch, and a couple other things to compare with those in Alaska that I had air-dried in laboratory drying ovens in order to bring them into the country. Technically, you're supposed to have a permit from the US Department of Agriculture to bring any animal forage into the country, which I didn't have, so I was taking a chance.

It had been a long flight and I got to Anchorage in the wee hours of the morning, like 3:00 a.m., so there weren't that many people going through US Customs. The agent opened my suitcase and the first thing he found were those ivory carvings I'd been given, which he immediately confiscated. He started to put back the pieces that were obviously bone, and then he saw all these little paper bags in my suitcase. He said, "What's this?" I said, "It's just dried specimens of grass and other things." "Agriculture?! You know, you've got to have a permit." I said, "They're all specially air-dried and they're to be used for scientific purposes." He looked at me again, and sort of took some dirty underwear and covered them up. He closed up the bag and said, "We've given you a pretty tough time already." So he let me go through with those.

1976 The second exchange visit was to the Taimyr region for about three weeks in 1976. The exchange visit was arranged through the Extreme North Agricultural Research Institute (IENAR) in the Soviet Union, the Alaska Cooperative Wildlife Research Unit (ACWRU) at UAF, and the Department of Environmental Population and Organismic Biology at the University of Colorado (EPOB). Pat Webber, a botany professor and expert in Arctic vegetation based in Boulder, Colorado, represented EPOB and I represented ACWRU. Pat's and my trips were supposed to be separate visits, but because of bureaucratic delays in Washington and Moscow we both arrived in Moscow at the same time. Given the difficulties Pat and I were having with the Soviet system in terms of visas and other paperwork, it quickly became apparent that merging the two exchange visits would best serve our interests, as well as those of IENAR by greatly reducing the overall costs. Pat was interested in vegetation where the caribou were and so was I, but I was coming at it more from the caribou standpoint where he was coming from the botanical side. Since we had originally each been assigned an interpreter, Natasha Maligina for Pat and Nadya Polyakova for me, they would remain with us throughout the entire visit. Natasha was affiliated with IENAR and was more familiar with the relevant caribou and vegetation terminology in the region, while Nadya was a more experienced interpreter and an urban intellectual from Moscow. At first, they appeared to be competing with one another, but once they got to know each other, they quickly realized that they were more effective and appreciated if they worked as a team. We were lucky to have them both.

Our field party consisted of Drs. Zabrodin and Borozdin, our two interpreters, Pat and me, and a grad student, Tatyana Vlasova, who volunteered to be camp cook. We spent ten days camping at Lake Ayan in a beautiful wilderness area about 200 kilometers east of Norilsk in the mountainous Putorana Plateau at the head of the Khatanga River, now protected as a Nature Reserve and listed as a UNESCO World Heritage Site (Putoransky State Nature Reserve established in 1987). Located at about 69° North, the open larch-lichen forests in the valleys and on the lower mountain slopes were the northernmost extension of the taiga or boreal forest in Siberia. This area was the primary wintering area for a large portion of the Taimyr wild reindeer herd, as well as habitat for the westernmost mountain sheep in the USSR, known as the snow sheep (*Ovis nivicola*). Numbering about 400,000, the Taimyr herd was the largest wild reindeer herd in the Soviet Union at that time. Pat and I considered ourselves fortunate to be able to spend time camping in this ecologically rich and scenically beautiful landscape where spectacular waterfalls fell over basalt cliffs from the plateau above to feed the lake and river in the valley below.

L–R: Nadya Polyakova (David's interpreter), David,
Natasha Maligina (Pat Webber's interpreter), and a
biologist who was assisting their host Dr. Zabrodin
in the mountains of the Putorana Plateau, Taimyr
Peninsula, Soviet Union, 1976. COURTESY OF DAVID KLEIN.

On short walks from camp, Pat and I were able to do reconnaissance of lichen-dominated plant communities in the valley and on the two or three narrow benches that were present on the sparsely forested mountain slopes. The lichens showed only light grazing pressure by reindeer, especially on the benches. The fine weather and beautiful landscape also enabled us to attempt a couple group hikes, but Natasha and Nadya did not have adequate boots or experience for long walks in rough or mountainous terrain so they were forced to drop out and return to camp with sore feet. They were not really needed as interpreters on such hikes, but we did enjoy their company and contribution to our conversation when we stopped for breaks and lunch.

Tatyana was keenly interested in seeing snow sheep and had missed out on an earlier hike into snow sheep habitat when she accompanied the two interpreters back to camp. So I offered to guide her on a quick and somewhat

Volunteer and graduate student Tatyana Vlasova with an arctic loon caught in a subsistence fish net but uninjured, Putorana Mountains, Taimyr Peninsula, Soviet Union, 1976. PHOTO BY DAVID KLEIN.

physically challenging climb to the snow sheep habitat. We briefly saw a couple of sheep before they disappeared from sight into more rugged terrain. I particularly enjoyed hiking with Tatyana as we both really enjoyed being in the beautiful terrain in such fine weather. We flushed a female rock ptarmigan with a brood of recently hatched chicks, one of which I handed to Tatyana so she could appreciate the thrill of briefly holding a live ptarmigan chick. I could see the excitement in her eyes as she felt the warmth of the tiny, downy chick in her hand. I recall reflecting at the time on similar experiences in the field in Alaska, realizing that a large part of my satisfaction from working with students in the field came from the excitement I saw in their faces when they began to comprehend and appreciate the complexity of nature and realize the beauty in it.

Our campsite was an excellent location for grayling and arctic char fishing, which was an attraction for both Zabrodin and Borozdin. They spent all of their "free time" fishing primarily for their personal subsistence use. They used gill nets set overnight at the edges of larger stream channels and fished from the bank with poles and lures. The ready availability of fish apparently had been a major reason for the reindeer herding Nenet people to establish a seasonal camp in this area in the 1930s before they were collectivized. For me, my hikes were like walking through a museum where artifacts from a past culture were frequently encountered. In the forest, the artifacts were mostly carved out of the available larch wood into utilitarian items, such as a ski, sled runner, or toggles used in sled reindeer harnesses. Along the lakeshore, driftwood pieces were used to make reindeer packs and riding saddles. The largest item was a stylized image of a man's head carved with a few strokes from a sharp axe into the five- to six-inch base of an entire larch tree that had been cut and the bark peeled off. This piece was inverted and propped up among the branches of a live tree with the totem-like head overlooking their campsite, perhaps as a good omen. The Nenets in the Lake Ayan area were able to carry on their traditional herding lifestyle until the 1930s when government policy to collectivize reindeer herding forced them to move their reindeer closer to Norilsk. Government policy also sought to expand reindeer production closer to Norilsk to help feed the workers at the nickel mines.

Our second field excursion out of Norilsk was to the Pura River via helicopter where the IENAR had a small research station located in the middle of the calving grounds of the large Taimyr wild reindeer herd. A major portion of the Taimyr reindeer herd calves in this western portion of the Taimyr Peninsula and moves to the northeast during post-calving to optimize foraging when the local forage quality is at its peak. The nearby confluence of the Pura River with the Pyasina River creates a delta-like complex of river channels, vegetated river bars, and islands that provide prime nesting habitat for waterfowl, like the endangered red-breasted geese and shore birds. On the adjacent tundra, the lemmings were at the peak of their cycle and were so abundant that year and so easily caught by arctic foxes, snowy owls, and jaegers that the effect of these predators on the red-breasted geese and other waterfowl was negligible.

Nenets boys riding forest reindeer, Taimyr Peninsula, Soviet Union, 1974. PHOTO COURTESY OF A. D. MUKHACHEV AND DAVID KLEIN.

In this area, Pat recorded plant species diversity and described plant community structure, while I attempted to assess recent reindeer grazing levels in several areas farther up river that we accessed by motorboat. Pat and I made rough comparisons of the tundra vegetation in this region with the central Alaska tundra with which we both were familiar, and after we came back we synthesized the Russian information into an article (Webber and Klein 1977).

Back in Norilsk, there were a number of large greenhouses that were heated and lit all year round with the energy surplus generated by the mining and processing of nickel and other metals, which had piqued Pat's and my curiosity. We asked if it would be possible to get a tour of the greenhouses. They were happy to do this because here was something positive they could show us. It wasn't the Gulag. The greenhouse complex was managed mostly by senior women well trained at the university in greenhouse management, and they were thrilled that here were two male scientists from the US with botanical training and experience with home greenhouses and gardening. As we walked through multiple greenhouses with ripe cucumbers and tomatoes on the vines, the greenhouse ladies would pick a few and pass them to Natasha who was carrying a large purse, commenting that our meals in the Arctic would be incomplete without fresh vegetables. As part of this complex, they also had this low building without windows where they grew mushrooms in a soil mixture fertilized by horse manure. The horses were raised specifically for this purpose, thus accounting for the occasional horse seen in the city pulling a wagon. They showed us multiple varieties of mushrooms and pointed out the best type for each culinary use, including what they considered to be their prize-winning variety for sautéing in olive oil or butter. They said, "These are really a super kind of mushroom. They're so wonderful when you cook them up." Then all of a sudden, they threw together a little lunch-type meal and insisted we eat with them, even though the tour was supposed to be completed prior to lunch. They didn't have any facilities to do much, but they sautéed some of their prime mushroom varieties in butter over two Bunsen burners in a lab in their small administration building, made an attractive salad of cucumbers, tomatoes, green onions, and even lettuce from the greenhouse, served Russian brown bread, and poured berry juice and enough champagne and vodka for the necessary toasts and to lighten the hearts of all. It was a most enjoyable lunch, especially for me and Pat, who were being doted on by six considerate and attractive women. Pat and I fell in love with these senior women who were so terrific.

Another outcome of our visit to the greenhouses was that the greenhouse ladies volunteered to help organize and prepare the banquet to be held the evening before Pat and I left Norilsk. They did an outstanding job in preparing the mushroom and salad courses as promised, as well as beautifully decorating the large table and room with flowers from the greenhouses. Pat and I were tasked with using champagne to propose multiple toasts acknowledging the success of our exchange visit from a scientific and international perspective, as well as restoring a bond of friendship between Siberia and Alaska in the interests of a more peaceful world. We also acknowledged the women, that being our interpreters, the camp cooks, and the greenhouse ladies, who were all important in making our visit both successful and enjoyable.

1989 The third exchange was in 1989, and Mikhail Gorbachev was in power in the Soviet Union. It was so different from the previous two trips. The Communist Party had been dissolved and Gorbachev's policies of *glasnost* ("openness") and *perestroika* ("restructuring") had been instituted. Russians were optimistic about their future and openly talked politics among themselves and with foreign visitors. The Extreme North Agricultural Research Institute in Norilsk was again the sponsoring institute for this exchange, and I was to visit the Taimyr Peninsula again, this time with my primary focus being on muskoxen and their habitat use patterns. Muskoxen had been reestablished here using muskoxen from both Canada and Alaska. I was going to work with Gregory Yakushkin, the institute's biologist in charge of the Taimyr muskox project. He was in his sixties and had been the key player working with the muskoxen located at the outlet near the eastern end of giant Lake Taimyr. The Soviets had built the Bikada Research Station there about six miles upstream from Lake Taimyr, and he spent a lot of time doing research there on habitat use by the introduced muskoxen and had monitored dispersal rates and habitat selection. When the muskoxen first arrived at the research station, they fenced them in. But building a big fence was super costly because everything had to be helicoptered in. Eventually, they turned all the muskoxen loose because maintaining the fence was too difficult, and also there wasn't enough forage to sustain them inside the fenced area for a long period. When they turned them loose, they mostly stayed in the area at first, but then they broke up into groups and some gradually moved around the peninsula. Eventually, they reestablished themselves fairly successfully with minimum mortality and the population increased.

I was met on arrival in Moscow by Tatyana Vlasova, now fluent in English, with an advanced degree in botany and a specialist in lichen response to atmospheric pollution. It was gratifying to see that she had done so well in her educational pursuits in the thirteen years since I had gotten to know her as a student at Lake Ayan. Her scientific interest in lichen ecology had enabled her to find secure, high-paying employment with the mining industry in Norilsk at a time when jobs in applied ecology were decreasing in the Russian Arctic. The next day we traveled together to Norilsk. It was then a five-hour flight from Norilsk to the muskox research station in a large helicopter heavily laden with supplies and extra fuel. There was no room for seats, so passengers were encouraged to find comfortable positions among the baggage and supplies and close to windows if you wished to see the landscape below on the relatively low altitude flight. Clear weather most of the way made it possible to view the diversity of terrain features and vegetation types of the Taimyr Peninsula. After the propellers began to rotate, the crew climbed aboard and immediately lit up cigarettes. I pointed out to Natasha Magalina, once again my interpreter, that I did not think it was wise to smoke when there were so many full fuel containers aboard. She agreed, and after prolonged discussion with the crew warning them that I was an official visitor and might report them to government authorities, they refrained from smoking on the flight.

When we arrived at Bikada, Gregory Yakushkin was already there with a few of his seasonal technicians, as well as the station cook and support staff. The next day we did a hike around the adjacent, low and hilly tundra where the muskoxen originally had been fenced in. I was impressed by Gregory's depth of understanding of how the introduced muskoxen had adapted so quickly to their new environment and were expanding in population numbers and distribution in the Taimyr tundra. Holding the muskoxen in large enclosures to allow them to adapt to their new environment and develop hierarchal structure within social groupings prior to their release had proved key to their successful establishment.

A few days after I arrived at the research station, Tatyana arrived and there was obvious disagreement over the schedule for my visit. Tatyana had suggested the possibility of shortening my visit with Gregory in order for me to visit areas in the downwind pollution plume in Norilsk so she could show me the effects of pollution on lichens and other vegetation. The added cost for helicopter time and so forth was to be covered by her employer, the nickel mining industry. I appreciated the chance to see the pollution effects on vegetation, a major threat to range use by reindeer/caribou, however, I emphasized that I firmly wanted to follow through on the commitment I had made to focus the exchange visit on muskoxen. I pointed out to Tatyana that there would likely be other opportunities in the future to address the pollution issue via the US-Russian exchanges. The controversy over my visit was resolved and Tatyana remained with us, contributing her botanical expertise to assessment of the habitat needs of the muskoxen and her social talents to the sense of community at the research station.

While the helicopter was still available, Gregory arranged for a day trip into a mountainous area northeast of the research station where willows, predominantly *Salix alaxensis*, sheltered from high winds by the mountains, grew to ten feet or more with stems two and a half inches in diameter. I questioned whether such luxurious growth would continue after the willows were discovered by the muskoxen. Muskoxen in Alaska's Arctic National Wildlife Refuge heavily browsed shrub willows in early winter until they were drifted over by snow, so they did not ever get this tall.

Also at the research station was a botany professor from the University of Moscow, Elina Pospelova, who was leading a group of students in a field course located at a tent camp about fifteen miles upriver. They were invited to visit the research station ostensibly to do their accumulated laundry and bathe in the station's *banya* (a combination bath house, laundry, and sauna). One of the station's small motorboats was used to transport them back and forth. Their visit coinciding with my presence was justification for a Russian-style dinner celebration. Most of the students were women, who helped in preparing traditional Russian foods, such as *piroshki* (potato and meat dumplings), small pies, pancakes, char caught daily with nets in the river, and char egg caviar cured overnight with salt. It was certainly a joyous occasion, and the party lasted late into the night, lubricated by champagne, beer, and vodka. A couple of guitars provided musical background for Russian songs, and I recall the beautiful voices of several of the women singers.

Elina accompanied Gregory and me to a place a few miles from the station where Gregory had found a group of muskoxen foraging on new-growth vegetation in a recently drained lake bed. Elina was an expert in high Arctic plant ecology and was particularly helpful in our attempts to assess the possible consequences of thaw lake drainage on range quality for muskoxen in that portion of the Taimyr. Eventually, we jointly wrote an article comparing habitat selection by the muskoxen in Alaska's Arctic region with the muskoxen in the Taimyr (Klein et al. 1993).

Another trip with the skiff was downriver to Lake Taimyr to kill a reindeer to replenish the meat supply at the station. We expected to find a few reindeer on the islands in the estuary of the river as it entered the lake.

David helping to skin and butcher a wild reindeer shot under a special permit they had to obtain food for the Bikada Research Station, Soviet Union, 1989. COURTESY OF DAVID KLEIN.

With binoculars, we easily spotted four reindeer bulls that had swum to one of the islands to feed on the high-quality forage. They were alarmed by the approaching skiff and entered the water to swim back to the mainland, but we were able to force one bull to swim back toward the island where I was given the "honor" of shooting it. Our hunt was successful and I quickly began butchering it with a small sheath knife I carried primarily to dig out roots of plants that we collected. Fortunately, I had just sharpened the knife so that I had the field dressing mostly completed by the time Gregory's technicians found the large knife they had brought along from the station kitchen for the butchering. It was sunny but a cool breeze was blowing and there were no large shrubs to offer protection from the wind. We quickly loaded the reindeer in the skiff and motored downstream to where a high riverbank offered protection from the wind. We built a warm fire of driftwood, mostly roots and large stems of willows from the eroding riverbank. Our appetites had been stimulated by the morning's activities, and we were

Gregory Yakushkin (left) drying his sock and Natasha Magalina (right) preparing a whitefish caught in a net by the Bikada Research Station on a lunch break during a boat trip upriver, 1989. They made a fire mostly from roots of dead willows because there was not much wood around. PHOTO BY DAVID KLEIN.

eagerly looking forward to lunch. Pots of river water were set on a folding grill over the fire for tea and to cook the potatoes while Natasha, the only woman in our hunting party, sliced the fresh liver and heart to be fried in a frying pan. To the surprise of the two young technicians, Natasha, who had grown up in the Russian North, ate a couple pieces of fresh-sliced raw liver, stating she liked raw liver almost as well as cooked. She then offered freshly cut pieces of the raw liver to all of us, and I was the only one who tried it. After that, the two young technicians showed a little more humility and respect to Natasha as they reminisced about hunting and camping out.

Yet another unanticipated add-on to the muskoxen exchange visit included the visit of Leonid Kolpashchikov, a wildlife biologist with the agricultural research institute. He landed a Soviet AN-2 biplane on the cobbly beach on the opposite side of the river from the research station. The AN-2 is a huge double-winged, single-engine aircraft well designed for short field landings, good for wildlife observation because it is slow flying, so you can fly pretty low, and has a high cargo and passenger capacity. He was taking advantage of the usually favorable late-summer weather to determine current distribution of the Taimyr wild reindeer herd. If appropriately aggregated, he wanted to try to obtain sex and age composition estimates of the herd. Leonid invited me to join the flight so that I could see the terrain and vegetation types being used by the reindeer and possibly to locate groups of muskoxen that were expected to be dispersing. He was a relatively young, eager guy, and he wanted to make contacts with people in Alaska about how to count the 350,000 or 400,000 animals of the herd, use radio collars, and so on. The Soviet Union had the largest caribou herd in Eurasia, and it was being harvested commercially (Klein and Kolpashchikov 1991).

Leonid, considerate of my desire to take photographs from the air, removed the small plexiglass window in the door of the aircraft so I would have better visibility. I thought this was great, but there was no place to sit there. You couldn't sit on the floor, it was too low. So he found an orange crate at the station and put a cushion on top of it, and I sat on that. Nobody wore seatbelts. The visibility was terrific for me, and I was able to get beautiful pictures. It was just fabulous to do this. In the three hours of flying, I appreciated being able to view the diversity of landscape types and vegetation around much of Lake Taimyr, including where large groups of the wild reindeer were feeding primarily in wet tundra of high- and low-center polygons. While flying north of Lake Taimyr to the coast of the Arctic Ocean, we spotted twelve muskoxen feeding in an extensive area of almost-rectangular high-center polygons nearly a hundred miles from their original release site. The flight more than filled my expectation, though the plane came down so hard on the only small section of beach available for landing near the research station that my orange crate seat was completely crushed under me. We had all been holding on, so no one was injured.

This exchange visit to the muskoxen research station was a great success. What I learned about the Taimyr region and its muskoxen, caribou, and vegetation and the bonds of friendship formed exemplified the value of these exchanges. Continuation of such endeavors seemed assured under the *glasnost* and *perestroika* of the new Russia. While working in the Soviet Union was not always easy, I accepted the challenges of it, enjoyed

Aerial view of muskoxen in low-centered polygon terrain who had moved over 100 miles to the north from the Bikada Research Station where they initially had been fenced in upon reintroduction to the region. PHOTO BY DAVID KLEIN.

the adventure, and my scientific thinking was expanded by observation of caribou and muskoxen in different places and under different circumstances. I thought it was good for the well-being of science and felt it was a worthwhile way to better understand people in other countries and the sciences.

I felt I didn't have to agree with the government to have an exchange in science. In fact, I believed strongly that the Nixon-Brezhnev accord was good for both countries and good for the world because it lowered tensions between these two world powers. Some of this was in my mind then, and is always part of my thinking when I'm thinking about international work. Not only did I learn about science and the species we were studying, but I learned so much about how people approached environmental problems in these different areas (Klein 2005).

Completing the Russian Exchange: Return Visits to Alaska

The agreement for the exchange visits to the USSR required reciprocal visits to the US by the Soviet/Russian scientists that had been primarily involved with our visits there. There were two primary visits of Soviet/Russian scientists to Alaska of which I was involved. The first was in 1977 in response to the 1974 and 1976 exchanges that focused on reindeer and caribou and their ecology, habitats, and management. The second visit to Alaska was in 2002 and dealt with muskoxen, their reintroduction, their adaptation to new habitats, their productivity, and their dispersal.

Those involved in the 1977 visit included Dr. V. Zabrodin, director of the Extreme North Agricultural Research Institute; Dr. E. K. Borozdin, head of Tundra Reindeer Research and Management; Dr. A. D. Mukhachev, head of Taiga Reindeer Research; and Professor V. N. Andreev, botanist and expert on lichen ecology with the Botanical Institute at the University of Yakutsk. The US State Department provided an interpreter for the visit who did her job well and seemed to enjoy being key to facilitating effective communication between this all-male group of Russians and Americans. She got along well with Dr. Zabrodin, who was leader of the Soviet group.

The itinerary for their visit started in Fairbanks with a meeting with Jack Luick and his reindeer research team and a tour of the Institute of Arctic Biology, the research laboratories, and their reindeer holding and research facilities. They met with caribou biologists from ADF&G, FWS, and the University of Alaska. In response to Professor Andreev's request, we found time for them to visit the Agricultural Research Station and the associated botanical gardens. They then traveled to Barrow (now Utqiaġvik) to visit the Naval Arctic Research Laboratory (NARL), where they talked with biologists involved in ongoing research with polar and brown bears and studying adaptations of other Arctic mammals. They also met with Barrow residents to talk about proposed oil development and subsistence hunting activities. The BLM provided a Grumman Goose aircraft and pilots to fly the group from Fairbanks to Barrow, Kotzebue, Shishmaref, Nome, and return to Fairbanks.

L–R: Professor V. N. Andreev (wearing beret and glasses), Dr. A. D. Mukhachev, the Russian-speaking interpreter provided by the US State Department (name unknown), and reindeer herder, Clifford Weyiouanna, their host in Shishmaref, Alaska, 1977. PHOTO BY DAVID KLEIN.

At Shishmaref, the villagers appreciated our visit and were good hosts, sharing their Native foods. The village was without hotels or restaurants, so we had brought along air mattresses and sleeping bags to be sure everybody had something to sleep on and the necessary groceries to supplement the meals prepared in the Weyiouanna household who helped organize our visit. Clifford Weyiouanna took us out to his reindeer herd and explained his herding practices, and the Russians appreciated being able to talk with him and see his animals and how he handled them. In order to have enough spots for everyone in our large group to sleep, we were spread out around town between the school, National Guard Armory, and the church. I was in the church where the only place to sleep was on the floor between the rows of pews. Dr. Zabrodin was surprised, but pleased, that he was allowed to sleep in the church. He thought, "When I go back to Russia, they'll never believe that we slept in a Christian church." He saw it as a joke, you know.

But I can imagine what it must've felt like, since the Soviet government repressed any proselytizing by churches.

Nome provided a different perspective to our Soviet visitors. Nome exhibited the seamier side of human society and was not the best locale for our Russian visitors to compare their system to ours. However, I felt that it was important for them to see the negative as well as the positive side of the evolving social system in the American Arctic. When the Saturday nightlife was accelerating we, with our Russian visitors, planned to visit the two most popular, or notorious, bars in town. Then Zabrodin announced that the Russians would not be going to the bars, saying that they were not interested in seeing a bunch of drunk Natives. I emphasized to the Russians that the Native people in Alaska, like indigenous Russians, are complex and have a lot of pride in their own culture. After speaking with Zabrodin in private, I learned that the real reason they were not going to the bars was that they had not been allotted US dollars to pay for drinks. With help from our interpreter, we explained that we Americans would buy the drinks for them as our guests. As it turned out, a city policeman who patrolled the two bars had already removed persons who were drinking excessively that night, thus minimizing the likelihood of rough behavior. It was well past 3:00 a.m. when we all went to our respective hotel rooms, and as I was about to head for bed, there was a soft knock on the door. There was Mukhachev standing there with an armload of Russian food and a bottle of vodka. He invited himself in to have a drink and, more importantly, offer excellent preserved Russian foods that at least partly explained his huge and heavy suitcase. Both of us had indulged moderately earlier in the evening and I was ready to adjourn for the night, but I welcomed Mukhachev's late arrival with food and "last drink of the night" in view of the social bonding and mutual respect that he and I had developed during my visit to the Taimyr.

We did host a community meeting in Nome to discuss the current problem on the eastern Seward Peninsula of caribou moving into the reindeer grazing areas and mixing with the reindeer. Several regional reindeer herders had come into Nome for the meeting, as well as state caribou management biologists who had flown in the day before. Unfortunately, after the events of the night before, attendance was poor, and it was brief because no one seemed energetic enough to debate the complex issue.

L–R: David Swanson, Gregory Yakushkin, and Tatyana Vlasova camping at Sadlerochit River, Alaska National Wildlife Refuge, Alaska, 2002. PHOTO BY DAVID KLEIN.

I also organized the reciprocal visit to Alaska in 2002 by Gregory Yakushkin and Tatyana Vlasova. I asked David Swanson, a botanist and plant community ecologist with the Soil Conservation Service who later went to work for the National Park Service and whose academic studies and subsequent field investigations had been in Siberia, to assist me. He was fluent in Russian and familiar with plant species of the taiga and Siberian wetlands, as well as the reindeer range in northwestern Alaska. As a muskox biologist, Yakushkin was most interested in the kind of habitat that the Alaska muskoxen were in, so Dave and I first accompanied them up to the Arctic National Wildlife Refuge. Primarily, we focused on the Sadlerochit River area, because muskoxen had been reintroduced there, similar to the Taimyr. After this, Yakushkin and I published a joint paper on comparative forage consumption by muskoxen in the Taimyr and in the Sadlerochit

(Klein et al. 1993). Then, given Tatyana's interest in lichens and their vulnerability to pollution, we drove to caribou wintering habitat in the Alaska Range near Cantwell to where a ten-by-ten-foot fenced enclosure had been established more than fifty years earlier to enable comparison of growth of lichens and other plants in timberline winter habitat moderately grazed by caribou of the Nelchina Caribou Herd. The enclosure had been reasonably well maintained and it was pretty impressive to see the improved lichen growth inside the enclosure versus a little too heavy grazing of lichens outside. We also set up a lichen workshop for students in the hills around Cantwell taught by Tatyana and a lichen ecologist who had been a student at UAF and lived in Anchorage.

I also took Tatyana to the Alaska Peninsula where I had a student working with the caribou herd there. Roger Ruess, a plant physiologist and ecologist from UAF, came along with us. Unfortunately, we were unable to get out in the field because we had to fly from Cold Bay in a small plane on floats and the weather wasn't good enough for flying. So we spent most of our time staying there at the headquarters of the Izembek National Wildlife Refuge, which provided Tatyana opportunities to talk with a lot of people there. We finally did get out in the field there a little bit, and she was able to see this country where the lichens had been severely overgrazed.

There were several other activities involved to give Gregory and Tatyana a comprehensive overview of Alaska in relation to their interest areas. Gregory was able to visit with state and federal biologists involved with management of muskoxen that had been reestablished in areas throughout Alaska's Arctic. And Tatyana had meetings with representatives of the Environmental Protection Agency (EPA), the Geophysical Institute, and the National Park Service to discuss possible collaboration on assessment of the extent and consequences of air pollution associated with the metallurgical complex at Norilsk. This collaboration subsequently came to fruition after Tatyana was able to talk with Soviet authorities and work out a deal where the EPA flew their pollution-sensing aircraft to the Taimyr. After all of this working with Tatyana, she and I later jointly authored a paper about lichens and air pollution (Klein and Vlasova 1992).

I was pleased that Tatyana's and Gregory's exchange visit had proved productive beyond my expectations. I think both the US and Soviet scientists who participated in these exchanges got something out of it, found them worthwhile, and were satisfied with their experiences. Like with Tatyana, I think she learned from her experience in the US that there was more chance of her playing a role in doing something about their air pollution problem than she had thought. I felt so good about her, and the connections I could offer with the EPA. That seemed ideal because I couldn't do much for her in the Soviet Union. The exchanges fostered this type of thing. Perhaps the Nixon-Brezhnev détente agreement for scientific exchanges played a role in the eventual peaceful dissolution of the Soviet Union.

Discussing national park management with some of the local village residents, Peneda-Gerês National Park, Portugal, 1972.
PHOTO BY DAVID KLEIN.

12
Expanding Horizons Beyond the Arctic

Although my focus was on Arctic ungulates and their habitats, I was interested in other places, so when given the opportunity I was excited by the chance to relate my knowledge and experience to different types of ecosystems and human cultures at lower latitudes. And I was always eager to learn new things and broaden my ecological understanding. Portugal and South Africa were two places where I spent significant time and was able to make interesting connections between north and south.

Portugal

The opportunity to visit Portugal was unanticipated as part of my 1971–72 Fulbright Grant to Norway. Under the Fulbright program, my primary commitment was to Norway, my host country, but I also was invited to visit and give lectures in other Fulbright member countries in Europe. I went to the University of Lund in Sweden, which was easy because it was a short train trip from Oslo, and I traveled to Northern Ireland. I also had an invitation to go to Yugoslavia that was interesting, but I couldn't take it because it conflicted with research I was doing in Norway.

Then I was invited to visit Peneda-Gerês National Park, located in the northwest of Portugal, to provide advice on management of the park's wildlife. It was the only national park in the country and was established in 1971. I was humbled by the invitation, feeling that as a wildlife biologist/manager from Alaska with no experience in the Mediterranean life zones of southern Europe, I was not appropriately prepared to provide the technical advice being sought regarding management of wildlife in Portugal. But I was the only

Villagers carrying spiney brush that they have cut on hillsides just outside of the village where it has not been overgrazed that they will use for absorptive bedding for their cattle and sheep inside barns in the winter. After the winter, the urine-soaked brush is spread on terraced fields as fertilizer and hand turned over into the soil, which, after years of this practice, has made their previously poor soil highly productive. Portugal, 1973. PHOTO BY DAVID KLEIN.

Fulbrighter in Europe at the time with wildlife and wildlife management training. This first visit to Portugal was far more than I had expected and was particularly enlightening to me both as an ecologist, as well as a humanist with a growing interest in human cultural development and understanding how the natural environment shapes human cultures.

Portugal, being long and narrow from south to north, encompassed several bioclimatic zones. The native forests in the northern region where the park was located were primarily deciduous hardwoods, particularly oak. It was a forester who came up with the idea of protecting this area as a national park. The "core area" of Peneda-Gerês National Park included mountain valleys with similar native wildlife species as in the eastern hardwood forests in

The beautiful granite and alpine landscape of Peneda-Gerês National Park, Portugal, 1973.
PHOTO BY DAVID KLEIN.

North America. Being familiar with the woods of southern New England and having taken forestry courses at the University of Connecticut, I realized the similarities, and was able to gain confidence in my ability to provide the advice and guidance that was expected of me.

Things were complicated in Portugal in terms of use of the land and wildlife. There was no wildlife program in the government, which is why people were still allowed to hunt roe deer, even though the population was

A village on the Portugal-Spain border with a new road built into the village.
The national park did not like this type of road building because it scarred the
landscape and would take years to repair. Men would go to places like France
to work as field laborers and when they returned they spent their newly earned
money to make their village look better and be easier to access with a road. The
stream in the bottom of the valley is the border between Spain and Portugal;
the Spanish side is on the right with terraced fields located higher up the
hillside and not on such steep ground as on the Portuguese side. After Portugal
created a national park in this area, Spain created one as well and they made it
an international park spanning across the border. PHOTO BY DAVID KLEIN.

pretty low. And range management was unheard of. Foresters blamed local
people's livestock for overgrazing the landscape. It wasn't really overgrazed;
people would let their animals graze and then they sometimes would burn
it to get rid of the shrubs that wouldn't be eaten by the grazing animals. The
local people also would harvest some of the prickly shrubs to use as winter
bedding for their sheep and cattle in barns, which when soaked with animal
urine made good fertilizer. When it was partly decomposed, they'd spread
it on terraced fields to build up the soils for growing vegetables, maize, and
barley. Seeing these people being relatively self-sufficient opened my eyes
to how people in the mountain communities were living the same way they
had for centuries and using the land extremely efficiently.

Following my visit, I submitted a wildlife management plan for Peneda-Gerês National Park to the park's director, José Lagrifa Mendes, in which I pointed out that I was unable to make detailed suggestions for park management on the basis of such a short visit, but I appreciated the opportunity, and discussions with him and his staff spurred my interest in the challenge to do a more in-depth survey if financial support became available in the future. It was an understatement to imply that my interest in continuing work in Peneda-Gerês was solely because I saw it as a challenge to assist Portugal in its efforts to use the national park concept to protect a portion of its beautiful natural and cultural landscape for future generations. I recognized that it would also allow me to pursue my interest in and fascination with how mountain environments shape the cultures of mountain-dwelling peoples. This interest was stimulated by the work I was doing with wild reindeer in Norway, but it had deeper roots from my youth in the mountains of northern New England and my graduate research focus on mountain goats, mountain sheep, and black-tailed deer in Alaska and their ecological connections to the alpine habitats that they occupied.

I also appreciated the openness of the Portuguese people, the forest engineers, and the university students in the applied sciences who accompanied me on visits to the park. In my numerous visits to Portugal, I was pleased that the university-trained people with whom I most frequently was associated were appreciative of Portugal's complex history and took pride in the melding of cultures that has resulted in the present Portuguese people. With some financial help from the USAID program (United States Agency for International Development), I was able to return in 1973 and spent three weeks carrying out a more in-depth ecological reconnaissance of the Peneda-Gerês National Park.

During my first visits to Portugal, João Bugalho was my interpreter. At that time, fluency in English was uncommon there, so his assistance was invaluable in facilitating effective communication. João had been doing graduate studies in ornithology in England under Peter Scott, the internationally known ecologist, founder of the World Wildlife Fund, and artist. When working with João, I appreciated that he was a fellow ecologist by training, that we shared similar interests in seeking further understanding of the natural environment, and we both were fascinated by the long human cultural association with wildlife and nature through hunting, art, and photography. After the bloodless coup that deposed the dictator Caetano, João was appointed director of Wildlife Management within the Ministry of Forestry. Having established a strong bond of friendship with João and both of us appreciating the emerging need for managed use of wildlife and their habitats, he asked me to assist him in the establishment of a politically sound and ecologically based system for management of Portugal's wildlife and their diverse habitats. They were trying to introduce good land-use management, and he invited me back to tour Portugal with him and provide advice. He also was working through the Technical University of Lisbon and trying to get more science education into the schools, which was an interest of mine in Alaska.

I got to know João increasingly well as we toured Portugal from north to south from October 18 through November 7, 1975. Accompanied by some of his young biologists, we visited different habitats and talked with local hunters, farmers, and private and public land managers about specific wildlife species and habitats for hunted and nonhunted species, migratory birds, and so on. The trip provided a view of a cross-section of wildlife habitats from the moist temperate woodlands of the north to the semiarid subtropical south. In the process, I was rewarded by exposure to the latitudinal cultural and culinary diversity that characterizes Portugal.

As in interior Alaska, it was apparent that fire played an important role in the ecology of wildlife habitats throughout much of Portugal. However, in both the United States and Portugal, the role of fire as a tool in land management and the influences of uncontrolled wildfire on public lands were poorly understood. This was further complicated by changes in land-use practices taking place in both countries. Although I had interest in and some understanding of the role of wildfire in Alaska, I was not qualified to provide advice on fire management in Portugal. I did have connections with Edwin and Betty Komarek at the Tall Timbers Research Station in Tallahassee, Florida, having visited there earlier in the 1970s. Their research on fire ecology and fire management in the southern pine forests had been successful in demonstrating how the use of fire could lead to sustainable productivity of forest lands for wildlife and wood production (Komarek 1969). I suggested that the Komareks could help define how fire could fit into habitat and wildlife management in Portugal, and they went to Portugal for a two-week visit in the fall of 1976. They produced a report that detailed the dynamics of fire ecology and suggested fire management strategies for the three dominant forest types in Portugal (Komarek and Komarek 1976).

As with my other international work, my time in Portugal led to continuing connections. For example, in 1975 I presented a paper at the 12th Congress of the International Union of Game Biologists (IUGB) in Lisbon (Klein 1975), and in 2003 I presented a paper at the 26th Congress of IUGB at the relatively new University of Minho at Braga, coauthored with the current director of Peneda-Gerês National Park, in which we reviewed aspects of park management policy still in place that had been adopted from my 1973 assessment report (International Union of Game Biologists 2003). I also subsequently visited Portugal to give invited lectures during a special graduate-level symposium on wildlife management offered at the Technical College of the University of Lisbon that had been organized by Professor Fausto Reusse and Miguel Bugalho, João's son. The most recent occasion resulted from an invitation in 2004 to be a keynote speaker at the 25th anniversary celebration of the Portuguese Society of Pastures and Forages (SPPF), which is an organization comparable to the Society for Range Management in the United States.[10]

I had never expected how an initial invitation in 1972 would develop into so many years of collaboration and friendship. I have valued my friendship with João and all that I have learned from him. With more than forty years of visits to Portugal to work with João, I felt somewhat guilty that I had enjoyed so many wonderful and productive trips there, but he had never been to Alaska. So in June 2005, I was finally able to host João and his wife, Nela, and show them some of Alaska's diversity. We visited active raptor nest sites in the Interior, stopped at Denali National Park, where we saw a female willow ptarmigan feeding young chicks similar to how female red-legged partridge in Portugal behave, and visited the Kenai Peninsula, where we went whale

---

10. For more about the Portuguese Society of Pastures and Forages, see J. M. Potes, E. V. Lourenço, and T. Carita, "Portuguese Society of Pastures and Forages," abstract in *XX International Grasslands Congress: Offered Papers*, ed. F. P. O'Mara, R. J. Wilkins, L.'t Mannetje, D. K. Lovett, P. A. M. Rogers, and T. M. Boland, 935 (The Netherlands: Wageningen Academic Publishers, 2005).

L–R: David, his daughter PeggyEllen Kleinleder, Nela and João Bugalho at Homer when they visited Alaska in 2005. COURTESY OF DAVID KLEIN.

watching and glacier viewing out of Seward and enjoyed the mountain and coastal scenery around Homer. I made my last trip to Portugal in 2013 and visited João and Nela at their new home in a small village overlooking the Algarve coast of southern Portugal. I enjoyed sharing memories with João now that we were older, was happy to see his children and grandchildren all grown up, and appreciated exploring the Portuguese countryside, learning more about their culture, and eating their delicious food.

South Africa

Some will wonder why a wildlife manager and research biologist who had worked professionally in northern latitudes and gained recognition as an authority on the ecology of Sitka black-tailed deer, caribou, moose, muskoxen, mountain sheep, and mountain goats, would become interested in African wildlife and their ecology. In college, I learned that most ungulate species existing in the world today had their evolutionary origins in the African continent. Research on Alaska ungulates focused on their morphological, physiological, and behavioral adaptations to the seasonal extremes of the Arctic stimulated my curiosity to ask how these adaptations could evolve in ungulates pre-adapted for life in the tropical and subtropical habitats of Africa. I concluded that in order to try to answer such a question I needed to gain a better understanding of African ungulate evolution and habitat diversity. Therefore, I looked for an appropriate opportunity to take part in ungulate research in Africa.

The opportunity came about in 1982 at an International Theriological Conference in Helsinki, Finland, where I met several biologists with the Mammal Research Institute (MRI) at the University of Pretoria in South Africa who were doing some excellent biological, ecological, and behavioral research broadly focused on the physiology, related habitat adaptations, and general ecology of African mammals, particularly ungulates. I asked about the possibility of going there and doing some research on the foraging dynamics and differences in water uptake of two closely related antelopes, the impala and blesbok. Neil Fairall, a researcher with the MRI who was part English and part Afrikaner and who was a specialist on the physiology, water transfer, and water relationships of ungulates, had already been doing eco-physiological studies on captive impala and blesbok (Fairall 1969; Fairall et al. 1983; Killian and Fairall 1983). He agreed to collaborate with me, and I spent four months in 1983 as a visiting professor at the Research Institute, with funding from the South African Council for Scientific and Industrial Research to help cover some of my salary and living expenses.

Neil Fairall's efforts were primarily directed toward quantifying water turnover rates of the animals, and their relation to energetics and gut morphology. I assisted Neil with his studies of impala and blesbok at the two-hundred-hectare, fenced-in Derdepoort Nature Reserve. I also did field observations on my own to assess differences between impala and blesbok in their selection and use of habitat and forage as influenced by the availability of water, forage types, predation risk, and diurnal temperature variation. I also was able to collect habitat use and related behavioral data at Derdepoort, Kruger National Park, and the S. A. Lombard Nature Reserve,

Neil Fairall with a blesbok
injected with tritiated
water and horns marked
with colored tape to
identify individual animals,
Derderpoort Wildlife Reserve,
South Africa, 1983. PHOTO BY
DAVID KLEIN.

a 2,800-hectare fenced area of natural habitat in western Transvaal near
Bloemhof (Klein and Fairall 1984, 1986).

Neil Fairall and I teamed up and developed some unique techniques to
determine water turnover. Derdepoort Nature Reserve was a fenced area
right close to Pretoria that had been stocked with wildlife, but where hunting was not permitted. This was a place where we had the animals under
control, therefore, we decided to use radioactive isotopes for studying them.

Impala drinking at a water hole, South
Africa, 1983. PHOTO BY DAVID KLEIN.

We injected tritiated water into the impala and a blesbok (Klein 2001a:247),
and since it was radioactive we couldn't do this out in the wild where people
were harvesting animals to eat. Neil was trained in using radioactive isotopes, and I had some experience with it when working with Bob White in
Alaska. For doing radioactive isotope work, collecting urine was usually the
simplest and least invasive method for assessing an animal's water turnover
rate. When doing this work in Alaska, the research animals were in a stall,
which made it pretty easy to collect urine. To obtain a urine sample, you
would have a stick with a small beaker taped to the end of it that you would
hold under the animal. In Africa, the animals at Derdepoort Nature Reserve
were within a fenced area, but were not tame by any means, so we wondered
how we were going to get the necessary urine samples. We couldn't get the

urine unless we captured the animals, which was difficult and complicated, so I suggested we collect fresh feces and use water extracted from the feces to test for water turnover. We ended up darting the animal, giving it an injection of the radioactive isotope, and then marking the horn with colored tape, so we could identify the individual animal. As I watched the animals for my behavioral studies and noted how frequently they drank water, the minute a marked animal dropped a group of fecal pellets, I was able to rush out there and pick up that fresh pile of pellets with a plastic Ziploc bag. This method paid off and we were able to extract the water from the samples and developed a technique for assessing the rate that the water was passing through their body (Fairall and Klein 1984; Klein and Fairall 1984).

Doing this research was fascinating because of the different physiological adaptations of these two types of antelopes. The impala is a bit smaller than the blesbok and lives more in the savannah and grazes, or browses on evergreen shrubs and trees during the dry season. This food has a lot of alkaloids and other secondary chemicals that they have to get rid of via the kidneys, so they have to have a high turnover rate of water in order to excrete most of these. And that means they have to go to water at least once a day to keep up with this high excretion rate. Whereas the blesbok lives in the highest upland dry plateau areas, which is mostly grassland with shrubs and plants related to grasslands and occasional scattered acacia trees, so they are able to support healthy body conditions with less water. Both regions go through a period of summer drought with poor-quality forage followed by rains that produce high-quality forage, and I wondered how these animals survived. During the hot and dry period, the temperature can be well over a hundred degrees. The blesbok stay out in the hot sun, whereas the impala go to shade because they lose too much water if they are out in the bright sun with the hot temperatures. During the dry season, there's often no available water, so the blesbok are adapted to get what water is present in living tissues of plants. They can go for several days without water because they can get enough water from the forage and they don't have the problem of needing to flush out secondary chemicals from the plants.

Studying these different species, such as the roe deer in Scandinavia and these antelopes in Africa, is helpful for comparison purposes and understanding the behaviors and responses of animals in different habitats and

Blesbok in the high veldt of South Africa basking in the morning sun to warm their bodies, 1983. Blesbok body temperature drops overnight as the air cools, so they use the morning sun to bring their internal temperatures back up in order to get them through the day and following night. PHOTO BY DAVID KLEIN.

under varying conditions. Comparing species, both physiologically and behaviorally—the caribou and muskoxen versus the blesbok and the impala—I could see similar habitat adaptations of the impala and caribou, who are selective feeders with energy-costly lifestyles, versus the blesbok and muskoxen, who are bulk feeders that lead energy-conservative lives (Klein and Fairall 1984, 1986; Klein 2001a).

Besides the exchange of scientific knowledge, one of the benefits of working with other scientists like this was learning from each other and learning new techniques. This radioactive isotope work especially was really important in the broader field of wildlife studies. I remember one person saying to me, "Well, how come you're going to South Africa? They've got this Afrikaner government where the blacks don't have a vote." I said, "It's about science. It's not political. There are good scientists there and we can all learn from each other." I believed in the value of this type of scientific collaboration.

There were many additional opportunities outside of my involvement in the impala and blesbok research to broaden my knowledge and understanding of African plant and animal ecology, human cultural complexity, and associated politics. These came about through invitations to visit other universities throughout South Africa where there were faculty with wildlife interests that intersected with mine, including the universities of Witwatersrand, Cape Town, Pietermaritzburg, Stellenbosch, and Durban. During some of these short visits, I was fortunate to be shown the diversity of local and regional wildlife habitats and their associated plant communities and fauna. I was impressed by the excellence of many of the papers on the ecology of southern Africa published by faculty based at the universities I visited. English botanists played a founding role in the establishment of South African universities, thus accounting for the early integration of ecology in the education and research in the biological sciences associated with these universities (Anker 2001).

These opportunities to visit several of the unique regional wildlife habitats of South Africa, visit fellow wildlife scientists whom I previously had met at international conferences, and make new friends added enrichment to my stay in South Africa. For example, time in the field with Norman Owen-Smith, professor at the University of Johannesburg, and one of his PhD-level graduate students provided a unique opportunity for discussion of our common interest in the role of secondary chemicals in ungulate forage selection. Or timing my visit to the University of Natal in order to sit in on a three-day, graduate-level field course at the Cathedral Peak Center for Resource Ecology, which demonstrated that teaching about ecological processes can be enhanced when done within the natural environment. Or a visit with Elizabeth Vrba, an expert on African ungulate evolution and taxonomy at the Transvaal Museum, that helped verify my assumption of the relatively close evolutionary relationship of the impala and blesbok and of the importance of comparing their adaptations to their respective habitats.

Being in Africa was a terrific experience for me. I achieved the goal I had set for myself of broadening my understanding of African ungulate ecology for comparison with my knowledge of high-latitude ungulates. It was a totally new environment and I learned so much ecology, as well as about the evolution of all of the African large mammals. But you couldn't help but begin also to learn about vegetation and the habitat and the birds and other members of the environment. It was such a complex system that you had to look at it closely to truly understand it.

Employees of the US Fish and Wildlife Service in Alaska at an annual meeting in Juneau, 1958. David Klein is second from right in the middle row. Other people David mentions include: Front row, first on left is Sig Olson and seventh from left is Clarence Rhode, regional director, and third from right is Bob Scott. Back row, fourth from left is Will Troyer, fifth from left is David Spencer, and John Buckley is second from right. COURTESY OF US FISH AND WILDLIFE SERVICE.

13

Managing Wildlife in Alaska: Territorial Days, Statehood, and the Era of Big Oil

I do not intend to offer an entire history of the field of wildlife management, but having spent more than sixty years of my life involved with it in some capacity, from studying wildlife in the late 1940s and early 1950s, working as a wildlife biologist and manager in Southeast Alaska in the 1950s, conducting research on wildlife and management issues from the 1950s into the 2000s, to participating in land use and wildlife conservation committees and panels throughout my career, I have seen significant changes with how wildlife management is carried out. My work and beliefs clearly were being shaped by these changes, while I also was being an agent of change for others. I was specifically involved with and affected by how these changes in wildlife practices manifested themselves in Alaska, and wanted to share some of my observations and thoughts about the implications of this.

I believe I made the right choice to go into wildlife management. I've become more of an ecologist as I've matured, but basically that was my start. I still feel that trying to understand natural systems is important. A lot of it is related to land use and that's one of the attractions of being in Alaska, a state where agriculture occupies less than 3 percent of its total land, rather than say Missouri. Of course there are wildlife management problems here, but they are different kinds of problems. For example, attempts to ranch cattle in brown bear country on Kodiak Island. Or the small, introduced bison herd near Delta, where the amount of time that management biologists have spent on those bison has been huge compared to what they should have spent on management of caribou or moose. This is comparable to getting hung up on wolf and bear management, where politics intervene, and managers lose focus on trying to understand the basic relationship between the animals and their environment. Wolves or bears are important factors in understanding this, but the vegetation is an important part of it also.

Wildlife management in Alaska underwent major change during my career. When Alaska was a territory, technically wildlife management was under the federal Fish and Wildlife Service; however, to give Alaska residents some voice in management they established a Game Commission. The commission was comprised of four citizens representing guide outfitters, sport hunters, fur buyers, and trappers and was responsible for setting hunting, fishing, and trapping seasons and bag limits. The nonvoting chair of the commission was Clarence Rhode, the regional director of the Fish and Wildlife Service in Alaska at the time. They were informed about the few studies that Fish and Wildlife Service did on habitat and animal population dynamics in order to help them make decisions. Through our annual meetings with Rhode and other Fish and Wildlife people, us young biologists had a good avenue for input to the Game Commission. The big change, of course, occurred during Alaska's transition to statehood in 1959, and the newly formed Alaska Department of Fish and Game took over management of wildlife. It worked surprisingly well.

In early Territorial times, enforcement of wildlife laws was carried out by game wardens, who were employees of the Fish and Wildlife Service. In addition to catching people for hunting violations, some game wardens collected information on animal population numbers or animal behavior, things that were needed for management decisions. Often these game wardens did not have advanced degrees, although some of them were doing the same thing that biologists would have been doing. There also were Predator and Rodent Control agents employed by the Fish and Wildlife Service who were responsible for controlling animals that were thought to be detrimental to the interests of Alaskans, including wolves, coyotes, and seals. Even eagles were unprotected in Alaska until about 1952.

When I was based in Petersburg, there was a Predator and Rodent Control agent stationed there, and another one in Wrangell. Even though the hunters were getting enough deer, these agents were still attempting to kill wolves. The more wolves they killed, the more justification there was for their job to continue. There were some cases in territorial times where

Leamen "Lee" Ellis, senior Predator and Rodent Control agent for Alaska, picking up a poisoned wolf carcass on frozen Martin Lake, Prince of Wales Island, Alaska, January 26, 1957. PHOTO BY DAVID KLEIN.

the Fish and Wildlife Service was starting to get the Predator and Rodent Control agents to agree to do wolf control only in those areas where biologists could say there was a real need for it. But that was the rare case. One thing agents in Southeast did was to poison wolves in winter on the frozen lakes that the wolves were using as routes to move across the larger islands. To attract the wolves, the agents inserted the poison strychnine tablets inside chunks of seal blubber, put these in plastic bags loaded with smelly, rotten fish waste, and dropped them from airplanes so when the bags hit the lake ice, they would burst open and scatter the rancid contents. The wolves would normally hang around the bait long enough so that they'd die from the strychnine poisoning before they got off of the ice, which made it easy to spot wolf carcasses from the air, land on the ice, and quickly pick them up. Alternatively, if the lakes didn't freeze up in time, agents would put poisoned bait inside whole seal carcasses that they set out along beaches above the high tide line. It was a little more difficult to retrieve the dead wolves using this method, because they traveled along the beach picking up things as they went and would be more likely to keep moving instead of sticking around and dying right there.

And then there was the debate about shooting wolves from the air, which the Division of Predator and Rodent Control had been doing. For example, several airplanes would fly to the North Slope in winter where they could pretty easily track wolves in the treeless terrain and shoot quite a number in one joint effort. The program resulted in killing a couple hundred wolves. The whole idea was not ecologically sound. The Fish and Wildlife Service was criticized for killing wolves when the caribou population wasn't being hunted significantly or being threatened. The reasoning was, "If we eliminate their predators, the caribou numbers will go up." At that time, the idea was that if a herd got too big it would fracture into new herds that would move south into forested habitat. Of course, we now know this did not happen.

In some areas, like the Tanana Hills in the Interior and on the Kenai Peninsula, cyanide guns were used to kill predators. They were called coyote getters. A metal conduit pipe was driven into the ground and loaded with a cartridge filled with cyanide powder and a packet impregnated with a lot of odors, along with a triggering device. It was designed so that if a coyote or other carnivore tried to pull off the smelly top part, it would fire the cartridge and shoot the cyanide directly into its mouth. The poison then would usually kill them within minutes.

In that era, there were bounties on everything from wolves to coyotes to eagles, with the exception of brown bears because they were so valuable for trophy hunting. Eventually, there was also a bounty on seals to control them in some areas where it was believed they were taking salmon from fishermen's nets. For the bounty in Southeast Alaska, you could turn in the scalp of a seal and get paid about five dollars each. But Native people on the north coast of Alaska, whose culture had been dependent on seals for food, clothing, and fuel for cooking and lighting, felt discriminated against because they received no bounty for the seals they killed for their own consumption and use of the skins. They said, "This is unfair to us. We should get five dollars for each of the seals we kill." The territory then extended the bounty to include seals in other parts of Alaska.

There were no organized environmental groups at that time in Alaska, which could have pointed out the illogical basis for what they were doing with bounties. If there were places where wolf control was needed, then, okay, having a bounty probably made sense. However, the bounty system was implemented in places whether it was needed or not, like what happened with seals, and by paying people for killing animals it appeared to be more of a welfare program for people living in the bush rather than a mechanism for predator control and wildlife management.

When statehood occurred, the state legislature kept the bounty on wolves and the federal government was still using poison. The idea was that wolves were killing caribou, mountain sheep, and moose, which were prime targets for hunters, so wolves and other predators had to be controlled. There were limited investigations being done on wolves (Murie 1944), but there was not a major effort to study the ecology of wolves and no studies underway to show the need for wolf control. The Game Division within the newly formed Alaska Department of Fish and Game was assigned the job of wildlife management. Well-trained biologists were hired, many of whom were graduates of the Wildlife Unit at UAF. One of the things these biologists focused on initially was getting rid of the bounties and stopping the use of poison to kill wolves and other wildlife. The bounties only lasted for a few years and finally were eliminated.

During territorial times and the early days of statehood, there wasn't much effort by wildlife management agencies to serve the interests of Alaska Native people. There were game regulations, but frequently they were not appropriate and only intended for urban hunters. For example, the caribou hunting season might not open until the weather was getting cool and that was when the caribou were not in the area used by Native people. In early territorial days, Alaska Natives were not required to have hunting licenses, or if they were, they did not have to pay much for them. And, of course, the issue of who had priority in terms of subsistence hunting rights and who had authority over management of subsistence hunting was not even being discussed. This didn't become a serious issue until the 1970s when the Alaska National Interest Lands Conservation Act (ANILCA) defined subsistence with priorities for Native peoples and the state and federal governments began fighting over who had authority over wildlife management on federal lands (Case 1984).

The controversy over wolf and bear management has persisted as long as I've been in Alaska and continues to this day. Professionals and the public have come down on both sides of the issue in terms of predator control as an effective management method. When I was Wildlife Unit leader, the state was having the problem that a large segment of sport and trophy hunters were arguing that there were too many predators and there should be more intensive predator control because there weren't enough moose to go around and/or the caribou were declining. They wanted to put the blame solely on predators. Then environmental groups and some anti-hunting groups, as well as animal rights groups in the Lower 48, threatened to boycott tourism in Alaska because the Board of Game was advocating shooting and killing wolves from aircraft without adequate justification. The killing of wolves was being used as a simplistic way to bring about recovery of moose populations. Often, other factors were ignored. For example, the effect of severe winters was ignored, when some of the good-quality food was buried in the snow and the reduced availability of forage made it more energetically costly for calves of the year to forage for their food. Or the role of fire was not adequately understood and was overlooked in terms of its impact on moose habitat. Generally, habitat itself was not being adequately examined and addressed. Some studies were done, and some of the better ones were through the Cooperative Wildlife Research Unit, but a problem with habitat studies is that little is learned unless they are carried out over the long-term. Things change slowly. Whereas, if moose hunters wanted something to happen fast, then killing predators seemed to be the best approach from their perspective. It was a simplistic way, but seldom the justifiable way. The different approaches to moose and/or wolf management by ADF&G were not well designed or carried out according to scientific principles, were not planned in a systematic manner, and were poorly explained to the public.

The main criticism I had at the time, and I think I wrote a column to that effect for Alaska newspapers, was when Dr. Wayne Regelin, who was the director of the Wildlife Conservation Division, argued that their method of extrapolating from other areas was science-based and so that was sufficient. I disagreed with him. I said, "Not all habitats are alike. In fact, they're all different. And if you extrapolate, then you can't argue that it's all science-based."

There were questionable situations that he couldn't rationalize away with that argument. The point that I stressed strongly was that ADF&G had failed because it lacked sufficient funding, not because it was negligent. They were doing some studies, but in most cases they weren't able to explain what they were doing to the general public. This was because the legislature had cut ADF&G funding for producing public information reports about their wildlife investigations, including predator-prey relationship studies. In the early days of statehood, there was a line item in the ADF&G budget for putting out a quarterly journal explaining their studies, what they were doing, and what they were finding out. Later, the legislature cut this funding, but they didn't say why. The real reason seemed to be that the legislature didn't want the public to be too informed. They wanted the Board of Game to be able to make wildlife management judgments and extrapolate beyond science-based findings, and the legislature to be free to exercise a stronger voice in management of wildlife without knowledgeable public support.

When Tony Knowles was governor of Alaska, he was confronted with the seemingly irresolvable problem of how to deal with wolf and bear management in a way that wouldn't have serious negative effects on Alaska's economy, including tourism. He provided ADF&G funding that enabled the National Research Council (NRC) to establish a panel to assess the effectiveness of predator management in Alaska. Members selected for the panel included a cross-section of people, including university academics who had experience with animal population dynamics and understood whole ecosystem dynamics and were not necessarily focused solely on predator relationships. There was one Canadian, Bruce McLellan, who was a bear specialist from British Columbia, and three Alaskans: me, Patricia Cochran, and George Yaska. I was selected as a wildlife ecologist and because I was leader of the Alaska Cooperative Wildlife Research Unit and had remained neutral or objective regarding the controversy. Patricia Cochran, an Iñupiaq woman from Nome, was executive director of the Alaska Native Science Commission, and George Yaska, an Athabascan from Huslia had a bachelor's degree in wildlife management from UAF and represented the Tanana Chiefs Conference. Others on that panel included Fran James, a respected ornithologist and good ecologist, who was head of the American Biological Society, and Gordon Orians, who was an ornithologist, ecologist, and professor at the University of Washington, and served as the panel's chairperson. The NRC avoided appointing panel members who were polarized on this issue one way or another. I've always tried to be deliberate in avoiding polarization on controversial issues that aren't strictly biological or science based. I tried to stick to having a good scientific basis behind my position and restrict it to the biological, ecological relationships.

The National Research Council panel met with groups in Alaska involved in the wolf control and predator-prey conflict. We examined the different wolf control efforts, and looked to see if there was any sound basis for their results. Wolf control in the recent past had been costly, but nobody seemed to know whether it accomplished the objectives, as poorly defined as they were. There didn't seem to be a good sense of how many wolves were left. The major findings of that report were that in some cases there can be scientific justification and ecological justification for wolf control, but if there's any control to be done it should be done as a well-designed experiment where someone is assigned to follow up afterward and see what happens. I felt relativity good about what we accomplished with that panel.

And then with waterfowl, the Natives hunted migratory waterfowl when they were available and when they needed them, not according to what the law said about when it was open season. Traditionally, Native peoples used several methods for harvesting waterfowl. When the birds were in flight, a bolo, spear, net, or a gun was used, whereas in the past in the Yukon-Kuskokwim Delta, groups of women and children drove young birds that were almost ready to fly and flightless adults that were molting and unable to fly into a net on the ground. This had proven to be an effective method that could kill hundreds of birds in a single drive. It did require a cooperative effort between two or more villages, and by the 1960s it had become a rare event. The Migratory Bird Treaty Act of 1916 prevented the killing of waterfowl during the spring breeding season; however, this was the only time such birds were available in northwestern and northern Alaska. Therefore, management and enforcement requirements of the Migratory Bird Treaty became problematic in Alaska. The seasons wouldn't open until the first of September and the waterfowl were usually gone by that time. That meant that the Natives who hunted them when they were available in their areas were hunting them illegally.

In 1964 and 1965, I did a study of waterfowl harvest in Yukon-Kuskokwim Delta villages, where I recorded approximately how many of each waterfowl species the local people were harvesting, with an emphasis on geese. I hired local Native residents to work on this project because I recognized how much knowledge they had of the local area and resources, something I lacked. They taught me so much about their region and cultures, which was wonderful for me, and their traditional knowledge and experience were critical to accomplishing the study's goals. The results demonstrated how dependent the Yup'ik people were on waterfowl as a food source in spring (Klein 1966). After the long winter when the supply of fish that they had caught the previous summer was pretty much gone and there were no caribou and only a few moose, this fresh meat of waterfowl in the spring was an essential subsistence resource. This study was one of the first of its kind to combine biology with anthropology to show the critical importance of wildlife in the subsistence economies and cultures of rural Alaska peoples.

The Native people were reluctant to stop what was an age-old practice, so they had a couple of confrontations with the Fish and Wildlife Service over enforcement. One was at Bethel where two young Natives took their boat across the river in spring and started hunting waterfowl. That was a tough one because they were obviously sport hunting rather than subsistence hunting. A worse case was when Fish and Wildlife enforcement agents flying in the Yukon-Kuskokwim Delta saw a couple of Natives hunting waterfowl near the village of Tuntutuliak. As the plane circled around to land, the hunters jumped on their dogsled and headed for the village as fast as they could go. The hunters arrived in Tuntutuliak before the agents, and when the agents arrived the whole village came out to confront them. At this point, the agents wisely thought it was best to avoid an aggressive situation and left. There wasn't any gunfire at that confrontation, but it showed that they weren't able to enforce the law under those conditions.

In 1961, there was another confrontation over enforcement of waterfowl hunting that is known as the "Duck-In." It happened at Barrow (Utqiaġvik) where the local Iñupiat people joined together to oppose Fish and Wildlife Service's seasonal restrictions on duck hunting. Two local subsistence hunters were arrested for shooting eider ducks out of season, and in protest most of Barrow's hunters appeared at the federal game warden's office with dead ducks in hand (Blackman 1989). Like in the Bethel and the Yukon-Kuskokwim region, if Native people wanted to hunt waterfowl to provide food for their families as they had done traditionally for generations, they were forced to hunt illegally because spring was the only season when these birds were in the Arctic. This protest succeeded in getting the charges dropped for the two hunters, as well as getting wildlife officials to only enforce protection of threatened or endangered species. In 1997, the Migratory Bird Treaty was renegotiated between the US and Canada, finally making Alaska spring subsistence waterfowl hunting legal (Case 1984).

Another complicated wildlife research and management situation arose with muskoxen. Muskoxen were once widely distributed in northern and western Alaska, but by the late 1800s they had disappeared. In 1929, with support from the Alaska Territorial Legislature, a program was initiated to reintroduce muskoxen to the state as a domestication experiment (Palmer and Rouse 1936; Klein 1988b). The first introduction into the wild occurred in 1936, when thirty-one muskoxen from Greenland were introduced to Nunivak Island (Hicks 2001). After the Nunivak Island population had grown substantially, in 1969 and 1970 the ADF&G transplanted fifty-one of them to the North Slope to reestablish them in the Arctic National Wildlife Refuge. I was involved in this project.

When we did this, we made the mistake of capturing yearlings. These were the largest muskox we could handle, because they had to be put in crates and flown in aircraft. Of the ones we released on the North Slope, close to 60 percent to 70 percent of them died. This was a poor success rate. However, it was the first time we'd done anything like this, so there was a lot of trial and error as to what we were doing and how to best do it. We learned that since the muskoxen we captured and released were all juveniles, they didn't have any familiarity with the terrain in which we let them go, where to find the forage they needed, or how to defend themselves against wolves. For example, some of the muskox went out onto the sea ice because they couldn't tell the difference between the land and the ice, which is hard in late winter when we released them and everything is still covered in snow. While other individual muskox just disappeared. We realized all these factors led to issues with mortality rates.

David's graduate students Kent Jingfors (left) and Dan Roby (right) making winter observations of muskoxen on the Sadlerochit River, circa 1981. PHOTO BY DAVID KLEIN.

It was thought for a while that all these released muskoxen died, but then they found a few of them in the Sadlerochit River area and one or two other places where a small number of them had persisted. The ones that went inland found windblown ridges where there was some food that helped them make it through the rest of the winter. But the big problem up there, especially with the Sadlerochit population, was they just stayed together as one large group. As the group got larger and larger, it was better at defending itself from wolves and even bears, but because muskoxen don't move around very much, with so many animals being in one place they were starting to overgraze and deplete their food source. With their small hooves, muskoxen are not very good at digging through deep snow to find forage in the winter, because their hooves are more like cattle and much smaller per unit of body weight than those of caribou. The muskoxen could only feed on willows along the rivers in the early winter when the snow wasn't too deep, and after that they had to feed on windblown ridges and slopes with tussocks of sedges and prostrate willows where there was only a thin snow cover to dig through. We assume that there just wasn't enough forage to sustain their large group, but the big question was, why didn't they move. There was a lot of suitable habitat not very far away that could have sustained smaller groups of muskoxen.

Then there was the question of the type of science upon which to base wildlife management decisions. As I have mentioned, during territorial days, the Fish and Wildlife Service had the attitude that habitat was all important for wildlife, so they were doing a lot of studies that related to habitat and trying to understand how habitat related to numbers of animals. In comparison, when ADF&G was established, most employees and administrators presumed that their mandate for management was only related to populations of animals that were being hunted. They focused on understanding animal population dynamics and how that related to their productivity, and then how these species could be harvested without negatively affecting the long-term productivity of their populations. Whether it is sport hunting, subsistence hunting, or trapping, you have to know how many animals are out there in order to determine how much or how little harvesting there can be. Since the state was only interested in managing animal populations on a sustained harvest basis with no emphasis on habitat, there was little interest in hiring anybody who wanted to study the broader connections between wildlife and their habitat. So this led to the question of who was going to be responsible for habitat. The state's attitude was that the feds had responsibility for habitat, and since FWS was still doing good habitat studies, the state could save money and just let the feds continue doing them. There is still no specific state agency in charge of habitat management; it is split between different agencies within the Department of Natural Resources.

From a budget standpoint, it was easy for the state to focus only on factors that they could relate directly to animal population dynamics, but there was little appreciation for the fact that herbivores may have an impact on the environment. This attitude excluded the role of forage for herbivores, and how forage availability may change both in relationship to the density of the animal population and in relationship to environmental factors, as well as the influence of more human activity and climate change. This lack

Cartoon illustration by Sig Olson showing the use of hunter check stations for wildlife management.
USFWS FEDERAL AID IN WILDLIFE RESTORATION, QUARTERLY PROGRESS REPORT, PROJECT W-3-R-101, ALASKA, DECEMBER 31, 1955, VOLUME 10, NO. 2, P. 23.

of responsibility for habitat by the state meant little good research was being done on critical habitat issues. For example, there were no good quantitative studies being done that could prove the assumption that fires improve habitat generally for moose, but also show that it doesn't happen instantaneously. Three to five years after a fire is when it starts to become good moose habitat. Another example was that the caribou populations were known to fluctuate over time, but there was disagreement as to what caused the fluctuation. There was a tendency to put the blame on predators even though it may have been a combination of environmental factors.

One of the hardest things in managing any kind of wildlife is knowing what all the factors are that affect their complicated relationships with their habitat and with other animals, and which factors are most important in determining outcomes. You want to make decisions based on as much understanding as possible about the variables that influence the situation, but it's very difficult because you can't be aware of and have your eye on all of these factors all of the time. Because all these factors make it complicated

David with a mountain goat that he
harvested on the Kenai Peninsula,
late 1950s. COURTESY OF DAVID KLEIN.

to understand animal populations and what they're doing and why they're
doing it, it can be difficult to make a decision about management at any
one point in time. Now, we don't necessarily have absolute information. For
example, there can be different perspectives on the desirable size of an animal population and it can be hard to know which is the best to manage
for. In Alaska, of course, you also have to factor in the human element of
hunting, at least for some species, and how that affects population size. We
don't always have all of the information we need, so the question is, how do
you manage? You manage on the best information you have available and
sometimes it's not enough.

Managing wildlife is not just about managing animal populations.
Since in many places it is related to hunting and what is happening with a

particular species, wildlife managers are dealing with people and managing their behavior, too. In this way, on one hand wildlife management is a social science, while on the other, it's a biological science. It is very complex. You could say successful management is getting the users to understand what's going on. Sometimes, if they know what's going on, it can be something they can take some action on themselves. For example, if there's a decline in caribou in some area, then regionally people may decide to reduce their hunting in those areas that have been overharvested and shift their activity to areas where the caribou herd is more stable. That can sometimes happen, but it requires understanding by the users of the resource. And then you have tourists who want to see wildlife, which means balancing between consumptive and nonconsumptive users in certain areas. For those who want to observe wildlife, they are just as interested in seeing the predators as well as the prey species, whereas most Alaska hunters are primarily interested in the

Cartoon illustration by Sig Olson demonstrating the downside of hunting wildlife from the road. USFWS FEDERAL AID IN WILDLIFE RESTORATION, QUARTERLY PROGRESS REPORT, PROJECT W-3-R-10, ALASKA, DECEMBER 31, 1955, VOLUME 10, NO. 2, P. 33.

large prey species, especially moose or caribou, because they are the target species of their hunt.

Nowadays, the big thing that is talked about is sustainability. I have a problem with using that term *sustainability*. When we first started talking about ecology, it was new and people started thinking differently (Stauffer 1957; Anker 2001), but now it's gone so far that even candy bar sales are presumably increased if "ecological" is printed on the packaging. Most consumers do not have a clue as to what that actually means. Nowadays, at a lot of universities, ecology is no longer the core course in the sciences that it was previously. Instead, genetics is one of the core course requirements, based on the idea that we can better understand the evolutionary history of plant and animal populations through genetics. This is important, of course, and we didn't have the techniques for doing that in my student days, but we shouldn't ignore or forget ecology. So both *sustainability* and *ecology* are terms that are overused and not understood by most people, especially those who are not specifically educated in these subjects.

Having a scientific background and understanding ecology and sustainability are key for wildlife management, but have not always been a requirement for heads of wildlife management agencies in Alaska. Those who are not trained as biologists or wildlife managers lack a full understanding of the issues they are faced with. The first head of the Alaska Department of Fish and Game after statehood was Clarence Anderson, who had a PhD in fisheries, and he appointed people as deputy commissioner and as division heads who also were professionally trained. Subsequently, many of those who became commissioners were graduates of the Co-op Unit program, including Ron Skoog, who did a master's degree on caribou and served as Commissioner of Fish and Game from 1977 to 1982; and Jim Brooks, who was the first head of the Game Division within ADF&G after statehood, which later became the Department of Wildlife Conservation, and served as commissioner from 1972 to 1977. Governor Wally Hickel broke this pattern of appointing ADF&G commissioners with appropriate training and experience. He appointed a shoestore owner in Anchorage who was an ardent hunter as his ADF&G commissioner. Wildlife faculty at UAF protested this appointment, believing it set a bad precedent for putting someone in a position for political reasons, not because they necessarily had good qualifications. Indirectly, word came down that Hickel might consider cutting funding for wildlife programs at UAF if pushed any further, so that was the end of that.

Then it went from bad to worse under Frank Murkowski's governorship, because he didn't approve of the scientific work that the state was doing at Prudhoe Bay where the state and the oil industry mutually supported an ADF&G biologist doing research on caribou in the Prudhoe and Kuparuk oil fields. This biologist was Ray Cameron, who had a PhD through the Institute of Arctic Biology at UAF and was a pilot. He was monitoring the movements of the caribou within and adjacent to the oil fields to see if the Trans-Alaska Pipeline, the Haul Road, and associated infrastructure were fracturing the Central Arctic Caribou Herd. He did survey flights in a Super Cub, and showed the size of the herd was staying fairly stable and, in fact, increasing a little bit, but it was fracturing into two components. At the same time, other herds, like the Porcupine Caribou Herd, were increasing more rapidly.

The oil industry didn't like Ray's findings and hired a consulting firm that was known to do the bidding of the oil industry. That consulting firm used larger and faster aircraft less suitable for wildlife observations and flew some of the same routes that Ray had flown, and claimed they were coming up with different data. They said his counts were incorrect. So this got to be a real touchy issue. The oil industry biologists tried to publish their data, but when the paper was sent out for peer review, it was rejected as poor science, so they couldn't get it published. However, Cameron's work was published and has withstood critical peer review (Cameron and Whitten 1980; Smith and Cameron 1983; Dau and Cameron 1986; Nellemann and Cameron 1998). Although The Wildlife Society stood behind Ray and his findings, the oil industry withdrew their portion of funding for his position.

Then it got even worse under the Sarah Palin governorship from 2006 to 2009, and it has remained that way. In 2008, she appointed Corey Rossi as assistant commissioner for the newly created Abundance Management program at ADF&G, and then in 2010 he became director of the Division of Wildlife Conservation. He had minimal education in biology and wildlife conservation, with an undergraduate degree that he got through a correspondence course from the Lower 48, and was a hunting guide who also had lobbied for predator control on behalf of pro-hunting special interest groups. His focus was on managing for hunting, especially for moose, so in his mind that was the only thing of importance for the division to spend money on. They put all the attention on wolf control and largely ignored everything else. Instead of doing things based on science, it was clearly politically motivated. Governor Sean Parnell, who served from 2009 to 2014, carried on the same oil-corrupted politics surrounding wildlife management as did his predecessors in the Murkowski and Palin regimes.

Co-Management of Wildlife Resources

The importance of international and interagency cooperation has been particularly important in assessing status, patterns of habitat use, and well-being of the Porcupine Caribou Herd. While much of the range of the Porcupine Herd has usually been in the Arctic National Wildlife Refuge in Alaska, major wintering range and calving grounds encompass portions of Canada as well. Both countries share responsibility for protection of the herd and its habitat, so there has been good collaboration through a joint international agreement where the Canadian Wildlife Service plays the major role in herd and habitat assessment in Canada, and the US Fish and Wildlife Service has responsibility for habitat protection and assessment in Alaska.

Beyond this general practice of professional managers sharing responsibility for a caribou herd, the trend has been to establish co-management committees comprised of local stakeholders with direct knowledge of and dependence upon the animals. This has been a way to expand decision making and have users be involved in managing their own wildlife resources. The idea being that if you are participating, you are more likely to support the management practices that are carried out. There are a number of cases in Alaska where this type of co-management has been working. For example, there was a co-management committee set up to manage the Porcupine Caribou Herd that included the Canadian government, the Yukon Territorial government, and the Gwich'in people from Arctic Village in Alaska and Old Crow in Canada whose lives and subsistence-dominated culture are most dependent on harvesting Porcupine Herd caribou. There were different cultural attitudes about caribou hunting and use that became apparent when this committee was initiated. Native people said they didn't like the idea of putting radio collars on caribou. They felt that the rough handling during collaring didn't fit with their cultural respect for the animals. So the Canadian Wildlife Service stopped radio collaring for two or three years. Then the Natives began to realize, "Well, it's true that we need this information if we're going to do a better job of management." After they received assurances from wildlife biologists that they would be more respectful of the animals they were handling, the Natives agreed to let researchers use radio collars again. Subsistence hunters often aren't well represented on advisory boards because they don't think they're going to have as much voice and they will be overridden by urban people, so this was a step toward dispelling that belief.

Now there also is co-management of the Western Arctic Caribou Herd in northwestern Alaska. The Western Arctic Caribou Herd has been our largest herd for many years. At one point, and more recently, it got up to almost 400,000 caribou. It stayed fairly stable for several years with reasonable body condition, no brucellosis, liberal harvest allowed, and no massive buildup of predators. Their calving grounds are mostly in the headwaters of the Colville River and its tributaries. When they migrate south for the winter, they travel on the Kobuk and Noatak Rivers through the Brooks Range, sometimes even going close to Kotzebue. The extent of their winter range usually is related to the total population size, so they spread out more when their population is higher. At these times, some of them might move out onto the Seward Peninsula, or even go down as far as the Yukon River or over into the headwaters and the drainages of the Koyukuk River.

We know historically the size of the Western Arctic Herd fluctuated widely. There were varying causes for the fluctuation, including overharvest and competition for a limited amount of forage from introduced reindeer. It wasn't until the late 1940s that the Fish and Wildlife Service started using aircraft to count animals and see what was going on with these caribou herds, and by the 1950s, it was starting to look like the Western Arctic Herd was increasing. When I was a student doing my master's degree, I got to be an observer on a late-winter flight being conducted by Clarence Rhode. We flew in a Grumman Goose over where the Western Arctic Herd was located to get a general idea of how many animals there were. This was before radio collars were being used. We located an aggregation that must have been

Approximately 12,000 caribou of the Western Arctic Caribou Herd and their tracks seen from an airplane at the headwaters of the Nimiuktuk River in the Delong Mountains, when Dave, as a graduate student, joined Clarence Rhode, Regional Director of the US Fish and Wildlife Service in Alaska, on an aerial count of caribou aggregations, April 1953. PHOTO BY DAVID KLEIN.

about 12,000 caribou in one area. At the time, that seemed big to me. But I have since seen larger groups, especially when they really gather together at the calving grounds. I think it was around the mid-1960s that the Western Arctic Herd increased to a peak. They were still using a pretty rough process for estimating population size, but it was getting better because up there in the Brooks Range and the North Slope it's wide open and you can see the animals better than in herds that are in the Alaska Range, for example. I think they came up with about 250,000 to 280,000 caribou.

When the Western Arctic Caribou Herd was small, it didn't migrate very far from its breeding grounds north of the Brooks Range. But as the herd got bigger, it started migrating farther and farther and spreading out. Finally, in the 1970s some of them started moving down onto the Seward Peninsula. The majority of the villagers there were happy to now have this new food source, except for the reindeer herding families who had to spend more time trying to keep their reindeer from mixing with the caribou. The caribou would only stay down on the Seward Peninsula during the wintering period, and then they'd move back to their common breeding grounds to join with all the other groups from within the Western Arctic Herd that had spent the winter in other places. No matter where these subgroups went, they would all eventually be back on the calving grounds again at calving time.

In the 1970s, there was a big decline in the Western Arctic Herd again.[11] There were varying hypotheses for why the herd size went down, but it is important to acknowledge that there are a lot of unknowns and it was probably the result of a combination of factors. At the time, caribou populations were down all across Alaska and Canada. One reason might have been predation, but we didn't have really good numbers on predators even though we knew that the wolf populations had built up. Of course, the Native people got a lot of blame for overhunting the caribou, but no one was out there watching them or counting how many they were killing so it was hard to know whether this was a factor or not. Another reason might have been because there were a lot of fires during that period in the caribou's wintering areas that destroyed massive areas of winter habitat. Another possible factor could have been excessive insect harassment, which causes a decline in the body condition of the caribou. At that time, climate change as a factor was not yet really being discussed.

In 2003, a group called the Western Arctic Caribou Working Group was formed in order to work together to ensure the long-term conservation of the Western Arctic Herd and its habitat, and to implement the Western Arctic Caribou Herd Cooperative Management Plan. Membership is made

---

11. According to the Alaska Department of Fish and Game, "the Western Arctic Herd numbered 242,000 caribou in 1970, and then plummeted to 75,000 by 1976. The herd steadily increased until possibly peaking at 490,000 animals around 2003" (Steinacher 2008). In July 2007, ADF&G survey results estimated the population at 377,000 caribou. This was a decline of 113,000 animals since the last count in 2003.

up of local subsistence hunters, reindeer herders, hunting guides, conservationists, and representatives of the Bureau of Land Management, Fish and Wildlife Service, National Park Service, and Alaska Department of Fish and Game. They meet once or twice a year and biologists report on the current health and population status, range condition, and other biological factors affecting the herd. The Working Group identifies concerns, requests information, and advocates for actions that will conserve and benefit the herd. They also provide public information about their activities through a website and a newsletter, *Caribou Trails*. The participation of all these agencies also means some financial assistance to get the members of the board to meetings. This is needed particularly for Natives from villages who may not otherwise have the money to pay for their travel to meetings.

The way this co-management works is that actual management decisions, and that includes the survey work as well as radio collaring and all that, have to be cleared through a committee that is dominated by the users. Decisions regarding management of the Western Arctic Herd do not go to the Board of Game, like they do for other wildlife, they go to this co-management board where the users outnumber the managers. Even though biologists on the committee have a strong voice relative to the research and interpretation of data, the Natives have the majority of members of the board and so have a stronger potential vote in the decision-making process. While board-based management doesn't always work the best and can become politicized, it wouldn't work if they just had professionally trained biologists making decisions about harvest allocation, because they are not trained to consider the interests of special groups like Native people or rural communities, which are not all the same everywhere. That's where local representation is so important. The advantage of this is that all of these people with an interest have a voice, and the users that are on this board are informed about what's going on by all of the agencies so they can see it from different perspectives. The users can disagree with the biologists and managers, and they have a strong say in how the bag limits and harvests are designed and where emphasis should be placed in terms of research. That's good government when people talk to one another.

However, management of the Western Arctic Herd has not always gone so smoothly, partly due to a lack of understanding of different cultural attitudes about caribou and hunting. I witnessed this firsthand in the late 1970s, when I was working with some graduate students, Jack Shea and Henning Thing, on a study in the Waring Mountains about caribou energetics and the effect of digging craters through the snow to access their winter forage of lichen (Thing 1977; Shea 1979). The village of Noorvik was only about four or five miles from a big open area where the caribou were, and we were able to observe local hunting activities. Mostly it was open tundra, with a few little drainages with some tall willows in them, so it was easy traveling for the hunters. Using a spotting scope, we observed how this one elder and a teenage boy on a dog team hunted. They followed one of the small streams, and stayed down below the bank. Then they stopped, tied up the dogs, grabbed their rifles and binoculars, and snuck up through the willows to get to the high part of the bank in order to look over. They got down on their hands and knees and looked around to see whether there were any caribou within range. They were so quiet and stayed below the embankment that the caribou wouldn't see them. When they were within range, they fired, and usually killed three animals. Then they went back, got the dogs and the sled, and picked up the dead animals. That was the load. Then they headed back to the village.

Another time, we saw these two guys on a snowmachine pulling a toboggan come blasting out in the open and go at pretty high speeds until they saw caribou in the distance. They went directly toward the caribou for a while until the caribou got alarmed and started running. Then they caught up and got a little bit in front to slow the caribou down, stopped the snowmachine, jumped off with their two rifles, knelt down, and fired their guns into a group of running caribou. There were so many shots fired that it was hard to know how many they had killed or wounded. They did follow up on the wounded animals and came back to kill them. They might have five, six, or seven caribou down, but they could only carry about three average-sized adult caribou on their toboggan. They gutted out those that were well shot and put them on the sled as the first load, and left behind the others that weren't so well shot, but still had meat that could be salvaged. Of course, it was cold weather so these carcasses froze solid. In some cases, they tied yellow nylon rope around the carcasses to identify that they were going to come back for them. In other cases, they didn't even salvage them. Like if they were very badly shot and leaking stomach fluid that ruined the meat, they just left them.

Joe Doerr did a follow-up study to find out how many of these dead caribou were actually salvaged. He went back to the area right after the snow had melted and found many of these carcasses still there. He went into Noorvik and there were caribou carcasses stacked like cordwood. When he asked about all this, the people were kind of reserved about it because they knew there had been criticism about wasting animals. Finally, it was acknowledged that it was young guys who made money in the oil fields and got these new snowmachines and they wanted to help out by feeding the village but they never had been trained about how to hunt properly because they'd been off making money. These young guys wanted to be praised for being good hunters, so they didn't want to bring badly shot animals into the village. It appeared that they were killing more caribou this way with snowmachines than in the old dog-team days. Part of the problem was that the caribou stayed in that area that particular winter. Even though the total Western Arctic Herd size was low, there was this large aggregation of over ten thousand near Noorvik. The conclusion was that this segment of the population was late in migrating because the frost at the end of the summer was late in coming and it was still pretty good feeding so they stuck around. Then suddenly there was a big dump of snow and the caribou still had to go through the Brooks Range, but instead of moving, they just stayed where they were.

Joe did a good job of collecting information and provided it to ADF&G, who presented it to the Native elders in Kotzebue saying that this excessive waste was unacceptable, especially when the herd was in decline. At first, the Native community denied this behavior, but gradually they had to accept it. Once they accepted it, the state said, "Well, we'll let it go this time. It was a unique situation that the animals were there." The people in the village also said, "Well, we were told that there were plenty of animals. That there was no limit on our hunting. Fish and Game didn't come and tell us early enough that there was a shortage." Well, it appears that Fish and Game did tell people, but there was a lack of communication when it came to spreading the word around the region.

It may have been confusing, because Fish and Game had said the opposite only a year earlier. They said, "There are plenty of caribou out there. You can take as many as you want." Then suddenly, bingo, that was no longer the case. That's often the way it is with caribou. Of course, this was mixed with sport hunters starting to hunt trophy caribou out of Kotzebue who weren't careful and who wanted to put all the blame on the Natives and vice versa. Also, ADF&G didn't have the most accurate data on caribou at the time, so that added another layer of uncertainty and confusion to the situation. There's a good argument from both sides. It's not that simple. In other words, yeah, Fish and Game could have done a much a better job than they did of keeping in touch with the people, but in their defense, the administration in Juneau and the Board of Game was focusing more on sport hunting at the time. Their attitude was that caribou herds were so big and there weren't that many people that were dependent upon them, so the Natives were not going to have a significant effect on the overall population. The Nelchina Caribou Herd was getting more attention because there were more urban sport hunters hunting there than around Kotzebue where there were only a few commercial outfitters. Plus, it was a complicated situation and Fish and Game tends to avoid complicated things.

Then in 1988, Jim Dau went to work for Fish and Game in Kotzebue as the assistant area biologist, and by 2007 he was the lead caribou biologist for the region doing work with the Western Arctic Caribou Herd. Having someone like him there changed the whole situation. He did his master's degree at UAF in the early 1980s about insect harassment of caribou and the proposed location for construction of the Milne Point Road (Dau 1986; Dau and Cameron 1986). In Kotzebue, Jim conducted research on caribou migration, calving, and seasonal range use, and was largely responsible for developing the system of co-management for the Western Arctic Caribou Herd. Jim also helped create bonds between ADF&G and local communities by being able to work with culturally diverse user groups, valuing the input of the local people, and appreciating their knowledge as a valuable complement to science. Jim Dau retired from the Alaska Department of Fish and Game in 2016 after twenty-eight years of service with the Kotzebue office (Daggett 2016). He will be greatly missed by the Native and non-Native residents of the area, all of whom have benefited from his work in the science-based management of caribou and other wildlife in northwestern Alaska.

Research Methodology

Of course, the practice of wildlife management has changed since the early days when I started. People aren't doing fieldwork as much now or in the same way that we did. I think students and practicing wildlife biologists are missing out when they do not get out in the field. Part of the problem nowadays is that we have all these new technologies, like remote sensing with satellite imagery and radio collars, so management biologists don't need to spend as much time out in the field directly observing the animals. Using radio collars, wildlife biologists can learn a lot about where wildlife are spending their time, but much of Alaska habitat is not mapped in sufficient detail to know by remote methods how animals are using that habitat. It generally requires being in the field to directly observe and gain knowledge about the animals, especially their interaction with the environment and their food resources. Of course, there are so many amazing new technologies that answer questions that we couldn't answer before, and these are good developments. For example, in the past you couldn't get certain information in the field without killing animals and looking at their guts, but now you can go out in the field and just collect feces and with DNA testing you can tell the kind of plants the animals have been eating. The genetic information from the DNA is so valuable. You still have to mount an expedition to collect these samples, so it costs something, but it's less than in the old days because you don't have to be out in the field for as long.

And, of course, using radio collars makes counting and tracking animals like caribou a lot easier. However, you can only get an idea of where some of the animals are. It does not give you a total population count. It used to be that to monitor the size of caribou herds, ADF&G would do an aerial survey once every three to five years. This could be very difficult and require a lot of time and effort when you had a large herd with components fractured out into different areas. Plus, it required collaboration with a bunch of other people and lining up planes, and everything got complicated and expensive. Then, of course, you had to have good flying weather. And in the summertime in the Arctic on the coastal plain and in the foothills on the north side of the Brooks Range, which is where the caribou were, it's frequently foggy or overcast or sometimes snowing. They used a Beaver airplane with a special camera mounted on the bottom of the plane to take photographs of

Professor Bubenik, originally from Czechoslovakia and working in Canada, holding a styrofoam caribou head that he would put over his head and look out through the eye holes to try to observe male caribou behavior during rut without being detected by the bull caribou. This experiment was with the Western Arctic Caribou Herd in the Selawik Hills, circa 1970, at the beginning of rut when the bulls start to join up with cows during migration from summer to winter range. He also had a tail with a string that he could pull to make the tail move. David assisted by filming Bubenik's interaction with the caribou. He did not accomplish as much as he had hoped, because it was hard for him to move around in this brushy area. He did almost interact with one bull, but it was becoming dangerous as the caribou looked like it was going to start head butting Bubenik. He quickly took the head off, and the caribou backed off because now he was a human. PHOTO BY DAVID KLEIN.

aggregated animals from the air. Back in the office, the caribou were counted in those aerial photos, with a pinprick made for each animal. You might have over a thousand animals in one photograph, and sometimes the calf is so close to the mom you couldn't tell for sure if it was one or two animals. In areas where the caribou were more scattered, actual counts were done using the standardized procedure of flying transects with one observer on each side of the plane. You hung ribbons from the struts of the airplane to limit the area in which you were counting. In order to ensure accurate results, the people doing these counts had to be well trained and experienced so that the

Cartoon illustration by Sig Olson spoofing the challenges of using aircraft for wildlife management. USFWS FEDERAL AID IN WILDLIFE RESTORATION, QUARTERLY PROGRESS REPORT, PROJECT W-3-R-10, ALASKA, MARCH 31, 1956, VOLUME 10, NO. 3, P. 21A.

methods would be consistent on different flights and with different people. Still, the reliability of these counts was not all that great. When you tried to put a population estimate together for the whole herd, you ended up asking yourself whether you actually got photographs of all the aggregations.

If you have a lot of radio-collared animals in a herd, well, you can have better confidence in your survey results in terms of numbers, but it means having to collar a lot of individual animals for best results, which adds a lot more time and money to a project. When they first put radio collars on caribou in the coastal plain of the Arctic Refuge, the batteries were big and cumbersome. They put one on this cow caribou and the researchers were just so thrilled to have a satellite collar on her that they didn't pay attention to how it hung. When they went to check on it again a week later, they realized that she was having a hard time running and was really lagging behind from

Cartoon illustration by Sig Olson questioning the reliability of aerial wildlife surveys and how easy it would be to miss animals, such as the caribou shown hiding behind a tree. USFWS FEDERAL AID IN WILDLIFE RESTORATION, QUARTERLY PROGRESS REPORT, PROJECT W-3-R-10, ALASKA, MARCH 31, 1956, VOLUME 10, NO. 3, P. 25A.

her group because the collar was too loose and was just flopping around. By slowing her down, the collar was making her easier bait for predators. Fortunately, they were able to dart the cow again and tighten up the collar.

During this time, I was raising questions about collaring animals and how this was impacting the caribou and the herds. I was saying that even if the collar is not flopping around, if you're going to make an animal carry that big thing around its neck, it's still going to make it more of a target for and attractive to predators, because it won't be able to move as fast. I also had concerns that they were putting radio collars on everything, yet didn't have any control group. Like how do you know that this is not having an effect on how the animals move, how they survive, how they feed, how they avoid predators? Nowadays, with all the small, computerized technology, it's easy to put satellite collars on animals that are not too disruptive.

Probably back in the early 1990s, there began to be a focus on modeling because ecological and biological systems were understood to be horribly complex. There's a limit to what the human brain can handle in dealing with complexity, so that's why we go to computer modeling. While modeling is a way of dealing with complexity and making it more understandable, it doesn't mean that you can duplicate the natural environment and draw conclusions as to how to proceed in the future. Studying and managing wildlife is not an exact laboratory type of science where you have control over all of the variables.

I was very skeptical in the beginning when models first became so popular. One of the reasons was because I was never very strong in statistics and modeling required a pretty high level of understanding of computers, which I also didn't have. Mainly, I was concerned that people would be seduced into thinking models were good predictors and they weren't. If you're really good with a computer, you can make things look good when they're not really good, and vice versa. I've subsequently appreciated the value of models, but computers aren't going to solve our problems. They are just tools. The models also are tools, and you've got to know their limitations if you're going to use them. Of course, the quality of the output of a model is only as good as the data you have to put in.

There are times when a model can be useful and important, and other times you don't need a model, you need to do data collection. For example, when the oil industry said they wanted to build a road between Prudhoe Bay and the Kuparuk oil field, but wanted to have the minimal impact on wildlife, the question was how were we going to address this. You don't need a model for that. You needed data on movements of animals and how it might change with a road or pipeline, or to help determine whether you should build a pipeline alongside the road versus separate from the road. There were a lot of things that we were able to test in the field, and could learn from. In comparison, a model would be more important when trying to figure out why the caribou population in an area is going up or down or is stable. Or if the caribou want to move to the coast and they can't get there because of traffic on the road, that's where a model works well. What are the variables, what are their influences? There is justification for modeling at the ecosystem level, like when you start asking questions about oil development in large areas, like in the National Petroleum Reserve–Alaska (NPRA), but there's a difference between modeling components of ecosystems and the components of species.

The value of a model is that it helps us to understand the complexity of a system, but a model is not very reliable for prediction because there are all these variables and we don't always have enough detailed information about them all. This leaves us with only being able to say if things change the way we think they're going to change, then this might happen, but that's all speculation, too. The problem is it's tempting for people that don't understand models, and even for the modelers themselves, to think they can model something and determine what the future's going to be. It doesn't work like that. We're dealing with information from the past, and when everything is changing, it doesn't work to base the future on the past. We can make models for the animals and if we do a good job with the vegetation assessments and everything, then we might be able to say, "Well, if the weather is as it was for the last five years and doesn't vary too highly from it, this is what is likely going to happen." But then there are all these unknowns. No matter how hard we try, something new could come up. Those are some of the problems with modeling.

Despite my skepticism, I have been involved in some modeling projects, the last one being with the Porcupine Caribou Herd. I was retired and was mostly an advisor. They had top-notch modelers who were modeling the Porcupine Caribou Herd in relationship to the Gwich'in people that depended on it. There was a sociological study collecting data to go into the model, too. The Gwich'in were interested in the model because we had pretty good data on the caribou: their numbers, their distribution, their use of habitats, and their physiological condition. And all of this information was getting more reliable all the time. The model was interactive, which was great for taking into the schools to show them how a model works. For example, the summer temperature could be raised in the computer model, and, bingo, the model would zip out a result. It also did a good job of showing groups of caribou moving across a map in relationship to going to the calving ground, and how if you manipulated snow cover it would affect the timing of their arrival there. This was terrific, because it convinced the local people that this was a useful tool for them. They already knew a lot of this information, but they could see how these things were interacting. It's a very complex system, but just because it's complex doesn't mean you should ignore it. You shouldn't just say, "Well, last year it did this, it'll probably do the same thing this year."

The people in the community could relate what was in the model to their own life. Like if you need some cash income in the community and you want it from tourism, you can plug that in to the model and see what the costs and benefits are going to be from different types of tourism. Of if they wanted roads into the village, they could see if those roads were going to interfere with the movement of the animals and make them less available. The model allowed them to see results from these types of decisions and could help them decide if they wanted that kind of change. This model was meant to help people to stop expecting the impossible, whether they're oil people, biologists doing the studies, the media, or politicians. So that model has done a lot of good in helping local people consider options for the future.

The sad thing was that a lot of money went into this project and the creators had real pride in it, and so they wanted to publish it, but the Native people had concerns. They said, "Well, wait a second, this could have political ramifications." They were afraid that the model would be misused to prove something that might be detrimental to their efforts to protect the Porcupine Caribou Herd and their calving grounds. They said, "We want more control over whether it's going to be published, because it may be hurtful to us if people do not understand the complexities of our cultural relationship with caribou that are not in the model." After a lot of discussion, finally, an agreement was made that gave the Natives a say on publication, and they agreed that it could be used with some qualifications (Kruse et al. 2004).

After the previous lengthy description of my experience with whole-system modeling, the following jocular and rhyming satire on modeling titled *Afterthoughts on Models* that I wrote in 1989 is perhaps appropriate:

> Modeling ungulate systems presents a major conundrum,
> If models are too simple, they tend to be humdrum,
> But in living systems the variables are innumerable and non-random.
> However, if models are too complex, we can't understand um.

Interest in modeling has increased exponentially,
Each model points up gaps in our knowledge differentially,
If we continue at this rate with our modeling proclivity,
Our knowledge gap is bound to grow to infinity.

Even though I admit that at that stage of my career I was a skeptic on the role of modeling in wildlife management, this assessment of models went over big when I wrote it during a conference about animal physiology in Fort Collins, Colorado. People enjoyed it so much that they printed it in the proceedings (Klein 1989a). Word of my sarcastic poetry spread, so that I was asked to give a summary at the end of the American Society of Mammalogists meeting in Fairbanks in 1989 in the same rhyming way (Klein 1989b). I believe that humor will always trump boredom in the professional world.

At age 85, David goes on one last
expedition to St. Matthew Island,
2012. PHOTO BY NED ROZELL.

14
Not Quite Retired: Staying Connected to Science

While the job as unit leader was enjoyable and fulfilling for me, and provided a wealth of opportunities for fascinating research and enriching international collaborations, by the late 1990s I was approaching retirement age. I was only seventy years old and still in good physical health, and not all that eager to retire because I was still enjoying the scientific, research, and teaching parts of the job. However, I was not going to miss all the administrative work of running the Co-op Unit. As I was considering retirement, senior FWS employees in Washington, DC, were trying to establish an official senior scientist position as an advancement step for outstanding Co-op Unit leaders, which also would have included a salary increase like other steps in the federal merit system. While I became senior scientist in 1991 when the joint Fish and Wildlife Research Unit formed and I was no longer running the unit, it did not include a change in salary. When I indicated that I was considering retirement, FWS requested that I remain until this process was complete so I could qualify for the new position. However, they were constrained by a federal requirement that such advancement required approval by a panel of peers. No such panel existed within FWS and there were not enough qualified people to create one, so efforts to create the position were stymied.

Eventually, I got tired of waiting and did not want to keep holding up the Alaska Unit from filling the long vacant assistant Unit leader positions because they were having to pay my high salary from a limited budget. I retired officially from the Cooperative Unit program in 1997, after thirty-five years of service. Earlier, when the federal budget was particularly tight, I had indicated that I would not retire unless it was agreed that the money from my top-level salary would stay with the Alaska Unit to allow for the hiring of two assistant leaders at the beginning salary level. Unfortunately, my former salary was not used directly in this manner; however, the Alaska Unit did find a way to hire two new assistant leaders. In retrospect, it was a good decision to retire when I did, because it took another three years before it became possible for advancement to the senior scientist position within FWS. Similar to other retiring university faculty members, I was designated professor emeritus that allowed me to continue to serve on graduate student committees and retain an office on campus. Even though retired, I also was still conducting research of my own, publishing articles, and participating in scientific panels and advisory committees.

Some of the graduate students to whom I provided assistance after I was retired included Fiona Danks, Kyle Joly, Claudia Ihl, and Archana Bali. In 2000, Fiona Danks's master's thesis was on remote sensing of potential muskoxen habitat in the National Petroleum Reserve–Alaska (Danks 2000). She had accompanied me to north Greenland as an assistant on research Christian Bay and I were doing on resource partitioning by mammalian herbivores in the high Arctic (Klein and Bay 1994), and after that she was able to enlist Christian as a collaborator on her PhD research at the Scott Polar Research Institute at the University of Cambridge that involved mapping domestic reindeer grazing habitat in the remote Archangelsk district of Russia (Danks 2007). Kyle Joly, who was a biologist with the Bureau of Land Management involved with assessing lichen growth rates in the Western Arctic Caribou Herd winter habitat area, completed a PhD dissertation where he showed how climate warming, although accelerating vascular plant growth, inhibited growth of lichens (Joly et al. 2009).

Claudia Ihl completed a master's degree in 1999 with me as her major advisor where she compared habitat use by muskoxen and privately owned reindeer on the Seward Peninsula (Ihl 1999). After this, the National Park Service offered her funding to do a PhD on muskoxen in Cape Krusenstern National Monument, where she conducted annual counts of muskoxen for the Park Service. Despite both Claudia and the Park Service learning that earning a PhD at UAF was a much more rigorous process than they had anticipated and that the student's graduate committee played a dominant role in assuring that the standards set by the university were met and respected, she completed her PhD on seasonal patterns of muskoxen habitat use in Cape Krusenstern National Monument (Ihl 2007). Upon completion of the PhD, Claudia obtained a tenure-tract position with the Northwest Campus of UAF at Nome, where she teaches and continues investigations on muskoxen resident in the area.

Archana Bali was one of my last graduate students and one whom I was particularly fond of. With funding from the Liz Claiborne and Art Ortenberg Foundation and help from the Conservation Society, I and my former classmate and friend, George Schaller, set up a competitive PhD-level scholarship program at UAF that would support the best-qualified applicant from a country seeking to restore populations of threatened and endangered species. Archana Bali, from India, won the competitive award

Archana Bali, one of David's last graduate students, circa 2009. PHOTO BY DAVID KLEIN.

and proved to be the ideal candidate. I served as an advisor to Archana and her graduate committee, but, unfortunately, the interdisciplinary design of her PhD proved problematic. Co-advisors could not agree on the general focus of her dissertation research, resulting in the social science advisor attempting to redirect Archana's dissertation from wildlife biology to anthropology, and the wildlife biology co-advisor resigning. Eventually, she was able to form a new thesis committee and made good progress on modeling the impact of mosquitoes and other insects on the foraging dynamics and associated well-being of caribou in Arctic Alaska. Unfortunately, Archana died of ovarian cancer in 2014 before completing the PhD dissertation, although she had completed a documentary titled *Voices of the Caribou People* that received the first-runner-up prize at the Fourth Annual Fairbanks Film Festival. Through her vivacious, yet profound, nature, Archana enriched the lives of her fellow graduate students and others of us at the university who were fortunate to be able to befriend her. Her death was both a professional and personal loss for me.

At the time of my retirement, the joint Alaska Cooperative Wildlife Research Unit and Cooperative Fish and Wildlife Research Unit was considered perhaps the most important in all of the United States largely because of the vast amount of federal lands within the state that required management and associated wildlife research. And they had an admirable record of turning out good students, doing good science, and producing research on and resolution of controversial resource development issues. We enjoyed respect from the federal and state governments and the University of Alaska. I am proud that I played a role in building the unit's good reputation, and delighted that all the graduate student training and mentoring I did helped to create a cadre of excellent wildlife professionals who to this day continue to influence the course of wildlife management and conversation in Alaska and around the globe.

THE HUMAN PERSPECTIVE: ESSAYS BY DAVID KLEIN

David wrote the chapters in this section to reflect his thoughts on philosophical issues ranging from ethical wildlife management, to general ideas about eco-philosophy and the conceptualization of wilderness, to the social and environmental impacts of modern society. Note the change in tone from the previous chapters that were based on oral narrative. David has been thinking about these issues for a long time, which has given him significant opportunity to formulate ideas and ways of expressing them. Through these essays, we get to know another side of David beyond the wildlife manager and researcher—someone who is concerned about our world's environmental, social, and cultural future and feels that we all have a responsibility as citizens to get involved.

Aldo Leopold examining a
gray partridge specimen, 1942.
PHOTOGRAPH BY ROBERT OETKING.
COURTESY OF THE ALDO LEOPOLD
FOUNDATION AND THE UNIVERSITY OF
WISCONSIN-MADISON ARCHIVES.

15
Walking in the Footsteps of Aldo Leopold: A Scientific Legacy

David Klein originally wrote "Walking in the Footsteps of Aldo Leopold" in 2000 for *The Wildlife Society Bulletin* (Klein 2000). It spotlighted remarks he made in 1999 upon accepting the Aldo Leopold Award, The Wildlife Society's highest honor, at their annual conference in Austin, Texas (The Wildlife Society 1999). David has revised the original to reflect his current thinking in light of modern circumstances.

Aldo Leopold died in 1948, before most of us in wildlife work today had the opportunity to meet him and come to know him as a person. Yet the legacy he left us, through his originality in defining wildlife management and developing a methodology for its practice, remains alive today. In my own development, I don't recall appreciating the positive influence that Leopold must have already had on me in my early years. Later, I became more familiar with the evolution of his ecological thinking and accompanying nature-oriented philosophy. In retrospect and within the context of the times, it has been easy to relate to Leopold's early impetuousness in striving to manage the "good" ungulates at the expense of the "bad" predators. After he gained experience abroad and acquired a more detailed understanding of the ecological complexity of the natural systems he was charged with managing, he adjusted his views consistent with his intellectual development.

We all have been guilty of the impetuousness of youth, but it takes real humility to acknowledge when our thinking has become outmoded. Leopold's intellect grew throughout his life, and it did so because he was a keen and objective observer of the land and the life it supported. He saw examples of how humans used and abused the land, and realized that they could be models from which we could learn. Having spent much of my professional career in an academic environment where exposure to questioning young minds is a daily occurrence, I have come to appreciate the importance of keeping an open mind throughout life. Once some knowledge has been gained, it is tempting to want to apply that knowledge without being impeded by the uninformed, but knowledge is a moving target, advancing with time. If we are wedded too strictly to our own ideas, our minds are closed, and we fail to recognize the limits of our knowledge. We soon become the uninformed.

Through travel, Leopold exposed himself to broader worldviews of land-use practice and policy than those prevalent in the then-developing field of natural resource management in North America, at the time largely considered the purview of federal agencies. In Germany in the 1930s, he saw and admired examples of centuries of land use that respected the land and sustained its productivity. On the other hand, he was perplexed by the artificiality of German wildlife management, a system that had deliberately eliminated large predators and had relied on winter feeding to sustain game populations that exceeded the carrying capacity of available habitats. He brought back with him both positive and negative perceptions—things to emulate and others to avoid. His efforts subsequently shaped the evolution of the North American brand of wildlife management.

Wildlife biologists are confronted with ecological complexity—often unique to our own regions—that makes our work both difficult and challenging. Through travel, we can step back from the myopic view of our own research or management activities and open our minds to understanding how other systems function, be they ecosystems or human societies. Travel gives the observant individual the opportunity to compare familiar systems with those newly encountered. For me, the opportunity to travel broadly, both in North America and abroad, advanced my own education beyond that gained formally in the classroom and from the written word. This inevitably led to a greater depth of understanding of my own local environment, from the ecological relationships of wildlife species that have been the focus of my work to the human involvement in their management.

It is a maxim of ecology that exposure to a changing environment challenges all organisms to adapt to those changes or perish. For humans, the entire world is our environment and today it is changing, largely as a consequence of our own understanding of the processes and functioning of biological systems. If we are to assure the continued productivity and sustainability of those systems, we must influence change where we can, in both rate and direction. Where changes in the environment, whether natural or human-caused, are beyond our power to influence, our job then is to help manipulate biological systems to assure their sustainability and the values we humans derive from them. Alternatively, or perhaps simultaneously, we must assist human society to adapt to the changing environment in ways that sustain the well-being of wildlife and the human benefits derived therein.

As biologists, we understand that animals occupy habitats unique to their species, and that in an evolutionary sense they are the products of these habitat characteristics. In a similar way, the cultures, beliefs, and attitudes that we humans identify with, believe in, and espouse are shaped by the environments in which we live. But both the biological and sociological components of the human environment are changing. In North America, our history has been one of close association with the natural world. This has included exploiting its renewable and nonrenewable resources, nurturing the productivity of its soils for the food and fiber needed to support our growing population, and enjoying the recreational opportunities and aesthetic returns that come from living close to the land. We have led the world in our appreciation for the natural environment and in our attempts to protect portions of it. Whereas early in this century most Americans lived in rural areas, most of us now are urban dwellers. The average American no longer has daily contact with the land. Our increasingly urbanized society is losing contact with nature.

Although the public retains an interest in nature, that interest is being shaped and, for some, satisfied by anthropomorphized distortions of ecology through seductively attractive images of wildlife on television and in other media. But commercial television's reason for existence is to promote consumerism. It has no social consciousness, and it cannot be expected to play a positive role in informing the public about the ecology and values of wildlife and the role wildlife has played and can continue to play in our society.

The major threats to wildlife, their habitats, and their effective management in this country is the eroding interest in wildlife values among the increasingly urbanized public, and the lack of understanding of the complexity of natural biological systems among even those with strong interests in wildlife, such as hunters, birdwatchers, photographers, and animal rights activists. If our democratic society is to be functional, our job is to assure that all of the public becomes much better informed about wildlife, the issues that threaten wildlife, the complexity of ecological relationships, and the need for public support of wildlife habitat protection and management efforts. After all, it is the public who ultimately sets wildlife management policy.

Those of us in wildlife work have also been guilty in the past of oversimplification in addressing management issues. Not very many years ago, species management was the primary focus. It was simpler that way. Although our efforts often produced the intended short-term results, consequences for other components of ecosystems were generally overlooked. Although we often need to focus on specific ecological relationships of a single species, if we are to manage for its consumptive use or to work to protect habitats critical to it, we must understand a species in relation to the total ecosystem of which it is a part. Because of the complexity that exists at the ecosystem level, we as individuals cannot be expected to undertake the task of investigating all aspects of an ecosystem simultaneously. This means that management at the ecosystem level requires cooperation among all those working for the protection and management of the natural environment, including wildlife managers and biologists, foresters, park naturalists, and conservation biologists, both within and outside state and federal government agencies.

Although Aldo Leopold's influence on me as a mentor was posthumous, it was the natural philosophy he developed and eloquently wrote about that captured my admiration. Leopold was clearly a man of his times, but he also kept abreast of the changing times. Today, we live in a world that is changing at an ever-increasing rate. My advice is to live as Leopold did. Keep up with the times, but don't get caught up in the times, else you may get left behind. Particularly relevant in this regard are the words of Albert Einstein spoken early in the Second World War. While it was over a half century ago, these words remain relevant: "The significant problems we face today cannot be solved at the same level of thinking we were at when we created them" (Hyerle and Alper 2014:4).

The technological advances since Leopold's time are overwhelming. We wildlife biologists have been quick to adopt relevant new technology, be it animal-mounted radio transmitters, computer modeling at the population and ecosystem levels, gene sequencing to differentiate animal populations, or GIS mapping. These advances have enabled us to refine our methods for monitoring animal population dynamics, movements, and ecosystem relationships, and have greatly improved the reliability of the data used for management. Technological advances also have given us an opportunity to ask complex questions about the ecology of animals that could not have been addressed in the past. But we must be careful that in our fascination and preoccupation with the new technology—particularly the computer keyboard and monitor screen—we do not lose direct contact with the natural world that should be the focus of our attention.

In the 1930s, Leopold cautioned against the trend for Americans to forsake their feet, the horse, and the canoe for the automobile and outboard motor in pursuit of hunting and other outdoor activities. He foresaw the erosion of many of the historical values associated with our outdoor activities as a result of an increase in the use of mechanized equipment. He particularly noted the deadening of our senses associated with the noise, speed, and smell of mechanized travel, senses so critical to those who should be keen observers of nature, be it the hunter, the birdwatcher, or the field biologist. As biologists who now effectively use and have become increasingly dependent on the computer for data acquisition, analysis, and modeling of ecosystem relationships, we must avoid the associated tendency to lose sight of the real world. Ecologists have long been aware that although natural processes can often be simulated in the laboratory, they cannot be duplicated there. The same analogy applies to computer modeling. If we are to understand natural systems, we must continue to get out into the field. Don't get me wrong, however. In today's world, wildlife management can advance only if we take advantage of the technology that is available to us. We must become "technological naturalists."

We biologists are well aware of the complexity that characterizes all living systems, from the cell to entire ecosystems, and we appreciate the difficulty of investigating complex ecosystem relationships. The public, however, naïvely views ecology as an exact science, comparable to chemistry, physics, or genetics. Our job includes informing the public about ecological relationships, but it also includes the responsibility to convey to the public an appreciation for both the complexity of natural systems and the difficulty of acquiring an understanding of how they function. The public seeks simple answers to complex questions about environmental management. We attempt to find answers to these questions, but we must be honest about the limits of our ability to do so.

More than a half century ago, Aldo Leopold wrote about the dichotomy between maximizing wildlife productivity and maintaining the health of natural systems:

> In all of these cleavages, we see repeated the same basic paradoxes: man the conqueror versus man the biotic citizen; science the sharpener of his sword versus science the searchlight on his universe; land the slave and servant versus land the collective organism. (Leopold 1949:223)

Nevertheless, as scientists and public servants working for the wise use and conservation of our wildlife resources, we are expected to use our best interpretive skills as a basis for advising management. In providing advice to those who may view us as all-knowing experts, it is tempting to assume that indeed we are. However, if we are to maintain intellectual credibility and, thus, the longer-term support of the public, we must have the humility to acknowledge the limitations of our ecological understanding.

Three cows of the Porcupine Caribou Herd en route to their calving grounds showing little concern for an airplane at the crest of the Brooks Range. PHOTO BY DAVID KLEIN.

16
Ethical Considerations in Caribou Management

In 1987, at the Third North American Caribou Workshop held at Chena Hot Springs Resort near Fairbanks, Alaska, David Klein asked, "Is it appropriate for wildlife professionals to be discussing ethics at a workshop on caribou research and management?" (Klein 1988a:189). This question about ethical practices within the profession of wildlife management remains relevant today, so a revised version of that original presentation appears below.

Opinions may vary in response to this question about professional ethics, nevertheless, ethics are often at issue when controversy exists between professionals, and this is particularly true when the public becomes involved. Public involvement is part of wildlife management, it is part of the political process in our democratic system, but when biological questions become politicized, pressures are generated that may challenge the professionalism of wildlifers. We must walk a fine line between wildlife professionalism and the politics of resource management.

Ethical guidelines do exist in our profession (Gilbert and Dodds 1987), and responsibility as wildlife professionals goes beyond loyalty to employers. However, biologists often must decide between loyalty to those who provide their paychecks and their own professional integrity. By establishing the following code of ethics, The Wildlife Society has recognized the underlying ethical principles that provide the foundation for their profession:

1. To develop and promote sound stewardship of wildlife resources and of the environments upon which wildlife and humans depend;

2. To undertake an active role in preventing human-induced environmental degradation;

3. To increase awareness and appreciation of wildlife values, and;

4. To seek the highest standards in all activities of the wildlife profession. (MacDonald 1987)

The Wildlife Society's ethical guidelines must also include the following principles by which wildlife managers should abide when carrying out their jobs: (1) subscribe to the highest standards of integrity and conduct; (2) recognize research and scientific management of wildlife and their environments as primary goals; and (3) encourage the use of sound biological information in management decisions.

In their book, *The Philosophy and Practice of Wildlife Management*, Gilbert and Dodds (1987) provide thoughtful discussion of the ethical responsibilities of wildlifers. They stress that in order to justify their activities as scientists, wildlife researchers must adhere to the scientific method. Research design must be rigorous and based on testable hypotheses. If we make generalizations based on inadequate data, we should be aware that we may be setting ourselves up, as well as the wildlife profession in general, for loss of credibility in the future. Gilbert and Dodds point out that where our data are not adequate to yield statistically reliable results, the error that may be involved in management decisions based on these results should seek to benefit wildlife populations and not the short-term interests of the using public. If we must err, it should be on the side of wildlife conservation.

It is apparent that wildlifers view the world in which they live and work with biases that parallel those of the general public. Stephen Kellert has done extensive surveys of public attitudes toward wildlife and has shown their relationship to childhood experiences that are often culturally related, as well as to social and economic associations (Kellert 1979). Attitudes toward wildlife are likely to be negative if past associations have been negative, as in the case of a farmer who experiences crop damage by wildlife. Conversely, positive associations, such as hunting and recreational viewing of wildlife, yield favorable attitudes toward wildlife. Wildlife biologists, however, are expected to have positive attitudes or biases toward wildlife given that wildlife is the very basis of their profession, employment, and economic well-being. We cannot deny our humanness, but we should not allow bias favoring wildlife to guide wildlife management decisions, nor should we allow it to carry over into our research design and execution (Gilbert and Dodds 1987). Are wildlife biologists who work for industry suspect? If our logic remains consistent, the answer is yes. But just as wildlifers working for wildlife management agencies should be able to be objective in their research and assessment of data, so should industry biologists. They can remain ethical as long as their biases do not limit their ability to be objective in their professional work.

Caribou research is one arena wherein such objectivity and adherence to ethical practices come into question. Why does caribou ecology generate so much controversy that colors our professional meetings, enters the technical literature, and provides fuel for our detractors? The complexity of the ecological relationships of caribou and our only superficial understanding of such may be major factors contributing to differing biological results and explanations. Considerable variation in food and habitat selection, predator relationships, and general ecology have been shown to exist in caribou from the woodland populations (*R. t. caribou*) at the southern limits of distribution to Peary caribou (*R. t. pearyi*) in the North. These variations invariably allow for broad generalizations about the species that are vulnerable to criticism. In spite of the considerable effort that has been devoted to the study of caribou throughout circumpolar regions, there remain more unanswered questions about the ecology of caribou than for other North American ungulates.

In contrast to other North American *cervids*, caribou (*Rangifer tarandus*) appear to provide a greater number of obstacles in our efforts to understand them. Because of their migratory habits, their annual cycle spans two or more ecosystems so they may be preyed upon by quite discrete populations of predators in their summer versus their winter ranges. Predator species also may vary seasonally and regionally. The complex sociality of caribou, with behavioral hierarchical structures that change seasonally in relation to antler growth and retention in both sexes, sets them apart from other *cervids*. Harassing and parasitic insects have an important influence on their behavior, movements, physiological status, and demography, and have been an important selective factor in their evolution. Caribou exhibit long-established traditions of movement and range fidelity that may, nevertheless, show annual variations related to weather or perhaps other environmental variables. Their main winter food item is lichens, which is little understood ecologically and physiologically. Lichens are a unique association of fungi and blue-green algae that vary significantly from vascular plants and are relatively indigestible by most herbivores. Consequently, lichens are little used by herbivores other than caribou. This main winter food supply is often snow covered, and its availability is complicated by snow characteristics and the energy cost of digging through the snow to obtain the lichens.

Controversy between professionals can be healthy. It focuses attention on issues that merit our attention. It stimulates thought and generates ideas. Controversy that has revolved around caribou has generated research efforts that have increased our factual knowledge of caribou ecology, thus helping to resolve the controversy. Witness, for example, that as a consequence of intensive studies of early mortality in caribou, we have an increased appreciation of the role of bears and eagles in caribou calf predation.

Controversy can also be detrimental. When wildlife professionals become involved in heated debate among themselves over issues where they claim expertise, their credibility may be eroded in the eyes of the public. Controversy may also lead to polarization of thought. There are numerous examples of individual scientists who have doggedly championed a controversial hypothesis to the extent that concern for their self-image overrides scientific objectivity, and they seemingly try to fortify their position through suspect research and subsequent publications defending their initial conclusions. Professional ethics become subverted in the interest of egotism, and the whole profession suffers. No matter how important an issue of the day may appear at the time, there will be future issues of equal or greater importance that will be difficult to defend in the public eye if we have sacrificed our professionalism on a past issue.

Controversy that develops over conflicts between resource uses may pit wildlifers against one another if their employers represent the uses in conflict. How should we handle situations that challenge our professional ethics? How should we respond to a request from an employer to build a case that exceeds the supporting data? Do we have any recourse when employers shut down our research efforts because the preliminary findings are inimical to their interests? If an employer "pigeonholes" our research results that are particularly relevant to an issue at hand, do we have any recourse? When is it legitimate for a public agency to withhold information from the public? Is it ethical to distort the truth in the presumed interest of society?

These are the kinds of questions that at times confront us wildlife professionals. And the answers may not always be obvious. Ecological relationships are complex, and particularly so in the case of caribou. Ecology is not as exact as most other scientific disciplines, and public perception of ecological relationships is often laced with emotion. But these should not be excuses for our failure to abide by a rigorous code of professional ethics. If we wish to be perceived as scientists among our colleagues, as well as by the public, we must behave accordingly, no matter how complex the field of ecology may be or how much emotion it engenders.

Skiing with graduate students in
upper Riley Creek over the pass to
Windy Creek, Denali National Park.
PHOTO BY DAVID KLEIN.

17
Valuing Northern Lands

This chapter is based on a paper David Klein presented at the International Conference on Inventorying Forest and Other Vegetation of the High Latitude and High Altitude Regions held in Fairbanks, Alaska, on July 23–26, 1984. It was never published, so David has revised and edited it for this book to reflect his current thinking in light of modern circumstances on issues surrounding the practice of wildlife management.

Aldo Leopold recognized that the philosophical valuing of land was based on an appreciation and understanding of the complexity of life that the lands support. Although the ecosystem concept was not well developed in Leopold's time, the land and its soils were acknowledged as basic to the primary processes that supported higher life forms. Understanding that lands have nurtured life's diversity from the time of geological origin to the present, Leopold felt that a personal familiarity with the land was not required if it was to be valued by humans. In this regard, when writing about conservation aesthetics, he asked: "Is my share in Alaska worthless to me because I shall never go there? Do I need a road to show me the arctic prairies, the goose pastures of the Yukon, the Kodiak bear, the sheep meadows behind McKinley?" (Leopold 1949:176). Regardless of whether you have to be familiar with a place or not to appreciate it, environmental values are human constructs that vary with the social, economic, and cultural diversity present within society. And they change alongside shifts in the dominant societal views. For example, Leopold foresaw the effects of the increase in urbanization and products of technological advances, inclusive of the automobile, as major elements in the erosion of American cultural values related to the land.

It often is not possible to separate and prioritize the aesthetic, recreational, economic, scientific, and cultural values of a land area. For example, there may be agreement that wilderness designation primarily serves to protect aesthetic, recreational, and perhaps psychological values; arguments for the protection of wilderness areas generally also emphasize their value for science, their cultural significance to local people, the economic returns from tourism, and protection they can provide for a broader ecosystem or watershed that other land designations cannot. At present, northern ecosystems are often less valued for their ecological or aesthetic significance and are only superficially understood, largely due to their remoteness from the major population centers of the world. Yet their relative freedom from human impacts makes them appear as ideal subjects for increased attention and research.

The socially agreed upon values of northern lands can be realized only if the potentials and limitations for their use are also understood. Inventory of vegetation is one way to accomplish this. Such an inventory is an essential prerequisite to sound land management decisions and sustainability of wildlife populations. Assessing the importance of northern vegetation as a primary food base for wild and domestic herbivores must also include its value as forage for grazing animals, availability of the forage as influenced by snow cover, and response of the plants to their use by herbivores.

Vegetation inventories are a necessary prerequisite for the assessment of range resource values for reindeer and caribou and should be an integral part of land-use planning. But an assessment of vegetation alone will not provide the information necessary to predict patterns of use of the vegetation. Some vegetation types occupying extensive areas may offer limited foraging potential and, conversely, relatively small expanses of other vegetation types may be of critical importance to the caribou. Therefore, inventory of range vegetation must go hand in hand with research into patterns of use of the range by the grazing animals, as well as assessment of the influence of other factors that may limit availability or access to forage, such as snow cover or interruption of seasonal movements.

Inventory of range vegetation is understandably done in summer during the plant growth period, so how lichen species composition, biomass productivity, and amount of forage available for consumption are related to snow cover is not well understood. Although snow cover is of obvious importance in limiting availability of forage in winter, it is also an important factor influencing the selection and use of calving grounds by caribou (Lent 1980). The significance of early snowmelt on the calving grounds may be related to having a benign environment for the newborn calves, but it also accelerates green-up of forage plants that are required to meet the high nutritional demands of the lactating females.

The apparent presence of seasonal range components, such as optimal winter lichen forage or summer alpine habitat, does not assure that these areas are useable by reindeer and caribou. An abundance of high-quality forage in specific areas is of little value to caribou and reindeer if they are precluded from using it. Seasonal range components must lie in proximity to one another or at least be accessible from one another via unobstructed migration routes. The length of the migration routes may determine whether range components are used (Klein and Kuzyakin 1982; Syroechkovskii 1995; and Klein and Magomedova 2003).

Unfortunately, resource inventories prior to development activities in the North usually have placed emphasis on petroleum and other minerals, rather than on the renewable resource value of native vegetation and the wildlife populations that it supports. The importance of natural vegetation in northern areas as the primary trophic level directly supporting wild herbivores and indirectly all other life forms at higher trophic levels is seldom appreciated and rarely assessed for its importance to both subsistence and cash economies dependent upon wildlife. Exceptions have been where plant resources yield direct economic return, as in the case of grazing areas important to the reindeer industry. In many areas, the importance to the local economy of wildlife as food, and as a basis for support of tourism, recreational hunting, and the fur industry may exceed that of all other resources, but a quantitative assessment of the economic values involved is difficult because of the diffuse nature of their contribution to the economy.

In the majority of cases, conflict over uses could have been avoided or minimized if these types of inventories of resources to be affected by a development activity had been carried out as part of the planning phase. Hydroelectric and oil field development, pipeline and road construction, forestry and other northern development activities should be planned to minimize their consequences to reindeer and caribou. However, the complexity of the relationship of such large grazers to their rangelands is frequently overlooked. Some examples where loss of grazing lands in the North for both wild and domestic animals have occurred as a byproduct of northern development and that have had ecosystem-wide repercussions include: (1) development of oil fields close to the coast in the Alaska Arctic and the subsequent maze of roads, pipelines, drill pads and other human activity that have impeded the free movement of caribou with a subsequent loss of access to summer grazing areas, calving grounds, and coastal insect-relief areas (Smith and Cameron 1983); (2) hydroelectric developments in northern Scandinavia, Newfoundland, and Labrador that have reduced grazing lands for reindeer and caribou and interrupted their movements (Klein and Magomedova 2003); (3) scarification of the soil and intense fertilization in Finland's forest industry that have resulted in the loss of production of lichens in reindeer wintering areas, and ditching of open marshes and bogs to allow tree growth that has eliminated important summer range for both domestic and wild reindeer that offers high-quality forage and relief areas from harassing insects when windy; and (4) damage to vegetation by vehicles on the tundra in summer, which was a common occurrence during early oil exploration activities in the Arctic, although most northern countries have now adopted regulations to limit this activity.

The loss of caribou rangelands as a consequence of oil field development is often passed off as inconsequential because the areas influenced represent only a fraction of the total Arctic tundra presumed to be available to the caribou. This assumption overlooks the relatively low productivity of the northern tundra in relation to grazing lands farther south, as well as the influence of predators and harassing and parasitic insects on movements and optimal grazing by caribou, necessitating wide-ranging foraging behavior and the ecological importance to caribou of discrete and unique range units.

Vegetation inventories and assessment of range value in the Arctic must also include the potential use by muskoxen. Muskoxen are the only other large herbivore characteristic of the Arctic that plays an important role in converting Arctic vegetation into meat available for human consumption. At present, muskoxen throughout their range provide only an incidental portion of the subsistence base for any northern peoples, although archaeological evidence indicates that on Banks Island and in northernmost Greenland and Siberia, earlier human cultures existed with muskoxen as their primary food (Knuth 1967; Uspenski 1984; Will 1984). Following the reestablishment of muskoxen in former habitat areas in Alaska and Russia, and to new habitats in West Greenland, these new herds increased rapidly and expanded into new range areas (Jingfors and Klein 1982). More recently, the numbers and distribution of the introduced herds have fluctuated widely as they adapt to regional variations in habitat quality and predator relationships. Although the diet of muskoxen is superficially similar to that of caribou and reindeer, the forage requirements of muskoxen are sufficiently different to cause relatively little overlap in range use except under the most extreme conditions of the High Arctic. In Alaska and on the Canadian mainland, muskoxen show a strong affinity for riparian vegetation (willows and other gravel bar and riverbank plants), which have higher growth rates and greater species diversity than the surrounding tundra. As a result, both forage quality and productivity are high. Assessment of range use by muskoxen in the population recently established and expanding in the Arctic National Wildlife Refuge in northeastern Alaska shows that not only have the muskoxen localized along streams, but those chosen appear to contain the most productive of the preferred forage species. Differences in productivity of riparian systems in this region appear to be strongly controlled by the annual hydrological regime of the particular drainage system (Constance O'Brien, pers. comm.).

The value of Arctic riparian vegetation to muskoxen, moose, and seasonally to caribou, ptarmigan, hares, and several other mammals and birds has only recently been recognized. It is apparent that a clearer understanding of the variability and importance of these riparian plant communities are necessary before vegetation inventories can be effectively used in establishing land-use priorities. There is, however, a need for urgency in the completion of this basic research. Northern development tends to focus on riparian ecosystems, for mining of gravel for road, pipeline, airstrip, and drill pad construction, or through the use of major rivers and streams as preferred transportation corridors.

A separate research focus is necessary for the assessment of High Arctic plant resources in relation to the grazing animals they will support. In the High Arctic, plant biomass and growth rates are extremely low, as is plant species diversity. Forage is extremely limited, especially for the high-energy lichens in the winter, and long migratory movements between winter and summer ranges are not possible. Compensatory factors are the absence or low presence of harassing insects and predators and highly developed energy conservative behavior. Not unexpectedly, the relationship of High Arctic herbivores to their food base appears to be quite tenuous, subject to the widely variable regional weather patterns, and quite different than among continental caribou and reindeer (Reimers 1980; Thomas and Edmonds 1983). Therefore, direct extrapolation of ecological relationships characteristic of reindeer and caribou on continental ranges to the High Arctic is not possible. In addition, wildlife in the High Arctic may be much more vulnerable to the influence of human activities than are comparable animal populations farther south (Klein 1972b).

Northern vegetation has until recently been relatively free of the impacts of northern development, however, there is increasing evidence that the waste products of industrialization are now penetrating even into the High Arctic. This has been observed in the fallout of heavy metals on the Greenland ice cap (Murozumi et al. 1969), the increase in Arctic haze in the past decade from atmospheric pollution generated in industrial centers farther south (Shaw 1981), and the increasing northern penetration of acid precipitation. With these trends occurring, it is urgent that more accurate monitoring of atmospheric fallout and vegetation changes that may result from these influences be undertaken throughout circumpolar areas. Biosphere reserves offer the potential for the establishment of long-term monitoring sites in circumpolar areas.

Conclusion

Northern ecosystems have been the focal point of scientific interest for a variety of reasons, including detailed investigations that have emphasized differences between specific plant communities in the North, the importance of their interrelationships, and their relationship to higher trophic levels, but the ecological importance of northern lands at present is only superficially understood and appreciated. There is a decreasing complexity within ecosystems from temperate to Arctic regions associated with decreased species diversity and slower rates of nutrient turnover. This lends a "simplicity" to northern ecosystems that makes them appropriate subjects for research. Individual influence within such systems can be more easily tracked and thus are more manageable within the framework of research design.

The pronounced seasonality in the North has selected for adaptations in the plants and animals that are unique to the high latitudes. An understanding of the importance and modes of influence of the basic prerequisites for living systems (heat, light, moisture, and nutrients) can often be more effectively investigated where pronounced seasonal extremes exist. Thus, the effects on vegetation of long day length, temperature and nutrient limitation, and short growing season have received considerable attention from scientists working in the Arctic and Subarctic. As a result of the International Biological Program (IBP) from 1964 to 1974, the Tundra Biome studies, the Research into Arctic Tundra Ecosystems program (RATE), and the International Man and the Biosphere program (MAB), there has been significant research on coastal and inland biological systems of the North with emphasis placed on plant-herbivore relationships, and research results published in numerous technical papers and several comprehensive volumes (Rosswall and Heal 1975; Brown 1975; Brown et al. 1980; Bliss et al. 1981). This work has been far reaching in terms of advancement of knowledge of northern lands, development of cooperative research efforts between countries, and free exchange of information and stimulation of continuing research interest in the North.[12] While this research has shown the value of vegetation to northern lands and wildlife, much more research is needed to clarify our understanding of the herbivore-plant relationships and Arctic plant communities under the influence of current climate change.

Continued exploration and development of oil, gas, and other subsurface resources will result in increasing conflict with resources on the surface. The comprehensive inventory of vegetation in northern land areas in relation to both existing and potential use patterns for wildlife and domestic animals and other human uses should be continued in order to provide a basis for establishing land-use priorities and minimizing future resource-use conflicts.

---

12. Norway's MAB program has been largely carried out on Svalbard with major research on the endemic reindeer (*R. t. platyrhynchus*) and their relationship to the sparse flora of the island complex. In the USSR, MAB research in the Arctic has largely been a continuation of their tundra biome studies under IBP, and, as a result, comprehensive long-range studies have been possible and are now resulting in the publication of detailed floristic and ecological descriptions of northern vegetation. The system of International Biosphere Reserves, which has received sponsorship through MAB via UNESCO, has stimulated some research on northern vegetation in circumpolar countries, but like the other MAB projects, the level of national support has been considerably less than seems justified. In the United States, funding for work in northern biosphere reserves has been largely through a consortium supported by the US Forest Service and the National Park Service.

Richard Watt (right) and Gary
Kenwood absorbing a beautiful
view during a wilderness hike
they did with David in the Brooks
Range, 1962. PHOTO BY DAVID KLEIN.

18
Defining the Wilderness Concept

Wilderness, like beauty, is a concept that dwells in the minds of those who would perceive it. The 1964 Wilderness Act defines wilderness as "where the earth and its community of life are untrammeled by man and where man himself is a visitor who does not remain" (United States Congress 1964). This treatment of wilderness is at odds with the culturally based evolution of the concept in North America. In 1949, Aldo Leopold emphasized that "wilderness is the raw material out of which man has hammered the artifact called civilization. To the laborer in the sweat of his labor, the raw stuff on his anvil is an adversary to be conquered. So was wilderness an adversary to the pioneer" (Leopold 1949:188). This notion of conquering the wilderness was shared among Euro-American pioneers involved in "opening up the West" and transforming it for agricultural production. It was only then that the "wild west" would become civilized. Simultaneously, these early settlers viewed the Native indigenous cultures, be they Algonquin, Navajo, Cherokee, or others, as dwellers within the American wilderness, or perhaps more gratuitously, as keepers of the wilderness equally appropriate for subjugation as was the wild country in which they lived.

My fascination with the evolution of the wilderness concept and its cultural variability has dominated my development as an ecologist. As a boy in Vermont and Connecticut, my imagined concept of wilderness was the product of a New England bias in which the Adirondacks and the Maine woods were emblematic of wild lands. Boy Scouting and associated campouts helped continue to shape my love for the outdoors and understanding of the natural environment. Upon arriving in Alaska, it became apparent to me that there was no broadly accepted concept of "wilderness." Compared to the relative tameness and long period of human occupancy in New England where I had come from, in my eyes much of Alaska was untrammeled, save for the widely scattered but localized effects of mining exploration and extraction and agriculture to feed the miners. However, for others, even these rare signs of former human occupation were too much. They wanted wilderness to be a place where there was no sign of previous human use. Of course, this failed to take into account the long history of Native Alaskans sustainably living off the land and leaving no sign of permanent occupation.

My own concept of "wilderness" has undergone major change as I gained experience and appreciation for the diversity of Alaska's wild lands, their ecosystems, the fish and wildlife they support, and how we humans, from the diverse Alaska Native cultures to the Russian and American exploiters and settlers, have used the fish and wildlife resources. Of course, experiences gained during numerous visits with colleagues and resource users from northern European and Circumarctic cultures and from cross-cultural contacts have broadened my understanding of the important role of culture in shaping how humans view the environment in which they live. Someone's view of wilderness is one of those concepts deeply rooted in cultural traditions.

Aldo Leopold, in his essay "The Green Lagoons," observed that "it is part of wisdom never to revisit a wilderness, for the more golden the lily, the more certain that someone has gilded it. To return not only spoils a trip, but tarnishes a memory" (Leopold 1949:150). I would say that this closely parallels how I have come to feel about the concept of wilderness. That much of it is an intangible concept within our own minds based on personal experience and cultural values, rather than hard and fast empirical fact. I first publically expressed this concept of wilderness in testimony I gave in 1977 before the United States Senate's Committee on Interior and Insular Affairs chaired by Senator Morris Udall where I spoke in favor of protecting the Arctic National Wildlife Range as an intact ecosystem (Klein 1977b). In 1994, I then published, "Wilderness: A Western Concept Alien to Arctic Cultures" as an essay where I strove to demonstrate how wilderness perceptions vary between cultures, and that it is important to remember that what is good for one culture is not always good for another (Klein 1994).

The evolution of the wilderness concept within American culture that I discuss below is a compilation of my previous article "Wilderness: A Western Concept Alien to Arctic Cultures" and an old unpublished manuscript of mine titled "Wilderness—Nature Unvanquished and a Land Use Category" with some minor editorial restructuring and updating. It also is indicative of the development of my personal connections with wilderness philosophy.[13]

The Concept of Wilderness

Aldo Leopold described wilderness as raw nature to be subdued, but also "to the laborer in repose, able for a moment to cast a philosophical eye on his world, that same raw stuff is something to be loved and cherished, because it gives definition and meaning to his life" (Leopold 1949:188). These few perceptively chosen words encompass two important aspects of the evolution of the wilderness concept in Western society. First is the human striving to transform nature; and second, the more recent nostalgic and aesthetic valuation of wilderness by an affluent society no longer in direct contact with nature. This pattern, perhaps not surprisingly, parallels the historical shift in Western society from its land-based origin to the technological/industrial dominance of this century.

The concept of wilderness in Western culture has its roots in Judeo-Christian fundamentalism. Europeans brought this concept with them to North America, as they set out to tame the wilderness of the western frontier. It was only after the wave of settlement had reached the Pacific coast that the desire to protect samples of wilderness was born. Humans now controlled the land and viewed themselves as separate from nature.

Western civilization has its roots in the city-states bordering the Mediterranean Sea, where separation of the urban dweller from nature was considered a desirable outcome of civilization. Wilderness was an obstacle to human dominance over nature, and became antithetical to the development of Western society. As humans increasingly became separated from the natural environment, familiarity with it was lost. Thus, wilderness, which

---

13. See also Klein 1976a and 1976b for more about David Klein's views on the wilderness concept.

had nurtured humans throughout their evolution from the Stone Age, was now abandoned by civilized man and was relegated to the realm of the unknown, engendering fear and foreboding.

The emerging new religions in the Mediterranean basin provided reinforcement for the belief that wilderness was threatening to human society, harboring the spirits of pagan animism, as well as demons and devils identified by the new religions. Religious ideology underwent a transformation from the nature-based spirit world of hunter-gatherer societies to the abstract single, human, and male all-powerful God of Judaism, Christianity, and Islam. Between 3000 and 2000 BC, Hebrews won a political victory by renouncing worship of graven images, which were the symbolism of nature-based religions, while substituting their new anthropocentric religion that flourished in the expanding Western civilization (Mander 1978).

Much later, the Industrial Revolution brought about acceleration in the rate of human exploitation of the earth's environment, fostered by the Reformation and the emergence of fundamental Protestantism. Max Weber ascribed the rapid development of industrialization and the associated growth of capitalism to the Protestant ideology that viewed the earth as a storehouse of resources explicitly available for human exploitation (Weber 1930). Protestantism also provided a work ethic that was supported by the rapid rise of capitalism. Human populations were exploding at the expense of wilderness.

Nonetheless, by the beginning of the nineteenth century, the dominant view of wilderness in the West was shifting from the fundamentalist Judeo-Christian negative image of darkness and the home of evil and threatening elements to a more positive view that melded the rural pastoral landscape with undisturbed nature. An appreciation for wild nature was evolving, particularly in North America where European immigrants pushed the frontier westward across the continent and developed the land in proximity to wilderness.

Appreciation of wild nature had become the central theme among an emerging cadre of American writers, including Charles Carleton Coffin, Henry David Thoreau, and John Muir. Thus, the wilderness movement born in North America was a satellite of the growing conservation movement that had been instrumental in bringing about the establishment of the world's first national parks. For many, the culmination of the wilderness movement in the United States was the recognition by the US Congress of the values of wilderness and the importance of wilderness preservation through passage of the Wilderness Act in 1964. This act designated federal lands, primarily within existing national parks, national forests, and national wildlife refuges, as wilderness and offered protection to assure its wild, untrammeled character was maintained.

Official recognition of wilderness values by the US Congress was largely a consequence of the strong educational and lobbying activity of the environmental movement through citizens' advocacy organizations, primarily the Wilderness Society, the Sierra Club, and the National Audubon Society. At the time, the Wilderness Act was branded by outspoken opponents, perhaps validly, as elitist legislation serving the interests of a wealthy minority of the population. Subsequently, however, areas designated as wilderness throughout the United States have experienced rapidly increasing visitation, dominated by young people, often with only moderate and meager levels of income.

Nevertheless, for most people in Western society today, wilderness is a concept, the reality of which they have not personally experienced. Only a minority of the American public actually visits wilderness areas. The image of wilderness in the minds of many urban Americans, however weak it may be, has been derived almost totally from television (the average American adult spends four hours per day in front of the TV screen). The proportion of TV time in support of wilderness preservation in the United States is probably a fraction of 1 percent (and most of that is on public TV, which is watched by less than 5 percent of the TV viewing public). Contrast this with about 20 percent of commercial TV time in the United States devoted to advertising products that either directly or indirectly contribute to loss of the natural environment or damage to it through pollution, deforestation, development, overharvest, and extraction of nonrenewable resources.

Even when the effort is made to promote wilderness through television, it lacks the potential to convey complexity to the viewer. The electronic media is flat, affecting only the visual and auditory senses in a filtered superficial manner. It is not possible to represent the depth, smells, and feel of wilderness. It cannot convey the nuances of life or the complexity of ecosystem relationships. Those who have not experienced nature by being in it and being a part of it cannot understand the beauty and richness of nature solely from the television screen. The aura of living systems does not lend itself to an abstract form of communication. It must be experienced in situ (Mander 1978).

There is no simple solution to the conundrum of the perceived reality of the natural environment as depicted on TV versus the reality discovered through actually spending time outdoors. TV has captivated the minds of many in Western society, but is technologically incapable of conveying an understanding, appreciation, and reverential respect for wilderness values. In rare instances when television is able to engender support for wilderness protection, it is only through the viewing public's willingness to accept the voice of electronic media as authority. Unfortunately, the voice for wilderness that comes from television is minuscule in comparison to the dominant materialistic, consumer-oriented, resource-exploitive voice that occupies the majority of primetime TV.

I do not intend these comments as merely a generalized attack against television, but rather to emphasize the ineffective role that television specifically plays in conveying the concept and reality of wilderness to the viewing public. TV plays an effective role in shaping the views of the public, however distorted from reality they may be.

It is ironic that Western society, with its materialistic, technological preoccupation, its present economy that is clearly unsustainable through its dependence on massive, worldwide exploitation of nonrenewable resources, and its dissociation from nature, has also been the source of political activism to provide protection for remaining areas of the world's wilderness. The wilderness preservation movement has its roots in America, fostered by the bio-centric writings of John Muir and Aldo Leopold, and more recently supported by advocates of deep ecology (Devall and Sessions 1985). The concept of humans as part of nature, which has remained an integral component of non-Western cultures, is viewed as a threat to the environment by many Western wilderness advocates (Guha 1989). The act of offering legal protection for wilderness that is far removed from our everyday lives but provides salve for our conscience, is perhaps in recognition of the fact that we have lacked the will to initiate the major governmental and economic restructuring necessary if we are to move toward sustainability of Western society.

However, indigenous peoples whose cultures have evolved within wild lands based on hunting and gathering are at home in these lands. Their lifestyles and very existence have been dependent upon a sustained harvest of resources from the land without altering nature. Indigenous peoples are at the top of trophic relationships within ecosystems and view themselves as part of nature.

Wilderness advocates are now turning their eyes northward and are beginning to perceive the as yet unrealized potential for wilderness opportunities in the Arctic. If the Arctic is to serve the growing interests of wilderness seekers from the south, those interests must be compatible with the interests and well-being of the indigenous residents of the Arctic. This is particularly relevant in view of the current, and presumably continuing, future trend in world politics toward recognition of rights of the indigenous peoples relating to the lands they occupy and their desire to protect values they cherish in their cultures. Indigenous peoples of the Arctic are gaining deserved legal authority and responsibility for administration of their homelands—lands that only recently have been viewed as such by Western society. Although conservation of nature in the Arctic is today a common goal of both the indigenous cultures and elements of Western culture, increased understanding of culturally-based differences in perceptions of nature is essential if mutually acceptable conservation efforts are to succeed. But how differently do people who live south of the Arctic and indigenous people of the Arctic view the concept of wilderness?

Specifically, I want to look at the meaning of wilderness in the Arctic, because it remains a place with a small population and vast areas of land that have not been as heavily impacted by human development as other parts of the world. My main question is what wilderness means in the Arctic and whether wilderness is a concept alien to Arctic cultures. Cultures have evolved within the constraints imposed by the environments where they occurred. Indigenous people that have lived compatibly with nature have done so by necessity. Cultures have waxed and waned in relation to resource abundance, sustainability, and level of exploitation. Those that exceeded the bounds of their environmental constraints died out, and there are numerous examples where artifacts left upon the landscape have provided fertile fields for archaeologists. When cultures persisted and human populations remained stable, it was usually because the level of technology available for exploitation of resources did not permit overexploitation of resources. When new technology became available, either through innovation or by adoption from other cultures, increased exploitation of resources became possible. Human populations then expanded until either a new level capable of sustainable resource exploitation was reached or overexploitation occurred and the human population declined, often to extinction, and taking with it the associated culture.

When advances in technology have led to increased human density, social interaction flourished and time became available for activities in addition to those essential for subsistence. Artistic skills developed and spirituality became more complex, often incorporating feedback from resource limitation. If the food base was diverse, overexploitation of one resource may not necessarily have led to the demise of human populations; however, it is apparent that awareness of the need to regulate future use of an overexploited resource may have existed. Constraints on overexploitation of renewable resources have become adopted in some indigenous cultures over time via taboos that were relatively free from influences of other cultures (Nelson 1983).

Cultures undergoing rapid change, whether from the introduction of new technologies and ideologies, exploitation of newly available resources, domination and absorption of minority cultures, occupation of new lands, or population explosion, are likely to lose those constraints against resource overexploitation that had evolved with the cultures. In cultures undergoing rapid social change, all aspects of culture, including value systems, become flexible and subject to change. Cultural attributes that yield long-term social benefits often are lost when there is associated population growth. Cultures in isolation, with stable or even declining population, are often resistant to change. Witness the stability of the Norse culture in Iceland during its isolation throughout the Little Ice Age. The written Icelandic language and agrarian-based culture remained intact, even though the sustainability of the land for livestock and crops declined to submarginal levels as a consequence of the cooling climate, widespread overgrazing, and soil erosion. A similar pattern appears to have preceded the demise of the Norse settlements in

Greenland, who were so inflexibly tied to an agrarian economy that they failed to transfer their dependence from land that could no longer support them to the more abundantly available resources from the sea that sustained the Inuit population (Fredskild 1988; Kinitsch 2016; Folger 2017).

Westerners often apply their wilderness label to areas that encompass the homelands of indigenous peoples. In indigenous cultures, the land is the source of being and is understood as such. In urban, industrialized, and monetarily based cultures, the individual has lost direct contact with the land and has no real appreciation for the relationship of culture to the land via the commodities that are products of the land (e.g., food, clothing, materials to construct homes, and paper that brings the printed word). Wilderness within the homeland of indigenous peoples is valued by them for its productivity, but in Western urban society that wilderness is valued for its lack of productivity for human consumption. A great disparity obviously exists between the Western view of Arctic wilderness and the indigenous view of Arctic homeland.

For example, according to Gwich'in leader Sarah James, the Gwich'in living close to the northern limit of forests in northwestern Canada and adjacent Alaska have a saying that "to understand our way, you must stop for a moment and feel the rhythm of the land, for we are part of it" (pers. comm. 1993). Before contact with Western culture, the Gwich'in knew of the caribou only in fall and winter, when they were present in their homeland. The caribou left their wintering grounds in spring to migrate north to the calving grounds located in the land of the Inuit, the people who lived at the edge of the sea. The Cree of the northern coniferous forests of central Canada have had a similar relationship with caribou (Engstad 1993). Their culture evolved largely in relation to and dependent upon caribou, and they only had intricate knowledge of the caribou's winter ecology because the animals were absent from their lands in summer. In fact, the Chipewyans have a saying about these mystical and unpredictable creatures that states: "Nobody knows the way of the wind and the caribou" (Munsterhjelm 1953:97).

For these caribou hunting cultures, the calving grounds of the caribou might be viewed as an analogue to the Western concept of wilderness—a land beyond the realm of the known homeland. Wilderness for them also might include those areas of the Arctic that could not support indigenous people, areas that were without harvestable resources and therefore of no utilitarian value, such as the tops of high mountains, icecaps, and expanses of the sea beyond safe exploitation. Such areas were usually endowed with spiritual power. They commanded respect even though they were never visited at all or perhaps only by shamans seeking powers from the spirit world. This indigenous concept of wilderness is far removed from the ideal of Western culture, where wilderness is a place of retreat and restoration of self and soul, and can be appreciated and exploited only through visitation.

Is a marriage of the Western concept of wilderness with indigenous peoples' views of land possible? Can protection of natural areas in the Arctic serve the interests of Western society, while respecting and protecting the interests of indigenous peoples within their homeland? Because surviving cultures are not static, and with both Western and Arctic indigenous cultures undergoing rapid change, the Arctic wilderness areas that legal action is trying to protect are moving targets. It is not surprising that a divergence of views about measures for land protection exists within both cultures.

Designation of wilderness areas in the homeland of indigenous peoples of the Arctic is an ethnocentric act that reflects ignorance of, and insensitivity to, the cultures, interests, and concerns of Arctic peoples. Although wilderness designation may protect the fish, wildlife, and other resources that are essential to the subsistence economy of Arctic peoples, this benefit is usually incidental to the primary intent and Western cultural bias of the designation. Similar results can be achieved without invoking or reflecting cultural dominance. Intercultural negotiation can lead to land-use classifications designed to maintain the productivity of the land and waters for sustained harvest by indigenous peoples, while also offering opportunities for visitors to experience the pristine nature that usually characterizes such environments. It is encouraging to note such a trend in Canada, where several new parks and other protected areas in the Arctic are the product of joint negotiations and efforts of cross-cultural groups.

Visitors from the south should be fully aware when visiting the Arctic that they are usually guests in the homelands of cultures other than their own. Gaining understanding of these cultures offers the potential to enhance rewards from their visit. Conversely, since the first explorers and whalers entered the Arctic, Westerners have assumed or claimed possession of the land and resources without consideration for the endemic cultures and peoples of the Arctic. The recent trend by Arctic countries to recognize claims of the Arctic peoples to lands and resources is an encouraging sign that this historical perception held by Westerners is being revised.

It is only through mutual understanding and respect between cultures that there can be a marriage of interests to assure the long-term protection of natural areas in the Arctic. Failure of peoples from diverse cultures to understand one another and to respect their differences inevitably leads to increasing polarization and alienation. Witness the opposition originating in southern urban centers to the harvest of marine mammals by Arctic peoples, and the subsequent boycott of sealskins in Western markets.

The future offers promise for the protection of nature in the Arctic, but it only can be accomplished through increased mutual understanding and communication between the peoples of the Arctic and those of Western society. Westerners must learn to find wilderness gratification when visiting homelands of the Inuit, Saami, Evenki, and other Arctic peoples without their specific designation as wilderness. We must continue to support protection of the Arctic environment and the sustainability and productivity of the biological systems it encompasses. But its protection should be negotiated within terms acceptable to Arctic residents, rather than by imposing alien cultural concepts upon them.

Western culture is an amalgam of cultures (largely, but not exclusively, European) that has and is undergoing accelerated change as a result of the industrial/technological revolution. Unlike most of the cultures that evolved over millennia of relative stability, Western culture is now in transition, fueled by rapid increase in human population density and exploitation of largely nonrenewable resources that are far removed from their consumers. It is a culture with little likelihood of adopting timely self-imposed constraints on resource exploitation that could lead to population and cultural sustainability.

Wilderness, as a concept, is also undergoing change in Western society. In the decades since passage of the 1964 Wilderness Act, there has been a rapid growth in users of areas designated as wilderness. The wilderness experience, as defined by the Wilderness Act, should provide opportunities for solitude. Now, however, the experience must be shared with an increasing number of other users. For many people, the consequence is that the wilderness character of these areas is being lost. Even though the land remains largely unaltered, the concept of wilderness is being eroded. Jay Hansford Vest has pointed out the difficulty that federal agencies have encountered in attempting to manage wilderness areas through objective management techniques while also trying to serve the aesthetic and poetic ideals encompassed in the Wilderness Act (Vest 1987). The Wilderness Act is an attempt to designate and protect the naturalness of areas by legal mandate, but the naturalness and solitude that can be experienced in wilderness are lost to the wilderness seeker if numerous other humans are encountered. Because concepts are in the human mind and not in the land itself, merely designating areas as wilderness could not assure that they would continue to fit the definition. Now, when I wish a wilderness experience, I increasingly select de facto wilderness because it remains less visited than those areas officially designated as wilderness and advertised as such by the ecotourism industry and government agencies responsible for administering them.

It is obvious that the association of wilderness with solitude is being eroded in Western society. Since the wilderness concept has changed during the history of Western civilization, as explained above, it would be naïve to assume that it would not continue to evolve. The pressures of increasing human population density and urbanization that have occurred in the last century is one of the factors driving this change. Despite the changes, the wilderness concept remains a Western one.

To most Americans and Europeans of the eighteenth and nineteenth centuries, the term *wilderness* conjured up a vision of remote and dense forest; the home of wild animals. This view was colored by a sense of the unknown and foreboding that is a product of childhood fantasies and religious teachings that were a part of our cultural heritage. In more recent times, a small but growing segment of society has looked upon wilderness as those remaining domains of unspoiled nature that deserve protection from further encroachment by human development because of their intrinsic value to mankind. This value is measured by opportunities for primitive recreational experiences and spiritual enrichment and in the contribution that wilderness can make toward society's increased understanding and appreciation of nature.

According to *Webster's New Twentieth Century Dictionary* (1975), *wilderness* is "a region uncultivated and uninhabited or an uncultivated tract of land." The 1964 Wilderness Act expands on this to define wilderness as:

> An area of undeveloped Federal land retaining its primeval character and influence without permanent improvements or human habitation, which is protected and managed so as to preserve its natural conditions and which (1) generally appears to have been affected primarily by the forces of nature with the imprint of man's work substantially unnoticeable; (2) has outstanding opportunities for solitude or a primitive and unconfined type of recreation; (3) has at least five thousand acres of land, of sufficient size to make practical its preservation and use in an unimpaired condition; and (4) may also contain ecological, geological, or other features of scientific, educational, scenic, or historical value (United States Congress 1964.)

In contrast, Stephen H. Spurr stated in 1966 that there was no such thing as true wilderness, because every community of life on earth's surface had already been influenced by man (Spurr 1966). He cited examples such as the presence of DDT in animals in Antarctica and in the oceanic depths, places that previously had been thought beyond the influence of man. Spurr emphasized that all "pure" or "virgin" wilderness had been destroyed or eliminated, and the degree of wilderness any area possessed was relative to man's impact upon it. He believed that although there was no pure wilderness remaining, wilderness in a less ideological sense could be restored, or created by man. Spurr's attitude appears to have been a minority viewpoint, at least in North America, where applying the term *wilderness* to artificially created or restored areas was viewed by purists as prostitution of the wilderness concept.

Given man's connection with wilderness as explained by Spurr, nature writer Sigurd F. Olson saw wilderness as part of our cultural heritage and therefore as a cultural entity (Olson 1961; Backes 2001). While wilderness is a way of perceiving and describing portions of the natural environment, it is not a cultural item in and of itself. Cultural items are man-made.

However, the concept of wilderness is a component of our cultural language. This confusion appears to be more of a problem of semantics than of disagreement. The *Oxford English Dictionary* defines *culture* as "the training, development, and refinement of mind, tastes, and manners; the intellectual side of civilization" (*Oxford English Dictionary* 1989). On the basis of this definition, wilderness acquires cultural relevance when man reaches that stage of intellectual development that enables him to derive aesthetic return from it. Aldo Leopold expressed this view by stating that "the ability to see the cultural value of wilderness boils down, in the last analysis, to a question of intellectual humility, and it is only the scholar who understands why the raw wilderness gives definition and meaning to the human enterprise" (Leopold 1949:200).

Wilderness Appreciation

The cultural basis for wilderness appreciation has deep historical roots. In an essay on the wilderness concept, function, and management, Ian McTaggart Cowan implied that wilderness is a product of man's increasing awareness of the rapid destruction of the natural environment, as well as being the result of the hybridization of man's culture (Cowan 1968). In his view, modern man's reverence for wilderness was merely striving for cultural identity by holding on to a perspective from his past. Cowan goes on to suggest that past appreciation of wilderness in the Western world was suppressed by our religious heritage. Christian fundamentalism has traditionally looked upon wilderness as the unknown beyond the security of the human domain; something to be feared, but also to be overcome and subdued.

On the other hand, in 1967 Roderick Nash advocated a vitalistic approach toward nature (Nash 1967). He ignored the negative influence of early Christianity that Cowan emphasized, and viewed wilderness appreciation as a direct outgrowth of religion and appreciation of God's handiwork in nature. Also starting in the late 1960s and early 1970s, Paul Shepard approached the subject as an interdisciplinarian, integrating the viewpoint of the humanities with that of biology (Shepard 1967, 1973). Shepard saw our Christian heritage as a strong negative influence on Western man's appreciation of nature, but he also stressed that "both transcendental romanticism and ecology, the two most potent forces for the preservation of nature, are products of a Christian culture" (Shepard 1967:220). According to Shepard, nature hating was intimately connected to the Judeo-Christian system, where the orthodox, medieval Christian attitude toward nature was derived essentially from prejudices and pride of men engaged in equatorial pastoralism and trade where forests posed threats to their animal herds and were places where travelers could be ambushed. He saw the Persian duality of light and dark, of good and evil, of sky and earth, as central dichotomies in Christian thought. On the other hand, the other-worldliness of Christian asceticism provided the perspective from which the earth and its natural world, exclusive of man, could be viewed as potential wealth for man, available through exploitation.

Shepard also saw a relationship between man's views of nature and his attitudes toward women. Similar associations of fear, hatred, and danger applied to nature were also attached to the female body and persona. Terms like fertile ground, trees bearing fruit, or virgin wilderness demonstrate the connections drawn between female fertility and the fecundity of nature; the concept of virgin nature being derived from the notion of it being unchanged or "unviolated" by man. For example, Charles Carleton Coffin, writing about the American prairies in the mid-1800s, described his feeling of being "surrounded by nature in all her purity and bloom" (Coffin 1869). There also were parallels within the Judeo-Christian belief system of man's dominance over nature and his subjugation of women. Man's ultimate control over nature occurred in a garden setting, where he could manipulate it to serve his own uses. In contrast, wilderness was despised because it was a place that was unproductive for man and where he had the least control over nature. It was obvious, however, that for the most part wilderness was yielding to man, being literally pushed back and subdued. It was no longer conflicting so directly with the immediate interests of man. It appeared that man would ultimately be the victor.

By the beginning of the nineteenth century, the common view of nature was moving away from that of fundamentalist Christian-Jews who looked upon nature as being cursed and an embodiment of evil to a melding of the rural and wild landscapes. As the inhabitants of the countryside were looked upon as free from the corrupting influences of urban life, such rural scenes were more frequently being visualized as relatively pure and wholesome.

As the frontiersman, the pioneer, and the colonizer were becoming more and more urbanized, industrialized, and separated from nature, he began to feel nostalgia for the past, for the "good old days," when he was using his wits to overcome nature. There was also a growing recognition that nature had been responsible for a way of life that yielded many elemental or basic satisfactions that were not possible in the city. Nostalgia for man's earlier closeness to nature and a longing to return to nature became dominant elements in the origin of the wilderness movement. Aldo Leopold recognized this and emphasized the importance of employing primitive methods of living and transportation when visiting wilderness. He felt that man must try to re-create the past in his recreational enjoyment of wilderness.

Late in the past century, the youth culture, and its antecedent the hippie movement, both spawned a variety of "back to nature" enthusiasts. However, these movements were often motivated by reaction against technological society per se, rather than by a recognition or appreciation of values in nature. The benefits of self-reliance and independence from conventional society were gained by returning to nature, wresting a living directly from the land, and experiencing personal dominance over nature. Ironically, these subcultures protested the deification of technology by modern society and its indifference to ecology, yet in most cases, their own "return to nature" was merely a step backward in time to a frontier setting when man was in more direct and personal conflict with nature.

Robert Marshall, a prolific writer on wilderness in the 1930s and one of the founders of the Wilderness Society in 1935, emphasized that wilderness serves man whether he is able to use it or not. One of his premises was that "knowing" that it is there allows the desire to visit it to exist. That even though a person may never get to a wilderness area, at least he can entertain the desire to visit it. Marshall emphasized the value of unsuppressed desires; of having broader perspectives as a result of the existence of things known but not yet experienced (Marshall 1930).

In some ways this is akin to an ethic put forth by Norwegian philosopher Arne Næss, which he developed during a mountain climbing trip to Nepal in the early 1970s. One of the original objectives of the trip was to scale Gauri Shankar (Tseringma), an unclimbed Himalayan mountain, at the time considered one of the few remaining outstanding climbing challenges in the world. While in base camp, Næss and his colleagues decided to discontinue the climb to the peak and leave the mountain unclimbed. Strongly influenced by the local Sherpa community's cultural/religious respect for the mountain, Næss and his colleagues proposed that some mountains should remain unclimbed. They felt that man is too much the conqueror of nature, and that some of the natural world should remain unvanquished by him. The basic principle of this ethic seems to be a reverence or respect for the mountain itself, as well as its symbolic representation of nature. Respect for the human ethos—that man needs to know that there still are unexplored regions and unclimbed mountains—was apparently not a strong motivating force behind Næss's action (Næss pers. comm. 1972; Næss 1973).

In many ways, wilderness has values that do not exist in other aesthetic entities, such as painting, sculpture, and music. Wilderness experience tends to affect all of the senses simultaneously and in this respect differs from experiencing conventional forms of art. One can value or appreciate a scenic landscape by viewing it through a car window, much as one would a painting, but this is not experiencing it in the same sense as the person who is actually within it. In fact, actually being a part of the wilderness scene appears to be an essential aspect of wilderness recreation. This valuing of nature immersion for gaining the full wilderness experience is what led some to speak out in favor of protecting wild places.

Protection of nature for its own sake is not a recent North American ethic. John Muir's advocacy for nature protection in the late 1880s rested to a large extent on his belief in the "right to existence" of all living things. The current environmental movement also stems from the anthropomorphizing of animal life by Walt Disney–type advertising and promotion associated with society's increasing separation from nature. This often leads to the focus of public concern for the well-being of individual animals, while the importance of habitats and ecosystems to wildlife populations and their preservation may be overlooked. Paul Errington and Douglas Pimlott, both wildlife ecologists, emphasized the need for ecological diversity as a basis for man's psychological well-being (Errington 1963; Pimlott 1969). Errington also believed that undisturbed ecosystems could serve to exemplify man's respect for nature as well as deserving protection for their own sake.

In addition to serving as reserves for wildlife, wilderness areas also have value for scientific study of undisturbed ecosystems. This may be particularly important for wildlife that may already have been eliminated from areas where human impact on the environment is great. The most readily apparent value of undisturbed ecosystems as scientific reserves lies in their potential as laboratories for the study and understanding of these systems and as controls for where changes in disturbed ecosystems can be compared. In some parts of Europe, closure of reserves or portions of them to the public has been done to protect segments of natural vegetation or habitats of importance for threatened species. The value of the diversity of genetic material within wilderness systems to the future welfare of mankind can only be guessed at, but it may prove to be far greater than we can foresee today.

In spite of growing environmental concern and increased public support of the wilderness movement, there still remains strong opposition to establishment of wilderness areas. Some of this opposition appears, at least superficially, to have a sound logical basis. Several studies conducted in the late 1960s in North America have shown that the wilderness movement at that time was largely restricted to the upper middle class, and included primarily well-educated people. The movement tended to exclude the poorly educated, the poor, and old and infirm people who were not physically able to participate in wilderness recreation. It was argued that because of these characteristics wilderness served only a minority of the population, and setting areas aside as "Wilderness" tended to violate our society's democratic principles. In recent decades, there has been a trend toward wider interest in wilderness recreation, especially among the youth who are willing to travel without the luxuries of contemporary society. Money no longer plays such an important role in visitation to wilderness areas. This is apparently a result of the current challenge to the work ethic of Western society by young people, which tends to free them to pursue nonmaterial goals. In comparison, wilderness use in Scandinavia traditionally has been less exclusively class oriented, probably because of their society-wide enthusiasm for outdoor recreation and a less well-defined class system than in North America.

A basis for the general lack of enthusiasm for wilderness recreation in our traditional society derives from our cultural heritage and is therefore entrenched within our social system. We emphasize work as the dominant aspect of human life essential for maintaining productivity and as the primary objective of Western industrialized society. The emphasis on work as desirable, and leisure as wasteful, has its roots in fundamental Protestant ethics. Calvinistic Puritanism provided an ideology that justified the relentless pursuit of gain (Weber 1930). In fact, not to do so would be to deny the duty of one's calling. The Puritan admonition against the use of wealth for pleasure provided the incentive for reinvestment, thus accelerating the rise of capitalism. Karl Marx, in his theory of the evolution of capitalism, failed to appreciate this relationship and instead treated capitalism as a product of the feudal social system (Marx 1912). In this way, Protestantism also influenced the development of industrialization as individuals worked harder and harder (Weber 1930).

In modern society, we may look upon work as an unpleasant daily chore, but we acquiesce to a moral obligation to work. While leisure activities are acknowledged to be enjoyable, they are still viewed as something that must not interfere with production. That is, with work. Traditionally, we have justified leisure on religious grounds, with socially approved leisure restricted to the Sabbath or to religious holidays when the time was not "wasted" by paying homage to God. While times have changed and most of society no longer feels guilt associated with leisure activities, the work ethic continues to influence our lives. We look forward to "earned" vacations and excuse the inactivity of older members of society by reference to their retirement deservedly garnered after a lifetime of work. It would be much more realistic and psychologically healthy to recognize that both work and leisure can be enjoyable as well as being essential components of life. If this change of attitude could be accomplished, it would tend to eliminate our inhibitions about spending money and time for leisure activities, and in dedicating land for purposes of leisure.

Support for wilderness as a land-use category is not only based upon acceptance of dedicating land for leisure purposes, but for protection of it for its own sake. It must be viewed as having intrinsic value to man separate from what it can produce from resource extraction or harvest. Proponents of the wilderness movement in North America value this "untrammeled" wilderness for the connections it gives humans back to the natural world, for the spiritual, mental, and emotional rejuvenation that can be found away from day-to-day urban life, and for the reminders it provides of a past way of life where humans lived in concert with the ecosystem around them instead of trying to conquer and manipulate it for their own personal gain.

Conclusion

The role of man in the wilderness and whether humans and nature can co-exist in a sustainable fashion continue to be debated. In this day and age, is it possible to have places on our planet that have not in some way felt the influence of man? Perhaps, as Stephen Spurr suggested, the wilderness label is a matter of degree in relation to man's impact on the land (Spurr 1966). Nevertheless, it is important to continue to protect natural areas, both for the value they give to humans mentally and physically, and for their scientific value where intact ecosystems can continue to be studied.

The concept of wilderness will continue to evolve as our cultures and environments shift over time. It will be interesting to see where we go from here.

Skiing in the Reindeer Hills in the
Talkeetna Mountains to conduct
winter fieldwork, circa 1978. PHOTO
BY DAVID KLEIN.

19

Environmental Philosophy: People and the Environment

Environmental philosophy can mean different things to different people. As a generic term it means the patterns of curiosity about how people live with the environment in a reasonably compatible way. So it's how we humans in different parts of the world, in different cultures, use the environment. Environmental philosophy is tied to ecology, evolution, and adaption to environment. People adapt to the environment and the environment adapts to the people in terms of how they use it. The way the environment shapes people is the same as the evolution of organisms, especially mammals and birds. Culture influences people's relationship to their environment. It takes a group of people living together in one area to create a culture or a culture develops in relationship to humans living that way.

The first humans who moved into Europe from Africa or into the Americas from Eurasia were nomadic and had no bounds, but once these hunters and gatherers settled down in one location you got agriculture and domestication of animals. As humans settled more, cleared land for agriculture and towns, cut down forests for firewood or lumber, moved water, and raised domestic animals, the more we changed the landscape around us. Then what was happening with the environment affected the lifestyle of the people. It's about learning how to live with the environment in such a way that you as humans benefit from it. But problems can develop when people who were used to living in relationship to the environment a certain way don't want to change when the environment changes. To live more in accordance with our environment, it's common sense that we have to understand the environment around us better than we do.

Of course, the term *environmental philosophy* is a human-biased term. So the question is, how do we, as humans and people that are educated, use that term? For some of us who understand evolution and ecology, it's still a biased term, because if we say environmental philosophy is oriented toward protection of the natural environment, then you have to ask, why protect the natural environment? Well, it really doesn't make any difference to the environment if humans are there or not. Environmental processes are going to go on in terms of what's a natural way.

My interest in the role of environmental philosophy, or *eco-philosophy*, as it relates to the development of culturally related environmental values came about through my lifelong love of the outdoors and a desire to understand the world in which we live. This stemmed from childhood experiences and parental emphasis on the importance of living close to nature and the land. This was followed by educational and professional experiences in Alaska and other northern countries, where I was able to observe a diversity of endemic cultures and my ecological investigations were largely among people who were living relatively in tune with nature. These cultures that were shaped by their natural environments contrasted sharply with urban cultures, where people were largely removed from elements of nature. My focus within eco-philosophy became trying to understand how humans value nature and how it varies among cultures.

When I joined the faculty at UAF, I had a lot of these questions about people and the environment in my own mind. I was doing some reading on my own in philosophy, and I had taken one philosophy course and participated in evening discussion groups at the University of British Columbia when I was working on my PhD there. When it came to evolution, it wasn't as widely accepted by faculty members as you might think, especially in the physical sciences. Some people tend to think about it as science versus religion, but it's impossible to compare religion, which is a faith, to science, where scientific methodology is not a faith. It doesn't make sense to put these at the same level. Although the Bible has got a lot of information in it, it's observational information of the time that it was written. It's interpreted by people and written by people who were strong believers in Christianity, while with published scientific findings, whether it's about the physical world or the biological world, the information is there without interpretation. It's subject to challenge if new information becomes available, and if it is a theory, it can be substantiated by experimentation. Yes, some science methodology is observational, like we can watch what's happening to the moon and gradually predict a lot of things that are happening up there, but then you draw hypotheses that may or may not prove out.

Of course, my thinking about environmental ethics and philosophy was highly influenced by Henry David Thoreau and Aldo Leopold, but my own ideas really started to develop after my sabbatical year at the University of Oslo in 1971–1972 when I came into contact with a group of Norwegian philosophers, including Arne Næss and Sigmund Kvaløy, who had been leaders in founding an environmental movement in Norway promoting the idea of deep ecology and environmental values being rooted in Christian religious beliefs (Næss 1973; Kvaløy 1974). Næss promoted the idea of eco-religion where nature is deified because humans gain humility toward and appreciation of nature through an emotional sense of their place in a unified system. More recently, Peder Anker has written about the development of eco-philosophy and the environmental movement in Norway (Anker 2007 and 2013). I also brought home from Norway a desire to see discussions about eco-philosophy among students in the Department of Wildlife Management at the University of Alaska Fairbanks. I collaborated with philosophy professor Rudy Krejci to host a one-credit weekly seminar with students to talk about a variety of philosophical and ethical issues, largely related to aspects of applied ecology. Rudy provided balance to the conversations, often explaining how classical philosophy historically had provided grounding for human attempts to define our place in nature. I found these gatherings personally inspiring, as well as helpful in advancing the students' understanding of a broader range of issues than they otherwise obtained in their regular coursework.

The first part of this chapter, titled "The Emerging Eco-Philosophy," has never been published, but was presented at the Fifth World Wilderness Conference in 1993 in Tromsø, Norway. The major and initial inspiration behind this essay was a seminar held in February 1972 at Tømte Gård, a botanical research station near Oslo, Norway, where a group of philosophers and scientists spent a few days discussing issues of eco-philosophy and eco-religion. It was a perfect setting for conversation and the sharing of ideas, with group meals in the main lodge's homey dining room and midday breaks to enjoy the cross-country ski trails that wound through the rolling hills.

Throughout my career, I have given much thought to environmental ethics as it relates to my work as an ecologist and have focused on the human side of eco-philosophy, where as humans we value nature because of how it relates to us, not necessarily for its own sake. But eco-philosophy as it was being presented by Næss and Kvaløy was new intellectual territory for me. Næss saw religion as a source of insight for understanding the deeper meaning of ecology, and Kvaløy was fascinated with Buddhism and how its animistic view of nature added a spiritual dimension to understanding the web of life. I was concerned about this new eco-religion and its reliance on theology and argued for formulation of a new eco-ethics or philosophy based on a scientific foundation. I said that we gain an appreciation for the environment through science-based understanding of it rather than from religion's sense of protecting "God's creation." Norwegian scholar Peder Anker has summarized my participation in and perspective on these eco-philosophy discussions:

> To him [Klein] this was a question of intellectual hierarchy: science and not religion should be the core of environmental debate. Yet he recognized that the "mass media capitalizing on the public interest in ecology, plus the inexactness of ecology as a science," made his field vulnerable to absorption into existing cultural conceptions and religions (Klein 1972:1). . . . What worried Klein was the bending of ecological research in support of what easily could end up as authoritarian religious dogmas. (Anker 2013:192)[14]

According to Anker, I had some influence on Norwegian philosophical thinking because the eco-philosophers at the Tømte seminar "took Klein's

---

14. The 1972 citation in Anker's writing refers to David Klein's unpublished manuscript, *The Emerging Ecophilosophy* that he personally provided to Peder Anker.

warnings to heart, as their subsequent writings focused on philosophical and not theological arguments" (ibid.:193).

The second part of this chapter titled, "Cultural Influences on Landscape Aesthetics," was originally published in the *Boston College Environmental Affairs Law Review*, which is a quarterly publication about issues related to law and science (Klein 1972a). It was a product of the time I spent in the Fennoscandian region in the early 1970s, when I had many opportunities to visit a wide diversity of rural and urban landscapes and gain familiarity with the history of land-use practices throughout the region. It is also based on my interests in landscape architecture and land-use planning that sparked conversations with professors, students, and others at universities in Norway, Sweden, and Finland.

While both of these essays were originally written in the 1970s, I have edited and revised them for this book to reflect my current thinking and modern circumstances.

The Emerging Eco-Philosophy

> Howbeit that is not first which is spiritual, but that which is natural; and afterward that which is spiritual. (1 Corinthians 15:46, the Bible)

In the developed countries of the world, the end of the Second World War brought with it a shift in focus from concerns for the basic survival of society to something beyond the devastations wrought by war. It was again possible to refocus on environmental values and begin a reemergence of environmental consciousness. A reaffirmation of environmental values was stimulated by human confrontation with the obvious devastations within the war zone, the undesirable results of industrial development and associated urban expansion stimulated by the war effort, and pronounced environmental degradation tied to air and water pollution. The roots of the emerging postwar environmental consciousness also grew from the rapidly broadening base of ecological knowledge that flowed from its scientific sources to the public. This flow of information continues today, although it has often been unrecognizably altered or diluted by the mass media.

If a majority of those in the developed countries are gaining at least a superficial understanding of the processes of life on Earth, and are becoming alarmed about the future well-being of humankind because of increasingly apparent indicators of environmental deterioration, what form can we expect the changing attitudes toward the environment to take in the near and more distant future? Is interest in ecology just another fad or fancy of society that will soon be left behind, or can we expect the emergence of a true eco-philosophy (some philosophers prefer the term *ecosophy*) that will dominate human thought and profoundly influence the future course of civilization? If we, perhaps optimistically, assume the latter to be the case, what form will this new eco-philosophy take? Will it supplant, alter, or be absorbed into existing religious theology and become the new eco-religion that offers the salvation of mankind as a substitute for salvation of the individual, or will it be merely another parameter of human understanding, outside of religion, scientifically based, but recognized for its importance to the future of human society?

Although the initial fascination of the public with the concept of ecology as a driving process in the natural environment seems to have waned, there is strong evidence that interest in ecology is not a fad and that we can anticipate continued substantial and important changes in our way of looking at nature. The character of these changes is what remains in question and what will determine their impact on human society in the future. Changing attitudes toward nature have been largely the product of information made available through the mass media—TV, newspapers, radio, popular and semipopular literature, and the internet. Most of this information is conveyed and its relevance to the human species interpreted by laymen who often have no special competence in the subject, although their emotional interest may be strong. Rare are the biologists or other scientists and philosophers who are involved in popularizing their own views of man and nature, although they often have optimum perspectives for such philosophizing. There are, however, a few outstanding exceptions. For example, the biologist and Nobel award recipient Jacques Monod, the humanist René Dubos, the naturalist F. F. Darling, and the philosopher Paul Weiss. It is ironic that while the mass media has capitalized on increased public interest in ecology, an inexact science, ecological knowledge has been much more readily absorbed into existing cultural conceptions than has been true of knowledge generated by the hard sciences. The emerging new conceptions of humans and their relation to nature, while stimulated by new ecological understanding, are nevertheless strongly influenced by past cultural and religiously dominated views of nature.

Attitudes toward nature, even in modern Western society, are deeply rooted in ancient myth and cultural traditions that are often inseparably interwoven with religion. Perhaps the changing attitudes toward nature are an inevitable and desirable outcome of increased understanding of our place in the universe. It is a debatable point whether such optimism is justified. Many philosophers, psychologists, and sociologists have argued that beyond the personal, and often creative, spiritual experiences that religion provides, man requires religion because religion has been an integral part of our cultural evolution throughout history. This view suggests that it is the biological nature of humans to seek an authoritarian and exterior basis for their system of ethics, and that the complexity of the universe and of living systems are beyond human comprehension and require metaphysical explanations. Reliance on authoritarian dogma, whether emanating from the state, church, community, or family, has been a dominant factor in our cultural background and an attitude of acceptance of authority continues to be a characteristic of the human mind. Thus, even those who are trained to be analytically critical, to employ logic in deriving conclusions, and to challenge historical "authority" often tend to compartmentalize their minds. They hold on to the past, cherishing and defensively protecting cultural ideologies instilled during childhood, which often are inconsistent with their acceptance of rational scientific knowledge. Such persons include noted scientists who appear to be "playing the game" of science with the otherwise unbiased portions of their minds.

It is not surprising then that the current ecological movement, reflected in increased environmental awareness and stimulated by expanded scientific knowledge, is also strongly infused with a "religious" emotionalism and a revival of vitalism in attitudes toward nature. In the context discussed here, "religious" refers to faith or belief in the supernatural or metaphysical as distinct from emotionalism per se, which is acknowledged as an important element in philosophy as well as being a motivating force for scientists.

For example, Pierre Teilhard de Chardin, a French Jesuit philosopher who trained as a paleontologist and geologist, postulated a goal of human evolution leading to ultimate complexity, universal consciousness, and reunion with Christ (Teilhard de Chardin 1966, 1969, 1971, 1975, 1979). This pantheistic concept was initially rejected by the Catholic Church because it undermined Christian monotheism. Nevertheless, it broke the literary ground for such post–World War II philosophers as Alan Watts and Eric Fromm. James Lovelock's book *Gaia: A New Look at Life on Earth*, first published in 1970, went one step further toward creating an eco-religion by reviving the ancient Greek view of the unity of the Earth's physical and biological components, and advocating the concept of "the oneness of life" or "the universality of matter" (Lovelock 1970). In effect, this eco-religion deified nature as an all-encompassing, unifying concept and believed that man, recognizing his biological origins and his dependence on and relationship to all living systems, achieved humility through perspective of his place in nature. Nature took on maternal significance; being the source of all life, of all biological productivity, and within which humans have evolved as a self-aware species. Thus, we humans could assume a filial affection toward the totality of nature and a kinship toward other organisms.

In comparison, *vitalism* is the belief that the processes of life are not explicable by the laws of physics and chemistry alone and that life is in some part self-determining (*Merriam-Webster Dictionary* 2017). The concept of vitalism dominated biology in pre-Darwinian times. Because eighteenth- and nineteenth-century vitalism was so strongly supported by, and so deeply entrenched within Christian theology, it has been one of the primary obstacles to the acceptance of the theory of evolution. The assumption is made that rationality exists in nature and that nature is purposeful with inherent goals and morality. This is exemplified by such statements as: "Life exists in its own right, which man must acknowledge"; "What right has man to determine the future existence of other species?"; or "Nature should be protected for its own value, exclusive of man's interests." These statements presuppose rights and values that are not of human origin. Nevertheless, vitalism as an explanation of life and its processes has been displaced in modern scientific and philosophic thinking during past decades by the evidence-based mechanistic viewpoint, which explains life based on chemical and physical conditions.

Evolution of a new eco-religion necessarily involves reaction against man-centered Judeo-Christian religious theology and the anthropocentrism of modern scientific technology. The phenomenal development of Western technology rests largely on the emergence of Protestantism, which freed mankind from the nonrational and benign "acceptance of life" of medieval Catholicism. Max Weber in his book *The Protestant Ethic and the Spirit of Capitalism*, first published in 1904, pointed out that capitalism, contrary to accepted opinion, was not the direct outgrowth of the feudal system but rather had its roots in the ideology of puritanical asceticism (Weber 1930). Under Puritanism each person had the responsibility to work in his "calling" to "honor the glory of God," a god who could only be known after an individual had proven himself in this world and then taken leave of it. The accumulation of wealth and the profit motive were justified as long as the pursuit of pleasure was avoided. Reinvestment of surplus income was therefore encouraged and the modern concepts of economic growth and industrialization were both born and sanctified.

Under the rationalism of capitalism, scientific technology flourished and provided an essential element in the realization of the Industrial Revolution. While science has never been "understood" by the public at large in Western society, it has been revered for the technological wonders that it wrought. Concurrently, however, there has been a rejection of science for its so-called "failure to provide the answers to present-day problems." This belief results from the confusion of science with technology. Or put another way, the failure to distinguish between the art of the accumulation of knowledge and our ineffectiveness in applying existing knowledge toward the solution of world problems.

Religious movements capable of attracting large followings have in the past demonstrated their effectiveness in overcoming great obstacles in order to achieve their desired goals. Partly in recognition of this potential, some philosophers and ecologist-conservationists have also become spokespersons for the developing eco-religion. They argue that the survival of the human species in the face of an impending "eco-crisis" is dependent upon the widespread adoption of a religious humility toward nature. They are searching for a "panacea for the masses" on the premise that the end, the survival of mankind, justifies the means. Their motivations, while sincere, are pragmatic rather than epistemological. Nevertheless, it must be acknowledged that respect for nature, whether it stems from an eco-religion or a science-based philosophy, must be generally acceptable to a large segment of the public if it is going to be effective in changing the ways of society. If people are already inclined to be emotional about nature, the appeal of a nature religion may be greater than that of an objectively based explanation of man's place in nature. I suspect, however, that when scientifically trained people forsake objectivity for metaphysical explanations of nature they are reflecting a frustration over the apparent limitations of scientific knowledge.

While, on first appraisal, the emergence of an eco-religion may appear to offer the most promising prospect for overcoming the obstacles to man's "coming to terms with his environment," there may be more drawbacks than benefits involved in such a development. Religious movements transfixed by emotional self-righteousness are notoriously uncontrollable and in the past have all too often justified irrational and destructive acts, all in the name of piety. Witness the Crusades, the Inquisition, witch burning, the slaughter of infidels by Muslims, and most recently, worldwide terrorism by fundamentalist Islamic, Christian, and other religious sects.

There is already a tendency for emotional vitalistic attitudes toward nature to supersede reason in influencing political action. In the eastern United States, pressure by activist "anti–animal cruelty" movements has been responsible for preventing the reduction of surplus deer through organized hunts in overpopulated habitats within wildlife refuges, where destruction of the food plants through overbrowsing and the wholesale starvation of the deer were inevitable without a substantial reduction in the number of deer. In some western states, feral horses have also generated similar controversies over management of wildlife habitats on public lands. The anthropomorphizing of nature by Disney, the Forest Service's "Smokey the Bear" imagery, and commercial TV in general, has contributed to a distorted view of nature by the public. Activist groups motivated by religious attitudes toward nature tend to be emotionally ideological rather than ecologically factual in selecting targets for their attention. Consequently, immediate, critical, and often dirty environmental problems, such as air and water pollution and the loss of wetlands through solid-waste disposal, are often overlooked among emotional concerns for the lives of individual animals or efforts to protect a seemingly remote wilderness area, apparently because the relationship between a sewer outfall and pristine nature may appear obscure. I do not mean to imply that the causes such groups are concerned with may not be worthy ones, but rather that they often are irrelevant to ecological reality or to major environmental problems.

An eco-religion that explains human relationship to other forms of matter through metaphysical or mystical constructs will ultimately suffer the same problem of dissolution as have religions in the past. As new knowledge develops, such dissolution is usually preceded by intransigence and militant opposition toward the dissemination of "offending" knowledge. One wonders how many Giordano Bruno's might be at least figuratively burned at the stake in the name of an eco-religion. Although an eco-religion might be popularly accepted as well as effective in countering human destruction of the environment today, it would appear to be a short-term solution to environmental problems, and short-sightedness already has the distinction of being the root cause of our current environmental dilemma.

An alternative to an eco-religion as the basis for explaining the human relationship to nature is a scientifically grounded eco-philosophy that can provide the foundation from which human beings can achieve an understanding of nature, as well as providing guidelines for those human activities that may influence nature. It is argued that a scientific eco-philosophy that fails to recognize the metaphysical concepts of the "uniqueness of life" and the "unity of nature," and which is dependent upon human knowledge and human ability to synthesize that knowledge, will necessarily be anthropocentric. Naysayers may conclude that humankind will continue to exert dominance over nature by manipulating, exploiting, and subduing nature as in the past, with the same spiraling sequence of detrimental consequences. This alternative is possible, however, it is less likely to occur if such an eco-philosophy provides a realistic view of nature and of our place within it. By a "realistic view of nature," I mean that view which most closely fits existing knowledge of living systems. Although such a view may be based on scientific objectivity, it need not exclude the existence of emotional feelings toward nature.

You may ask, "Are we capable of developing a system of ethics to govern our actions that is not dominantly egocentric?" This question perhaps cannot be answered now, and further, it may be meaningless within the context of human thought. Certainly any eco-religion that is a human construct is also subject to the same pitfalls of human egocentrism. Further, it seems illogical to expect that a philosophy whose primary objective is to guide our relationship to nature should not also focus principally upon humankind. Man is without question the organism with the most dominant impact upon the biosphere, and it is only through the regulation of human activities that we can have any conscious influence on our own future as a species or that of anything else. The greatest logical difficulty in the development of a scientific eco-philosophy is that of resolving the recognition of our non-preferential relationship to other organisms. Or stated differently, resolving man's ecological humility with the "need" for humans to place the interest of our own species first.

Cynics will cite this apparent inconsistency, which is exemplified by such misleading phraseology as "for the benefit of mankind" or "for our enjoyment or use." In everyday parlance such phrases most often refer to the avarice of individuals or small groups of individuals seeking short-term material gain, and they are quite unrelated to the altruistic concept of the long-term welfare of mankind that is incorporated into eco-philosophy. What may "benefit" an individual at an instant in time within a social system that emphasizes material values, such as the rapid exploitation of a natural resource, may be wholly detrimental to the long-term "benefit" of society or to mankind as a whole. There should be no shame in protecting endangered species and in setting aside wilderness areas and nature preserves solely for the satisfaction of human interests. On the other hand, it should not be considered ecologically immoral to use a resource when in light of the best available knowledge such use appears to be in the long-term interest of mankind, not just to produce jobs in today's economy.

Ethics are of human origin and the ethics of man's relationship to all other life and matter are and must be human constructs. There is no basis to assume that other organisms have special rights to existence and if we impose such rights we are in effect playing God. Nevertheless, we can be in awe of the integrity and complexity of nature and the uniqueness of organisms without being hypocritical. We can and should have the wisdom to recognize the present or potential value of living systems to mankind either through some direct benefit or use or through indirect ecological interrelationships. The concept of mankind represents a continuum through time and at any point in time we must recognize our responsibility as stewards of the Earth and its resources for future generations.

In the absence of knowledge leading to sound conclusions, wisdom always calls for caution. If we cannot predict with a high degree of reliability the consequences of our activities that alter the state of matter, we should proceed carefully. Inaction is preferable to irreversible destruction of the environment wrought in ignorance. But now I am guilty of using a word with very ambiguous meaning. Ecologists most often speak of "destruction" of the environment as any alteration of the environment by mankind that is inconsistent with natural ecological sequences. The word "destroy" must always have a frame of reference. In the extreme sense, with regard to the physical world "destroy" can mean any change in the physical state of matter because that state which preceded the change will be "destroyed" by the change. We can examine a more relevant example. Take the case where a super highway is to be built through a virgin forest. To ecologists, this act of man is classified as destructive because it will result in the irreversible alteration of the ecology of the area. It may even border on the sacrilegious to religiously motivated nature advocates. Motorists, on the other hand, will be impressed by the apparent utility of the highway, while the highway engineers and builders will see the highway as the culmination of their creative efforts; the very antithesis of the concept of destruction. What is the reality or "true analysis" of this situation? The answer must be that there is no reality except in the eyes of those who perceive it as such, for if that forest were to burn as a result of lightning the ecologist would be forced to acknowledge that it had been destroyed only within the current human time frame of reference. Given time, the forest would grow back. Indeed, the fire might well be an essential element in the overall ecology of that specific area which ultimately produced the forest.

Perhaps the greatest obstacle to the universal adoption of an eco-philosophy (or an eco-religion) is human reluctance to accept the concept of the unity of mankind. Although this concept can be biologically demonstrated, it is too often socially rejected. Man's kinship with his fellow man is obvious at the level of family, friends, and community, but it becomes more difficult to grasp and to believe in as distances and cultures become more remote. Physical remoteness in our modern world is no longer the significant barrier to cross-cultural understanding as it has been in the past. Nevertheless, cultural differences continue to remain real barriers to cross-cultural understanding in all parts of the world. There is no guaranteed solution to what might be called the "human environmental dilemma." It appears obvious, however, that the clarity of wisdom that we must have to meet the challenges that lie ahead can be achieved only through a deeper understanding of our place in nature and from the humility that this understanding will produce.

Cultural Influences on Landscape Aesthetics: Some Comparisons between Scandinavia and Northwestern North America

Who appreciates a particular landscape? Is it the people who live upon it, those who visit it, or perhaps those who understand its cultural or ecological history? Is a natural landscape "better," "more desirable," of "greater quality," or in some way superior to an altered landscape? Can man and his works be part of a natural landscape? What are unique elements in a landscape? Is the past worth preserving? If so, to what extent? These are only a few of the questions that must be answered if priorities are to be set whereby land will continue to be a positive force in man's aesthetic stimulation.

Throughout North America and Europe, there is unending discussion about environmental quality, and there is, of course, general agreement on the desirability of maintaining or enhancing such quality. There is not, however, universal agreement on what constitutes quality in the environment. One's judgments as to quality necessarily reflect the nature of your value system. Value may be represented in dollars and cents or in nonmonetary criteria, such as aesthetic, cultural, or historical worth. The quality of a work of architecture, for example, is often determined by the money and entrepreneurial efforts that have been expended upon it. Yet buildings and landscapes may also be venerated simply because they communicate history. One can appreciate that they are not readily duplicated and that a component of their beauty is their reflection of the passage of time.

The natural landscape, however, is too often taken for granted, particularly so in frontier areas, such as portions of the western United States and northern Canada, where there remain large expanses of undisturbed landscape. Our indifference is simply a function of our failure to understand the uniqueness of natural ecological systems. We cannot comprehend how complex and time-consuming a job it is to "make" a natural landscape. It requires only a few years to build the largest buildings, construct the highest dams, or span the widest rivers. And the United States fulfilled its objective of putting man on the moon in less than a decade. But it took millions of years to "build" the Grand Canyon, and thousands of years are required to produce a mature redwood forest (Miller 1965). It is obvious that man's time frame is microscopic in contrast to nature's. With such a limited perspective, it is not surprising that we fail to appreciate the dynamics of ecology, despite the recent incorporation of this word into our household vocabulary.

In the Western world, because of our preoccupation with economics, we too often tend to associate value with money. As an example, within such a value system, if land is not readily developable, it will be held in low regard. It is the norm that land be appraised only for its potential dollar return and not for its noncommercial value to mankind. This attitude appears to be at the base of our emerging land dilemma. In their accelerated evolution from a relatively stationary agrarian people to a highly mobile industrial society, Americans have lost their traditional ties to the land.

Understanding ecology and acknowledging its relevance to man, however, does not mean that man must somehow stop tampering with nature. Man is very much a part of the environment, and his physical presence inevitably will cause some modification or change. A "quality" environment is often more than just the undisturbed natural environment. But the evidences of man in the environment should reflect his understanding of his rightful place therein. Enhancing the quality of the environment need not result only from the conscious efforts of man. It may be accidental or coincidental. For example, a farm building constructed in the conventional manner of an area or a well-built log cabin in the woods are often compatible with their respective surroundings, because they are the products of long periods of trial and development and because they make effective use of native and recyclable materials to fulfill utilitarian purposes. Their structure is dependent upon a thorough knowledge of the evolution of local design. Such design is not merely fortuitous, but the result of deliberative action by earlier inhabitants to build into these structures characteristics reflective of their personal needs, their native materials, and their climate and terrain (Rudofsky 1964; Rapoport 1969). Unfortunately, however, too often such deliberation is absent from modern man's new activities in new environments.

When such structures have aged and weathered, their beauty is increased because of their apparent assimilation with the landscape. Also with time, the surrounding forests "compensate" for the openings made by man, as trees of the forest edge respond to the increased light and become foliated nearly to the ground. Such openings take on a "natural" or "no longer disturbed" appearance. Finally, the very appearance of age would seem to command a subconscious respect in the observer since that appearance calls to mind man's historical attachment to the area. To be able to visualize ties with one's ancestors, whether in the recent or ancient past, is to be able to appreciate more deeply one's heritage.

Cultural landscapes of long tradition are being lost at a rapid rate throughout the world as land-use patterns undergo change imposed by developments in agricultural technology and the pressures of expanding human populations (UNESCO 1970:31–46). Agricultural activity upon the landscape tends particularly to foster an appreciation by the viewer of the mutually restorative relationship of man with the land.[15] The abuse of that relationship, however, is strikingly manifest in several forms, such as erosion, unconsolidated accumulation of rubbish, quarries, and strip mines (Darling 1969). Increasingly, these visually offensive forms replace once prevalent pastoral scenes. For example, throughout much of Scandinavia, the pastoral landscape is disappearing as more and more subsistence farms are abandoned and forests take over (Ahlen 1966). While the abandonment of marginal farmland and their forestation may be desirable in some cases from an economic and social welfare viewpoint, many Scandinavians also value the pastoral landscape for its aesthetic worth. As a consequence, while certain branches of government encourage subsistence farmers to move to industrial areas where labor is in demand, and while they subsidize the forestation of

---

15. For an excellent discussion of man's changing attitudes toward the landscape, see Shepard 1967.

unused farmlands, other efforts in government are directed toward preserving the historical landscape (National Swedish Environmental Protection Board 1969; National Swedish Environmental Protection Board, Ministry of Local Government and Labour 1970).

The pastoral or "grazing" landscape of the Scandinavian region has been maintained in the past by heavy grazing of cattle, sheep, and horses, plus cultivation of crops on the less rocky sites. This type of subsistence farming has a long tradition, and, in terms of high production agriculture on the North American continent, it can be considered misuse of the land. Generally, there is no supplemental fertilization of grazed areas in addition to the excrement of the grazing animals; the soil is shallow and rocky and often has high clay content. Nitrogen and phosphorus in the soil are usually below standards for crop production (Berglund 1969; Fries 1969; Maimer 1969). Productivity from the land is low both in plant and animal matter. In drier or windier climates, severe erosion tends to follow such land-use practices, as has been the case in western North America, North Africa, the Middle East, China, and many other parts of the world (UNESCO 1970). In most of Scandinavia, a moist climate, the shelter of the surrounding forests, and the protection of the ground cover provided by the winter snows (livestock must be quartered in barns and fed hay during winter), virtually eliminate the threat of soil erosion. On the other hand, the aesthetic effect of this type of land use is very pleasing. In spring, the park-like vistas are colored by a diverse array of flowers. Artificial fertilization will increase the productivity of these lands, but it will destroy much of their beauty because the increased soil fertility favors grasses that crowd out the annual and perennial flowering plants (Ahlen 1966; Berglund 1969). Ecological diversity is then lost.

Some woody plants, such as solitary juniper shrubs and hardwood trees with fully foliated crowns, remain scattered throughout the fields; the former because of their resistance to grazing by cattle, and the latter because of special protection by farmers. In the past, oak was favored as an open grown tree because its acorns were used for animal food. Moreover, oak, birch, and other hardwoods were valued for special uses such as the building of boats, wagons, and sleds, and the creation of tools and utensils. Farmers allowed these desired trees to become established by fencing certain areas from grazing long enough for the young trees to grow above the reach of grazing livestock.

In order to preserve the pastoral landscape for its cultural significance and its aesthetic value, research efforts through the Institute of Economic Botany in Uppsala, Sweden, are directed toward increasing the efficiency and economy of cattle and sheep farming.[16] The objective is to provide economic incentive for farmers to stay on the land. It is recognized that loss of the pastoral landscape, apart from its cultural and aesthetic significance, will mean the loss of certain plant and animal associations that are unique to this ecological type. Wildlife such as the roe deer, hedgehog, badger, wood pigeon, and many songbirds are bound to local traditions and folklore. The "edge effect," which is a product of the field and forest interface, is important to these wildlife species (Ahlen 1966).

In some ways, the effort to maintain the grazing landscape in Sweden is analogous to recent attitudes toward clear-cutting of mature forests in northwestern North America (Behan 1967; United States Congress 1970). Because of their training, foresters look upon "over mature" forests as wasteful and inefficient use of the land, while second-growth stands of trees, with their more uniform, lighter green color, represent more efficient land use. In the latter, board feet produced per acre per year is greatly in excess of that in the over mature forests, where growth just replaces loss through decay, and the total marketable board feet of timber is less than will be available when the second-growth, even-aged stands reach marketable size (Behan 1967).

Foresters also often argue that second-growth forests are aesthetically more pleasing than the over mature virgin forests. Their emphasis on land for utilitarian purposes confuses the conceptual bases of beauty with those of utility. Psychologists and aestheticians agree that beauty is rooted in sensual pleasure and that conceptions of beauty are metaphorical extensions of the experience of sensory gratification.[17] Beauty, therefore, is an end in itself and needs no excuse for being, while utility is the means for the attainment of

---

16. Author's discussion with Dr. E. Steen, Institute of Economic Botany, Uppsala, Sweden, 1972.

17. For an excellent discussion of beauty in relation to its psychological and cultural roots, see R. G. Collingwood, *The Principles of Art* (Oxford, England: Clarendon Press, 1938).

something else. Many conservation-oriented people outside of the forestry profession, however, see beauty in the old, virgin forests and are offended by the geometrical patchwork appearance of logged areas and the uniformity of the second-growth trees. Among some of these conservationists, aesthetic appreciation of the climax forest may also reflect a cultural bias that results from a "purist" ideology, that the environment undisturbed by man is more desirable than the disturbed environment. Cultural biases, therefore, exist both among the foresters and the conservationists, but in opposite directions and often with entirely different motivating bases.

As to the pastoral landscape in much of Scandinavia, we find the situation somewhat reversed, in that an ecologist, agronomist, or soil expert appraising the situation there would most likely find the grazing landscape offensive to "what his training tells him." The abundance of herbs, the absence of shrubs, and the apparent lack of forest regeneration all may be technically undesirable (Berglund 1969:29–34; Dr. E. Steen, pers. comm. 1972). The high herb/low grass ratio is symptomatic of the overgrazing that has taken place on naturally poor soils without the addition of fertilizers, and from the professional viewpoint these lands would be "better off" in forest. The absence of shrubs and lack of forest regeneration reflect the failure of the forests to reproduce themselves (Ahlen 1966), and in terms of the most efficient productivity of the land, it might be better to let it return to forest and grow wood. The pastoral landscape can then be looked upon as poor use of the land and, from that point of view, undesirable.

The point here, however, is that the grazing landscape has beauty as a *result* of these so-called abuses of the land. The pattern of land use has created the ecological diversity that is the basis of its beauty. Ironically, fertilization would reduce the complex of flowering plants and increase the grasses (Berglund 1969). Allowing the forest to regenerate would eliminate the openings that provide the vistas necessary to achieve the park-like appearance and the open setting for the farm buildings, specimen trees, domestic animals, and fully foliated trees of the forest that face the field edge.

It is apparent in this situation that conflicts exist between cultural attitudes and scientific training. A person's profession and way of life obviously influences his attitude toward the land. Farmers tend to respect the land because it is the apparent source of their livelihood. Miners often deface the land in their efforts to reach what lies underneath its surface, which to others may seem like they have little respect for the land at the surface. Engineers and construction workers may look upon nature as an obstacle to their work. Trees are cut to make way for roads and other works of man, rivers are to be bridged or dammed, climatic extremes are to be ameliorated through construction of suitable shelters for man, and hills are to be lowered or tunneled to establish faster transportation corridors.

With such a wide divergence in attitudes about land values, who is to decide the highest priority of use for a given piece of land: those who appreciate its aesthetic worth independent of utility, or those who recognize its potential for productivity? If we relegate to a low priority the concept of greatest efficiency of productivity of the land for the benefit of man and place beauty first, is this in conflict with an increasingly more crowded planet with greater and greater demands being placed on the land to meet the "needs" of the expanding population? All too frequently, relative values of the land are couched in such phraseology so that aesthetic value is made to appear as a nonessential luxury that must yield to the material demands of an affluent society. Beauty, however, is a legitimate product of the landscape and should be more easily justified as essential to human well-being and quality of life than is a second TV set, a power lawnmower, or an electric can opener. Although the importance of beauty to human existence is a common subject of classic literature, modern man all too often loses sight of aesthetics in his devotion to economics. In spite of the obviously justified humanitarian pleas for increased availability of foodstuffs for the undernourished people of the world, "man cannot live by bread alone." Man only too readily alters his environment, but he cannot remove himself from environmental influences. He is, in spite of himself, a product of the environment he creates.

David using binoculars to scout
for game on a hunt on the Taylor
Highway, early 1950s. COURTESY OF
DAVID KLEIN.

20
Hunting Ethics and the Morality of Hunting

The ethical morality and standards associated with hunting as a sport have their roots in earliest human cultures. Wildlife was valued as a resource from the land that sustained their cultural existence. But as largely mobile hunter-gatherers transitioned to more stable agriculturists who were tied to cropping the land to feed themselves and their livestock, the traditional dependency on wildlife with its associated hunting ethics based on a melding of guidelines and taboos began to change. The foundation of the modern Western world's pattern of hunting ethics was defined and formalized in Europe in the Middle Ages, based on the attachments to the land and wildlife and cultural practices within the class hierarchy of feudalism in northern Europe. It was this style of traditional European hunting ethics that the colonists brought with them when they came over to settle North America.

In the British colonies in North America, harvest of wildlife provided an essential aid to early settlers attempting to establish farmsteads as they converted the natural landscape into largely agricultural production. Hunting of wildlife was also the source of meat sold in stores in communities developing as service centers; many of these later became the larger towns and ultimately cities. Wildlife was considered a natural resource of the land, available without restrictions to those who would seek it out. As the human population expanded in numbers and distribution through colonization and settlement, there was little concern over the impact of increasing harvest of wildlife and the subsequent habitat loss. Subsistence use of wildlife by the Indian tribes in the eastern colonies initially may have been acknowledged by the early European settlers as sustainable and compatible with the pre-settlement natural environment; however, as the landscape was altered by the advancing Western culture in the New World, hunting by the Native Americans became incompatible with land converted to pasture and crop production. The colonists came to see the Native Americans and their traditional hunting as competitors for a limited resource.

While hunting was still considered a necessary part of rural life, the focus for the settlers shifted toward agriculture as the main means of making a living and supporting a family. As the country developed and populations shifted away from rural and land-based lifestyles, hunting became more of a sporting activity instead of a survival skill. By the 1920s, sport and big game trophy hunting had become a popular pastime. For the wealthiest, wilderness hunting expeditions to Africa or Alaska in search of exotic prey were particular favorites. However, for some, especially in more urban settings, hunting began to be associated with the primitive or the savage, and came to be viewed negatively.

I first became aware that ethical standards were a traditional and essential part of hunting as a sport in America when I was a boy in Vermont in the 1930s. My father was a hunter who taught my older brother and me to respect the animals being hunted. My great-uncle and family friend, A. P. Curtis, was a strong advocate of sportsmanship, had a keen interest in all wildlife, not just the charismatic species, and was well read on the natural history of birds and mammals. Being sensitive to concerns I had expressed as a young boy over increased poaching of wildlife and killing of nongame bird species, A. P. presented me with his copy of the book *Our Vanishing Wild Life: Its Extermination and Preservation*, by William T. Hornaday, then director of the New York Zoological Society (Hornaday 1913). Hornaday, an early conservationist and ardent hunter himself, described and documented the decline in wildlife population numbers at the time and the increasing threats of extinction of several native bird species. He also was openly critical of the deterioration of traditionally valued sport hunting ethics, placing major blame on the production of semiautomatic, multiple-shot firearms that used ammunition with increased killing power, and the subsequent promotional advertisements by manufacturers for their sporting arms and ammunition. These industry-initiated actions designed to increase the killing efficiency of hunting firearms resulted in an increase in the daily harvest of game by individual hunters, but preceded action by state agencies to enact regulations that shortened the length of hunting seasons and set daily bag limits on wildlife.

Hornaday's book helped solidify my views as a nature-oriented child about the importance of maintaining high ethical standards if hunting was to be maintained as the sporting tradition that had been instilled in me. This concept gained further relevance in my mind during a course I took at the University of Connecticut titled *Wildlife Management* that was taught by Franklin McCamey, who placed major emphasis on Aldo Leopold's approach to wildlife and hunting. Throughout my subsequent professional life, the relationship between maintaining hunting ethics and managing wildlife and their habitats has been of major importance to me. It is particularly critical when attempting to manage wildlife populations while still providing sustainable harvests for both sport and subsistence hunters, as well as leaving enough animals for the nonconsumptive users of the wildlife (photographers, wildlife viewers, and those seeking to better understand the wildlife species). Things like not wasting game, abiding by prescribed hunting seasons and bag limits, and practicing "fair chase" are ways hunters can ensure their target animal populations will be maintained for the future.

One of the main elements of ethical hunting has been the concept of "fair chase." Fair chase is defined by the Boone and Crockett Club (BCC) as "the ethical, sportsmanlike, and lawful pursuit and taking of any free-ranging wild, native North American big game animal in a manner that does not give the hunter an improper advantage over such animals" (Boone and Crockett Club 2017). The BCC, established in 1887 by Theodore Roosevelt and other leading wildlife conservationists, many of whom were ardent trophy hunters, has long been an advocate for high ethical standards among hunters. The organization is the standard record keeper of North American "big game" trophies, and their policy is to only list those trophy animals killed using fair chase methods. Nevertheless, many hunters look upon BCC's fair chase standards as applicable only to wealthy trophy hunters, such as those of the early 1900s who would go on a month-long hunt just as much for the enjoyment of tracking animals and enjoying the wilderness as for harvesting animals. This practice has long since disappeared in the fast pace of our increasingly urbanized society. Despite BCC's admirable effort to improve ethical standards for hunting, it is apparent that in many places sport hunting has deteriorated into an obsession to get the biggest animal in the shortest time, with little regard for species populations or habitat issues.

It is interesting to note that BCC seems to violate its own ethical code of emphasizing respect for wildlife, when its journal, *Fair Chase*, contains full-page color advertisements for hunting ammunition that is "ideal for varmint and predator hunting" because it provides "rapid fragmentation upon impact" (Boone and Crockett Club 2015:29). The standard dictionary definition of *varmints* is "objectionable birds and mammals, inclusive of humans," a definition not likely acceptable to either hunters or nonhunters. As early as 1933, Aldo Leopold concluded that "vermin" control was irrelevant to wildlife management (Leopold 1933:385). It is more than ironic that after more than eighty years some US ammunition companies still attempt to sell bullets specially designed for killing vermin or varmints, which is what they label raccoons, foxes, bobcat, weasel, squirrel, opossum, skunk, porcupine, groundhog, and coyote. The implication is that they are "bad" animals and killing them will benefit other "good" wildlife. However, several of these are game species valued by hunters in many states with prescribed hunting seasons and bag limits.

The first part of this chapter, titled "Hunting: A Sacred Game or a Damnable Sport," was a treatise I first composed in the 1970s that represents my views on questions surrounding the morality of hunting and the conflicting views between those who hunt and those who oppose it. This was never published and I have edited and revised it for this book to reflect my current thinking in light of modern circumstances.

The second part of the chapter, titled "Ethics and Bear Management in Alaska: A Case Study," is based on a piece I wrote in 2012 titled "Bear Snaring Defies Our Values: Management Should Be Based on Respect for the Bruin's Ecosystem Role" that was published as a "Community Perspective" in the *Fairbanks Daily News-Miner* newspaper (Klein 2012). This was at a time when the snaring of brown bears at baiting stations was being proposed by the Alaska Board of Game as a way to reduce bear predation on moose calves. At that time, moose were targeted for increase because of public outcry about low numbers of moose available for hunting opportunities. Moose is favored as a food source by both subsistence and personal-use hunters in many parts of Alaska. However, many Alaskans opposed bear baiting as a standard harvest technique because it was not "fair chase," and it encouraged the bears to associate human food with humans. There is significant evidence that this sets a dangerous precedent and has caused numerous conflicts in communities around the state. As a member of the Alaska Chapter of The Wildlife Society, I participated in drafting a position statement titled "Baiting, Reductions, and Sale of Parts of Brown/Grizzly and Black Bears," which opposed baiting of bears as a standard harvest technique. Nevertheless, the Alaska Board of Game ignored this opposition from both traditional hunters and nonhunters and approved bear baiting.

I have included this example of bear baiting because it reflects my long-standing concern over the eroding valuation of wildlife and the apparent decline of hunting ethics among many of those who hunt and define themselves as sportsmen. I believe this weakening of hunting ethics is correlated with increased mechanization and commercialization of wildlife harvest methodology. In Alaska, I have witnessed a correlation between this change in ethical hunting and the state's system of wildlife management. The members of the Alaska Board of Game are appointed by the governor and are not required to have education or training in wildlife ecology or management, and sport hunters generally dominate the membership. Thus, decisions tend to be made in favor of sport hunting over species conservation or wildlife viewing, and there seems to be little consideration of what constitutes ethical practices. By doing this, our Board of Game is encouraging the degradation of ethical hunting and adding to the negative perceptions the nonhunting public already has toward hunting.

Hunting: A Sacred Game or a Damnable Sport?

Polarity in viewpoints characterizes the misunderstanding that surrounds hunting and has led to the proliferation of anti-hunting sentiment both within and between cultures in North America, as well as in Europe (Lynge 1992; Kerasote 1993; Nelson 1998). Increasing urbanization appears to have brought about increased commercialization of hunting and the associated loss of traditional hunting ethics, and, conversely, led to the increased political growth of the anti-hunting movement. Collectively, all of these factors have threatened the future of hunting as a sport.

Hunting, as a complex relationship of man to nature and a sport with strong historical roots, is characteristically misunderstood by nonhunters. The anti-hunting "passion" and loss of stature of the hunter in the eyes of a growing segment of the public seems tied to the increasing association of the gun with crime, war, violence, and the direct agent of death and destruction, and to emotional attitudes toward nature stimulated by the current focus on ecology. Anti-killing sentiment directed toward hunting also appears to derive from the projection of Judeo-Christian morality into nature, which has fostered the proliferation of vitalistic attitudes toward nature. In the associated melding of cultures, including those with strong emphasis on the role of hunting, hunters have contributed to their own deteriorating public image by failing to emphasize and maintain the qualitative aspects of the hunt and by assuming a defensive stance with regard to the ethics of hunting.

The traditional justifications given in defense of hunting have failed to provide the basis for understanding the sport, which is essential if it is to be accepted by the nonhunting public. For example, hunting has been promoted as a merciful act that is preferable to leaving animals to die in nature by predation, starvation, illness, or bad weather. Or that hunting is a form of wildlife management because hunters intervene to eliminate what are considered "bad" animal populations and protect the "good" ones. This view of nature as being "good" and "bad" has been common among the general public, whether they are associated with strong opinions about hunting or not. They appear to result from the projection of Christian morality into nature: that the "weak" and the "defenseless" animals, primarily the herbivores, are the innocent ones to be protected, while the carnivores, those animals that must kill to live, are the "evil" or "sinful" ones to be eliminated. Humans have even taken this categorization one step further by our tendency to anthropomorphize animals, as evidenced by classic folklore with creatures such as the big bad wolf, the sly fox, the gentle lamb, and more recently Mickey Mouse, Bambi, and Smokey the Bear.

Another justification often given for man to continue to yield to this primitive urge to hunt is that it is neither ethically nor morally wrong, but is the way of nature. If hunting is part of nature, then the hunter qualifies as a top predator, whether he is an urban sport hunter or a Native American for whom hunting remains part of his or her culture. This explanation tends to avoid critical analysis, because it is extremely difficult to establish the relationship of modern man's behavior to that of his evolutionary past. Nevertheless, several authors have attempted to do this, for example, Konrad Lorenz in 1952 in *King Solomon's Ring* (Lorenz 1952), Robert Ardrey in 1961 in *African Genesis: A Personal Investigation into the Animal Origins and Nature of Man* (Ardrey 1961), and Desmond Morris in 1967 in *The Naked Ape: A Zoologist's Study of the Human Animal* (Morris 1967). These, and others, have been controversial works, and they have by no means resolved the question. There is, however, little question of man's hunting ancestry. Washburn and Lancaster, in their 1968 article, "The Evolution of Hunting," point out that man has been a hunter for 99 percent of his history and emphasize that "the biology, psychology, and customs that separate us from the apes—all these we owe to the hunter of time past" (Washburn and Lancaster 1968:303). Although the record is incomplete and speculation looms larger than fact, for those who would understand the origin and nature of human behavior, there is no choice but to try to understand "man the hunter."

Paul Shepard, writing about the role of hunting in human evolution in his 1967 book *Man in the Landscape: A Historic View of the Esthetics of Nature*, saw hunting as "a sacred game," which, in contrast to agrarian pursuits and the technological society stemming from it, fosters the veneration of nature (Shepard 1967). He viewed hunting as the optimum stimulant for development of the human mind, which itself is the evolutionary product of natural selection as influenced by hunting. In comparison, Aldo Leopold in his 1949 book *A Sand County Almanac*, saw hunting as representing man's effort to re-create an aspect of his more primitive past when he was bound more closely to nature than he is at present (Leopold 1949). Leopold placed emphasis on man's cultural history rather than his evolutionary origin. He stressed the importance of restricting the application of man's modern technological advantages to the hunt if this value of hunting was to be preserved. Similarly, Ortega y Gasset observed: "As the weapon became more and more effective, man imposed more and more limitations on himself . . . as if passing beyond a certain limit in that relationship might annihilate the essential character of the hunt, transforming it into pure killing and destruction" (Ortega y Gasset 1972[1995]:53).

The deteriorating image of hunting in the public eye seems at least partly associated with apparent contradictions of sportsmanship with the increasing use of aircraft, all-terrain vehicles, and other highly sophisticated products of technology in order to accomplish a hunt. While a case can be made for the relationship of hunting to our cultural traditions, it is certainly debatable whether it is essential to human well-being that we hunt, or that we must find outlets for hunting motivations by actually hunting.

While the "hunting ancestry" argument attempts to explain man's psychological motivation for hunting, it avoids the basic issues of ethics and morality as they relate to hunting. It is like saying that if man has been a killer in his evolutionary past, then it is natural for him to kill, and therefore justifiable. This is not good logic, however, because modern man is no longer living in a "natural" way, and there is ample precedent for the need as well as the ability of man to control certain aspects of his biologically motivated behavior in the broader interests of society.

The popularization of ecology and the associated environmental concern that has developed in recent decades has also been accompanied by emotional and quasi-religious attitudes toward nature, as in *The Biophilia Hypothesis* (Kellert and Wilson 1993) and "Gaia and Geognosy" (Margulis and Lovelock 1989). These attitudes often focus on individual animals rather than populations and ecosystems, and provide the basis for much of the current anti-hunting sentiment. Pantheism, with its denial of the superiority of humans over nature, and a new "vitalism" that suggests life is sustained and explained by an unmeasurable force or energy and cannot be reduced to a mechanistic process, characterize many of the nature-oriented and anti-hunting movements that emerged with the countercultures and social change of the 1960s and 1970s. Such views of nature usually emphasize the uniqueness of life, and the implicit assumption is made that rationality exists in nature, and that nature is purposeful and with inherent goals and morality.

In the past, anti-hunters often claimed support from Albert Schweitzer, particularly from his concept of "reverence for life." Schweitzer's reverence for life ethic, expounded in his 1950 book, *The Animal World of Albert Schweitzer*, holds that life is a unique entity beyond human comprehension and is the gift of God (Schweitzer 1950). Man should, therefore, respect life in all living organisms, and he should avoid causing suffering and death if at all possible. Schweitzer's renown as a theologian, humanitarian, and philosopher made his "reverence for life" ethic virtually an authoritarian one. It seemed to be unchallengeable by the layperson, because of the human tendency to believe, or at least to want to believe, that a man like Schweitzer must be right in one area of thought because his philosophical pronouncements in so many other areas are believed to morally "correct," of high ethical standards, and imbued with human compassion.

Paul Shepard, in his 1967 book *Man in the Landscape* devoted an entire chapter to analysis and critique of Albert Schweitzer's ethical perspective in relation to hunting. Shepard's analysis elaborated on how Schweitzer's reverence for life dictum was an absolute ethic with no qualifications and no exemptions, as was the Hindu Ashima upon which it was modeled a commandment against all killing (Shepard 1967). If Schweitzer is to be interpreted literally—and he himself stressed that this is what should be done—then we must assume that he conceived of all living things as wards of humankind. This would include predators, plants, and disease organisms. In spite of this strong commitment to the ethic, he made rather arbitrary qualitative distinctions and exceptions in practice. For example, he kept a gun in Africa and used it to shoot snakes, predatory mammals, and birds, which he justified as protection for the domestic animals that were kept within the compound. And in his writings, he frequently refers to the struggle to subdue and destroy the ever-encroaching tropical vegetation. So, ironically, many of his efforts in Africa were devoted toward destroying life despite his "reverence for life."

The extreme projection of Schweitzer's ethic to include plants and disease organisms may appear to be deliberately clouding the issue, but it is necessary to emphasize the contradictions inherent in his position. Paul Shepard pointed out that Schweitzer did not arrive at this concept from the perspective of one who loves nature, but rather he looked upon nature as the "cruel drama of the will-to-live divided against itself" (ibid.:191). Man, as God's agent, could intervene to limit the cruelty of nature. Ironically, this is the same ethical justification discussed above in support of hunting.

Another viewpoint common to those opposed to hunting was expressed in a 1957 *Saturday Review* article by Joseph Wood Krutch where he states:

"Any activity which includes killing as a pleasurable end in itself is damnable" (Krutch 1957:9). Krutch viewed the hunter as one who "does evil for evil's sake." This viewpoint expresses a lack of understanding of hunting as a complex sequence of activities among which killing is only one of many components. It is like asking, "How can the farmer find enjoyment in raising animals to be slaughtered?" It should be obvious that killing or causing pain is neither the objective of animal husbandry nor of hunting, but they are incidental although indispensable parts of both of these human activities. The hunter's veneration of the prey toward which the violence of the hunt is directed is difficult for the nonhunter to appreciate. As José Ortega y Gasset said in his 1972 classic book, *Meditations on Hunting*, where he tries to get at the root of man's hunting history:

> Strictly speaking, the essence of sportive hunting is not raising the animal to the level of man, but something much more spiritual than that: a conscious and almost religious humbling of man which limits his superiority and lowers him toward the animal. (Ortega y Gasset 1972[1995]:111)

Viewed superficially by the nonhunter, Ortega y Gasset's provocative assessment of hunting may appear as a confession confirming generally held views that in hunting man returns to a primitive and savage state. While this view is not denied by Ortega y Gasset, his statement was made in defense of the behavior of the hunter.

Anti-hunters may have lost sight of this distinction when they argue that man has evolved, at least culturally, beyond his savage ancestral ways. In the view of some anti-hunters, the modern man who hunts is exhibiting an atavistic urge and has not matured psychologically, socially, or culturally. This argument does not make a case against hunting, but rather maligns its supposed therapeutic values.

Along a similar vein in the 1960s, those who hunt were often accused by anti-hunting groups of doing so because of the conscious or subconscious feeling of masculinity that they derive from the sport (Gilbert 1967). Most men who hunt would acknowledge that an enhanced feeling of manliness derives from the hunt, albeit incidental to other aspects of hunting. However, should such men be labeled as sexually insecure and the gun portrayed as a phallic symbol to them? If so, then it would seem that the sexual consciousness that is so much a part of our daily lives is also to be condemned. As with the previous argument, this one also fails to make a case against hunting. Instead, it relates hunting to man's psychological health rather than challenging it on the basis of ethical or moral grounds.

The question of the justification for hunting is part of a much larger question: that of the morality of man's exploitation of other organisms. By exploitation, I mean any manipulation of other organisms by man that results in altering their ways of life, or imposing upon them hardship, injury, or death. For practical purposes of this discussion, in addition to hunting, this would include domestication, experimentation with animals, and destruction of wildlife habitat. However, the list could be extended to include the impact of man on all forms of life without greatly altering the logic involved in its justification.

The complicated relationship humans have with animals apparently lies deep in our evolutionary past. Sigfried Giedion, architect, philosopher, and writer, emphasized that animals were simultaneously objects of adoration, life-giving food, and hunted quarry. He thought the two-fold significance of the animal as object of worship and source of nourishment was an outcome of a mentality that did not confine the sacred to the thereafter, suggesting that the sacred and the profane were inseparable (Giedion 1963). Giedion saw modern man's attitude toward nature as anthropomorphic, in contrast to a zoomorphic attitude of primitive man.

Man has traditionally attempted to justify his exploitation of other animals on the basis of the value of such action to mankind. Such justification has been of utilitarian or pragmatic nature with very little reference to, or consideration of, ethics or morality. Man has argued that his use of other animals is essential for human well-being and survival, and that he is dependent upon them for food, clothing, and as beasts of burden. Man as an individual, however, is not dependent upon animal protein to live a healthy life, although there is a common misconception to this effect in the Western world. The sacred cow may seem incongruous with a shortage of protein and wholesale malnutrition in the East, but it is symbolic of a religious heritage that is quite foreign to our meat-eating habits. Nor are animal skins and fibers or animal traction essential for human survival. If we are realistic, it is very difficult to justify man's use of other animals solely on the basis of his dependence on them.

When we destroy the habitat of wild animals, we are in effect exploiting these animals and are using them poorly by placing negative influences on their lives. We do this in the name of improvement of man's well-being, that is, to create areas for homes, highways, or industry. We display animals in zoos to satisfy the curiosity of the public, which we also categorize as education. We exploit pets by subjecting them to regimentation in their lives, primarily for the recreational and emotional satisfaction that this close relationship provides us. It is true that we shower our pets with affection and that they return some of this affection; however, we do this for our own satisfaction, and the animals involved are not free to choose this relationship. The most controversial category in man's use of animals is that of the blood sports, which include hunting, bullfighting, cockfighting, falconry, and any of those sports resulting in either injury or death to the animals involved. Opponents and advocates of these activities both acknowledge that they provide recreation and satisfaction directly to humans, despite what happens to the animals. The various uses humans make of animals may or may not result in the injury or death of individual animals, however, all uses at least alter the way of life of the animals involved; a consequence that we as humans rarely think about.

Although we do not usually consider all types of exploitation of animals on an ethical or moral basis, the principle involved is similar in each case. In regard to the value to mankind, hunting has utilitarian value, and similar to animal husbandry, keeping a pet, or poisoning rats in the city dump, it serves our interests. In comparing hunting to other uses of animals, the question of ethics or morality is one of degree in relationship to the relative impact on humans. For example, if we can justify exploiting animals for food, then hunting should also be justifiable. And conversely, if any exploitation of animals is considered morally wrong from the standpoint of the interest of the animals themselves, then all exploitation should fall in the same category. If a defensible logical analysis is to be made, any ethical distinctions that exist in the justification of hunting versus the justification of any other uses of animals must relate to the relative values of these activities to humans, or in conflicting values between various uses, and not to differences in the effects on the animals involved.

The redeeming social value of hunting has been eloquently elaborated by Ortega y Gasset, and Leopold and Shepard have been outstanding literary advocates of the sport. The latter consideration is one for the biological management of species. We can logically argue against hunting in special cases where hunting is in conflict with other uses of wildlife that may provide comparable or greater returns to society. It may also be necessary to curtail specific hunting to honor cultural traditions and beliefs out of respect for the groups that hold them. Such a situation occurred in Alaska shortly after it became a state in 1959. Native Alaskans in the southern coastal regions traditionally looked upon ravens as the reincarnation of their ancestors and honored them in their art and clan structure. They understandably were offended if ravens were deliberately killed. At that time, ravens were not protected under the International Migratory Bird Treaty. In recognition of the beliefs of these people, the state of Alaska through the Territorial Board of Game prohibited the hunting of ravens in Southeast Alaska. The territorial wildlife management agency acquiesced to cultural tradition, which presumably had a stronger claim against hunting than any recreational value hunting of ravens would have provided non-Natives. The decision was made on the basis of how the hunt would impact humans and which group would be more severely affected, not on a question of morality in the dominant culture with regard to killing ravens.

In a 1967 article, "The Ethical Relationship between Humans and Other Organisms," Dale Guthrie pointed out that the dilemma or logical trap that Schweitzer found himself in, as do many others who oppose hunting and other uses of animals by man on ethical grounds, resulted from the belief within Western culture that the basis for our ethical values and moral standards has been some outside agency (Guthrie 1967). Moral principles and the standards by which they are judged, however, are human constructs, and can be evaluated on an empirical basis. The only underlying *a priori* assumption in this system is that man's rules of conduct should be in his own (i.e., society's) interest. Aristotle, and in more recent times Kant, have both stressed that ethics have no relevance except in governing relationships between human beings. Although Kant's views on the irrelevance of religious motivation to the development of morality have been largely superseded, his argument that modern ethics, be they of religious or nonreligious derivation, need not draw their support from transcendental sources remains viable. It is acceptable to Western theologians as long as the question of motivation is excluded.

Guthrie maintains that morality and ethics, being human constructs, relate only to man and cannot be extended to other organisms. That is, moral judgments can be made of man's actions, but not of those of other animals. Therefore, all other organisms are amoral bodies. There is no place within such a system for judgments of "the bad wolves that kill the good deer" or "the bad insects that bite us or carry disease and the good ones that pollinate plants." Schweitzer included all of life within the human ethical system, so was forced into these categorizations. He classified predators as bad because they killed or caused pain, acts which he had already defined as evil or cruel.

Obviously, all those who have extended ethics to other organisms have been faced with the problem of creating moral classifications within nature. This is not to deny the relationship of man to other life forms as was characteristic of Cartesian philosophy, nor to fail to be awed by the complexity and beauty of life as we may see it, but rather to recognize the boundaries of our ethical system. Man's actions toward other entities, be they living organisms or inanimate objects, should be evaluated by the relative impact of such actions on man and not by any absolute or inherent value these things are thought to possess, or of moral classification of their "goodness" or "badness." Neither should the acts themselves be judged good or bad; these judgments only gain relevance in relation to mankind. Human acts committed toward other animals, such as hunting or domestication, can only be evaluated realistically through their human effects. However, these effects should be interpreted in their broadest possible sense.

We can argue, for example, that whereas hunting may provide immediate recreational or nutritional returns, in some situations hunting of an animal species may destroy the opportunity for its observation and enjoyment by people either now or in the future and therefore hunting should be constrained or avoided. Similarly, if hunting under certain circumstances fosters disrespect for life and nature or is otherwise degrading to man, it should not be condoned. It follows from the preceding discussion that there are valid moral and ethical obligations, as well as restraints, associated with hunting, but only those that relate our hunting conduct to ourselves and other humans—both those living and yet unborn. Justifications for opposing the act of hunting should therefore fall within this concept. Each hunting situation should be considered on its own merits, including its total impact on mankind. Within such a framework, we can logically question the methods and means employed and their impact on all segments of society, including the hunter, but not the act of hunting itself.

A final consideration that relates to hunting is our human attitude toward death. In our concern over death in other organisms, we are primarily anthropomorphizing. The human tendency to accept a "sanctity of life" concept is associated with projection of our own self-biased valuation of life to other organisms, or we might say, projection of our own fear of death to other organisms. Darwinian evolution presumes that death of the individual has been essential for the evolution of life and living systems as we know them today. Without death of individuals, there can be no continuation of the life forms that now exist. An expected criticism of the justification for hunting through rationally based ethics is that such a system is too coldly objective, too hard, and lacking in compassion for life. Rational ethics, however, can provide the basis for a very humane ethic toward the totality of life, an ethic that can yield to mankind a large return of both social and aesthetic values. It provides a basis for deep and realistic understanding of life.

It is a further extension of the growing recognition that an appreciation for and understanding of the complexity of nature is essential if we humans are to benefit from our relationship with nature rather than be destroyed by it. Hunting provides one avenue for the development of such an understanding and appreciation of all life and its complexities, its beauty, and its relationship to man. With keen perception and simplicity, Ortega y Gasset expressed the elemental relationship of the hunter to nature:

> The hunter, while he advances or waits crouching, feels tied through the earth to the animal he pursues . . . that automatically leads the hunter to perceive the environment from the point of view of the prey without abandoning his own point of view" (Ortega y Gasset 1972[1995]:141–42).

Philosophical logic stresses that morality and ethics have relevance only to human interrelationships and are inappropriate to the relationship of man to other organisms. Hunting is a human use of animals and it should be judged on essentially the same basis as other human uses of animals, be it as pets, work animals, or domestic livestock. Hunting is a use of animals that yields benefits to society and is therefore justifiable to the extent that it does not conflict with the long-term social welfare of humans.

Ethics and Bear Management in Alaska: A Case Study

The approval of bear baiting in Alaska demonstrates how the erosion of ethical values of hunters may occur when a subgroup of hunters lobbies for legalizing their mode of hunting at the expense of traditional ethical values held by other hunters and many environmentalists.

At its March 2012 meeting in Fairbanks, Alaska, the Alaska Board of Game considered and discussed proposals for baiting and snaring of bears. This raised ethical questions for me about bear management in Alaska. In 1959, right after statehood, I began employment with the newly established Alaska Game Division, later to become the Division of Wildlife Conservation within the Alaska Department of Fish and Game. I worked as a wildlife management biologist based in Petersburg and later Juneau, but had worked for five years previously in a similar capacity for the Territorial Alaska Game Commission. Although I worked primarily with deer management, I also was closely involved with bear management issues and associated investigations related to intensified logging to supply the newly established pulp mills at Ketchikan and Sitka. At that time, many of the loggers lobbied for reduction of brown bears out of fear or concern for their own safety. They were supported by the US Forest Service, who appeared to be blindly focused on timber harvest and shunning their responsibility for the wildlife resources on national forest lands in Alaska.

Nevertheless, at that time, bears were generally highly valued for their contribution to local economies, mainly through guide outfitting for "Outside" (non-Alaskan) trophy hunters. In contrast to other western states, in Alaska there was also an appreciation for and recognition of bears as emblematic of the coexistence of human activities with the state's unique and abundant wildlife. In addition, there was traditional respect for bears among most Alaska Native cultures. This well-established tradition of "valuing" bears and other charismatic wildlife by Alaskans played an important role during the Alaska Constitutional Convention in the structuring of state government to enable development of an equitable system for management of Alaska's wildlife.

In these early days, the correlation between the abundance of both salmon and bears in Alaska had long been accepted though not fully understood. At that time, bears were not appreciated for their ecological role in distributing the nutrients that the five species of Pacific salmon brought from the sea into the watersheds where they spawn and then die. It was only through the modern technique of stable isotope analysis that it became known that the large size and abundance of bears in coastal Alaska was directly tied to the marine nutrients brought in by the dying salmon. This method has also shown that the bears play a dominant role in spreading these nutrients around the landscape to fertilize coastal ecosystems, although they are aided by eagles, other birds, and mammals that feed on the dead and dying salmon. The giant Sitka spruce tree, the lush growth of plants, the high productivity of other wildlife, including grouse, waterfowl, furbearers, deer, and moose from Southeast Alaska to Northwest Alaska, all have benefited from this salmon-bear relationship. Even in interior Alaska, wherever salmon reach major spawning areas, such as the Teklanika Springs, grizzlies have been known to concentrate, and hunters and trappers have long known of the high productivity of wildlife associated with these salmon spawning areas.

Bears have played a prominent role in the cultural history of all Alaskans and have long merited admiration and respect for their charismatic presence in our northern ecosystems. For the most part, bears have been managed as a highly valued component of Alaska's wild fauna. Management has varied regionally in relation to state, federal, and Native land status and specific management goals, and has included sustainable harvest levels; reductions in bear numbers where bears have been shown to be limiting the increase of harvestable prey populations; protection of bears from hunting to facilitate viewing by the public; public education to minimize bear-human conflicts, particularly in urban and suburban areas; and removal of nuisance bears.

Permitting the baiting of bears challenges these ethical and cultural standards that have guided wildlife management in Alaska since statehood. It would contradict existing management policy that discourages attraction of bears to human foods in order to minimize risks from human-bear interaction. It would increase the risk of human injury from bears associated with hunter harvest of bears. It would degrade bears in the eyes of both the hunting and nonhunting public. Bear baiting goes against the standards of "fair chase" consistently touted as the basis of ethical hunting, and so would degrade those hunters who employ it in the eyes of ethical hunters. In addition, by following unethical practices like this that are disrespectful to the animals, approval of bear baiting would lend support to the already growing anti-hunting sentiment present in society. This would likely have a negative impact on Alaska's tourism economy by dampening enthusiasm for viewing bears as a wilderness species.[18] Finally, it would be inconsistent with bear management guidelines published in 1997 by the National Research Council's Committee on Management of Wolf and Bear Populations in Alaska (National Research Council 1997).

Conclusion

It seems evident that the future of hunting as a sport remains threatened unless a change in the trend in public attitudes is forthcoming. Specific action toward achieving such a change should include research to more clearly define the elements of psychological conflict existing between the hunter and the anti-hunter. Such studies will likely emphasize the differing values held by these two groups and could therefore provide the orientation for educational efforts aimed at altering those values that are based on a too superficial understanding or misunderstanding of nature, on a lack of appreciation for the social criteria for ethical standards, and on an unawareness of the complexities of hunting as a sport. Finally, it is up to hunters themselves and those would-be advocates of the sport to bring about a reemphasis on quality in hunting, and to return the high ethical standards to hunting that won it respect in the past.

---

18. In 1992, when the Alaska Board of Game approved aerial shooting of wolves as a method of predator control in order to increase popularly hunted prey populations, such as moose, national environmental groups launched a campaign to encourage tourists to boycott Alaska. There were economic consequences from this action (Egan 1992).

David capturing overwintering
ducks in Wrangell Narrows near
Petersburg, circa 1957. COURTESY OF
DAVID KLEIN.

21
On Being Objective

In 1961, David Klein gave the following lecture to the Juneau Toastmaster Club to emphasize what he saw as the importance of objectivity in order to accomplish the best scientific research possible. It illustrates the depth of his philosophical thinking early in his career, and how his ideas have expanded from this basic platform into his deeply held current views and perspective. It is interesting to note how relevant this piece remains to current affairs of today.

None of us can truthfully say that he is completely without bias. We are products of the environment in which we have been raised, and all of our thoughts are colored to a greater or lesser extent by past experience. But to consciously and wholeheartedly work for objectivity in our thought and action is one of the highest ideals for which man can strive.

Webster defines objective thought as that which is characterized by the tendency to view events, phenomena, and ideas as external and apart from self-consciousness; hence detached, impersonal, or unprejudiced. This is in contrast to subjective thought, which is dominated by personal bias or emotional background.

We are living in a troubled world, and if we as human beings, endowed with the power of thought and the ability to reason, are to preserve ourselves, our civilization, and perhaps life itself in this ever more complex world society, we have got to face up to our problems in an objective fashion. The present state of world affairs requires action but not necessarily military action. Modern world societies can no longer protect themselves through the instrument of war. Barring accidental nuclear war, we are faced with the prospect of coexistence with unfriendly governments or else destruction of civilization as we know it today through nuclear war. We have no logical alternative. With the present destructive potential of major world powers, total war is no longer likely. Future world struggles will be won by wits, rather than weapons.

Life is a struggle not to be avoided, but to be met as a challenge with the utmost confidence and urgency. We have been lulled into a false sense of security by our very own system of government. Democracy, which was a product of reason and objective thinking, became a working reality in the United States. However, we seem to have forgotten that our forefathers were guided by a code of ethics. Today, we apparently feel that democracy means each of us is guaranteed "life, liberty, and the pursuit of happiness" with emphasis on happiness and with no obligations on our part.

We measure our well-being in comparison to the communist world in terms of material benefits, standards of living, 200-horsepower automobiles, 30-inch TV sets and $40,000 homes. Aren't these measures of quantity rather than quality? True, we often use these as defensive tactics when confronted with communist boasts of increased production and raised living standards, but this is not justification for such action.

The true merits of a democratic form of government are the right of each citizen to a free voice in the government, and the guarantee of maximum individual freedom of action and expression compatible with the principle of equality of mankind and the efficient functioning of society. However, democracy has no priority on these principles. On the contrary, they have been expounded by philosophers for centuries, but because our form of government was the production of rational, objective individuals guided by unselfish motives, we are enjoying its liberties and benefits today.

You may say, "I appreciate our system of government and actively support it. What more do you ask?" However, if a free government of intelligent and educated people is to survive for any appreciable length of time, those people must do more than merely pay lip service to it. They must accept and practice the philosophy upon which it is based.

It is up to every individual for his or her own welfare, and the welfare of society and mankind, to strive for objectivity in thought and action and to be sure that our decisions, which may affect other members of our society, are based on ethical principles, rather than the desire for material gain or personal security.

Michael Hansen (left), one of David's Phd students, and a visiting Norwegian researcher by the Trans-Alaska Pipeline on a spring ski trip to observe sheep in Atigun Canyon, circa 1994. PHOTO BY DAVID KLEIN.

22
Alaska's People, Economics, and Resources

David Klein wrote this in 1970 as an editorial essay published in the "Main Trails and Bypaths" section of *Alaska Magazine* (Klein 1970c). It was written in response to growing concern at the time about how to balance industrial growth with preservation of the natural environment, largely its biological productivity and aesthetic values. He asked what types of controls on human use of the environment, if any, should be in place to assure the kind of life Alaskans envisioned for themselves in the future. Despite this essay being written forty-nine years ago, David believes that it remains relevant and still reflects his thinking on these critical issues. It provides a useful summation of underlying views and values that motivated his life and career.

Americans have a tendency to look upon the population explosion as an abstract statistical phenomenon, certainly of international concern, but since it has had no apparent effect on food supply or our material wealth our concern is superficial. And particularly so here in Alaska, the largest state with the smallest population. But even here in Alaska we have problems of too rapid population growth. In the Eskimo villages of western and northern Alaska, the annual rate of increase is over 4 percent; a rate that will double the population in just seventeen years and which exceeds even that of Mexico. This unprecedented rate of growth in an economically undeveloped area imposes a considerable tax burden on us, as well as on all US taxpayers who must shoulder the responsibility of providing for the welfare of these people. In the area of education alone, we have not been able to provide the opportunity for schooling through the secondary level, which we have come to consider a requisite for our level of social and economic development.

But my primary objective now is not to arouse concern over the population explosion. I would like, however, to raise a few questions for consideration that relate to population growth and to our present attitude toward economic development and use of resources. What I really want to do is to challenge some existing philosophies that are akin to motherhood in their entrenchment as accepted dogma in our modern technological and materialistic society.

Here in the United States, an expanding economy and expanding population have come to be associated with our high standard of living. Every businessman knows that a growing population is good because it means more customers for everything from diapers to caskets. Industrial development means more jobs for an ever-increasing labor force. But it is becoming increasingly apparent (although certainly not universally so) that many of the present-day ills confronting society on a local as well as a national basis are the products of too rapid growth. Consider the state of our schools, both overcrowded and understaffed. We seem to be at least a pace or two out of step with our needs to provide adequate schools, hospitals, libraries, and other social services, and in the face of such rapid growth any hesitation seems to put us so far behind in meeting these needs that our hopes for success become almost fantasy. It was Vachel Lindsay who observed that "a hasty prosperity may be raw and absurd. A well-considered poverty may be exquisite" (Lindsay 1925:xlvii).

Perhaps less pertinent to the Alaska scene, but certainly a problem in the "Lower 48," is the apparent deterioration in the qualitative aspects of living associated with the constantly increasing population pressures. Indeed, many of us have come to Alaska to avoid the traffic problems, air pollution, water shortages, disfiguration of the landscape, and general congestion that are plaguing most of the US population centers.

At some time in the not too distant future, we will have to arrive at a state of relative equilibrium with our environment. At what level will this be? Do we have any obligations with regard to the use we make of "our" environment (and I use the possessive pronoun "our" guardedly because our environment will no longer be ours in later generations)? What are our alternatives? Do we utilize the Earth to maximum efficiency, and if so, what is maximum efficiency? Is this sustaining the greatest number of people the Earth can possibly support? Should we qualify this by adding "without hardship"? Is quality of life a consideration? Many scientists maintain that we have a capability to adequately feed a world population two or three times that of the present. But now we are comparing man to cattle in a feedlot with no consideration for the deterioration in quality that may accompany such high-density living. Is a human life of value if opportunities are not available to it for its psychological development and enrichment?

Perhaps we can adapt physiologically and psychologically to high population pressures, but the question is "should we?" Isn't it more desirable to attempt to control our population and stabilize our economy at a level that will guarantee maximum development of culture and knowledge?

What are our obligations to future generations? Do we have any, and if so, how far ahead do we look? Obviously, we are concerned for the welfare of our own children and perhaps to a lesser extent their children, but how about humanity in general? How do we establish priorities? What value do we give to life now versus ten years from now, or twenty-five or one hundred or five hundred, for that matter? We seem to be engaged in a headlong race to no one knows where and we won't stop long enough to ask ourselves where we are going for fear of being left behind.

Inevitably, a discussion of people, economy, and resources leads to the issue of conservation, but conservation means different things to different people. At one extreme, conservation means protection: preserving and keeping in an entire state. This concept of conservation is nearly synonymous with non-use. At the other end of the spectrum, the talk is of use of resources now with emphasis on the "now," and with such phraseology as maximum use or yield, the greatest good for the greatest number of people, and so forth. Is some middle road more reasonable? Obviously, we cannot lock up our resources and still live the "good life of the Great Society." But it is equally true that we cannot provide all of the material needs of an ever-expanding world population; convert our landscape to concrete and old car bodies; pollute air and waters, and at the same time improve or even maintain the quality of our present-day lives.

As long as we remain wedded to a policy of rapid economic growth, intangible qualitative aspects of life will lose out to material or monetary values whenever a conflict of interests develops. We are tempted to associate our lack of foresight with the rapid pace of modern society and our obsession with the technological world. These are undoubtedly compounding factors, but the roots of this problem appear to lie deeper in our past. In 1906, William James graphically described the problem as "the moral flabbiness born of the exclusive worship of the bitch-goddess SUCCESS. That—with the squalid cash interpretation put on the word success—is our national disease" (James 1906).

Americans have a compulsion to convert everything to dollars and cents. When a traffic problem exists in a major city, the least expensive and most direct route for construction of a new highway is almost always chosen even if it may mean the loss of aesthetic values already in short supply. A dam is built because it will yield badly needed electrical energy or will furnish water for irrigation, both of which are of obvious monetary value, while the values that may be lost through the construction of the dam such as scenery, opportunities for hunting and fishing, or other recreation cannot readily be given a dollar value.

Even when economic surveys are made to equate a monetary value to recreational resources, intangibles still exist. Wilderness areas cannot usually be justified on the basis of objective economic surveys. Yet wilderness has value to a certain percentage of the population. Ardent wilderness advocates will argue, and I believe validly, that wilderness has a quality that cannot be measured in dollars and cents. This "value" might be compared to that of a work of art, which may be meaningless and worthless to some people yet to others it may have a value that no price tag can define. Aesthetic and material values are not common denominators and attempts to treat them as such are fraught with failure.

The "multiple use" concept that is given so much lip service by government agencies involved in resource management is not a panacea to problems of competing uses of resources. Certain uses of resources are just not compatible. You cannot sell recreation sites on a lake that is polluted by industrial waste nor can the wilderness value of an area be maintained if roads penetrate it or if logging is permitted.

There seems to be a prevalent attitude among politicians, and people in general, that resources should be developed and used as rapidly as possible and that an unused resource is a wasted one. Foresters, throughout their training, are instilled with the idea that a forest is being wasted if uncut, and we are told of the vast amount of water power that is wasted annually in the Yukon River each year that the Rampart Dam remains unbuilt. The frantic haste of oil men to probe Alaska's North Slope is reminiscent, and perhaps analogous as well in its single-mindedness, to the frenzied swarming of arctic mosquitoes over a freshly bared arm. In spite of protestations to the contrary, it is difficult to disassociate such an attitude from man's self-serving quest for greater material wealth; a quest that has shown little concern for lessons learned from the past or obligations to the future, but that emphasizes only the present.

Man has met God's challenge in Genesis; he has truly "subdued the wilderness" and has emerged victorious with a level of social and technological advancement undreamed of in biblical times. Man must now come to the realization that *that* battle is over. To further "subdue the enemy" is to destroy the very source of our cultural heritage and to threaten the future well-being of mankind. The challenge is no longer one of expanding frontiers into the wilderness. The new threat to mankind is man himself.

Is the momentum of our technological world society so great and our infatuation with material things so overpowering that we are helpless to alter the course of mankind? Is our Nirvana to be a mass society of congestion, concrete, cacophony, and conformity; the chance result of man's independent striving for greater material wealth? Or is man capable of utilizing the same intellectual potential that has brought about the technological revolution to consciously plan and direct the future course of society in such a way that quality of life is not lost?

References

Ahlén, I. 1966. "Landskapets Utnyttjande och Faunan," *Sveriges Natur*, Arsbok (Yearbook) 1966: 73–99.

Allende, Isabel. 2001. *Portrait in Sepia*. New York: HarperCollins.

American Heritage® Science Dictionary. n. d. "Barcan." Houghton Mifflin Company. Accessed April 14, 2017. www.dictionary.com.

Anker, P. 2001. *Imperial Ecology*. Cambridge, MA: Harvard University Press.

———. 2007. "Science as a Vacation: A History of Ecology in Norway." *History of Science* 45 (4): 455–79.

———. 2013. "The Call for a New Ecotheology in Norway." *Journal for the Study of Religion, Nature, and Culture* 7 (2): 187–207.

Arctic Climate Impact Assessment (ACIA). 2005. *Arctic Climate Impact Assessment: Scientific Report*. Cambridge, England: University of Cambridge Press. Accessed February 14, 2018. http://www.acia.uaf.edu/pages/scientific.html.

Ardrey, Robert. 1961. *African Genesis: A Personal Investigation into the Animal Origins and Nature of Man*. New York: Athenaeum.

Backes, David. 1997. *A Wilderness Within: The Life of Sigurd F. Olson*. Minneapolis: University of Minnesota Press.

———, ed. 2001. *Sigurd F. Olson: The Meaning of Wilderness, Essential Articles and Speeches*. Minneapolis: University of Minnesota Press.

Behan, R. W. 1967. "The Succotash Syndrome, or Multiple Use: A Heartfelt Approach to Forest Land Management." *Natural Resources Journal* 7 (4): 473–84.

Ben-David, M., T. A. Hanley, D. R. Klein, D. M. Schell. 1997. "Seasonal Changes in Diets of Coastal and Riverine Mink: The Role of Spawning Pacific Salmon." *Canadian Journal of Zoology* 75 (5): 803–11.

Ben-David, M., T. A. Hanley, D. M. Schell. 1998. "Fertilization of Terrestrial Vegetation by Spawning Pacific Salmon: The Role of Flooding and Predator Activity." *Oikos* 83, no. 1 (October): 47–55.

Berg, E. E., and R. S. Anderson. 2006. "Fire History of White and Lutz Spruce Forests on the Kenai Peninsula, Alaska, over the Last Two Millennia as Determined from Soil Charcoal." *Forest Ecology and Management* 227:275–83.

Bergerud, A. T. 1969. *The Population Dynamics of Newfoundland Caribou*. PhD dissertation, University of British Columbia, Vancouver.

———. 1974. "Decline of Caribou in North America Following Settlement." *Journal of Wildlife Management* 38, no. 4 (October): 757–70.

Berglund, B. E., ed. 1969. "Impact of Man on the Scandinavian Landscape during the Late Post-Glacial." *Oikos*, Supplementum 12.

Blackman, Margaret. 1989. *Sadie Brower Neakok, An Iñupiaq Woman*. Seattle: University of Washington Press.

Bliss, L. C., O. W. Heal, and J. J. Moore. 1981. *Tundra Ecosystems: A Comparative Analysis*. International Biological Programme 25, 257–84. Cambridge: Cambridge University Press.

Bliss, L. C., and D. R. Klein. 1981. "Current Extractive Industrial Development, North America." In *Tundra Ecosystems: A Comparative Analysis*, edited by L. D. Bliss, J. B. Cragg, D. W. Heal, and J. J. Moore. Cambridge: Cambridge University Press.

Boone and Crockett Club. 2015. *Fair Chase* (Spring/March) 2015.

———. 2017. Boone and Crockett Club web page. *Fair Chase Statement*. Accessed April 27, 2017. https://www.boone-crockett.org/huntingEthics/ethics_fairchase.asp?area= huntingEthics.

Brewster, Karen, ed. 2004. *The Whales, They Give Themselves: Conversations with Harry Brower, Sr.* Fairbanks: University of Alaska Press.

———. 2012. *Boots, Bikes, and Bombers: Adventures of Alaska Conservationist Ginny Hill Wood*. Fairbanks: University of Alaska Press.

Brown, Jerry. 1975. *Summaries of 1975 AAAS Tundra Biome Symposium Presentations*. U.S. Tundra Biome Data Report, 75–76. Washington, DC: U.S. International Biological Program.

Brown, Jerry, K. R. Everett, P. J. Webber, S. F. MacLean Jr., and D. F. Murray. 1980. "The Coastal Tundra at Barrow." In *An Arctic Ecosystem: The Coastal Tundra at Barrow, Alaska*. US/IBP Synthesis series, 12, 1–29. Stroudsburg, PA: Dowden, Hutchinson & Ross.

Burn, Douglas. 2012. *St. Matthew Island Integrated Science Expedition of 2012*. Video supported by the USFWS and Alaska Maritime National Wildlife Refuge. Accessed January 25, 2019. https://www.youtube.com/watch?v=vjFkc9BO75s.

Burris, O. E., and D. E. McKnight. 1973. *Game Transplants in Alaska*. Alaska Department of Fish and Game, *Technical Bulletin*, No. 4. Juneau, AK: Alaska Department of Fish and Game.

Cameron, R., and K. Whitten. 1980. *Effects of the Trans-Alaska Pipeline on Caribou Movements*. Vol. 5, Project Progress Report, Federal Aid in Wildlife Restoration Project W-21-1, Job no. 3.18R. Juneau, AK: Alaska Department of Fish and Game.

Case, David. 1984. *Alaska Natives and American Law*. Fairbanks: University of Alaska Press.

Child, K. N. 1973. *The Reactions of Barren-Ground Caribou* (Rangifer tarandus granti) *to Simulated Pipeline and Pipeline Crossing Structures at Prudhoe Bay, Alaska*. Completion Report, Alaska Cooperative Wildlife Research Unit, University of Alaska, Fairbanks.

Child, K. N., and P. C. Lent. 1973. *The Reactions of Reindeer to a Pipeline Simulation at Penny River, Alaska*. Interim Report by Alaska Cooperative Wildlife Research Unit, University of Alaska Fairbanks.

Coffin, C. C. 1869. *Our New Way Round the World*. Boston: Fields, Osgood, and Company.

Cohen, David William. 1994. *The Combing of History*. Chicago: University of Chicago Press.

Collingwood, R. G. 1938. *The Principles of Art*. Oxford, England: Clarendon Press.

Committee on Cumulative Environmental Effects of Oil and Gas Activities on Alaska's North Slope, National Research Council of the National Academies. 2003. *Cumulative Environmental Effects of Oil and Gas Activities on Alaska's North Slope*. Washington, DC: The National Academies Press.

Cowan, I. McTaggart. 1968."Wilderness: Concept, Function, and Management." Eighth Horace M. Albright Conservation Lectureship, University of California School of Forestry, Berkeley, CA.

Daggett, Carmen. 2016. "Caribou Biologist Jim Dau Retires after Almost Three Decades of Service." *Alaska Fish and Wildlife News.* January 2016. Accessed March 24, 2017. http://www.adfg.alaska.gov/index.cfm?adfg=wildlifenews.view_article&articles_id=758.

Danks, Fiona S. 2000. *Potential Muskox Habitat in the National Petroleum Reserve Alaska: A GIS Analysis.* Master's thesis, University of Alaska Fairbanks.

———. 2007. *A Multi-Scale Assessment of Landscape in the Barents Region: Reindeer Habitat in a Climate of Change.* PhD dissertation, University of Cambridge, England.

Darling, Frank Fraser. 1969. "The Impact of Man on His Environment," Second Reith Lecture 1969. In *Wilderness and Plenty*, edited by F. F. Darling, 18–36. 1970. London: Ballantine Books.

Dau, Jim. 1986. *Distribution and Behavior of Barren-Ground Caribou in Relation to Weather and Parasitic Insects.* Master's thesis, University of Alaska Fairbanks.

Dau, J. R., and R. D. Cameron. 1986. "Effects of a Road System on Caribou Distribution during Calving." *Rangifer*, Special Issue 1:95–101.

Dawson, G. M. 1894. "Geological Notes on Some of the Coasts and Islands of Bering Sea and Vicinity." *Bulletin of the Geological Society of America*, No. 5.

Devall, B., and G. Sessions. 1985. *Deep Ecology: Living as If Nature Mattered.* Layton, UT: Gibbs M. Smith.

Dixon, E. J. 1999. *Bones, Boats, and Bison: Archeology and the First Colonization of Western North America.* Albuquerque: University of New Mexico Press.

Dunaway, David. 1991. "The Oral Biography." *Biography* 14, no. 3 (Summer): 256–66.

Egan, Timothy. 1992. "Facing Boycott, Alaska Drops Plan to Kill Wolves." *New York Times*, December 23, 1992. Accessed August 13, 2017. http://www.nytimes.com/1992/12/23/us/facing-boycott-alaska-drops-plan-to-kill-wolves.html.

Elliott, H. W. 1875. "Polar bears." *Harper's Weekly* 19 (957): 1–2.

———. 1882. "Monograph of the Seal Islands of Alaska." In *St. Matthew Island and Its Relation to St. Paul*, 115–17. Washington, DC: U.S. Department of the Interior.

Elliott, Nan, ed. 1978. *The Alaska Public Forum 1978 Year-End Report.* A Program of the Alaska Growth Policy Council. May 1978. Juneau, AK: State of Alaska, Alaska Growth Policy Council.

Engstad, H. 1993. *The Land of Feast and Famine.* New York: Alfred A. Knopf.

Errington, P. L. 1963. "The Pricelessness of Untampered Nature." *Journal of Wildlife Management* 27 (2): 313–20.

Estes, James A. 2016. *Serendipity: An Ecologist's Quest to Understand Nature.* Oakland: University of California Press.

Fairall, N. 1969. "Prenatal Development of the Impala *Aepyceros melampus.*" *Koedoe* 12 (1): 97–103.

Fairall, N., A. K. Eloff, and I. S. McNaim. 1983. "Integration of Metabolism and Digestion in the Hyrax." *South African Journal of Animal Science* 13 (1): 79–80.

Fairall, N., and D. R. Klein. 1984. "Protein Intake and Water Turnover: A Comparison of Two Equivalently Sized African Antelope—the Blesbok *Damaliscus dorcas* and Impala *Aepyceros melampus.*" *Canadian Journal of Animal Science* 64 (Suppl.): 212–14.

Fay, F. 1963. Field trip to St. Matthew Island, July 17–August 7, 1963. Correspondence to Chief, Zoonotic Disease Section, Arctic Health Research Center, Anchorage. September 6, 1963.

Folger, Tim. 2017. "Why Did Greenland's Vikings Vanish?" *Smithsonian*, March 2017. Accessed August 3, 2017. http://www.smithsonianmag.com/history/why-greenland -vikings-vanished-180962119/.

Finnegan, Ruth. 1992. *Oral Traditions and the Verbal Arts: A Guide to Research Practices.* London: Routledge.

Fredskild, B. 1988. "Agriculture in a Marginal Area: South Greenland from the Norse Landnam (985 A.D.) to the Present (1985 A.D.)." In *The Cultural Landscape: Past, Present, and Future*, edited by H. H. Birks, H. J. B. Birks, P. E Kaland, and D. Moe, 381–93. Cambridge: Cambridge University Press.

Fries, M. 1969. "Aspects of Floristic Changes in Connection with the Development of the Cultural Landscape." In *Impact of Man on the Scandinavian Landscape during the Late Post-Glacial*, edited by B. E. Berglund, 29–34. *Oikos*, Supplementum 12.

L. Frink, D. Corbett, A. Rosebrough, and M. Partlow, 2001. "The Archaeology of St. Matthew Island, Bering Sea." *Alaska Journal of Anthropology* 1:131–37.

Geist, Valerius. 1998. *Deer of the World: Their Evolution, Behavior, and Ecology.* Mechanicsburg, PA: Stackpole Books.

Giedion, S. 1963. *Constancy, Change, and Architecture.* Cambridge, MA: Harvard University Press.

Gilbert, Bil. 1967. "A Close Look at Wildlife in America." *Saturday Evening Post*, September 9, 1967, 32–48.

Gilbert, Frederick F., and Donald G. Dodds. 1987. *The Philosophy and Practice of Wildlife Management.* Malabar, FL: R. E. Krieger Publishing Company.

Goforth, W. Reid. 2006 (1994). *The Cooperative Fish and Wildlife Research Unit Program: Serving the Nation since 1953.* Special Publication, February 2006, U.S. Geological Survey Cooperative Research Units, Reston, VA (Original publication by National Biological Survey). Accessed February 22, 2018. Pdf of 2006 edition: https://usgs-cru-department-data.s3.amazonaws.com/headquarters/unit_docs/CRU_Program_BookletS-1.pdf.

Grele, Ron. 1975. *Envelopes of Sound: Six Practitioners Discuss the Method, Theory, and Practice of Oral History and Oral Testimony.* Chicago: Precedent Publications.

Griffin, Dennis. 2017. "A History of Human Land Use on St. Matthew Island, Alaska." *Alaska Journal of Anthropology* 2 (1–2): 84–99.

Guha, R. 1989. "Radical American Environmentalism and Wilderness Preservation: A Third World Critique." *Environmental Ethics* 11:71–83.

Guthrie, R. D. 1967. "The Ethical Relationship between Humans and Other Organisms." *Perspectives in Biology and Medicine* 11, no. 1 (Autumn): 52–62.

Haeckel, Ernst. 1900. *The Riddle of the Universe at the Close of the Nineteenth Century.* Translated by Joseph McCabe. London: Harper & Brothers.

Hanna, G. D. 1920. "Mammals of the St. Matthew Island, Bering Sea." *Journal of Mammalogy* 1:118–22.

Hardin, G. 1968. "The Tragedy of the Commons." *Science* 162 (3859): 1243–48.

———. 1985. "An Ecolate View of the Human Predicament." A talk that was later developed into his book *Filters against Folly: How to Survive Despite Economists, Ecologists, and the Merely Eloquent* (New York: Viking Penguin, 1985). Accessed October 22, 2017. The Garrett Hardin Society website: http://www.garretthardinsociety.org/articles/art_ecolate_view_human_predicament.html.

Healy, M. A. 1889. *Report of the Cruise of the Revenue Cutter* Corwin *in the Arctic Ocean in the Year 1884.* Washington, DC: Government Printing Office.

Hicks, Mary V., ed. 2001. *Muskox Management Report of Survey-Inventory Activities, 1 July 1998–30 June 2000.* Juneau, AK: Alaska Department of Fish and Game, Division of Wildlife Conservation.

Hornaday, William Temple. 1913. *Our Vanishing Wild Life: Its Extermination and Preservation.* New York: New York Zoological Society.

Horne, Esther Burnett, and Sally McBeth. 1998. *Essie's Story: The Life and Legacy of a Shoshone Teacher.* Lincoln: University of Nebraska Press.

Hunt, W. R. 1975. *Arctic Passage: Turbulent History of the Land and People of the Bering Sea, 1697–1975.* New York: Charles Scribner's Sons.

Hyerle, D. N., and L. Alper. 2014. *Pathways to Thinking Schools.* Thousand Oaks, CA: Corwin, A Sage Company.

Ihl, Claudia. 1999. *Comparative Habitat and Diet Selection of Muskoxen and Reindeer on the Seward Peninsula, Western Alaska.* Master's thesis, University of Alaska Fairbanks.

———. 2007. *Foraging Ecology and Sociality of Muskoxen in Northwestern Alaska.* PhD dissertation, University of Alaska Fairbanks.

International Union of Game Biologists (IUGB), Sociedade Portuguesa de Vida Selvagem, ed. 2003. "Integrating People with Wildlife": 26th Congress, International Union of Game Biologists, 1–6 September 2003, Braga, Portugal. Book of Abstracts.

Isto, Sarah Crawford. 2012. *The Fur Farms of Alaska: Two Centuries of History and a Forgotten Stampede.* Fairbanks: University of Alaska Press.

James, William. 1906. Letter to H. G. Wells, September 11, 1906. In *Oxford Dictionary of Quotations,* 3rd ed. Oxford: Oxford University Press, 1979, 272.

Jingfors, K. T., and D. R. Klein. 1982. "Productivity in Recently Established Muskox Populations in Alaska." *Journal of Wildlife Management* 46 (4): 1092–96.

Joly, Kyle, Randi Jandt, and David R. Klein. 2009. "Decrease of Lichens in Arctic Ecosystems: The Role of Wildfire, Caribou, Reindeer, Competition, and Climate in Northwestern Alaska." *Polar Research* 28:433–42.

Joly, Kyle, David R. Klein, David L. Verbyla, T. Scott Rupp, and F. Stuart Chapin. 2011. "Linkages between Large-Scale Climate Patterns and the Dynamics of Arctic Caribou Populations." *Ecography* 34 (2): 345–52.

Joly, Kyle F., Stuart Chapin III, and David R. Klein. 2010. "Winter Habitat Selection by Caribou in Relation to Lichen Abundance, Wildfires, Grazing, and Landscape Characteristics in Northwest Alaska." *Ecoscience* 17 (3): 321–33.

Kaye, Roger. 2006. *Alaska's Last Great Wilderness: The Campaign to Establish the Arctic National Wildlife Refuge.* Fairbanks: University of Alaska Press.

Kellert, Stephen R. 1979. *Public Attitudes toward Critical Wildlife and Natural Habitat Issues.* Washington, DC: Department of the Interior, U.S. Fish and Wildlife Service.

Kellert, Stephen R., and Edward O. Wilson, eds. 1993. *The Biophilia Hypothesis.* Washington, DC: Island Press.

Kerasote, T. 1993. *Bloodties: Nature, Culture, and the Hunt.* New York: Random House.

Killian, W., and N. Fairall. 1983. "Food Selection in the Blesbok on Pasture with Low Plant Diversity." *South African Journal of Animal Science* 13 (1): 38–40.

Kinitsch, Eli. 2016. "Why Did the Norse Disappear?" *Science,* November 10, 2016. Accessed August 3, 2017. http://www.sciencemag.org/news/2016/11/why-did -greenland-s-vikings-disappear.

Klein, David, R. 1953. *A Reconnaissance Study of the Mountain Goat in Alaska.* Master's thesis, University of Alaska Fairbanks.

————.1956. "Natural Mortality Patterns of Black-Tailed Deer Populations in Southeast Alaska." Abstract in *Science in Alaska, Proceedings of the Alaska Science Conference, 1956.* Vol. 7:8.

————. 1957a. Trip report submitted to the Wildlife Administrator, Fish and Wildlife Service, Juneau, Alaska, January 15, 1957. Copy of report in possession of authors.

————. 1957b. "The Black-Tailed Deer in Alaska: An Outline of Management Methods." In Wildlife Management Series, No. 1. Fish and Wildlife Service, Juneau, Alaska.

————. 1959a. *St. Matthew Island Reindeer-Range Study.* Special Scientific Report–Wildlife, No. 43. Washington, DC: U.S. Fish and Wildlife Service.

————. 1959b. "Track Differentiation for Censusing Bear Populations." *Journal of Wildlife Management* 23 (3): 361–63.

————. 1963. *Physiological Response of Deer on Ranges of Varying Quality.* PhD dissertation, University of British Columbia, Vancouver.

————. 1964. "Range-Related Differences in Growth of Deer Reflected in Skeletal Ratios." *Journal of Mammalogy* 45:226–35.

————. 1965. "Ecology of Deer Range in Alaska." *Ecological Monographs* 35:259–84.

————. 1966. "Waterfowl in the Economy of the Eskimos on the Yukon-Kuskokwim Delta, Alaska." *Arctic* 19, no. 4 (December): 319–36.

————. 1968. "The Introduction, Increase, and Crash of Reindeer on St. Matthew Island." *Journal of Wildlife Management* 32, no. 2 (April): 350–67.

————. 1970a. "An Alaskan Population Explosion." *Explorers Journal* 48 (3): 162–72.

————. 1970b. "The Impact of Oil Development in Alaska." In *Productivity and Conservation in Northern Circumpolar Lands,* edited by W. A. Fuller and P. G. Kevan, 202–42. New Series, No. 16. Morges, Switzerland: International Union of Conservation of Nature and Natural Resources.

————. 1970c. "People, Economics, and Resources." Main Trails and Bypaths. *Alaska Magazine,* February 1970, 6–7.

————. 1971. "Reaction of Reindeer to Obstructions and Disturbances." *Science* 173:393–98.

————. 1972a. "Cultural Influences on Landscape Aesthetics: Some Comparisons between Scandinavia and Northwest North America." *Boston College Environmental Affairs Law Review* 2 (1): 80–89.

————. 1972b. "Problems in Conservation of Mammals in the North." *Biological Conservation* 4 (2): 97–101.

————. 1973a. "The Impact of Oil Development in the Northern Environment." In *Proceedings of the Third Interpetroleum Congress: Petroleum and Environment,* 109–21.

————. 1973b. "The Reaction of Some Northern Mammals to Aircraft Disturbance." *Proceedings of the Eleventh International Congress of Game Biologists, Stockholm, Sweden,* 377–83.

————. 1973–1974. "Alaska's St. Matthew Island: Scene of a Recent Population Explosion." *Polarboken,* 33–52.

————. 1975. "New Perspectives on Wildlife Management in Parks and Reserves." Presented at the 12th International Congress of Game Biology (ICGB), Lisbon, Portugal.

————. 1976a. "Wilderness, Part I: Evolution of the Concept." *Landscape* 20:36–41.

————. 1976b. "Wilderness, Part II: The Conundrum of Management." *Landscape* 21:28–31.

————. 1977a. "Winter Food Preferences of Snowshoe Hares (*Lepus americanus*) in Interior Alaska." *Proceedings of the Thirteenth International Congress of Game Biologists,* 266–75.

———. 1977b. Testimony before Udall Wilderness Committee. United States Senate. Congressional Record, October 20, 1977.

———. 1979. "The Alaska Oil Pipeline in Retrospect." *Transaction of the North American Wildlife and Natural Resources Conference* 44:235–46.

———. 1980. "Reaction of Reindeer and Caribou to Obstructions: A Reassessment." In *Proceedings of the Second International Reindeer/Caribou Symposium, 17–21. September 1979, Røros, Norway*, edited by Eigil Reimers, Eldar Gaare, and Sven Skjenneberg, 519–27. Direktoratet for vilt og ferskvannsfisk, Trondheim, Norway.

———. 1985. Oral history interview with Dan O'Neill, November 25, 1985, Fairbanks, Alaska. Tape No. ORAL HISTORY 85–321, Parts 1 and 2, Alaska and Polar Regions Collections & Archives, Elmer E. Rasmuson Library, University of Alaska Fairbanks.

———. 1987. "Vegetation Recovery Patterns Following Overgrazing by Reindeer on St. Matthew Island." *Journal of Range Management* 40 (4): 336–38.

———. 1988a. "Philosophical and Ethical Concerns in Caribou Research and Management." In *Proceedings of the 3rd North American Caribou Workshop at Chena Hot Springs, Alaska, November 4–6, 1987*, edited by Raymond D. Cameron and James L. Davis, 189–95. *Wildlife Technical Bulletin*, No. 8. Juneau, AK: Alaska Department of Fish and Game.

———. 1988b. "The Establishment of Muskox Populations by Translocation." In *Translocation of Wild Animals*, edited by Leon Nielsen and Robert D. Brown, 288–15. Milwaukee, WI: Wisconsin Humane Society and Kingsville, TX: Caesar Kleberg Wildlife Research Institute.

———. 1989a. *CODA: Third Workshop on the Energetics and Nutrition of Wild Ungulates*. Fort Collins, CO, January 17–20, 1989.

———. 1989b. "69th ASM Meeting Organizers Lament." *Journal of Mammalogy* 70 (4): 883–84.

———. 1990. "Variation in Quality of Caribou and Reindeer Forage Plants Associated with Season, Plant Part, and Phenology." *Rangifer*, Special Issue 3:123–30.

———. 1991. "Limiting Factors in Caribou Population Ecology." *Rangifer*, Special Issue 7:30–35.

———. 1994. "Wilderness: A Western Concept Alien to Arctic Cultures." *Information North* 20, no. 3 (September): 1–6.

———. 1995. "The Introduction, Increase, and Demise of Wolves on Coronation Island Alaska." In *Ecology and Conservation of Wolves in a Changing World*, edited by L. N. Carbyn, S. H. Fritts, and D. R. Seip, 275–80. Edmonton, Canada: Canadian Circumpolar Institute, University of Alberta.

———. 1999. "The Roles of Climate and Insularity in Establishment and Persistence of *Rangifer tarandus* Populations in the High Arctic." *Ecological Bulletin* 47:96–104.

———. 2000. "Walking in the Footsteps of Aldo Leopold." *Wildlife Society Bulletin* 28 (2): 464–67.

———. 2001a. "Similarity in Habitat Adaptations of Arctic and African Ungulates: Evolutionary Convergence or Ecological Divergence?" *Alces* 37 (2): 245–52.

———. 2001b. "The Conundrum of Caribou Complexity." In *Arctic Refuge: A Circle of Testimony*, compiled by Hank Lentfer and Carolyn Servid, 43–47. Minneapolis: Milkweed Editions.

———. 2002. Oral history interview with Roger Kaye, December 12, 2002, Fairbanks, Alaska. United States Fish and Wildlife Service Archives. Accessed February 23, 2018. http://digitalmedia.fws.gov/cdm/singleitem/collection/document/id/1172.

———. (lead author). 2005. "Management and Conservation of Wildlife in a Changing Arctic Environment." In *Arctic Council, Arctic Climate Impact Assessment*. Cambridge: Cambridge University Press. Electronic version available at http://www.acia.uaf.edu/pages/scientific.html, accessed July 30, 2017.

———. 2012. "Bear Snaring Defies Our Values: Management Should Be Based on Respect for the Bruin's Ecosystem Role." Community Perspective. *Fairbanks Daily News Miner*, February 26, 2012.

———. 2013a. "Restore Quartz: This Favorite Interior Alaska Lake Needs Water; We Can Help." Community Perspective. *Fairbanks Daily News Miner*, July 28, 2013. http://www.newsminer.com/opinion/community_perspectives/restore-quartz-this-favorite-interior-alaska-lake-needs-water-we/article_98247632-f660-11e2-9592-0019bb30f31a.html, accessed February 23, 2018.

———. 2013b. Oral history interview with Karen Brewster, November 4, 2013, Fairbanks, Alaska. Tape No. ORAL HISTORY 2018-05-01, Alaska and Polar Regions Collections & Archives, Elmer E. Rasmuson Library, University of Alaska Fairbanks.

———. 2013c. Oral history interview with Karen Brewster, December 5, 2013, Fairbanks, Alaska. Tape No. ORAL HISTORY 2018-05-02, Alaska and Polar Regions Collections & Archives, Elmer E. Rasmuson Library, University of Alaska Fairbanks.

———. 2013d. Oral history interview with Karen Brewster, December 13, 2013, Fairbanks, Alaska. Tape No. ORAL HISTORY 2018-05-03, Parts 1–3, Alaska and Polar Regions Collections & Archives, Elmer E. Rasmuson Library, University of Alaska Fairbanks.

———. 2014a. Oral history interview with Karen Brewster, February 6, 2014, Fairbanks, Alaska. Tape No. ORAL HISTORY 2018-05-04, Alaska and Polar Regions Collections & Archives, Elmer E. Rasmuson Library, University of Alaska Fairbanks.

———. 2014b. Oral history interview with Karen Brewster, February 13, 2014, Fairbanks, Alaska. Tape No. ORAL HISTORY 2018-05-05, Alaska and Polar Regions Collections & Archives, Elmer E. Rasmuson Library, University of Alaska Fairbanks.

———. 2014c. Oral history interview with Karen Brewster, February 20, 2014, Fairbanks, Alaska. Tape No. ORAL HISTORY 2018-05-06, Alaska and Polar Regions Collections & Archives, Elmer E. Rasmuson Library, University of Alaska Fairbanks.

———. 2014d. Oral history interview with Karen Brewster, March 6, 2014, Fairbanks, Alaska. Tape No. ORAL HISTORY 2018-05-07, Parts 1 and 2, Alaska and Polar Regions Collections & Archives, Elmer E. Rasmuson Library, University of Alaska Fairbanks.

———. 2014e. Oral history interview with Karen Brewster, March 20, 2014, Fairbanks, Alaska. Tape No. ORAL HISTORY 2018-05-08, Parts 1–3, Alaska and Polar Regions Collections & Archives, Elmer E. Rasmuson Library, University of Alaska Fairbanks.

———. 2014f. Oral history interview with Karen Brewster, March 27, 2014, Fairbanks, Alaska. Tape No. ORAL HISTORY 2018-05-09, Alaska and Polar Regions Collections & Archives, Elmer E. Rasmuson Library, University of Alaska Fairbanks.

———. 2014g. Oral history interview with Karen Brewster, April 3, 2014, Fairbanks, Alaska. Tape No. ORAL HISTORY 2018-05-10, Alaska and Polar Regions Collections & Archives, Elmer E. Rasmuson Library, University of Alaska Fairbanks.

———. 2014h. Oral history interview with Karen Brewster, April 10, 2014, Fairbanks, Alaska. Tape No. ORAL HISTORY 2018-05-11, Alaska and Polar Regions Collections & Archives, Elmer E. Rasmuson Library, University of Alaska Fairbanks.

———. 2014i. Oral history interview with Karen Brewster, April 24, 2014, Fairbanks, Alaska. Tape No. ORAL HISTORY 2018-05-12, Alaska and Polar Regions Collections & Archives, Elmer E. Rasmuson Library, University of Alaska Fairbanks.

————. 2014j. Oral history interview with Karen Brewster, June 6, 2014, Fairbanks, Alaska. Tape No. ORAL HISTORY 2018-05-13, Alaska and Polar Regions Collections & Archives, Elmer E. Rasmuson Library, University of Alaska Fairbanks.

————. 2014k. Oral history interview with Karen Brewster, June 12, 2014, Fairbanks, Alaska. Tape No. ORAL HISTORY 2018-05-14, Alaska and Polar Regions Collections & Archives, Elmer E. Rasmuson Library, University of Alaska Fairbanks.

————. 2014l. Oral history interview with Karen Brewster, July 17, 2014, Fairbanks, Alaska. Tape No. ORAL HISTORY 2018-05-15, Alaska and Polar Regions Collections & Archives, Elmer E. Rasmuson Library, University of Alaska Fairbanks.

————. 2014m. Oral history interview with Karen Brewster, July 24, 2014, Fairbanks, Alaska. Tape No. ORAL HISTORY 2018-05-16, Alaska and Polar Regions Collections & Archives, Elmer E. Rasmuson Library, University of Alaska Fairbanks.

————. 2014n. Oral history interview with Karen Brewster, August 21, 2014, Fairbanks, Alaska. Tape No. ORAL HISTORY 2018-05-17, Alaska and Polar Regions Collections & Archives, Elmer E. Rasmuson Library, University of Alaska Fairbanks.

————. 2014o. Oral history interview with Karen Brewster, August 28, 2014, Fairbanks, Alaska. Tape No. ORAL HISTORY 2018-05-18, Alaska and Polar Regions Collections & Archives, Elmer E. Rasmuson Library, University of Alaska Fairbanks.

————. 2014p. Oral history interview with Karen Brewster, September 11, 2014, Fairbanks, Alaska. Tape No. ORAL HISTORY 2018-05-19, Alaska and Polar Regions Collections & Archives, Elmer E. Rasmuson Library, University of Alaska Fairbanks.

————. 2014q. Oral history interview with Karen Brewster, October 11, 2014, Fairbanks, Alaska. Tape No. ORAL HISTORY 2018-05-20, Alaska and Polar Regions Collections & Archives, Elmer E. Rasmuson Library, University of Alaska Fairbanks.

————. 2014r. Oral history interview with Karen Brewster, October 16, 2014, Fairbanks, Alaska. Tape No. ORAL HISTORY 2018-05-21, Alaska and Polar Regions Collections & Archives, Elmer E. Rasmuson Library, University of Alaska Fairbanks.

————. 2014s. Oral history interview with Karen Brewster, October 23, 2014, Fairbanks, Alaska. Tape No. ORAL HISTORY 2018-05-22, Alaska and Polar Regions Collections & Archives, Elmer E. Rasmuson Library, University of Alaska Fairbanks.

————. 2014t. Oral history interview with Karen Brewster, October 31, 2014, Fairbanks, Alaska. Tape No. ORAL HISTORY 2018-05-23, Alaska and Polar Regions Collections & Archives, Elmer E. Rasmuson Library, University of Alaska Fairbanks.

————. 2014u. Oral history interview with Karen Brewster, November 8, 2014, Fairbanks, Alaska. Tape No. ORAL HISTORY 2018-05-24, Alaska and Polar Regions Collections & Archives, Elmer E. Rasmuson Library, University of Alaska Fairbanks.

————. 2014v. Oral history interview with Karen Brewster, November 21, 2014, Fairbanks, Alaska. Tape No. ORAL HISTORY 2018-05-25, Alaska and Polar Regions Collections & Archives, Elmer E. Rasmuson Library, University of Alaska Fairbanks.

Klein, D. R., and C. Bay. 1990. "Foraging Dynamics of Muskox in Peary Land, Northern Greenland." *HolArctic Ecology* 13 (4): 269–80.

————. 1991. "Diet Selection by Vertebrate Herbivores in the High Arctic of Greenland." *HolArctic Ecology* 14:152–55.

————. 1994. "Resource Partitioning by Mammalian Herbivores in the High Arctic." *Oecologia* 97:439–50.

Klein, D. R., H. H. Bruun, R. Lundgren, and M. Philipp. 2008. "Climate Change Influences on Species Relationships and Distributions in High-Arctic Greenland." In *High-Arctic Ecosystem Dynamics in a Changing Climate: Ten Years of Monitoring and Research at Zackenberg Research Station, Northeast Greenland,* edited by H. Meltofte, T. R.

Christensen, B. Elberling, M. C. Forchhsmmer, and M. Rasch. Vol. 40 of *Advances in Ecological Research*. Amsterdam: Elsevier.

Klein, D. R., and N. Fairall. 1984. "Comparative Thermoregulatory Behavior of Impala (*Aepyceros melampus*) and Blesbok (*Damaliscus dorcas*)." *Canadian Journal of Animal Science* 64 (Suppl.): 210–11.

———. 1986. "Comparative Foraging Behavior and Associated Energetics of Impala and Blesbok." *Journal of Applied Ecology* 23:489–502.

Klein, D. R., and J. E. Hemming. 1977. "Resource Development and Related Environmental Problems in Arctic Alaska: Impact on Fish and Wildlife." In *Symposium on the Geography of Polar Countries*, edited by J. Brown, 15–23. U.S. Army Corps of Engineers, Special Report no. 77.

Klein, D. R., and R. Kleinleder. 2015. "Differential Effects of Coastal Erosion on Colonial-Nesting Sea Birds on the St. Matthew Islands." In *Resource Management in a Changing World*, edited by Susan Sommer, 21–29. *Alaska Park Science* 14 (1). Anchorage, AK: National Park Service.

Klein, D. R., and L. A. Kolpashchikov. 1991. "Current Status of the Soviet Union's Largest Caribou Herd." In *Proceedings of the Fourth North American Caribou Workshop, St. John's, Newfoundland*, edited by C. Butler and S. P. Mahoney, 251–55.

Klein, D. R., and V. Kuzyakin. 1982. "Distribution and Status of Wild Reindeer in the Soviet Union." *Journal of Wildlife Management* 46:728–33.

Klein, D. R., and M. Magomedova. 2003. "Industrial Development and Wildlife in Arctic Ecosystems: Can Learning from the Past Lead to a Brighter Future?" In *Social and Environmental Impacts in the North: Methods in Evaluation of Socio-Economic and Environmental Consequences of Mining and Energy Production in the Arctic and Sub-Arctic*, edited by R. O. Rasmussen and N. E. Koroleva, 35–56. *Proceedings of the NATO Advanced Research Workshop on Methodologies in Evaluation of Socio-Economic and Environmental Consequences of Mining and Energy Production in the Arctic and Sub-Arctic, Apatity, Russia, 8–12 May 2002*. Netherlands: Kluwer Academic Publishers.

Klein, D. R., and S. T. Olson. 1960. "Natural Mortality Patterns of Deer in SE AK." *Journal of Wildlife Management* 24 (1): 80–88.

Klein, D. R., and F. Schønheyder. 1970. "Variation in Ruminal Nitrogen Levels among Some Cervidae." *Canadian Journal of Zoology* 48:437–1442.

Klein, D., and M. Shulski. 2009. "Lichen Recovery Following Heavy Grazing by Reindeer Delayed by Climate Warming." *Ambio* 38 (1): 11–16.

———. 2011. "The Role of Lichens, Reindeer, and Climate in Ecosystem Change on a Bering Sea Island." *Arctic* 64, no. 3 (September): 353–61.

Klein, David, and A. Sowls. 2011. "History of Polar Bears as Summer Residents on the St. Matthew Islands, Bering Sea," *Arctic* 64, no. 4 (December): 429–43.

———. 2015. "Red Foxes Replace Arctic Foxes on a Bering Sea Island: Consequences for Nesting Birds." In *Resource Management in a Changing World*, edited by Susan Sommer, 31–39. *Alaska Park Science* 14 (1). Anchorage, AK: National Park Service.

Klein, D. R., and H. Staaland. 1984. "Extinction of Svalbard Muskoxen through Competitive Exclusion: An Hypothesis." In *Proceedings of the First International Muskox Symposium*, edited by D. R. Klein, R. G. White, and S. Keller, 26–31. Biological Papers of the University of Alaska, Special Report, No. 4. Fairbanks: University of Alaska.

Klein, D. R., and H. Strandgaard. 1972. "Factors Affecting Growth and Body Size of Roe Deer." *Journal of Wildlife Management* 36 (1): 64–79.

Klein, D. R., and H. Thing. 1989. "Chemical Elements in Mineral Licks and Associated Muskoxen Feces in Jameson Land, Northeast Greenland." *Canadian Journal of Zoology* 67:1092–95.

Klein D. R., and T. Vlasova. 1992. "Lichens: A Unique Forage Resource Threatened by Air Pollution." *Rangifer* 12 (1): 21–27.

Klein, D., J. Walsh, and M. Shulski. 2009. "What Killed the Reindeer of St Matthew Island?" *Weatherwise* 62 (6): 32–38.

Klein, D. R., and R. G. White, eds. 1978. "Parameters of Caribou Population Ecology in Alaska: Proceedings of a Symposium and Workshop, November 17–19, 1977, University of Alaska, Fairbanks." Biological Papers of the University of Alaska, Special Report, No. 3. Fairbanks: University of Alaska.

Klein, D. R., G. D. Yakushkin, and E. B. Pospelova. 1993. "Comparative Habitat Selection by Muskoxen Introduced to Northeastern Alaska and the Taimyr Peninsula, Russia." *Rangifer* 13 (1): 21–25.

Kleinfeld, Judith. 1985. *Alaska's Small Rural High Schools: Are They Working?* ISER Report Series, Issue 58. Anchorage: University of Alaska Anchorage, Institute of Social and Economic Research.

K'Meyer, Tracy E., and A. Glenn Crothers. 2007. "'If I See Some of This in Writing, I'm Going to Shoot You': Reluctant Narrators, Taboo Topics, and the Ethical Dilemmas of the Oral Historian." *Oral History Review* 34, no. 1 (Winter/Spring): 71–93.

Knuth, Eigil. 1967. *Archaeology of the Musk-Ox Way.* Contributions du Centre d Études Arctiques et Finno-Scandinaves, no. 5. Paris, France: École Pratique des Hautes Études,

Komarek, E. V. 1969. "Fire and Animal Behavior." In *Proceedings, Annual Tall Timbers Fire Ecology Conference; 1969 April 10–11*, 161–207. Tallahassee, FL: Tall Timbers Research Station.

Komarek, Edwin, and Betty Komarek. 1976. *Comments on the Wildfire Problem in Portugal in Relation to Forests, Wildlife, and Range.* Report submitted to Portugal National Parks. In possession of authors.

Kruse, J. A., R. G. White, H. E. Epstein, B. Archie, M. D. Berman, S. R. Braund, F. S. Chapin III, J. Charlie Sr., C. J. Daniel, J. Eamer, N. Flanders, B. Griffith, S. Haley, L. Huskey, S. James, Bernice Joseph, D. Klein, G. P. Kofinas, S. M. Martin, S. M. Murphy, W. Nebesky, C. Nicholson, D. E. Russell, J. Tetlichi, A. Tussing, M. D. Walker, and O. R. Young. 2004. "Modeling Sustainability of Arctic Communities: An Interdisciplinary Collaboration of Researchers and Local Knowledge Holders." *Ecosystems* 7 (8): 815–28.

Krutch, Joseph Wood. 1957. "The Sportsman or the Predator? A Damnable Pleasure." *The Saturday Review of Literature* 40 (33), August 17, 1957: 8–10 and 39–40.

Kvaløy, S. 1974. "Ecophilosophy and Ecopolitics: Thinking and Acting in Response to the Threats of Ecocatastrophe." *North American Review* 259, no. 2 (Summer): 16–28.

Lent, Peter C. 1962. *Caribou Investigations, Northwest Alaska: Terrestrial Mammals Investigations, Ogotoruk Creek–Cape Thompson and Vicinity, Part C: Project Chariot Final Report.* Fairbanks: Department of Biological Sciences, University of Alaska.

———. 1980. "Synoptic Snowmelt Patterns in Arctic Alaska in Relation to Caribou Habitat Use." In *Proceedings of the Second International Reindeer/Caribou Symposium, 17–21 September 1979, Røros, Norway*, edited by Eigil Reimers, Eldar Gaare, Sven Skjenneberg, 71–77. Direktoratet for vilt og ferskvannsfisk. Trondheim, Norway.

Lentfer, Hank, and Carolyn Servid, compilers. 2001. *Arctic Refuge: A Circle of Testimony.* Minneapolis: Milkweed Editions.

Leopold, A. 1933. *Game Management.* New York: C. Scribner's Sons.

———. 1949. *A Sand County Almanac: And Sketches Here and There.* New York: Oxford University Press.

Leopold, A. Starker, and Frank Fraser Darling. 1953. *Wildlife in Alaska, An Ecological Reconnaissance.* Sponsored by the New York Zoological Society and the Conservation Foundation. New York: Ronald Press Co.

Lindsay, Vachel. 1925. *Collected Poems, Revised and Illustrated Edition.* New York: The Macmillan Company.

Lorenz, Konrad. 1952. *King Solomon's Ring.* New York: Time Inc.

Lovelock, J. E. 1970. *Gaia: A New Look at Life on Earth.* Oxford, England: Oxford University Press (reissued with new cover and new preface in 2000).

Luchin, V. A., I. P. Semiletov, and G. E. Weller. 2002. "Changes in the Bering Sea Region: Atmosphere-Ice-Water System in the Second Half of the Twentieth Century." *Progress in Oceanography* 55:23–44.

Luick, J. R., P. C. Lent, D. R. Klein, and R. G. White, eds. 1975. *Proceedings of the First International Reindeer and Caribou Symposium, August 9–11 1972, University of Alaska, Fairbanks, Alaska.* Biological Papers of the University of Alaska, Special Report, No. 1, September 1975. Fairbanks: University of Alaska.

Lutz, Harold. 1960. *History of the Early Occurrence of Moose on the Kenai Peninsula and in Other Sections of Alaska.* Juneau: U.S. Dept. of Agriculture, National Forest Service, Alaska Forest Research Center.

Lynge, F. 1992. *Arctic Wars: Animal Rights and Endangered Peoples.* Hanover, NH: Dartmouth College, University Press of New England.

MacDonald, D. 1987. "Constitution and Bylaws." *Wildlife Society Bulletin* 15:14–22.

Maimer, N. 1969. "Organic Matter and Cycling of Minerals in Virgin and Present Ecosystems." In *Impact of Man on the Scandinavian Landscape during the Late Post-Glacial*, edited by B. E. Berglund, 79–86. *Oikos*, Supplementum 12.

Mandelbaum, David. 1973. "The Study of Life History: Ghandi." *Current Anthropology* 14, no. 3 (June): 177–96.

Mander, J. 1978. *Four Arguments for the Elimination of Television.* New York: Quill Press.

Margulis, L., and Lovelock, J. E. 1989. "Gaia and Geognosy." In *Global Ecology: Towards a Science of the Biosphere*, edited by M. B. Rambler, L. Margulis, and R. Fester, 1–29. San Diego, CA: Academic Press.

Marshall, Robert. 1930. "The Problem of the Wilderness." *Scientific Monthly* 30, no. 2 (February): 141–48.

Marx, Karl. 1912. *Capital: A Critique of Political Economy.* Chicago: C. H. Kerr and Company.

Matsuoka, S. 2003. "Observations of Arctic and Red Fox on St. Matthew and Hall Islands." May 26–July 8, 2003. Tony Degange USFWS files, Anchorage, AK.

McMillen, Stuart. 2017. "St. Matthew Island." Comic about reindeer overpopulation. Accessed December 30, 2017. http://www.stuartmcmillen.com/comic/st-matthew -island/.

Meltofte, H., T. R. Christensen, B. Elberling, M. C. Forchhammer, and M. Rasch, eds. 2008. *High-Arctic Ecosystem Dynamics in a Changing Climate: Ten Years of Monitoring and Research at Zackenberg Research Station, Northeast Greenland.* Vol. 40 of *Advances in Ecological Research.* Amsterdam: Elsevier.

Merriam, C., ed. 1901–1910. *The Harriman Alaska Expedition (the Harriman Alaska Series).* Vols. 1–5. New York: Doubleday, Page and Company.

Merriam-Webster Dictionary, online edition. 2017. "Vitalism." Accessed April 25, 2017. https://www.merriam-webster.com/dictionary/vitalism.

Miller, D. C. 1965. "Last Stand of the Giants." *National Wildlife* 3 (1): 12–15.

Mitchell, Donald Craig. 2001. *Take My Land, Take My Life: The Story of Congress's Historic Settlement of Alaska Native Land Claims, 1960–1971.* Fairbanks: University of Alaska Press.

Morris, Desmond. 1967. *The Naked Ape: A Zoologist's Study of the Human Animal.* New York: McGraw-Hill Book Company.

Moss, R. 1973. "The Digestion and Intake of Winter Foods by Wild Ptarmigan in Alaska." *The Condor* 75, no. 3 (Autumn): 293–300.

Munsterhjelm, E. 1953. *The Wind and the Caribou: Hunting and Trapping in Northern Canada.* New York: Macmillan Publishers.

Murie, Adolph. 1944. *The Wolves of Mount McKinley.* Fauna of the National Parks of the United States, Fauna Series, No. 5, 1944. Washington, DC: U.S. Government Printing Office.

Murozumi, M., Tsaihwa Chow, and C. Patterson. 1969. "Chemical Concentrations of Pollutant Lead Aerosols, Terrestrial Dusts, and Sea Salts in Greenland and AntArctic Snow Strata." *Geochimica et Cosmochimica Acta* 33 (10): 1247–94.

Næss, A. 1973. "The Shallow and the Deep, Long-Range Ecology Movements." *Inquiry* 16:95–100.

Nash, R. 1967. *Wilderness and the American Mind.* New Haven, CT: Yale University Press.

National Research Council. 1997. *Wolves, Bears, and Their Prey in Alaska: Biological and Social Challenges in Wildlife Management.* Washington, DC: The National Academies Press.

National Swedish Environmental Protection Board. 1969. *Protection of Environment in Sweden.* Solna, Sweden: Planning Secretariat.

———. 1974. *XIth International Congress of Game Biologists, Stockholm, September 3–7, 1973. Conference Proceedings.* Stockholm, Sweden: National Swedish Environmental Protection Board.

National Swedish Environmental Protection Board, Ministry of Local Government and Labour. 1970. *Survey of Norwegian Planning Legislation and Organization.* Oslo, Norway: Fellestrykk.

Nellemann, C., and R. D. Cameron. 1998. "Cumulative Impacts of an Evolving Oil-field Complex on the Distribution of Calving Caribou." *Canadian Journal of Zoology* 76 (8): 1425–1430.

Nelson, Richard. 1983. *Make Prayers to the Raven: A Koyukon View of the Northern Forest.* Chicago: University of Chicago Press.

———. 1998. *Heart and Blood: Living with Deer in America.* New York: Alfred A. Knopf.

Nixon, Richard. 1972. "178–Joint Communique, Following Discussions with Soviet Leaders." May 29, 1972. USA/USSR Environmental Agreement Project V–2. Ecosystems of Northern Regions, the American Presidency Project website, *Public Papers of the Presidents Collection*: Richard Nixon, 1972. Accessed January 31, 2019. http://presidency.proxied.lsit.ucsb.edu/ws/index.php?pid=3439&st=&st1=.

Olson, S. F. 1961. "The Spiritual Aspects of Wilderness." In *Wilderness: America's Living Heritage*, edited by David Brower. San Francisco: Sierra Club.

O'Neill, Daniel T. 1994. *Firecracker Boys.* New York: St. Martin's Press.

Ortega y Gasset, J. 1972. *Meditations on Hunting.* New York: Charles Scribner (1995 re-print: Wilderness Adventures Press, Belgrade, Montana).

Oxford English Dictionary, 2nd ed. Vol. 4. 1989. "Culture" Oxford, England: Clarendon Press.

Palmer, L. J. 1926. *Progress of Reindeer Grazing Investigations in Alaska. USDA Bulletin* 1423. Washington, DC: U.S. Government Printing Office.

Palmer, L. J., and C. H. Rouse. 1936. *Progress of Muskox Investigations in Alaska, 1930–1935*. Reprinted by U.S. Bureau of Sport Fisheries and Wildlife, Juneau, Alaska, 1963.

———. 1945. *The Study of the Alaska Tundra with Reference to Its Reactions to Reindeer and Other Grazing*. Fish and Wildlife Service Report No 10. Washington, DC: U.S. Government Printing Office.

Patton, W. W., D. F. Barnes, and M. B. Estlund. 1975. *Reconnaissance Geologic Map of St. Matthew Island, Bering Sea, Alaska*. Miscellaneous Field Studies Map 642. Washington, DC: United States Geological Survey.

Pimlott, D. H. 1969. *The Value of Diversity: Transactions of the Thirty-Fourth North American Wildlife and Natural Resources Conference*. Wildlife Management Institute.

Portelli, Alessandro. 1998. "Oral History as Genre." In *Narrative and Genre*, edited by Mary Chamberlain and Paul Richard Thompson. London: Routledge.

Potes, J. M., E. V. Lourenço, and T. Carita. 2005. "Portuguese Society of Pastures and Forages." Abstract in *XX International Grasslands Congress: Offered Papers*, edited by F. P. O'Mara, R. J. Wilkins, L.'t Mannetje, D. K. Lovett, P. A. M. Rogers, and T. M. Boland, 935. The Netherlands: Wageningen Academic Publishers.

Quinlan, S. E. 1995. *The Case of the Mummified Pigs and Other Mysteries in Nature*. Honesdale, PA: Caroline Boyds Mills Press.

———. 2007. "The Mystery of St. Matthew Island." In *Reading Street, Grade 3.1, Edition 1*, edited by Scott Foresman Company, 658–67. Boston: Pearson Publishing.

Rapoport, Amos. 1969. *House Form and Culture*. Englewood Cliffs, NJ: Prentice Hall.

Rasmussen, R. O., and N. E. Koroleva, eds. 2003. "Social and Environmental Impacts in the North: Methods in Evaluation of Socio-Economic and Environmental Consequences of Mining and Energy Production in the Arctic and Sub-Arctic." *Proceedings of the NATO Advanced Research Workshop on Methodologies in Evaluation of Socio-Economic and Environmental Consequences of Mining and Energy Production in the Arctic and Sub-Arctic, Apatity, Russia, 8–12 May 2002*. Netherlands: Kluwer Academic Publishers.

Rausch, Robert L., and Virgina R. Rausch. 1968. "On the Biology and Systematic Position of *Microtus abbreviatus* Miller, a Vole Endemic to the St. Matthew Island, Bering Sea." *Sonderdruck aus Z. f. Säugetierkunde Bd.* 33:65–99.

Rearden, Jim. 1998. *Alaska's Wolf Man: The 1915–55 Wilderness Adventures of Frank Glaser*. Missoula, MT: Pictorial Histories Publishing Co.

Reimers, E. 1980. "Activity Pattern: The Major Determinant for Growth and Fattening in *Rangifer*?" In *Proceedings of the Second International Reindeer/Caribou Symposium, 17–21 September 1979, Røros, Norway*, edited by Eigil Reimers, Eldar Gaare, Sven Skjenneberg. Direktoratet for vilt og ferskvannsfisk, Trondheim, Norway.

Reimers, E., K. Flydal, and R. Stenseth. 2000. "High Voltage Transmission Lines and Their Effect on Reindeer: A Research Program in Progress." *Polar Research* 19:75–82.

Reimers, E., and D. R. Klein, 1979. "Reindeer and Caribou." *Nature* 282:508–59.

Reimers, E., D. R. Klein, and R. Sorumgard, 1983. "Calving Time, Growth Rate, and Body Size of Norwegian Wild Reindeer." *Journal of Arctic and Alpine Research* 15:107–18.

Roby, D. D. 1978. *Behavioral Patterns of Barren-Ground Caribou of the Central Arctic Herd Adjacent to the Trans-Alaska Pipeline*. Master's thesis, University of Alaska Fairbanks.

Rosswall, T., and O. W. Heal, eds. 1975. *Structure and Function of Tundra Ecosystems*. IBP Tundra Biome 5. International Meeting, Abisko, Sweden 1974. Reihe: *Ecological Bulletin*, No. 20. Stockholm: Swedish National Research Council.

Rozell, Ned. 2010. "What Wiped Out St. Matthew Island's Reindeer?" *Alaska Dispatch News*, January 16, 2010. Accessed February 23, 2017. https://www.adn.com/features/article/what-wiped-out-st-matthew-islands-reindeer/2010/01/17/.

———. 2012a. "Scientists Prepare for Voyage to Remote St. Matthew." Anchorage Daily News, July 29, 2012, p. E5.

———. 2012b. "When Reindeer Paradise Turned to Purgatory." Anchorage Daily News, August 12, 2012 p. E5.

———. 2014. "The Mammoth Mystery of St. Paul Island." KTOO Public Media, October 4, 2014. Accessed January 31, 2019. https://www.ktoo.org/2014/10/04/mammoth -mystery-st-paul-island/

———. 2015. "The Loneliest Camp on Earth." *Alaska Science Forum*, Geophysical Institute, University of Alaska Fairbanks. August 6, 2015.

Rudofsky, B. 1964. *Architecture without Architects*. New York: Doubleday.

Sandegren, Finn E. 1969. *Breeding and Maternal Behavior of the Steller Sea Lion* (Eumetopias jubata) *in Alaska*. Illustrations by William D. Berry. Master's thesis, University of Alaska Fairbanks.

Scheffer, Victor B. 1951. "The Rise and Fall of a Reindeer Herd." *Scientific Monthly* 73, no. 6 (December): 356–62.

Schneider, William. 2002. . . . *So They Understand: Cultural Issues in Oral History*. Logan: Utah State University Press.

———. 2005. "Lessons from the Storytellers." In *Resilience in Arctic Societies: Papers from the Third IPSSAS Seminar*, edited by Larry Kaplan and Michelle Daveluy, 111–18. Fairbanks, AK: International PhD School for Studies of Arctic Societies.

———. 2008. *Living with Stories: Telling, Retelling, and Remembering*. Logan: Utah State University Press.

Schneider, William, and Phyllis Morrow. 1995. *When Our Words Return: Writing, Hearing, and Remembering Oral Traditions of Alaska and the Yukon*. Logan: Utah State University Press.

Schweitzer, A. 1950. *The Animal World of Albert Schweitzer: Jungle Insights into Reverence for Life*. Edited by Charles Joy. New York: Ecco Press.

Scott Foresman Company, ed. 2007. *Reading Street, Grade 3.1, Edition 1*. Boston: Pearson Publishing.

Shaw, G. E. 1981. "Eddy Diffusion Transport of Arctic Pollution from the Mid-Latitudes: A Preliminary Model." *Atmospheric Environment* 15:1483–90.

Shea, John C. 1979. *Social Behavior of Wintering Caribou in Northwestern Alaska*. Master's thesis, University of Alaska Fairbanks.

Shepard, P. 1967. *Man in the Landscape: A Historic View of the Esthetics of Nature*. New York: Alfred A. Knopf.

———. 1973. *The Tender Carnivore and the Sacred Game*. New York: Charles Scribner's Sons.

Sherwonit, Bill. 2012. "Biologist Wants New State Park at Popular Interior Alaska Lake." *Anchorage Daily News*, October 31, 2012. Accessed February 23, 2018. https://www adn.com/outdoors/article/biologist-wants-new-state-park-popular-interior -alaska-lake/2012/10/31/.

Skarphédinn, T. 2010. "The History of Reindeer in Iceland and Reindeer Study, 1979– 1981." *Rangifer* 4 (2): 22–38.

Skuncke, F. 1958. *Renbeten och deras gradering*. Lapvansendet-Renfoskningen, Meddelande 4.

———. 1969. "Reindeer Ecology and Management in Sweden." Biological Papers of the University of Alaska, No. 8. Fairbanks: University of Alaska.

Smith, W. T., and R. D. Cameron. 1983. "Responses of Caribou to Industrial Development on Alaska's Arctic Slope." *Acta Zoologica Fennica* 175:43–45.

Spurr, S. 1966. "Untitled Lecture about Wilderness Management." Sixth Horace M. Albright Conservation Lectureship, University of California School of Forestry, Berkeley, CA.

Stauffer, R. C. 1957. "Haeckel, Darwin, and Ecology." *Quarterly Review of Biology*, 32:138–44.

Steinacher, Sue. 2008. "Census Shows Decline in the Western Arctic Caribou." *Alaska Fish and Wildlife News*, July 2008. Accessed March 24, 2017. http://www.adfg.alaska.gov/index.cfm?adfg=wildlifenews.view_article&articles_id=385.

Syroechkovskii, E. E. 1995. *Wild Reindeer*. D. R. Klein, scientific editor, Translations Publishing Program, Smithsonian Institution, Washington, DC. (Original Russian: Severnyi Olen, Agropromizdat Publishers, Moscow 1986.)

Teilhard de Chardin, P. 1966. *Man's Place in Nature*. New York: Harper.

———. 1969. *Science and Christ*. New York: Harper.

———. 1971. *Christianity and Evolution*. New York: Harcourt Brace Jovanovich.

———. 1975. *Toward the Future*. New York: Harcourt Brace Jovanovich.

———. 1979. *The Heart of Matter*. New York: Harcourt Brace Jovanovich.

The Wildlife Society. 1999. "David Klein Receives 1999 Aldo Leopold Memorial Award." *The Wildlifer* 294 (May–June 1999): 41 and 47.

The Wildlife Society. 2005. *Following Leopold's Footsteps: The Wildlife Society's Aldo Leopold Medal Winners 1950–2005*, 55. Bethesda, MD: The Wildlife Society.

Thing, Henning. 1977. "Behavior, Mechanics, and Energetics Associated with Winter Cratering by Caribou in Northwestern Alaska." Biological Papers of the University of Alaska, No. 18. Fairbanks: University of Alaska.

Thing, H., D. R. Klein, K. Jingfors, and S. Holt. 1987. "Ecology of Muskoxen in Jameson Land, Northeast Greenland." *HoloArctic Ecology* 10:95–103.

Thomas, D. C., and J. Edmonds. 1983. "Rumen Contents and Habitat Selection by Peary Caribou in Winter, Canadian Arctic Archipelago." *Arctic and Alpine Research* 15:97–105.

Tonkin, Elizabeth. 1992. *Narrating Our Pasts: The Social Construction of Oral History*. Cambridge, England: Cambridge University Press.

UNESCO. 1970. *Use and Conservation of the Biosphere*. Liege, Belgium: Vaillant-Carmanne, S.A.

United States Congress. 1964. Public Law, 88–577, Wilderness Act, September 3, 1964.

———. 1970. *A University View of the Forest Service*. A report of a Select Committee of the University of Montana for the Committee on Interior and Insular Affairs, U.S. Senate. Senate Document No. 91–115.

United States–USSR. 1972. Agreement on Exchanges and Cooperation in Scientific, Technical, Educational, Cultural, and Other Fields in 1972–73, April 11, 1972, United States–USSR, 23 U.S.T. 790, T.I.A.S. No. 7343. *Weekly Compilation of Presidential Documents* 8 (23): 921.1972.

Uspenski, Sava, M. 1984. "Muskoxen in the USSR: Some Results of and Perspectives on Their Introduction." In *Proceedings of the First International Muskox Symposium*, edited by David R. Klein, Robert White, and Susan Keller, 2–14. Biological Papers of the University of Alaska, Special Report, No. 4. Fairbanks: University of Alaska.

Veltre, Doug W., David R. Yesner, Kristine J. Crossen, Russell W. Graham, and Joan B. Coltrain. 2008. "Patterns of Faunal Extinction and Paleoclimatic Change from Mid-Holocene Mammoth and Polar Bear Remains, Pribilof Islands, Alaska." *Quaternary Research* 70, no. 1 (July): 40–50.

Vest, J. H. 1987. "The Philosophical Significance of Wilderness Solitude." *Environmental Ethics* 9:303.

Wang, Yue, Peter Heintzman, Lee Newsom, Nancy Bigelow, Matthew Wooller, Beth Shapiro, and John Williams. 2017. "The Southern Coastal Beringian Land Bridge: Cryptic Refugium or Pseudorefugium for Woody Plants during the Last Glacial Maximum?" *Journal of Biogeography* (April): 1–13.

Warren, Julianne Lutz. 2016 (2006). *Aldo Leopold's Odyssey: Rediscovering the Author of "A Sand County Almanac."* 10th anniversary ed. Washington, DC: Island Press.

Washburn, Sherwood L., and C. S. Lancaster. 1968. "The Evolution of Hunting." In *Man the Hunter: Symposium on Man the Hunter (1966: University of Chicago)*, edited by Richard B. Lee and Irven DeVore, 293–303. Chicago: Aldine Publishing Company.

Webber, P. J., and D. R. Klein. 1977. "Geobotanical and Ecological Observations at Two Locations in the West-Central Siberian Arctic." *Arctic and Alpine Research* 9 (3): 305–15.

Weber, M. 1930. *The Protestant Ethic and the Spirit of Capitalism.* New York: Charles Scribner's Sons.

Webster's New Twentieth Century Dictionary, unabridged. Wilderness 1975. 2nd ed. Cleveland: Collins World Publishing Company.

Weeden, R. B., and D. R. Klein. 1971. "Wildlife and Oil: A Survey of Critical Issues in Alaska." *The Polar Record* 15 (97): 479–94.

Weladji, R. B., O. Holand, and T. Almøy. 2003. "Use of Climatic Data to Assess the Effect of Insect Harassment on the Autumn Weight of Reindeer (*Rangifer tarandus*) Calves." *Journal of Zoology* 260 (1): 79–85.

Weladji, R., D. R. Klein, O. Holand, and A. Mysterud. 2002. "Comparative Response of *Rangifer tarandus* and Other Northern Ungulates to Climatic Variability." *Rangifer* 22 (1): 33–50.

White, R. G., and D. R. Klein. 1985. "Comparative Foraging Strategies of Northern Herbivores." Abs. 0651. Fourth International Theriological Conference, Edmonton, Canada. 13–20 August 1985.

Wilimovsky, Norman J., ed. 1966. *Environment of the Cape Thompson Region, Alaska.* John N. Wolfe, associate editor. Oak Ridge, TN: United States Atomic Energy Commission, Division of Technical Information.

Will, R. T. 1984. "Muskox Procurement and Use on Banks Island by Nineteenth Century Copper Inuit." In *Proceedings of the First International Muskox Symposium*, edited by David R. Klein, Robert White, and Susan Keller, 153–61. Biological Papers of the University of Alaska, Special Report, No. 4. Fairbanks: University of Alaska.

Yow, Valerie. 1995. "Ethics and Interpersonal Relationships in Oral History Research." *Oral History Review* 22, no. 1 (Summer): 57–59.

———. 1997. 'Do I Like Them Too Much?': Effects of the Oral History Interview on the Interviewer and Vice-Versa." *Oral History Review* 24, no. 1 (Summer): 55–79.

Index

Page numbers with an *f* refer to a figure or a caption; an *n* indicates a note.